The Chief Justiceship of
Charles Evans Hughes, 1930–1941

CHIEF JUSTICESHIPS
OF THE UNITED STATES SUPREME COURT

Herbert A. Johnson, Series Editor

The Chief Justiceship of Charles Evans Hughes, 1930–1941

William G. Ross

The University of South Carolina Press

© 2007 University of South Carolina

Published by the University of South Carolina Press
Columbia, South Carolina 29208

www.sc.edu/uscpress

Manufactured in the United States of America

16   15   14   13   12   11   10   09   08   07   10   9   8   7   6   5   4   3   2   1

Library of Congress Cataloging-in-Publication Data

Ross, William G., 1954–
    The chief justiceship of Charles Evans Hughes, 1930–1941 / William G. Ross.
        p.   cm.— (Chief justiceships of the United States Supreme Court)
    Includes bibliographical references and index.
    ISBN-13: 978-1-57003-679-8 (cloth : alk. paper)
    ISBN-10: 1-57003-679-9 (cloth : alk. paper)
    1. Hughes, Charles Evans, 1862–1948.   2. Judges—United States—Biography.   3. United
States. Supreme Court—Officials and employees—Biography.   4. United States. Supreme
Court—History—20th century.   I. Title.
KF8745.H8R67   2007
347.73'2634—dc22
[B]
                                                                                    2006038764

This book was printed on Glatfelter Natures, a recycled paper with 50 percent postconsumer
waste content.

To David J. Langum Sr.,
colleague, mentor, friend

Contents

Illustrations

Series Editor's Preface

It is critically important for U.S. constitutional history that scholars come to grips with the "enduring enigma" of the Hughes Court and its checkered role in response to the Great Depression. Unquestionably, Chief Justice Charles Evans Hughes played a central part in this drama of interbranch conflict within the federal government and ideological debate throughout American society. Those of us who are children of the Depression, as well as the much larger number who are inheritors of its impact on American life and constitutional law, need to know more about this "Jovian presence" who, according to his successor, Harlan F. Stone, ran Court conferences like a drill sergeant. Bill Ross accepts as his task the need to answer the question as to how Hughes affected the U.S. Supreme Court during one of the most critical periods of its history. In doing so he is able to contribute much to our understanding of the dynamics of decision making in both the contentious pre-1937 Court and the rapidly "liberalizing" Supreme Court that emerged with the newly appointed justices of FDR's second term. He also raises for us some important questions concerning the nature of the U.S. Constitution and the roles of the Supreme Court and the political branches in shaping fundamental law. Indirectly he ponders the interplay of politics, public law, and the electorate in a structurally federated republic that has become more and more unitarily nationalist in operating assumptions and ideological underpinnings. Not surprisingly, this perceptive and revealing analysis of Chief Justice Hughes and his Court does not resolve the "enduring enigma" of constitutional law's response to the Great Depression. Indeed the likelihood is that no historical study ever will fully encapsulate or explain this watershed in American constitutional development. However, Ross has given us much to think about and he has outlined carefully those issues with which academia must begin.

Focusing on Chief Justice Hughes proves to be an advantageous observation point from which to analyze broader issues. Among the growing list of men who have led the U.S. Supreme Court, Hughes ranks among the four greatest, the other three being John Marshall, William Howard Taft, and Earl Warren. These four share some common characteristics. They all had, in varying degrees, a significant amount of political experience and prominence before they were installed in the Court's central seat. Each one was of sufficient political standing that they were candidates for the presidency or vice presidency of the United

States. All, in quite individualistic ways, were dominant and perhaps even domineering personalities. Focused and clear headed, they were able to control Court conferences, minimize harsh and disruptive behavior, and move business forward in an expeditious manner. With the possible exception of Taft, each of them was faced with broad-based and serious challenges to the independence and status of the Supreme Court and the lower federal tribunals. Of course, it was Taft who took the lead in relieving the Court from an impossible burden of mandatory appeals through the enactment of "the Judges Act " of 1925, which made virtually all appellate cases subject to discretionary certiorari consideration.

However, Hughes, like all the others who have presided over the Supreme Court, was a unique individual who had been shaped by his background and his experiences. What emerges from this monograph is the remarkable degree to which he personified the pragmatism as well as the ideological inconsistencies of early twentieth-century progressivism. Prior to his first term of service on the Supreme Court (1910–16), he had been a reformer and progressive governor of New York. On the Court he demonstrated sensitivity to the needs of laborers and a willingness to utilize governmental regulatory power to lighten the burdens of the deprived and underprivileged. Most notably, Associate Justice Hughes was supportive of the evolving concept of the federal police power and usually deferential to state regulatory initiatives. Yet the frenzy of the Depression had apparently made Hughes's earlier preferences seem too modest and restrained for the circumstances of the 1930s, and his nomination as chief justice was strongly opposed by progressive and reformist groups and widely seen as an effort by President Hoover to appoint a pro-business lawyer to solidify the traditionalist bloc on the Court.

After a comprehensive examination of the Hughes Court's tightrope performance concerning the constitutionality of New Deal legislation, Ross concludes that Hughes played a moderating influence over his colleagues on the bench. This both facilitated the decision-making process and tempered political reaction to unpopular decisions. He points out that the Court more likely "followed the election returns" of 1936 rather than responding to President Roosevelt's ill-starred and poorly executed attempt to "pack" the Supreme Court in 1937. In addition there is evidence that even the so-called conservative justices, the "Four Horsemen of the Apocalypse," were aware of the critical situation of the American economy and, thus, were amenable to certain changes in constitutional philosophy that would permit broader legislative response to the needs of the people. This study represents a studied effort to deal fairly with all participants in this drama and to provide evidence that demonstrates the difficulties faced by the Court, by the New Deal majority in Congress, and by the opinion-shaping forces in American society. Ross has also given due consideration to the emerging historiographic controversies that have recently developed over the "Switch in Time That Saved Nine"; while benefiting greatly from his study of that scholarship, he has provided readers with a valuable synthesis of those theories while modifying his own understanding through a fresh examination of the evidence.

The Court under Hughes's chief justiceship also played a significant role in applying principles of due process to the criminal justice systems of the United States government and to state practices that offended the evolving concepts of "ordered liberty" and fair trial. Building upon earlier precedents, the Hughes Court utilized the theories of due process in varying degrees, but it also expanded the scope of the Fourteenth Amendment to incorporate into state criminal procedures the principles embedded in the federal Bill of Rights. Although in retrospect the Hughes Court was not exceptional in its efforts to advance racial justice, its criminal procedure decisions may well have carried with them benefits for some persecuted African American citizens, and its closer scrutiny of what was truly equal about the "separate but equal" doctrine anticipated more active Supreme Court engagement in the future.

In this volume and to a lesser degree in earlier monographs in this Chief Justiceships series, there has been a leit motif dealing with the relationship between constitutional law and the dynamics of the American political system. Certainly the initial conception of the rule of law was based on the premise that there could be a clear line of distinction between the law of the constitution and the function of politics. However, in the intense pressure of economic distress and human suffering that was typical of the Depression, there occurred a new understanding of the place of the U.S. Constitution and the broader American perception of constitutionalism. There also was a marked change in the role of the U.S. Supreme Court, both in American life and in the balance and separation of powers in the federal system. For better or for worse, we are still living within that paradigm, and it is refreshing that this book asks questions that may finally force us to confront the current understanding of the rule of law and how it operates *and should function* in twenty-first-century America.

Herbert A. Johnson

Acknowledgments

It is a pleasure to acknowledge and thank some of the many persons who made important contributions to this book.

I am especially grateful to Herbert A. Johnson, whose editorial advice, always delivered with modesty and courtesy, was invaluable. The prospect of having Herb's expert hands guiding the book throughout its preparation is what persuaded me to undertake this project.

Barry Cushman likewise deserves special thanks for his immensely thorough critique of my first draft of the manuscript. Barry challenged me to define my terms more carefully and to reject old shibboleths that clouded my views of the Hughes Court. Although we may continue to differ in our interpretations of various legal and historical issues, he has influenced me in many positive ways.

I am also especially grateful to my friend and Cumberland colleague David J. Langum Sr., who likewise read the manuscript and persuaded me to rethink some of my basic assumptions. David has now helped to guide me through three books on constitutional history. Brannon P. Denning, who carefully read the manuscript and offered helpful criticism, also deserves special thanks. Other Cumberland colleagues, particularly Howard F. Walthall Sr. and Miriam A. Cherry, also provided valuable insights. During my year as a visiting professor at Notre Dame, Walter F. Pratt Jr., the author of a fine volume in this series, was a source of help and inspiration.

Deserving of gratitude, too, are Cumberland dean John L. Carroll and associate dean Henry C. Strickland, who provided essential financial and technical resources and offered their constant good will and encouragement. Thanks also is due to Jeanette Lincecum, my secretary, who proofread the manuscript.

I also appreciate the services of Laurel Rebecca Clapp, the director of Cumberland's law library, and the assistance of research librarians Edward L. Craig Jr. and Brenda K. Jones. This book likewise benefited from the services of the librarians at the Manuscript Division of the Library of Congress.

Introduction

Charles Evans Hughes served as chief justice of the United States during a critical period of constitutional transition. The Supreme Court during the 1930s permanently abandoned restrictive doctrines of due process and interpretations of the commerce and taxing powers that the Court had invoked to nullify federal and state economic regulatory legislation during the previous half century. The Hughes Court therefore largely removed constitutional impediments to the development of the regulatory state. At the same time it was adopting a more deferential approach toward the review of economic legislation, however, the Hughes Court was pioneering a different form of judicial activism in its more careful scrutiny of legislation restricting personal freedom. Hughes is widely hailed for his statesmanship in guiding the Court through its often turbulent transition from a gatekeeper of economic legislation to a guardian of personal liberty.

Yet although the Hughes Court clearly changed the nation's constitutional landscape, the causes and extent of this transformation continue to provoke disagreement. Few issues in American constitutional history have generated more controversy than the Hughes Court's response to economic regulatory legislation in the wake of President Roosevelt's Court-packing proposal in 1937. Scholars differ sharply about whether there was a so-called judicial revolution during Hughes's chief justiceship and, if so, whether the revolution was the result of the natural evolution of the Court's jurisprudence or the product of external forces, particularly the threat of Court packing. These questions necessarily focus largely upon Hughes and Justice Owen J. Roberts, for neither the Court's "liberal" bloc (Justices Harlan Fiske Stone, Louis D. Brandeis, and Nathan B. Cardozo) nor the so-called Four Horsemen (Justices Willis H. Van Devanter, James C. McReynolds, George W. Sutherland, and Pierce Butler) significantly evolved or revolved in their attitudes toward the constitutionality of regulatory legislation.

Popular accounts of the Court often have portrayed the pre-1937 Court as implacably hostile toward reform legislation and therefore have trumpeted as a veritable "judicial revolution" the landmark decisions of 1937, which upheld significant regulatory statutes, including the Social Security Act and the National Labor Relations Act. Although one finds this caricature even in some early scholarly literature, there long has been a broad understanding that judicial nullification of regulatory legislation always was the exception rather than the rule. Even during the "Lochner Era," the Court sustained far more state and federal legislation than it struck down,[1] though the Court struck down many high-profile statutes, and the ever-present specter of judicial nullification of regulatory legislation may have discouraged the enactment of such laws.[2] In the most comprehensive recent study, Professor Barry Cushman has methodically cataloged the hundreds of cases in which even the Court's most "conservative" members joined the Court in rejecting challenges to legislation under theories of due process, equal protection, the taxing power, and the commerce clause. Such decisions help to underscore continuities in the Court's jurisprudence before and after 1937.[3]

The extent of that continuity and the timing of any discontinuity, however, remain subjects of intense controversy.[4] So-called internalists, particularly Cushman, G. Edward White, and Richard Friedman, contend that the Court's consistent approval of economic legislation beginning in 1937 was not revolutionary but, rather, was the natural result of an evolutionary process by which the Court gradually had accepted the regulatory state.[5]

Other scholars, the so-called externalists, however, draw upon a tradition of legal realism and behaviorism in contending that the Court's 1937 decisions constituted a distinct departure from its earlier scrutiny of regulatory legislation. To these scholars, particularly William E. Leuchtenburg, the Democratic mandate in the election of 1936 and the threat of Roosevelt's Court-packing proposal helped to persuade the Court—or at least Roberts and Hughes—to accept more deferential attitudes toward such laws.[6]

1. For example, John Semonche, *Charting the Future: The Supreme Court Responds to a Changing Society, 1890–1920* (Westport, Conn.: Greenwood Press, 1978); Melvin I. Urofsky, "Myth and Reality: The Supreme Court and Protective Legislation in the Progressive Era," *Yearbook 1983 Supreme Court Historical Society,* 55. For an analysis of shifting perspectives on the Hughes Court from the 1930s to the late 1970s, see Michael E. Parrish, "The Hughes Court, the Great Depression, and the Historians," 40 *Historian* 286–308 (1978).

2. See Felix Frankfurter, "The Red Terror of Judicial Reform," *New Republic,* October 1, 1924, 112; repr. in Philip B. Kurland, ed., *Felix Frankfurter on the Supreme Court: Extrajudicial Essays on the Court and the Constitution* (Cambridge, Mass.: Harvard University Press, 1970), 164.

3. Barry Cushman, *Rethinking the New Deal Court: The Structure of a Constitutional Revolution* (New York: Oxford University Press, 1998), and "The Secret Lives of the Four Horsemen," 83 *Virginia Law Review* 559 (1997).

4. For a recent survey, see Laura Kalman, "The Constitution, the Supreme Court, and the New Deal," 110 *Historian* 1052–80 (2005).

5. Cushman, *Rethinking the New Deal Court;* G. Edward White, *The Constitution and the New Deal* (Cambridge, Mass.: Harvard University Press, 2000); Richard D. Friedman, "Switching Time and Other Thought Experiments: The Hughes Court and Constitutional Transformation," 142 *University of Pennsylvania Law Review* 1891 (1994).

6. William E. Leuchtenburg, *The Supreme Court Reborn: The Constitutional Revolution in the Age of Roosevelt* (New York: Oxford University Press, 1995). See also Laura Kalman, "Law, Politics, and the New Deal(s)," 108 *Yale Law Journal* 2165–2213 (1999); David A. Pepper, Note, "Against Legalism: Rebutting an Anachronistic Account of 1937," 82 *Marquette Law Review* 146–50 (1998). Bruce Ackerman, *We the People: Transformations* (Cambridge, Mass.: Harvard University Press, 1998).

In attempting a synthesis of these views, Bruce Ackerman has contended that the trauma of the Great Depression and the subsequent expansion of federal economic regulation in the New Deal generated a transformation of popular attitudes toward the nature and purpose of government that found expression in a judicial revolution in 1937, even if the Court was not directly influenced by the threat of Court packing. This "constitutional moment," Ackerman contends, ranks in importance alongside the Revolution that produced the Constitution itself, and the Civil War and Reconstruction, which elevated human equality to the constitutional level of liberty.[7]

Although the externalist-internalist debate has flared brightly and often fiercely for more than a decade, the two schools never have been mutually exclusive. As Leuchtenburg has written, "The doctrines of the Old Court collapsed in a day—but only after a long period of disintegration."[8] Few scholars would disagree with Leuchtenburg's conclusion that the Court in 1937 "began a revolution in jurisprudence that ended, apparently forever, the reign of laissez-faire and legitimated the arrival of the Leviathan state."[9] In his wide-ranging study of the Constitution and the New Deal, White aptly characterized the constitutional revolution as a "crisis in adaptivity," in which the Court during the 1930s finally adapted itself to the "modern" concept of a "living Constitution."[10] Meanwhile, scholars on both sides of the divide are increasingly willing to acknowledge the validity of certain aspects of the interpretations of their academic antagonists. Friedman rejects the "internalist" tag,[11] Leuchtenburg does not regard himself as an "externalist,"[12] and Laura Kalman, who acknowledges that she has gradually moved closer to the "internalist" position, has called for rejection of the labels, which she aptly believes "obscure more than they clarify" and "collapse into one another."[13] Similarly, this volume is not intended to espouse an internalist or an externalist viewpoint. It adopts elements of both interpretations to the extent that both provide useful means for understanding the forces that transformed the Court during Hughes's chief justiceship.

The controversy over this "judicial revolution" has resonance far beyond the historiography of the Hughes Court, because it involves profound questions about the extent to which the Court is a political institution. It also affects discussions about the extent to which the Court tends to reflect prevailing public opinion, acts as a countermajoritarian lever, and mediates a modus vivendi between competing political forces. This book should help to explore these issues in the context of the Hughes Court. The principal purpose of the volume, however, is to explain how Hughes's chief justiceship affected the Court during one of the most critical periods of its history.

7. Ackerman, *We the People.*

8. Leuchtenburg, *The Supreme Court Reborn,* 235.

9. Ibid., 236.

10. White, *The Constitution and the New Deal,* 234–36.

11. Kalman, "The Constitution, the Supreme Court, and the New Deal."

12. William E. Leuchtenburg, "Comment on Laura Kalman's Article," 110 *American Historical Review* (2005).

13. Kalman, "The Constitution, the Supreme Court, and the New Deal."

The Chief Justiceship of
Charles Evans Hughes, 1930–1941

1

A Chief Justiceship
Begun in Controversy

The nomination of Charles Evans Hughes in 1930 to serve as the eleventh chief justice of the United States precipitated a controversy that was prophetic of the turmoil that would roil and transform the Supreme Court during Hughes's chief justiceship. Unlike most previous Supreme Court appointments, the Hughes nomination encountered abrasive resistance from a wide range of senators and members of the public. Critics of the nomination alleged that Hughes was in thrall to the corporate business interests that opposed the social and economic reform legislation that the Supreme Court had all too often nullified. Frustrated by more than a decade of political and judicial setbacks, disparate social reformers, progressives, and labor leaders execrated the Hughes nomination as a symbol of the triumph of corporate capitalism and political conservatism that had characterized the 1920s. Opposition to the nomination therefore provided the latest episode in a decades-old controversy concerning the constitutionality of social and economic reform legislation that would reach its denouement during Hughes's tenure as chief justice. In lambasting the Court for strangling hard-won reform legislation, foes of the nomination echoed long-standing complaints that would become steadily amplified until they reached a crescendo in the fateful year of 1937. After several tumultuous days, Hughes's nomination was confirmed by a margin of 52 to 26, with eighteen senators not voting—one of the narrowest confirmation votes in Supreme Court history.[1]

The virulent hostility to the nomination stunned the would-be chief justice and his proponents because Hughes's qualifications for the position were so stellar and his political credentials were relatively progressive. No one has ever ascended the nation's highest bench with a more distinguished record of service in both public office and the legal profession.

Hughes was born on April 11, 1862, in Glens Falls, New York, the only child of parents who instilled in him the sense of rectitude and earnestness of purpose that would characterize his long career. Although he came from a more modest social and economic background than any previous chief justice, with the possible

---

1. 72 *Congressional Record*, 71st Congress, 2d session, February 13, 1930, 3591.

exception of John Marshall, Hughes nevertheless enjoyed a privileged upbringing. His father, a Welsh immigrant, was a Baptist clergyman, and his highly educated mother provided a rigorous curriculum for her son at home until he entered public school at the age of nine. Although the Hughes family exemplified the values and mores of the small-town gentry of their era, Hughes grew up mostly in an urban environment, because the family moved to Newark when he was six years old and to New York City when he was twelve. The precocious Hughes matriculated at Madison University (now Colgate) in upstate New York at age fourteen. Seeking a more cosmopolitan and urban environment, Hughes later transferred to Brown University, where he remained devoted to his studies and his religious practices even as he began to enjoy worldly pleasures such as card playing, smoking, and the theater, upon which his parents frowned.[2] Elected to Phi Beta Kappa during his junior year, Hughes graduated third in his class at the age of nineteen.

Although his parents had expected their son to follow his father into the ministry, Hughes entered Columbia Law School after teaching Greek, Latin, and algebra for a year. Graduating from law school with highest honors in 1882 at the age of twenty, Hughes joined a New York law firm that represented large corporations in complex business transactions and litigation. By age twenty-five, he had become a partner in a firm that included the redoubtable lawyers Walter L. Carter and Paul D. Cravath.

Hughes's success at an early age reflected habits and a temperament that remained consistent throughout a long career. His formidable intellect was linked with an iron constitution that sustained his voracious capacity to endure the rigors of exacting and complex work. Masterful in his ability to pace himself, Hughes moved methodically through every task and tried to avoid any unnecessary haste or tension that would sap his strength. He conserved time so preciously that he claimed to have grown his famous beard so he could replace shaving with more productive tasks.[3] Hughes was decades ahead of his time in his recognition of the connection between physical health and mental alertness. Unlike many of his contemporaries, Hughes maintained a moderate weight, exercised regularly, consumed alcohol only sparingly,[4] and stopped smoking at an early age. He renewed his intellect and spirits by scheduling regular periods for reading literature and listening to music. Throughout his adult life he took European holidays, which he described as "joyous and uplifting experiences" that relieved "the unrequited drudgery" of much of his professional work.[5] His frequent visits to the Swiss Alps particularly refreshed him. Despite his public reputation as a "bearded icicle," Hughes was a genial man with a robust laugh and a clever sense of humor. As a journalist observed in 1931, "[H]is coldness and aloofness have been exaggerated," largely by persons who interrupted him while he was working or who asked

2. Merlo J. Pusey, *Charles Evans Hughes* (New York: MacMillan, 1951), 1:1–62.

3. David J. Danelski and Joseph S. Tulchin, eds., *The Autobiographical Notes of Charles Evans Hughes* (Cambridge, Mass.: Harvard University Press, 1973), 88 n. 27.

4. Ibid., 85, 114.

5. Ibid., 115.

for favors or information which he did not consider he had the right to give. . . .
He is by no means as receptive as Mr. Taft was to the time-wasters and the merely
curious who impose upon the good nature of officials."[6]

Hughes also drew much strength from a stable family life. At twenty-six, he
married Antoinette Carter, the daughter of his partner Walter Carter. Perhaps
even more than most women of her generation, Mrs. Hughes devoted herself to
providing a comfortable home in which her husband could take refuge from the
strains of his work. Married for fifty-seven years, until Antoinette died three years
before her husband, the couple had three daughters—Helen, Catherine, and Eliz-
abeth—and a son—Charles Evans Jr.

Hughes likewise benefited from the moral principles of his Baptist upbringing,
even though he eventually rejected most or all the theological tenets of orthodox
Christianity. As he urged a Baptist Sunday school class in 1925, Christians should
base their lives "not . . . upon dogma . . . but upon the spiritual verities of the
Sermon on the Mount."[7]

Despite his outward equanimity, his reputation for supreme self-confidence,
and an insatiable appetite for hard work, Hughes was troubled by self-doubt and
often pushed himself to the point of nervous exhaustion. His demanding work
periodically caused him to suffer from bleeding ulcers. Many who worked closely
with him remarked on Hughes's sudden and frequent shifts in mood, from exalta-
tion to depression, with arcane silences punctured by spurts of hilarity. Although
his patience in mastering prodigious quantities of intricate details helped make
Hughes a great lawyer, investigator, and jurist, he rarely relished such minutiae.
Instead, the aridity of much of this work often bored and frustrated him, while
the heroic concentration it demanded frequently drained his bones and spirit.
Despite his intricate network of acquaintances, Hughes appears to have had no
close friends. Herbert Hoover claimed that Hughes lacked any "instinct for personal friendship" and was the "most self-contained man" he had ever known,[8]
while Hughes's sympathetic biographer Merlo J. Pusey admitted that "[p]ersonal
friendships were less important to him than his work, which absorbed most the
time that other men gave to casual friendly intercourse."[9]

Hughes's remarkably multifaceted career may have reflected the underlying
restlessness of a man too talented and ambitious to remain forever at one occupation. A first shift in vocation occurred nine years after his admission to the bar,
when he stunned and dismayed his partners by forsaking a lucrative practice for
academia. Worn down by the practice of law, Hughes taught law at Cornell for
two years, a career that he later recalled as the most enjoyable of his life. The

6. R. L. Duffas, "Mr. Hughes the Chief Justice Emerges," *New York Times Magazine*, June 28,
1931, 3.

7. Pusey, *Charles Evans Hughes*, 1:111.

8. Betty Glad, *Charles Evans Hughes and the Illusions of Innocence: A Study in American Diplomacy*
(Urbana: University of Illinois Press, 1966), 109.

9. Pusey, *Charles Evans Hughes*, 1:220.

growing financial stringency of his academic post and a desire to be more actively involved in the law lured him back to his New York City practice in 1893. He later kept a hand in legal academia by teaching for several years at New York Law School and delivering occasional lectures at various other law schools.

After quietly practicing law for another decade following his return to New York City, Hughes was suddenly and somewhat reluctantly thrust into public attention in 1905, when he chaired a state legislative investigation that exposed corruption and fraud in the utilities industry and led to a reduction of gas and electric rates for consumers. Attracting widespread praise for the energy, courage, fairness, and technical acumen with which he conducted the investigation, Hughes soon was appointed to direct an even more challenging inquiry into corruption in the insurance industry that helped to reduce risk and premiums for policy holders. These investigations could not have been more auspiciously timed to capture the public imagination, for they occurred at the very time that the fledgling Progressive movement was demanding the reform of business and politics. Hughes's investigations complemented the temper of a decade in which journalists such as Ida Tarbell and Upton Sinclair exposed unsavory business practices and President Theodore Roosevelt tried to enforce the antitrust law against monopolies.

Hoping to cleanse scandal-ridden New York Republican politics and ensure the enactment of reform legislation in the nation's most populous state, Roosevelt encouraged Hughes to seek Roosevelt's old job as governor of New York. Despite misgivings about the independence of this political novice, Republicans nominated Hughes for governor in 1906 in a race against the publishing magnate William Randolph Hearst, who was then at the height of his popularity. Widespread respect for Hughes's competence and integrity ensured Hughes's victory in an election in which voters repudiated every other statewide Republican candidate.[10]

During his three years as governor, Hughes successfully promoted significant progressive legislation. Under his leadership, the state enacted pioneering labor laws, including the nation's first compulsory workers' compensation law, a child labor law, and an eight-hour day for selected railway workers. It also established safety regulations for railway engineers and firemen. Consistent with his lifelong belief in honest and open government, Hughes also persuaded the legislature to enact a law that limited spending by certain political candidates and required accounting for campaign expenditures.[11] Meanwhile, Hughes instituted administrative reforms that modernized and rationalized the state's government.[12]

Hughes's reforms did not please all reformers, for the disparate Progressive movement was rent by many divisions. Throughout his life Hughes embodied the moderate side of progressivism, which sought to instill honesty and efficiency in

10. Robert F. Wesser, *Charles Evans Hughes: Politics and Reform in New York, 1905–1910* (Ithaca, N.Y.: Cornell University Press, 1967), 49–101.

11. Pusey, *Charles Evans Hughes,* 1:181–217; Wesser, *Charles Evans Hughes,* 102–347 passim.

12. Wesser, *Charles Evans Hughes,* 345.

government, tame the excesses of capitalism, and mitigate the plight of the poor. Unlike the more radical progressives, Hughes never sought fundamental transformation of the nation's social and economic system. Although Hughes had high ideals, adhered to exacting standards of personal rectitude, and was not entirely free from self-righteousness, he lacked the passionate indignation that animated many of the more fiery reformers. Cautious by nature, he abhorred sudden change, preferring to reform society incrementally through carefully considered measures. As a realist, he pursued pragmatic goals that often were more modest than those sought by more impatient progressives. Hughes also lacked the class consciousness that characterized many progressives and socialists. In contrast to many other progressives who were born into the genteel professional middle class, Hughes never resented great wealth or sought to punish plutocrats. Unabashed in providing legal services for wealthy corporations and individuals, he moved comfortably in the salons of the upper classes even while he retained the physical and moral self-discipline that he had learned in the Baptist parsonage.

Rejecting William Howard Taft's offer of the Republican vice-presidential nomination in 1908, Hughes was reelected governor that year by a tepid margin that reflected the hostility of the party bosses and gambling interests that he had crossed by opposing racetrack betting. His truncated second term was notably less successful than his first, as the state's political bosses began to reassert their power. Early in his second term, Hughes failed in his effort to further curtail the power of party leaders through the enactment of a direct primary for the nomination of political candidates, one of the key elements in the progressive program.[13] The state assembly's rejection of the bill greatly frustrated Hughes, as did the legislature's hostility toward his plans for a far-reaching investigation into political corruption.[14] Hughes's growing ineffectiveness was partly the result of his studied aloofness from partisan politics. Placing his perception of the public interest above partisanship, Hughes refused to reward political services with patronage, make personal appeals to legislators for support of his programs, meddle in party nominations, or influence legislative committee assignments.[15] His high-minded scorn of party politics eventually alienated even Roosevelt.[16]

Weary of fighting acrimonious and often futile battles in an increasingly fetid political climate, Hughes gratefully accepted Taft's nomination of a seat on the Supreme Court in 1910, following the death of Justice David Brewer. Although many progressives complained that Hughes had abandoned New York to the detested party bosses, Hughes believed that the bench suited his abilities more than the hurly-burly of political life. In contrast to his nomination as chief justice twenty years later, Hughes's intelligence, integrity, and progressivism ensured that

13. Richard L. McCormick, *From Realignment to Reform: Political Change in New York State, 1893–1910* (Ithaca, N.Y.: Cornell University Press, 1981), 243–47.

14. Pusey, *Charles Evans Hughes,* 1:257.

15. McCormick, *From Realignment to Reform,* 228.

16. Wesser, *Charles Evans Hughes,* 345–46.

his nomination encountered no opposition in the Senate. Although his appointment received widespread public approbation,[17] complaints by the Hearst press and William Jennings Bryan that Hughes was too closely allied with corporate business interests presaged the furor over his nomination as chief justice two decades later. Bryan alleged that Hughes exemplified "the citizen who personally opposes vice and is a punisher of small crimes, but shows no indignation at the larger forms of legalized robbery."[18]

These criticisms of Hughes were part of broader complaints against federal and state courts that critics of laissez-faire economics had voiced since the 1880s, when courts began striking down economic regulatory legislation. These criticisms, which were accompanied by a bewildering array of proposals for curbing judicial power, reached a crescendo in 1912 before temporarily subsiding in the wake of a brief period of judicial restraint.

Populists, progressives, and labor leaders bitterly opposed "substantive due process," the doctrine that permitted courts to scrutinize the substantive content of regulatory legislation to ensure that such statutes did not deprive businesses or contracting parties of "due process of law" under the Fifth and Fourteenth Amendments. To the critics of the judiciary, "substantive due process" betrayed democracy by permitting unelected judges to read their own social and economic biases into the Constitution. One of the most controversial aspects of substantive due process was the doctrine of "liberty of contract," which posited that workers did not generally need protective legislation because they enjoyed equal bargaining power with their employers. The theory of liberty of contract reached its apogee in the Court's 1905 decision in *Lochner v. New York*, which struck down a statute limiting the hours that bakers could work.[19]

Similarly, courts during this era also often offended proponents of economic regulation by invoking the Fourteenth Amendment's equal protection clause to find that regulatory legislation was invalid because it discriminated between or among business entities. Critics of the courts also fumed with indignation that the Supreme Court and other federal and state courts had often nullified federal regulatory legislation by narrowly interpreting the scope of congressional power to regulate interstate commerce and impose taxes. Although it upheld much more regulatory legislation than it struck down, the Court invalidated many high-profile statutes, and the threat of judicial nullification chilled efforts to enact reform legislation. Even when the Court sustained regulatory legislation, its critics questioned why courts should presume to inquiry into the wisdom of any statute. As Robert Wiebe has aptly explained, judges' self-appointment as "social guardians" made the courts "yeasayers as much as naysayers."[20]

---

17. "The Appointment of Mr. Justice Hughes," *Green Bag*, June 1910, 335–36 (quoting various periodicals).

18. Ibid., 336.

19. *Lochner v. New York*, 198 U.S. 45 (1905).

20. Robert H. Wiebe, *The Search for Order, 1877–1920* (New York: Hill and Wang, 1967), 107.

During his six years as an associate justice, Hughes generally voted to uphold social and regulatory legislation. His voting record was similar to those of his colleagues, for he served during a tranquil period in which the Court, without deep divisions, sustained the constitutionality of much legislation, including the Pure Food and Drug Act, the Mann Act, and the Second Employers' Liability Act. Criticism of the Court, which had peaked during Roosevelt's presidential campaign in 1912, abruptly abated for several years. By 1914 the *Outlook,* a weekly magazine edited by Roosevelt, proclaimed that the Court, "once regarded as the very stronghold of extreme constitutionalism, has been steadily setting an example of liberal construction."[21]

Hughes's most notable opinions for the Court espoused a broad view of Congress's power to regulate intrastate commerce as an incident of its power to regulate interstate commerce. In the *Minnesota Rate Cases* (1913), Hughes stated that all commerce had become so interrelated that Congress had the power to regulate even ostensibly intrastate commerce.[22] Although the Court in that decision sustained a railroad rate set by a state commission in the absence of any federal regulation, Hughes's opinion declared that the "power of Congress to regulate commerce among the several states is supreme and plenary"[23] and that "the full control by Congress of the subjects committed to its regulation is not to be denied or thwarted by the commingling of interstate and intrastate operations."[24] The full implications of this doctrine emerged the following year in Hughes's opinion for the Court in the *Shreveport Rate Cases,*[25] in which the Court held that the Interstate Commerce Commission properly disallowed intrastate railroad rates that had an adverse affect on interstate commerce. Hughes declared that "Congress in the exercise of its paramount power may prevent the common instrumentalities of interstate and intrastate commercial intercourse from being used in their intrastate operations to the injury of interstate commerce."[26]

Similarly, Hughes deferred in state cases to the police power to regulate businesses in the interests of the public health, safety, and welfare. In 1914, for example, he dissented from the Court's decision striking down a state statute that prohibited employers from requiring their employees to promise not to join a labor union.[27] In a 1911 opinion sustaining an Iowa law that denied the validity of contracts between railroads and their employees limiting liability for personal injuries, Hughes declared that

> [F]reedom of contract is a qualified and not an absolute right. There is no absolute freedom to do as one wills or to contract as one chooses. . . . Liberty implies

21. "A Great Court," *Outlook,* July 4, 1914, 508.
22. 230 U.S. 352 (1913).
23. Ibid., 398.
24. Ibid., 399.
25. *Houston, East & West Texas Railway Co. v. United States,* 234 U.S. 342 (1914).
26. Ibid., 353.
27. *Coppage v. Kansas,* 236 U.S. 1, 27–42 (1915) (Day, J., dissenting, joined by Hughes, J.).

the absence of arbitrary restraint, not immunity from reasonable regulations and prohibitions imposed in the interests of the community. The scope of judicial inquiry in deciding the question of *power* is not to be confused with the scope of legislative considerations in dealing with the matter of *policy*.[28]

Hughes also compiled a liberal record on social issues. Ahead of his time on gender issues, Hughes, who later became an outspoken proponent of women's suffrage,[29] joined John Marshall Harlan in dissenting from an opinion that a wife could not sue her husband for assault and battery under the law of the District of Columbia.[30] Hughes also wrote the opinions of a deeply divided Court in the two of the most significant cases involving race that arose during his tenure, *Bailey v. Alabama* (1911) and *McCabe v. Atchison, Topeka, & Santa Fe Railroad* (1914). In *Bailey*, the Court invalidated a statute, enforced mostly against blacks, for violating the Thirteenth Amendment's prohibition against involuntary servitude by permitting employers to compel the labor of employees who quit their jobs without repaying wage advances. In *McCabe*, the Court relied on the Fourteenth Amendment's equal protection clause in striking down a state law that authorized railroads to furnish sleeping and dining cars only for whites even though the state could demonstrate that provision of separate luxury accommodations for blacks would be unprofitable for the railroad because few blacks could afford them. Hughes also wrote the Court's opinion overturning an Arizona statute that limited the number of aliens that an employer could hire.[31] Hughes was the only justice who joined Justice Oliver Wendell Holmes Jr.'s dissent from the Court's decision that Leo Frank, a Georgia Jew convicted of murdering one of his father-in-law's factory employees, had received a fair trial even though he had been tried in an atmosphere of intense religious, ethnic, and social prejudice.[32]

Hughes's tenure on the Court abruptly ended in June 1916, when the justice resigned to accept the Republican presidential nomination. Although he had actively opposed efforts to promote his candidacy, Hughes finally acquiesced after

---

28. *Chicago, Burlington, & Quincy Railroad Company v. McGuire*, 219 U.S. 549, 567, 569 (1911) (emphasis in original). Hughes declared that "Whether the enactment is wise or unwise, whether it is based on sound economic theory, whether it is the best means to achieve the desired result . . . are matters for the judgment of the legislature, and the earnest conflict of serious opinion does not suffice to bring them within the range of judicial cognizance." Ibid., 569.

29. As the Republican presidential candidate in 1916, Hughes inspired widespread surprise by publicly endorsing a federal women's suffrage amendment, even though the Republican Party platform merely called for enactment of women's suffrage at the state level. Woodrow Wilson, the Democratic nominee, refused to go beyond the Democratic platform's call for state-by-state suffrage. Christine A. Lunardini and Thomas J. Knock, "Woodrow Wilson and Women Suffrage: A New Look," 95 *Political Science Quarterly* 661 (1980).

30. *Thompson v. Thompson*, 218 U.S. 611 (1910).

31. *Truax v. Raich*, 239 U.S. 33 (1915).

32. *Frank v. Mangum*, 237 U.S. 309 (1915). For an account of the case, see Leonard Dinnerstein, *The Leo Frank Case* (New York: Columbia University Press, 1968).

party leaders persuaded him that he alone could bridge the chasm between conservatives and progressives, whose animosity had disastrously split the party in 1912. Even though many Democrats and critics of the Court professed indignation that a Supreme Court justice would forsake the bench for partisan politics, the resignation issue fizzled after President Wilson refused to exploit it in his reelection campaign. Contrary to the expectations of Chief Justice White and other defenders of the Court, the resignation did not seriously impair the Court's prestige, perhaps because there was little evidence that Hughes had exploited his judicial office to advance a presidential ambition.

Hughes was less adroit in reuniting the Republican Party, losing the election to Wilson by the thin margin of 277 to 254 electoral votes. A shift of only a few thousand votes in California would have thrown the election to the Republican, even though Hughes trailed Wilson in popular votes by the wider margin of 49.4 percent to 46.2 percent. Many observers contended that Hughes was a lackluster campaigner and that he was less than skillful in healing divisions among party leaders and articulating the themes of his campaign. Although he faced an incumbent president whose popularity was enhanced by his success in championing progressive legislation and keeping the nation out of the war in Europe, Hughes had the advantage of leading a majority party that did not lose any other presidential election between 1892 and 1932, except when the party split in 1912. Hughes later insisted that he did not regret his defeat, for he feared that presiding over the inevitable war and the making of the peace would have broken his health as it had broken Wilson's.

Following his defeat, Hughes returned to New York City, where he organized a new law firm. Hughes's public service work, however, severely limited his time for practicing law. In addition to serving as president of the New York State Bar Association and the Legal Aid Society, Hughes toured the nation during the First World War, making speeches to kindle support for American participation in the conflict. He also chaired the draft appeals board for New York City and later accepted Wilson's invitation to investigate charges of inefficiency and corruption in the production and delivery of military aircraft.[33]

After the war, Hughes devoted more time to his legal practice, though he continued to allocate about a third of his time to public service activities. When the New York legislature in 1920 expelled its five Socialist members solely because it objected to their political beliefs, Hughes waged a fierce, but ultimately unsuccessful, campaign for their reinstatement.[34] Hughes often acted as a lawyer's lawyer, providing advice on complex litigation to other members of the bar. Although Hughes nearly always provided advice on behalf of business corporations in cases for which he received compensation, he enhanced his independence by refusing to accept regular retainers. Although he continued to excel in the meticulous pretrial preparation for which he was so widely acclaimed, he also frequently

33. Pusey, *Charles Evans Hughes,* 1:367–82.
34. Ibid., 1:391–92.

appeared as an advocate, arguing dozens of cases before the U.S. Supreme Court and many more before the New York Court of Appeals and lesser state courts. Hughes's intellect and personality were so formidable in the courtroom that Judge Benjamin Nathan Cardozo of the New York Court of Appeals waited twenty-four hours before ruling in any case argued by Hughes in order to resist Hughes's magnetism.

When the Republicans returned to the White House in 1921, Hughes became secretary of state in the schizoid Warren Harding cabinet, in which the luminaries Hughes, Treasury Secretary Andrew Mellon, and Commerce Secretary Hoover served alongside Attorney General Harry Daugherty and Interior Secretary Albert B. Fall, whose careers ended in scandal and disgrace. Hughes won nearly universal admiration for masterminding a 1922 naval disarmament treaty among the world's leading military powers and an international treaty that respected China's territorial rights. Hughes also improved relations between the United States and Latin America by retreating from the interventionist policies of previous administrations.[35] He inspired an unsuccessful movement for American membership in the Permanent Court of International Justice, the so-called World Court.

Hughes left the State Department in 1925 to return to private practice in New York. Although he was widely encouraged to seek the presidency in 1928, he pleaded his advancing years as a reason for remaining in private life. He served happily as a judge of the World Court from 1928 until he resigned in 1930 to become chief justice of the United States.

Hughes's credentials for the nation's highest judicial post were so singular that he immediately emerged as a leading successor to Taft when the chief justice's health began to decline precipitously during the waning months of 1929. President Hoover later suggested that he never considered anyone other than Hughes, though there is evidence that the leading candidate at first was Harlan Fiske Stone, an associate justice and a personal friend of Hoover.[36] If the president

35. Glad, *Illusions of Innocence,* 257–60.

36. See Alpheus Thomas Mason, *Harlan Fiske Stone: Pillar of the Law* (New York: Viking Press, 1956), 273–84; Alpheus Thomas Mason, *William Howard Taft: Chief Justice* (New York: Simon & Schuster, 1964), 297–98. According to a persistent rumor, Hoover preferred Stone and offered the nomination to Hughes with the expectation that he would reject it after the acting secretary of state, Joseph P. Cotton, pointed out to Hoover that Hughes would not want his son to have to resign as solicitor general. See Henry F. Pringle, "Profiles: Chief Justice, III," *New Yorker,* July 13, 1935, 19; Drew Pearson and Robert S. Allen, *The Nine Old Men* (New York: Doubleday, 1937), 74–75. In correspondence with Hughes in 1937, Hoover denied discussing the nomination with Cotton and claimed that he discussed it only with Attorney General William Mitchell, who urged the nomination of Hughes, who Hoover believed was "the obvious choice." Hoover did not deny, however, that he may also have considered Stone. Herbert Hoover to Charles Evans Hughes, February 19, 1937, and February 25, 1937, reel 5, Charles Evans Hughes Papers, Manuscript Division, Library of Congress (hereafter cited as Hughes Papers). See also Hughes to Hoover, February 20, 1937 and March 8, 1937, reel 5, Hughes Papers. Mitchell likewise denied the account about Cotton. See James M. Buchanan, "A Note on the 'Joe Cotton Story,' " *Yearbook 1981 Supreme Court Historical Society,* 92. Felix Frankfurter, who had spoken with Cotton shortly after his conversation with Hoover, believed Cotton's account. Felix Frankfurter to Merlo J.

initially favored Stone, he appears to have harbored misgivings about the justice's jurisprudential predilections.[37]

Hoover's reluctance to his appoint his friend probably was influenced by Taft, who believed that Hughes was more conservative than Stone and could more effectively achieve harmony among the justices.[38] Regarding Hoover as dangerously progressive and Stone as "hopeless," Taft had not trusted Hoover to select his successor. Two months before his resignation, Taft had expressed hope that he and his fellow conservatives could outlive the Hoover administration because he predicted that Hoover would appoint "some rather extreme destroyers of the Constitution."[39] When his failing health made such a long wait impossible, Taft could only hope for the appointment of a conservative successor. With his reverence for the Court and the law, this self-described "evangel of constitutionalism" was confident that Court's interpretation of what he called "the ark of our covenant" would remain in "sound" hands under Hughes, and he may have given the White House advance approval of Hughes's nomination.[40] Taft himself had seriously considered nominating Hughes to the chief justiceship two decades earlier, when Chief Justice Fuller died only two months after Hughes became an associate justice. Undecided for months, Taft may have appointed the aged White rather than the youthful Hughes because he himself still hoped to realize his dream of becoming chief justice.[41]

Taft's role in Hughes's appointment was an appropriate valedictory for Taft, who had appointed four justices during his presidency and had influenced the appointment of five more—including himself—during the Harding and Coolidge administrations. With the succession of his anointed successor seemingly secure, Taft resigned on February 3, 1930, and died five weeks later.

Pusey, November 14, 1956, November 27, 1956, December 10, 1956, and December 15, 1956 , reel 1, Felix Frankfurter Papers, Manuscript Division, Library of Congress (hereafter cited as Frankfurter Papers). The possibility that he was not really Hoover's first choice so bothered Hughes that he took pains to rebut it in his autobiography, quoting at length from Hoover's 1937 letters. Danelski and Tulchin, *Autobiographical Notes,* 291–94. Pusey, who omitted any discussion of the issue from his biography of Hughes, privately insisted that he did not believe Cotton's story. Merlo J. Pusey to Felix Frankfurter, November 19, 1956, December 5, 1956, and December 11, 1956, reel 1, Frankfurter Papers. For an argument in favor of the Cotton story, see Frederick Bernays Wiener, "Justice Hughes' Appointment: The Cotton Story Re-examined," *Yearbook 1981 Supreme Court Historical Society,* 78–91.

37. Mason, *William Howard Taft,* 298 n.; Henry J. Abraham, *Justices, Presidents, and Senators: A History of the U.S. Supreme Court Appointments from Washington to Clinton,* rev. ed. (Lanham, Md.: Rowman & Littlefield, 1999), 198.

38. Taft told his son, "Stone is not a leader and would have a great deal of trouble in *massing* the Court." Henry F. Pringle, *The Life and Times of William Howard Taft* (New York: Farrar & Rinehart, 1939), 2:1044.

39. William Howard Taft to Horace D. Taft, December 1, 1929, series B, reel 316, William Howard Taft Papers, Manuscript Division, Library of Congress; William Howard Taft to Horace D. Taft, December 8, 1929, ibid.

40. Mason, *Harlan Fiske Stone,* 278.

41. Abraham, *Justices, Presidents, and Senators,* 127–28.

Unlike Taft, who had pined for the chief justiceship ever since his youth and preferred it to the presidency, Hughes accepted the nomination only with reluctance. Hughes's achievements in public life had already secured for him such a venerable place in American history that he is one of the few Supreme Court justices who is remembered as much or more for his nonjudicial career than for his service on the Court. Hughes, who at age sixty-seven remains the oldest person ever confirmed to a seat on the Court, had looked forward to enjoying more leisure time while continuing his service on the World Court, profiting from an immensely lucrative law practice, and performing occasional acts of public service. Hughes also sought to avoid a return to public office in deference to his wife, who yearned for a quieter and more private life after decades in the public eye. Moreover, Hughes's elevation to the Court required that his son resign as solicitor general, though Hoover promised that he would find him another prominent job in his administration.

Hughes's nomination, made on the same day that Taft resigned, was first greeted with the widespread plaudits that Hoover and Hughes had anticipated.[42] Within a week, however, the nomination had become a lightening rod through which western progressive Republicans and southern states' rights Democrats vented resentment against the northeastern social and economic elite that Hughes seemed to epitomize. Opposition against a Supreme Court nomination usually galvanizes only if there is a convergence of various factors, including widespread discontent over many of the Court's opinions, a politically vulnerable president, and a senator or organization willing to act as a catalyst. All of these factors were present during the spring of 1930. George W. Norris, the progressive Nebraska Republican who served as chairman of the Senate Judiciary Committee, triggered opposition to the nomination when he voted in committee to oppose the nomination and then offered a long broadside against the nomination in a Senate speech. Norris's disregard for the deference that senators usually accorded Supreme Court nominations encouraged other senators to attack the nomination.

Emboldened by Hoover's political vulnerability in the wake of the growing economic depression and the recent bruising fights over farm relief and the tariff, many prominent senators used the nomination as the occasion for complaining about the influence of corporate interests in both the Court and the Hoover administration. Hughes's nomination likewise provided an opportunity for progressive senators to voice old resentments against the Court for invalidating many federal and state regulatory and reform statutes during the previous four decades. It is ironic that the Court's hostility toward such legislation had markedly subsided during Hughes's tenure on the Court from 1910 to 1916, partly as the result of Hughes's influence, and that it had substantially increased after Hughes left the Court. The most notable examples were *Hammer v. Dagenhart* (1918), which invalidated a federal child labor law as beyond the commerce power;[43] *Bailey v. Drexel*

---

42. "Fate's Strange Way with Two Great Chief Justices," *Literary Digest*, February 15, 1930, 7–9.

43. 247 U.S. 251.

Furniture (1922), striking down a second child labor law as beyond the taxing power;[44] and *Adkins v. Children's Hospital* (1923), nullifying a minimum wage law for women.[45] Meanwhile, the Court had also continued to impose restrictions on the activities of labor unions, holding that the antitrust laws did not prohibit injunctions to prohibit secondary boycotts;[46] invalidating a state statute prohibiting judges from enjoining peaceful picketing,[47] and ruling that labor unions were liable for damages in lawsuits for torts committed by unions during strikes.[48]

During the hearings on the Hughes nomination, the Court's month-old decision striking down the Maryland Public Service Commission's limitation upon the fares charged by streetcar companies in Baltimore[49] provoked much discussion and criticism, for it provided the most recent example of the Court's alleged protection of private property at the expense of the public interest. Progressives expressed indignation that the Court—with Louis D. Brandeis, Holmes, and Stone in dissent—had held that the Public Service Commission's limitations upon fares that reduced a business's return on its investment to 6.26 percent could be regarded as confiscatory.[50]

Progressives complained bitterly that Hughes's long career as a corporate attorney demonstrated that he was irrevocably biased against government regulation of business. Norris alleged that "[o]ne has to have his hands filled with gold . . . before he can be admitted . . . to the outer office of Mr. Hughes. It takes big money to employ him."[51] In words that would acquire greater resonance as economic recession deepened into the Great Depression, Norris declared that "the man who has never felt the pinch of hunger and who has never known what it was to be cold, who has never associated with those who have earned their bread by the sweat of their faces, but who has lived in luxury, is not fit to sit in judgment in a contest between organized wealth and those who toil."[52] Norris had made virtually identical complaints against Taft in a bitter speech in the Senate in 1922 after the Taft Court began to hand down opinions that invalidated regulatory legislation.[53]

Similarly, Republican senator William E. Borah of Idaho alleged that "Hughes was representing his real views when he appeared for these companies."[54] Ignoring Hughes's record during his previous service on the Court, Borah warned that Hughes favored "practically no restraint . . . upon the vast corporate interests."[55]

44. 259 U.S. 20.

45. 261 U.S. 525.

46. *Duplex Printing Press Co. v. Deering,* 254 U.S. 443 (1921).

47. *Truax v. Corrigan,* 257 U.S. 312 (1921).

48. *United Mine Workers of America v. Coronado Coal Co.,* 259 U.S. 344 (1922).

49. *United Railways & Electric Co. of Baltimore v. West,* 289 U.S. 234 (1930).

50. 72 *Congressional Record,* 71st Congress, 2d Session, February 13, 1930, 3570–73 (remarks of Senator Norris); ibid.

51. 72 *Congressional Record,* 71st Congress, 2d Session, February 13, 1930, 3566.

52. Ibid.

53. 62 *Congressional Record,* 67th Congress, 2d Session, April 6, 1922, 5113–14.

54. 72 *Congressional Record,* 71st Congress, 2d Session, February 11, 1930, 3450.

55. Ibid.

Likewise, the *Nation* flayed Hughes for his "deadly conservative" mentality, his "worship of property rights," and his "readiness to take retainers from any great corporation."[56] And the *New Republic* declared that "[a] man may be far above the imputation of corruption and undue influence, and still have been trained in a school which makes probable his future bias for one class of litigant and against another."[57]

Criticism of Hughes swiftly spilled into criticism of the Court's conservatism amid warnings that the confirmation of Hughes would bolster a majority that persistently stymied reform by striking down state and federal economic regulatory legislation. Correctly foreseeing during the early months of the Great Depression the social and economic turmoil that would characterize the new decade, critics of the Court warned that it would need progressive leadership as never before. As the *Nation* predicted, "[T]he next few years may well be epoch-making. The overwhelming growth of great capitalistic organizations, the extraordinary combinations of great companies—these and other events reveal in part what is ahead. And what is needed at the head of the supreme tribunal is not a closed mind but one aware that the world and the old order change and must change."[58]

Decrying the Court as "the last resort of organized capital that plunders the common people," Democratic senator Clarence C. Dill of Washington denounced the justices for "writing their economic theories of the supremacy of property rights into the[ir] decisions."[59] Similarly, Wisconsin senator Robert M. La Follette Jr., a progressive Republican, accused the Court of nullifying legislation "because a majority of the members of the Court do not agree with the legislative objective, the social ends, and the economic theories involved in such legislation."[60] Proponents of economic reform legislation and the rights of organized labor warned that the nomination of Hughes was particularly critical because the Court was so sharply polarized between progressives and conservatives. Senator Smith W. Brookhart of Iowa, a progressive Republican, alleged that the Court "is now divided into two political parties,"[61] and the *New Republic* argued that the "two groups in the Supreme Court represent fundamentally divergent social philosophies in a much greater degree than do the two parties in Congress."[62] Because Taft, despite his basic conservatism, had tended to occupy a place in the middle of the Court's political spectrum, the addition of a new judge, particularly a chief justice, could therefore help to shift the Court's balance of power in a direction

56. "The New Chief Justice," *Nation*, February 19, 1930, 208 (editorial).

57. "The Supreme Court under Fire," *New Republic*, February 26, 1930, 31 (editorial).

58. "The New Chief Justice," *Nation*, February 19, 1930, 208 (editorial).

59. 72 *Congressional Record*, 71st Congress, 2d Session, February 12, 1930, 3500 (remarks of Senator Dill).

60. Ibid., February 13, 1930, 3561 (remarks of Senator La Follette).

61. Ibid., February 12, 1930, 3505 (remarks of Senator Brookhart).

62. "The Supreme Court under Fire," *New Republic*, February 26, 1930, 30 (editorial).

that could be either more receptive toward the constitutionality of economic legislation or more skeptical about it.

Meanwhile, southern Democrats attacked Hughes for the opinions that he wrote as an associate justice extending the federal government's power to regulate interstate commerce, particularly in the *Shreveport Rate Cases*.[63] Progressives, who still looked as much to the states as to the federal government for reform, also execrated the decision for derogating state power. Other critics of the nomination complained about Hughes's advanced age,[64] his ostensibly blasé attitude about corruption among his colleagues in the Harding cabinet,[65] his resignation from the bench in 1916 to seek the presidency,[66] his role in reducing American naval defenses at the Washington Disarmament Conference while he was secretary of state,[67] his willingness to resign from the World Court after serving less than two years of his nine-year term,[68] and his vigorous campaigns on behalf of Republican presidential candidates during the 1920s.[69] Echoing arguments made against the Taft nomination in 1921, some critics of the nomination further contended that a man rejected by the voters for the presidency should not merit appointment to the nation's second-most-prestigious office.[70] Senators also questioned his ethics in appearing as an advocate before his former colleagues on the bench.[71] The intensity of the Senate debate over the Hughes nomination was attributable in part to a 1929 Senate rule change that permitted open debates on judicial appointments, which previously were considered only in executive session.[72]

Even though they never seriously expected to defeat the nomination, critics of the Hughes appointment believed that their opposition had served the salutary purpose of making citizens more aware of the influence of corporate interests on the Supreme Court.[73] Moreover, they predicted that the widespread public criticism of the Court would make Hughes and his conservative brethren more

63. 72 *Congressional Record,* 71st Congress, 2d Session, February 3, 1930, 3581–83 (remarks of Senator Ransdell); ibid., 3585 (remarks of Senator George).

64. 72 *Congressional Record,* 71st Congress, 2d Session, February 12, 1930, 3500–3501 (remarks of Senator Dill); ibid., February 13, 1930, 3589 (remarks of Senator McKellar).

65. Ibid. (remarks of Senator Walsh).

66. Ibid., 3560 (remarks of Senator Nye); ibid., 3585–86 (remarks of Senator George).

67. See, for example, Matthew A. McCullough to George W. Norris, February 15, 1930 , box 29, George W. Norris Papers, Manuscript Division, Library of Congress (hereafter cited as Norris Papers).

68. Benjamin A. Howes to George W. Norris, February 12, 1930, box 29, Norris Papers.

69. 72 *Congressional Record,* 71st Congress, 2d Session, February 12, 1930, 3586 (remarks of Senator George).

70. Ibid., 3500 (remarks of Senator Dill); ibid., February 13, 1930 (remarks of Senator Dill).

71. Ibid., 3560 (remarks of Senator Nye).

72. Joseph P. Harris, *The Advice and Consent of the Senate: A Study in the Confirmation of Appointments by the United States Senate* (Berkeley: University of California Press, 1953), 253–55. See also George W. Norris to Hugh Russell Fraser, June 22, 1929, box 41, Norris Papers.

73. See, for example, George W. Norris to J. M. Hammond, June 13, 1931, box 41, Norris Papers; Webb Rice to George W. Norris, February 15, 1930, box 29, Norris Papers; "The Senate Speaks Out," *Outlook and Independent,* February 26, 1930, 337.

circumspect in their solicitude for business interests.[74] As the journalist Frank R. Kent explained, Hughes was "far too intelligent to permit all the criticism with which he was drenched to roll off his armor of self-esteem. Some of it will soak in."[75] Liberals likewise hoped that the furor over the Hughes nomination would encourage Hoover to nominate more progressive men to the Court.[76]

The contest over Hughes's nomination was only the prelude to the even more bruising controversy that erupted only a few weeks after Hughes's confirmation, when President Hoover nominated John J. Parker to succeed Edward T. Sanford, who died suddenly and unexpectedly on March 8, 1930, only five hours before Taft died. The Parker nomination was at first widely hailed, because the professional credentials of Parker, a judge of the U.S. Court of Appeals for the Fourth Circuit, were beyond reproach.[77] Like the nomination of Hughes, however, the Parker nomination quickly became entangled in a complex political web. After six stormy weeks, it was defeated by a vote of 41 of 39, the victim of a strange coalition of labor unions, blacks, middle-class liberals, midwestern progressives, and southern segregationists.[78] No previous nomination had galvanized such wide-ranging opposition from so many disparate quarters, and none would again until many of the same forces successfully opposed the Supreme Court nomination of another Fourth Circuit judge, Clement Haynsworth, in 1969.

Even though Parker had impressive credentials, he owed his nomination largely to Hoover's wish to reward the South, in which the Republican Party in the 1928 presidential election carried several states for the first time since Reconstruction. Republicans were particularly optimistic about their prospects of developing a two-party system in Parker's home state of North Carolina, which was one of the most progressive and industrialized southern states.[79] Fearing that Republican efforts to cultivate white southern voters would diminish the GOP's commitment to racial equality, the National Association for the Advancement of Colored People (NAACP) scrutinized Parker's record and found that he had assured white voters during his unsuccessful gubernatorial race in 1920 that the Republican Party did not seek participation by African Americans in the political process.[80]

74. Paul Y. Anderson, "The Hughes Rebellion," *Nation*, February 26, 1930, 238; Frank R. Kent, "War on the Supreme Court," *Literary Digest*, March 1, 1930, 7.

75. Kent, "War on the Supreme Court," 7.

76. "The Senate Speaks Out," *Outlook and Independent*, February 26, 1930, 337.

77. "From the 'New South' to the Supreme Court," *Literary Digest*, April 5, 1930, 12.

78. 72 *Congressional Record*, 71st Congress, 2d Session, May 7, 1930, 8487.

79. Donald J. Lisco, *Hoover, Blacks, & Lily-Whites: A Study of Southern Strategies* (Chapel Hill: University of North Carolina Press, 1985), 205–8.

80. *Hearings before the Subcomm. of the Senate Comm. on Judiciary on the Confirmation of Hon. John J. Parker to Be an Associate Justice of the Supreme Court of the United States*, 71st Congress, 2d Session, 74–79 (1930) (testimony of Walter White, secretary of the NAACP); Lisco, *Hoover, Blacks, & Lily-Whites*, 208–11; Rona Hirsch Mendelsohn, "Senate Confirmation of Supreme Court

Meanwhile, the American Federation of Labor (AFL) expressed alarm over a judicial decision[81] in which Parker had upheld an injunction against union efforts to organize workers against mine workers who enforced "yellow dog" contracts in which workers agreed not to join a labor union.[82] Although Parker's advocates pointed out that he was merely following precedent,[83] Parker's decision was a symbol of the persistent judicial hostility against union activity that for decades had hobbled the AFL's efforts to organize workers. To the AFL, Parker was yet another member of the long line of "injunction judges" about whom it had so bitterly complained. At a time when public support for the labor movement was rising, the AFL naturally hoped that the Court would begin to dismantle restrictions that it had imposed on union activities.

The AFL's opposition to Parker's ruling demonstrated that many critics of the Court who complained of judicial activism in striking down state and federal regulatory statutes did not oppose judicial activism in rejecting judicial precedents that imposed restraints on labor or legislation. In attacking Parker as a "weakling" for following precedent in his injunction decision, Senator Henry F. Ashurst, a Democrat from Arizona, argued that "[a] capable judge, a man of great intellectual capacity, would have said, 'Precedent or no precedent, I shall be a maker of precedents and I shall never follow a precedent that would tend to enslave men who are unable to help themselves.'"[84]

The NAACP and the AFL organized mass campaigns against the nomination that attracted the support of various liberal organizations, including the American Civil Liberties Union (ACLU) and the American Friends Committee. For the first time in U.S. history, substantial numbers of citizens and organized interest groups placed political pressure on senators in an attempt to influence the vote on a judicial nomination.[85] Political appeals to northern senators who had significant black and labor constituencies influenced the outcome, as did the fears of some southern Democratic senators that the nomination would assist GOP efforts to cultivate southern support.

Appointments: The Nomination and Rejection of John J. Parker," 14 *Howard Law Journal* 121–23 (1968).

81. *United Mine Workers v. Red Jacket Consol. Coal & Coke Co.*, 18 F.2d 839 (4th Cir. 1927).

82. Richard L. Watson Jr., "The Defeat of Judge Parker: A Study in Pressure Groups and Politics," 50 *Mississippi Valley Historical Review* 216–17 (1963).

83. *Parker Hearings, supra,* 19–23.

84. 72 *Congressional Record*, 71st Congress, 2d Session, May 5, 1930, 8344 (remarks of Senator Ashurst).

85. See William G. Ross, "Participation by the Public in the Federal Judicial Selection Process," 43 *Vanderbilt Law Review* 10–13 (1990). For example, Senator Henry J. Allen of Kansas received letters from more than two dozen organizations that opposed the nomination, including a broad spectrum of civil rights and religious groups and at least fifteen labor groups. See series C, box 58, Papers of Henry J. Allen, Manuscript Division, Library of Congress.

Although ACLU president Roger S. Baldwin complained after Parker's defeat that few persons perceived how significantly the selection of Supreme Court justices influenced the "social life of future generations,"[86] the widespread opposition to Parker's nomination demonstrated an unprecedented level of awareness about the importance of the Court's composition. The rejection of the Parker nomination taught liberals and labor unions that they could help to prevent the nomination or confirmation of objectionable judicial candidates. Liberals and organized labor understood, however, that Parker's defeat was the result of a felicitous convergence of propitious political circumstances that would not necessarily reemerge whenever a president nominated a conservative to the Court. Accordingly, many of them warned that reformers should not look to the Court for economic, social, and political change. For example, the *New Republic* remarked that "[n]o matter who is appointed and confirmed, the use of injunctions in labor cases ought to be regulated by the right kind of legislation."[87]

Understandably anxious to avert further embarrassment, Hoover nominated Owen J. Roberts, a prominent Philadelphia lawyer whose palatability among liberals was rather strange since he, like Hughes, had devoted most of his career to the representation of major corporate clients, particularly railroads. Roberts, however, was what one progressive journal described as "a conservative with liberal tendencies."[88] He had at least occasionally represented plaintiffs in actions against corporations and had endeared himself to liberals by serving as special counsel to the federal government in the successful prosecution of former Interior Secretary Fall and other miscreants of the Harding administration's Teapot Dome scandal. Assuring Justice Stone that Roberts would prove an ally, Harvard law professor Felix Frankfurter explained that "Roberts has a sense of perspective and a sense of humor—he realizes that the world was not born yesterday nor will it remain in the stereotypes of today. . . . Facts will find a ready access to his mind."[89] Although Justice Willis Van Devanter regretted Parker's rejection, he privately remarked that Roberts "is naturally a stronger man and has a better fundamental education in the law and has a wider experience and practice."[90] Roberts's numerous appearances before the Court had favorably impressed Van Devanter.[91]

Meanwhile, unions were willing to overlook Roberts's close ties to big business because Roberts had sometimes represented labor unions for nominal fees. African Americans had no apparent reason to worry about Roberts, who served as a trustee of the predominately black Lincoln College in Pennsylvania. An honors

86. Roger S. Baldwin to William E. Borah, May 13, 1930, box 301, William E. Borah Papers, Manuscript Division, Library of Congress.

87. "Judge Parker and the Injunction," *New Republic*, April 16, 1930, 232.

88. "Justice Roberts," *Outlook and Independent*, June 4, 1930, 175.

89. Felix Frankfurter to Harlan Fiske Stone, May 22, 1930, reel 3, Frankfurter Papers.

90. Willis Van Devanter to Branden Vandeventer, June 2, 1930, box 16, Willis Van Devanter Papers, Manuscript Division, Library of Congress (hereafter cited as Van Devanter Papers).

91. Willis Van Devanter to Dennis T. Flynn, May 22, 1930, ibid.; Willis Van Devanter to John C. Pollock, June 5, 1930, ibid.

graduate of the University of Pennsylvania's college and law school, Roberts was widely regarded for the intellectual ability he had displayed in private practice and his meticulous prosecution of the complex Teapot Dome cases. At fifty-five, he was a healthy and vigorous man in the prime of life. The Senate confirmed his nomination by acclamation on June 2. Many liberals would come to regret Roberts's appointment. In their 1937 book attacking the Court, Drew Pearson and Robert S. Allen derided it as "the biggest joke ever played upon the fighting liberals of the . . . Senate" and insisted that even Parker would have been more progressive.[92] They did, however, accurately conclude that liberals were "too tired" after their fights against the Hughes and Parker nominations to scrutinize Roberts more closely.[93]

Because seven of the nine justices were older than sixty-four at the time Roberts joined the Court, there was a common expectation that several vacancies would occur on the Court within the next few years. As Hughes remarked after Holmes's retirement, "What a shifting scene the Supreme Court, despite security of tenure, presents!"[94] After Cardozo's appointment in 1932, however, the scene remained more static than at most times in the Court's history. With the exception of the retirement of Holmes and his replacement by Cardozo, the Court's membership remained unchanged from 1930 until the middle of 1937, after which there were five vacancies in less than two and a half years. In terms of membership as well as philosophy, the Hughes Court was in many ways two Courts, the 1930–1937 Court, and the post-1937 Court.

Unlike any previous chief justice other than Edward Douglass White, who was elevated to the chief's seat from an associate justiceship, Hughes began his work with the advantage of having previously served on the Court. This provided him with invaluable working knowledge of the Court's arcane and complex operations that a neophyte would have needed to spend precious time mastering. Hughes also had the advantage of having already served on the Court with three of the justices—Holmes, James Clark McReynolds, and Van Devanter.[95] Hughes had developed a lasting personal friendship with Van Devanter during their years together on the Court. Moreover, Hughes had served in the cabinet for a year with Stone and was well acquainted with Brandeis as a brother at the bar. A favorable omen of Hughes's ability to promote greater harmony on the Court

92. Pearson and Allen, *The Nine Old Men,* 139–40. Parker's record on the Fourth Circuit between 1930 and his death in 1958 offers many insights into how he would have performed as a Supreme Court justice. The standard interpretation is that Parker's subsequent judicial record indicates that he would have been much more receptive toward the rights of racial minorities and organized labor than his opponents in 1930 predicted. Mendelsohn, "Senate Confirmation," 122; Abraham, *Justices, Presidents and Senators,* 31, 151. Not everyone, however, agrees. See Donald E. Lively, "The Supreme Court Appointment Process: In Search of Constitutional Roles and Responsibilities," 59 *Southern California Law Review* 567–72 (1986).

93. Pearson and Allen, *The Nine Old Men.*

94. "Address of Chief Justice Hughes," *American Bar Association Journal,* June 1932, 368.

95. Technically, Hughes also served with Brandeis, who took his oath of office five days before Hughes resigned from the Court on June 10, 1916.

appeared when both McReynolds and Brandeis, representing opposite ends of the Court's ideological spectrum, privately expressed satisfaction with Hughes's nomination.[96] Holmes told British political theorist Harold J. Laski that he was more pleased with Hughes's appointment than he could have been by any other,[97] and he predicted to Felix Frankfurter that Hughes would "make a pretty good Chief."[98]

Hughes returned to a Court that was in many ways more skeptical of the constitutionality of regulatory legislation and less cohesive than was the Court from which he departed in 1916. The dozen years before Hughes's return had seen a resurgence in the Court's nullification of state and federal economic regulatory legislation. This judicial activism, which began not long after Hughes left the bench, accelerated with the election of Harding as president in 1920 and his subsequent appointment of Taft to the chief justiceship and Pierce Butler, Edward T. Sanford, and George Sutherland to associate justiceships. The core of the so-called conservative bloc during both the Taft and Hughes Courts consisted of four justices—Van Devanter, McReynolds, Butler, and Sutherland. Two and sometimes three other justices during the Taft Court and the first seven years of the Hughes Court constituted a "liberal" bloc that tended to vote to uphold economic legislation and strike down laws that infringed on personal liberty. These were Brandeis, Stone (after his appointment in 1925), Holmes (until his retirement in 1932), and Cardozo (who replaced Holmes). Taft, Sanford, and Joseph McKenna (until his death in 1925) occupied a middle position on the Taft Court, voting sometimes with the "conservatives" and sometimes with the "liberals" when the Court divided. Until 1937, Hughes and Roberts likewise tended to be "swing" voters. Although their appointments therefore did not fundamentally alter the ideological dynamics of the Taft Court, their votes for regulatory legislation in a number of closely divided cases between 1930 and 1934, and their general skepticism about the use of restrictions on civil liberties, made the early Hughes Court generally appear more "liberal" than the Taft Court.

With Hughes and Roberts perceived as more moderate than Taft and Sanford, Van Devanter, McReynolds, Sutherland, and Butler became more identifiable as a distinct bloc. During the 1930s, some of their critics derogated these justices as "murderer's row" because they killed so much reform legislation. More frequently

96. Willis Van Devanter to Charles Evans Hughes, February 5, 1930, reel 5, Hughes Papers. See also Louis D. Brandeis to Charles Evans Hughes, February 14, 1930, ibid.; J.C. McReynolds to Charles Evans Hughes, February 4, [1930,] ibid. Hughes confided to Van Devanter that "[i]t is especially gratifying to learn that Justice McReynolds and Justice Brandeis have expressed themselves so generously." Charles Evans Hughes to Willis Van Devanter, February 7, 1930, ibid.

97. Oliver Wendell Holmes Jr. to Harold J. Laski, February 27, 1930, in Mark DeWolfe Howe, ed., *Holmes-Laski Letters: The Correspondence of Mr. Justice Holmes and Harold J. Laski, 1916–1935*, Vol. 2, *1926–1935* (Cambridge, Mass.: Harvard University Press, 1953), 1227. See also Holmes to Laski, February 14, 1930, ibid., 1224.

98. Oliver Wendell Holmes to Felix Frankfurter, March 5, 1930, in Robert M. Mennel and Christine L. Compston, eds., *Holmes and Frankfurter: Their Correspondence, 1912–1934* (Hanover: University Press of New England [for] University of New Hampshire Press, 1996), 250.

they were called the "Four Horsemen of the Apocalypse" because their strident warnings about the perils of governmental regulations seemed to prophesy the imminent demise of capitalism and republican government. This mocking label has forever clung to these men, whose losing battles against the rise of the administrative state have consigned them to low levels in lists that rank justices according to their reputation among scholars. Their rankings also have suffered because none, with the exception of Sutherland, was a particularly articulate or prolific author of judicial opinions. Even though each had a relatively long tenure on the Court, memories of them have faded because the papers of Butler and McReynolds were destroyed, and the documents of Van Devanter and Sutherland offer few penetrating insights into their lives. Moreover, Sutherland and Van Devanter are often perceived as stolid and colorless characters, while Butler and McReynolds are remembered as bullies and prisoners of their many prejudices. Even though these justices had far more complex personalities than these stereotypes would suggest, the received wisdom has enough truth in it that serious revision of their reputations is unlikely.

The antiregulatory predilections of the Four Horsemen reflected their roots in rural and frontier societies that valued rugged individualism. With the exception of McReynolds, each was a largely self-made man. As practicing attorneys, the Horsemen shared the political outlook of their clients, mostly corporations that often sought to circumvent, circumscribe, or nullify federal and state regulatory legislation. They retained these attitudes during their long years of service on the Court, even though they more often than not voted to uphold the constitutionality of regulatory legislation.[99]

Van Devanter, who joined the Court seven months after Hughes in 1910, was reared in a small Indiana town, the son of a prosperous attorney. Going west as a young man, he established a law practice in the socially chaotic Wyoming Territory, where he litigated cattle rustling cases and land disputes, prepared the territory for statehood by codifying its statutes, and helped organize the Republican Party. He served as a judge of the Eighth Circuit for seven years before Taft appointed him to the Supreme Court. Although Van Devanter won high respect from his colleagues for his deft participation in the Court's conferences and his useful contributions to their written opinions, he was himself a hesitant and often dilatory writer, authoring only 346 opinions, a single concurrence, and four dissents during his twenty-six years on the Court. His opinions tended to concern the subjects of land and water rights, railroads, admiralty, Indian affairs, and procedure, in which he was the Court's acknowledged expert. So great were his abilities in the area of procedure that he was the most influential member of the committee that drafted the Judiciary Act of 1925, which greatly broadened the Court's discretionary jurisdiction. Van Devanter's judicial philosophy, like the views of his

99. For an exhaustive list of the decisions in which these justices voted to sustain the constitutionality of regulatory legislation, see Barry Cushman, "The Secret Lives of the Four Horsemen," 83 *Virginia Law Review* 559, 561–645 (1997).

fellow Horsemen, underwent no apparent evolution during his many years on the Court. Two of his critics expressed a common sentiment when they wrote in 1937 that the justice "seldom has deviated from a viewpoint as outmoded as the law of the six-shooter which governed Wyoming in the days Van Devanter practiced there."[100]

McReynolds, the only southerner and the only Democrat who served on the Hughes Court until Hugo Black's appointment in 1937, was born and reared on a plantation on the Kentucky-Tennessee border in an area that retained many traces of the frontier. His father, a prominent planter and physician who opposed public education and other manifestations of modern egalitarianism, imparted to his son an elitism that often expressed itself in racism and an overbearing arrogance. Following graduation from Vanderbilt and the University of Virginia's law school, McReynolds practiced law in Nashville, representing railroads and other large corporations. McReynolds first attracted national attention when he served from 1903 to 1907 as assistant attorney general in the Theodore Roosevelt administration, where he prosecuted antitrust suits with immense vigor and considerable success. Although McReynolds established a private practice in New York in 1907, he served as special counsel to the federal government in various antitrust suits, contributing especially to the government's victory in its litigation against the tobacco trust. McReynolds continued his crusade against the trusts as U.S. attorney general in the Wilson administration, where his irascible personality created friction with his cabinet colleagues and members of Congress.

Even though Wilson had a high regard for McReynolds's abilities, he nominated McReynolds to the Supreme Court in 1914 partly to terminate the controversies and ill feelings that he had generated as attorney general. Few observers detected his reactionary tendencies, and his reputation as a trustbuster led many to predict that he would add a progressive or even radical tinge to the Court.[101] As a member of the Court during the 1920s, however, McReynolds was one of the most reliable opponents of regulatory legislation in divided decisions, though even he joined with all of his colleagues in voting to uphold most regulatory legislation that the Court reviewed. In civil liberties cases, he sometimes displayed the same libertarian streak that informed his votes in economic cases. Most notably, he was the author of the Court's pioneering personal liberties decisions in *Meyer v. Nebraska* and *Pierce v. Society of Sisters,* which struck down legislation that crippled parochial schools.[102]

McReynolds's eccentric personality continues to fascinate, puzzle, and repel historians. A bachelor, McReynolds was at once a reclusive misanthrope and a gregarious host whose invitations were widely sought in Washington. Though charitable with his considerable wealth, he was often bullied subordinates and was chronically rude toward those justices whose intellectual capabilities he regarded

100. Pearson and Allen, *The Nine Old Men,* 188.
101. "Mr. McReynolds's Promotion," *Literary Digest,* September 5, 1914, 405–6.
102. 262 U.S. 390 (1923); 268 U.S. 510 (1923).

as inferior to his own. A notorious anti-Semite, he embarrassed his fellow justices and created tension on the Court by snubbing Justices Brandeis and Cardozo. His attitudes toward blacks were retrograde even by the standards of his era and native region, and he was no supporter of the rights of women.

Sutherland, remembered—perhaps erroneously—as the most moderate of the Four Horsemen, was born in England, but was raised and practiced law in territorial Utah, where suspicion of the federal government was deeply entrenched in the political culture. After Utah attained statehood in 1896, he served in the state senate and the U.S. House of Representatives before his election in 1904 to the U.S. Senate, where he served two terms as a Republican. Although Sutherland's record generally was conservative, he advocated for women's suffrage, the Pure Food and Drug Act, and a federal workers' compensation law. After his defeat for a third Senate term, Sutherland practiced law in Washington, D.C., and served as president of the American Bar Association before President Harding, his former Senate colleague, appointed him to the Court in 1922. Like Van Devanter, Sutherland enjoyed a formidable intellect, a prodigious work ethic, and a genial disposition that enabled him to win and retain the affection of his brethren, including even the most liberal justices. Of the Four Horsemen, Sutherland is widely perceived to have had the most highly coherent judicial philosophy and yet to have been the least doctrinaire. A highly developed philosophy of natural law made him libertarian in cases involving both economic regulation and personal freedom, yet he also believed that the state often needed to act to preserve economic and personal liberties. Born the same year as Hughes, Sutherland was a still vigorous sixty-eight when Hughes became chief justice.

Butler, the most junior of the Four Horsemen, was born on a hardscrabble Minnesota farm to Irish immigrants, but he enjoyed the advantages of an intellectually rigorous home because his father, a graduate of Dublin's Trinity College, took great care with his son's education. After graduation from Carleton College, Butler read law in St. Paul and served as a county attorney before practicing for thirty years with a leading Minnesota law firm. Most of Butler's practice was devoted to sparing railroads from governmental regulation, a role Butler relished because he subscribed to a vigorously laissez-faire creed. The Taft administration drew on Butler's talent when it enlisted him to represent the government in antitrust prosecution, the only major exception to Butler's antiregulatory law practice. Harding nominated Butler to the Court in 1922 after Taft, Van Devanter, and many prominent conservative attorneys lobbied vigorously for his appointment. Butler's Roman Catholicism also influenced Harding's choice, because no Catholic had served on the Court since White died in 1921. In rambunctious confirmation proceedings that presaged the fight over the Hughes and Roberts nominations seven years later, labor leaders and progressive senators, including La Follette and Norris, vigorously opposed Butler's confirmation, alleging that Butler was hopelessly biased on behalf of corporations. Butler's opponents also objected to his role in persuading the University of Minnesota to fire several antiwar professors during the First World War. Although only eight senators voted against the confirmation, the tally might have been higher if Butler had not attracted sympathy after the Ku Klux Klan opposed his confirmation on the basis of his Catholicism. As a justice, Butler confirmed the worst fears of his opponents, for no member of the Court with the possible exception of McReynolds voted to invalidate more economic regulatory legislation and uphold more restrictions on civil liberties.

In contrast with the Four Horsemen, the "liberals" who served on the Court during Hughes's early years as chief justice are accorded high rankings by historians for their deference to economic regulation and their activism on behalf of noneconomic liberties. Holmes, who was eighty-nine years old in 1930, was completing one of the most distinguished careers in the Court's history. The son of the writer Oliver Wendell Holmes Sr., he practiced law in Boston for many years before achieving renown as a legal philosopher with his influential volume *The Common Law* (1881). After a brief stint as a professor at Harvard Law School, Holmes served twenty years as a justice of the Supreme Judicial Court of Massachusetts, where his terse opinions on the legal problems of a modern industrial society were influential far beyond the Bay State. Appointed to the Supreme Court by Roosevelt in 1902, Holmes soon demonstrated his tenacious devotion to judicial restraint, consistently voting to uphold regulatory legislation that he privately disparaged as a "humbug." Contrary to popular image, Holmes also tended to defer to legislation affecting noneconomic liberties in cases involving peonage, eugenics, and the rights of parents over the education of their children.[103] Only in free-speech cases was Holmes was considerably less deferential to legislatures. Together with Brandeis, he pioneered the law of free speech in dissents that long since have become the nation's law.[104] Thrice wounded in the Civil War, Holmes adhered to a fatalistic and pragmatic view of life that was reflected in numerous judicial opinions in which he argued that legislatures should be allowed to conduct economic experiments and that political radicals should likewise have the freedom to advocate novel ideas. Already eighty when Taft became chief justice, Holmes throughout the 1920s confounded predictions of his imminent retirement. Though he often napped in the courtroom, Holmes remained a productive jutice during the first year and a half of Hughes's chief justiceship, authoring two dozen opinions. By January 1932, however, the ninety-year-old Holmes was in rapid decline, and his brethren agreed that he should retire. When Hughes visited him at home on a Sunday afternoon and gently suggested that he might wish to spend more time pursuing his many intellectual interests, Holmes immediately and graciously offered to resign. While Holmes sat stoically in his study, Hughes left the sage's home in tears.

103. *Bailey v. Alabama*, 219 U.S. 219 (1911) (dissenting from invalidation of forced labor statute); *Buck v. Bell*, 274 U.S. 200 (1927) (authoring decision permitting forced sterilization); *Meyer v. Nebraska*, 262 U.S. 390 (1923) (dissenting from invalidation of statute prohibiting the teaching of German in non-public schools).

104. *Abrams v. United States*, 250 U.S. 616 (1919); *Schaeffer v. United States*, 251 U.S. 468 (1920); *Pierce v. United States*, 252 U.S. 239 (1920).

The departure of so distinguished a justice seemed to demand the appointment of a similarly stellar successor, and seldom has public opinion coalesced so widely in favor of a single potential nominee. So formidable was the reputation of Judge Benjamin N. Cardozo of the New York Court of Appeals that bar leaders and influential senators of both parties clamored for his nomination. As a judge of New York's highest court during a time of rapid industrial and commercial development, Cardozo had written trailblazing opinions that brought the common law into conformity with the exigencies of modern social and economic conditions. In addition to his carefully crafted opinions, Cardozo wrote several books, including *The Nature of the Judicial Process* (1921) and *Law and Literature* (1931), which remain standard works. Building on the ideas that Holmes expressed in *The Common Law,* Cardozo argued that, although a judge should respect precedent and defer to the will of legislators, he must also follow his conscience in adapting the law to the changing needs of society. Cardozo was also admired for his gentle temperament, unbending honesty, and far-reaching intellectual curiosity. "Slight, pale, white-haired, he looks like a man who might read Latin and Greek for the fun of it, and he does," one observer remarked in 1935.[105] Hughes recalled after Cardozo's death "[i]n conference, while generally reserved and reticent until it was his duty to speak, he then responded with an unsurpassed clearness and precision in statement. His gentleness and self-restraint, his ineffable charm combined with his alertness and mental strength, made him a unique personality."[106]

Hoover hesitated for a month after Holmes's resignation, loath to appoint a second New Yorker and a second Jew to the Court and perhaps wary of Cardozo's belief that property interests often needed to yield to the common good. The president eventually decided that intellect and temperament were more important than geography, ethnicity, or religion, and he recognized that so popular an appointment could help revive enthusiasm for his beleaguered presidency. As one journal observed, Hoover's nomination of Cardozo was "greeted with a tremendous outburst of approval in which there seems to be no note of dissent."[107] The Senate confirmed Cardozo by acclamation on February 24, 1932. The widespread acclaim for Cardozo's appointment, however, masked considerable misgivings among conservatives, who remained largely silent because Cardozo's credentials were so impeccable. It is not surprising that the Four Horsemen were less than enthusiastic about Cardozo's appointment. Van Devanter, who had favored Attorney General William Mitchell's appointment,[108] derogated Cardozo as an "unfortunate selection" because he was "unstable" and wished "to depart from old

105. "New Deal Meets Tests in Supreme Court," *Literary Digest,* January 19, 1935, 5.

106. "Remarks of Chief Justice Hughes in Response to Presentation of the Resolutions," *American Bar Association Journal,* January 1939, 37.

107. "America Judges Her New Judge," *Literary Digest,* February 27, 1932, 29.

108. Willis Van Devanter to Frank B. Kellogg, January 14, 1932, box 16, Van Devanter Papers.

landmarks and take up with new and uncertain experiments."[109] Rankled by the appointment of another Jew, McReynolds contemptuously read a newspaper at Cardozo's inauguration ceremony and consistently treated Cardozo with the discourtesy he continued to display toward Brandeis.[110]

Cardozo's performance as a justice more than fulfilled the expectations of his admirers, though his aggregate contributions were less than they anticipated because his tenure was cut short by his untimely death at age sixty-eight after only six years on the Court. His towering judicial reputation is therefore based largely upon his fourteen-year tenure on the New York Court of Appeals and his brilliant books about the judicial process.

Cardozo's judicial philosophy closely resembled that of Louis Dembitz Brandeis, who became the most senior member of the Court's liberal faction after Holmes's resignation. Born to a wealthy merchant family in Louisville in 1856, Brandeis practiced law in Boston for many years after graduating from Harvard Law School. Although Brandeis was phenomenally successful as a business attorney, he also championed so many public causes pro bono that he became known as "the People's Lawyer." A vocal opponent of monopoly, he also advised Woodrow Wilson on antitrust policy. Wilson's nomination of Brandeis to the Court in 1916 encountered formidable opposition among many conservatives, who feared that Brandeis's progressivism would leave businesses more vulnerable to regulation. The nomination of Brandeis, the first Jew to serve on the Court, also encountered both overt and covert anti-Semitism. Not surprisingly, Brandeis voted more often to sustain economic regulation than did most of his brethren. Unlike Holmes, Stone, and to a lesser extent Cardozo, Brandeis politically embraced the economic legislation that he voted as a judge to sustain. Although Brandeis exercised some influence in helping to move the Court toward greater acceptance of economic regulation, his most enduring legacy may be the doctrines of freedom of expression that he and Holmes pioneered in dissents that later formed the foundation for decisions by the Court.

Sharing the general judicial philosophies of Holmes, Brandeis, and Cardozo, Stone was a classic example of the justice who confounds the expectations of the president who appoints him. Calvin Coolidge, who nominated his attorney general and fellow Amherst classmate to the Court, probably never suspected that Stone would turn into one of the Court's most progressive members. The son of a middling New Hampshire farmer, Stone became a successful Wall Street attorney and served as a professor and dean of his alma mater, the Columbia Law School, before heading the Justice Department. Although Stone, a lifelong Republican, never shed his political skepticism about the benefits of economic

109. Willis Van Devanter to Mrs. John W. Lacey, February 29, 1932, box 16, Van Devanter Papers.

110. Richard Polenberg. *The World of Benjamin Cardozo: Personal Values and the Judicial Process* (Cambridge, Mass.: Harvard University Press, 1997), 171.

regulation, he believed that changing public attitudes about the role of government required a practical and dynamic response from the courts rather than devotion to a static theory of property rights.[111] Mindful of his anomalous position among the justices, Stone privately told Learned Hand in 1934, "I feel just about as far from the 'children of light' as I do from the Tories."[112]

With Cardozo's appointment, the Court's membership remained stable for more than five years. In contrast to many previous Courts, the Hughes Court included no justices who suffered from significant intellectual deficiencies or (with the exception of Holmes) long-term physical infirmities. Of course, as Sutherland wryly remarked in a 1937 letter to the president of Dartmouth College, many critics of the Court believed that "some us are a little bit under par in rational capacity."[113] Although the average age of the justices was 66.4 years at the time that Cardozo joined the Court and rose to 71.6 years by the time of Van Devanter's resignation in 1937, the Court during this time was no more geriatric than it has been at many other times in its history. With the exception of Hughes, Butler, and Roberts, however, each of the justices who served before 1937 suffered from physical or psychological problems that diminished their relish for their work, even if they generally were able to perform at their fullest capacity.

Feeling their ages, Van Devanter, McReynolds, and Sutherland first considered retiring during the early 1930s. Van Devanter had intended to retire after the 1932 election, regardless of the outcome, but he could not afford to retire after Congress in 1932 enacted a statute providing that no retired federal judge could receive more than ten thousand dollars per year, which was half his salary.[114] McReynolds probably would have retired long before 1941 if he had not burned with animosity toward Franklin Roosevelt. Meanwhile, Sutherland remained on the Court even though he suffered incessantly from a wide array of minor maladies.

Cardozo also suffered from declining health, loneliness, and depression during his years on the Court. A bachelor, he never recovered from the 1929 death of his sister, with whom he had shared a home. Because his fellow justices performed most of their work at home and met only for Saturday conferences, Cardozo missed the more intimate associations he had enjoyed with his brethren on the New York Court of Appeals, and the Court's sharp divisions during the last three years of his tenure bothered him deeply. He told Stone that the contentious 1935–1936 term "would have been almost intolerable without you."[115] Never at ease in

111. See Miriam Galston, "Activism and Restraint: The Evolution of Harlan Fiske Stone's Judicial Philosophy," 70 *Tulane Law Review* 137, 182 (1995).

112. Harlan Fiske Stone to Learned Hand, February 7, 1934, box 15, Harlan Fiske Stone Papers, Manuscript Division, Library of Congress (hereafter cited as Stone Papers).

113. George W. Sutherland to Ernest M. Hopkins, January 13, 1937, box 6, George W. Sutherland Papers, Manuscript Division, Library of Congress (hereafter cited as Sutherland Papers).

114. George W. Sutherland to Mrs. John W. Lacey, October 26, 1932, box 17, Sutherland Papers.

115. Benjamin N. Cardozo to Harlan Fiske Stone, July 2, 1936, box 74, Stone Papers.

Washington, he returned as often as possible to his homes in Manhattan and Long Island. Although he served on the Court until his death on July 9, 1938, his service effectively ended after he suffered a heart attack in December 1937.

Stone usually enjoyed vigorous health, but the Court's numerous decisions nullifying regulatory legislation vexed him so much that he was often restless and unhappy. He told Frankfurter in 1932, "I sometimes wonder whether the game is worth the candle, and whether I would not be having about as useful and interesting career if I were teaching aspiring youth or making money in Wall Street, or even sitting under a cocoanut tree in the South Sea islands."[116]

Although the Hughes Court from 1930 through 1936 was unanimous in four-fifths of its decisions,[117] the Court sharply divided in many cases that involved "cutting-edge" issues. So factionalized was the Hughes Court at times that some of the more "liberal" justices may sometimes have met privately to coordinate strategy, and the Four Horsemen are rumored to have conducted caucuses while sharing cab rides to oral arguments and conferences.[118] Despite the high level of factionalism and the inevitable tensions produced by often closely divided decisions in high-stakes cases, there was little personal animosity among the justices. Hughes's natural diplomacy helped to ease tensions, and the dispositions of the justices, with the notable exception of McReynolds and the partial exception of Butler, were of a naturally amicable nature. Brandeis, for example, had such a high regard for Van Devanter that he urged him in 1934 to refrain from retiring.[119] Such an esprit de corps was vital during a period of intense constitutional ferment when the Court was thrust as never before into the maelstrom of political controversy.

116. Harlan Fiske Stone to Felix Frankfurter, March 2, 1932, reel 3, Frankfurter Papers. See also Stone to Sterling Carr, January 4, 1933, box 8, Stone Papers ("I might be interested in going back to practice in New York, as I suppose I could do at any time").

117. For detailed statistics about voting patterns, see Russell W. Galloway Jr., "The Court That Challenged the New Deal (1930–1936)," 24 *Santa Clara Law Review* 66 (1984).

118. Joseph L. Rauh Jr., "An Unabashed Liberal Looks at a Half-Century of the Supreme Court," 69 *North Carolina Law Review* 214 (1990); Joseph L. Rauh Jr. et al., "A Personal View of Justice Benjamin N. Cardozo: Recollections of Four Cardozo Law Clerks," 1 *Cardozo Law Review* 9 (1979) (recollection of Joseph L. Rauh Jr.). Although Rauh, Cardozo's last law clerk, recalled late in life that Brandeis, Stone, and Cardozo often met privately on Friday nights, two of Cardozo's earlier clerks, who served between 1933 and 1936, could not recall such meetings. "Personal View," 18 (recollection of Ambrose Duskow); "Personal View," 21 (recollection of Alan Stroock). Justice Douglas recalled in his autobiography that Stone sometimes met privately on Friday afternoons to discuss cases with various justices, including Frankfurter, Douglas, Roberts, and Murphy. Douglas indicated, however, that such meetings were for the purpose of allowing fuller discussion rather than formulating liberal strategy, an assertion that Roberts's presence would seem to confirm. See William O. Douglas, *The Court Years, 1939–1975: The Autobiography of William O. Douglas* (New York: Random House, 1980), 222

119. Paul Freund, "Charles Evans Hughes as Chief Justice," 81 *Harvard Law Review* 16 (1967).

2

MIXED SIGNALS ON REGULATORY LEGISLATION, 1930–1934

The Hughes Court quickly confounded the dire predictions made by opponents of Hughes's appointment. For nearly five years after Hughes became chief justice, the Court was more deferential toward regulatory legislation than at any time since his previous tenure on the Court. In several important five-to-four decisions, Hughes provided the vote that spared such laws from judicial nullification. The Court also gratified liberals by demonstrating less deference toward laws that curtailed personal liberties. During its early years, the Hughes Court handed down several landmark decisions that expanded freedom of speech, liberty of the press, and the rights of criminal defendants. Several of these, too, were five-to-four decisions in which Hughes cast the critical vote. So swift and dramatic was the Court's apparent change of direction under Hughes that one commentator declared by October 1931 that Hughes had "shown himself to be just the sort of Chief Justice that his opponents insisted that he never could be. Those who voted against him are still rubbing their eyes."[1] Similarly, Joseph P. Pollard observed during the autumn of 1931 that the Court was "no longer running the government in the interests of a favored few. . . . The extreme conservatism that has dominated the Court ever since the World War has at last been driven into the dark corner reserved for dissenters, and a new and brighter light is shining in the courtroom."[2]

Nevertheless, the Court did not alter its fundamental course during the early years of Hughes's chief justiceship. It continued to carefully scrutinize economic regulatory legislation, and in several cases it struck down regulatory statutes as violating the due process or equal protection clauses. The Court also continued to adhere to a relatively restrictive interpretation of the commerce clause. As one study aptly has concluded, "[t]he early Hughes Court represented an uneasy compromise between the *laissez faire* and the social welfare conceptions of the state."[3]

1. Oliver McKee Jr., "A Liberal Supreme Court: The Position of Chief Justice Hughes," *Outlook and Independent,* October 7, 1931, 171.

2. Joseph Percival Pollard, "Our Supreme Court Goes Liberal," *Forum,* October 1931, 193.

3. Samuel Hendel, *Charles Evans Hughes and the Supreme Court* (New York: Russell & Russell, 1968), 136.

Stone privately complained in 1936 that "there has never been a time in the history of the Court when there has been so little intelligible, recognizable pattern in its judicial performance as in the last few years."[4]

The Court's decisions concerning economic regulation achieved increasing importance during the 1930s, as the Great Depression infused new urgency into questions concerning the constitutional scope of governmental powers. As opponents of the Hughes and Parker nominations had predicted, the Court's decisions would help to determine the extent to which state and federal authorities could experiment with efforts to relieve suffering caused by the Depression, promote recovery, and enact reforms to prevent future depressions. By 1933 a quarter of American workers, mostly heads of households, were unemployed. Gross national product was half its 1929 level, and business investment had shrunk to an eighth of its 1929 high. Several states and more than a thousand municipalities had defaulted on bonds.[5] The Depression devastated agriculture even more than industry, with farm income falling by 1933 to a mere third of its 1929 level.[6]

Despite the Depression's toll, Hughes refused to despair. At the depth of the Depression, in May 1932, Hughes remarked to the American Law Institute, "We are living in a time of many anxieties. But discouragement pays no dividends. . . . These are hard days, critical days, but they are days in which it is worth while to live and toil,—stirring days!"[7] Hughes, however, was sympathetic toward those whom the Depression had ravaged. Even the most conservative justices were not unaware of the widespread suffering. Van Devanter wrote to a friend as early as the fall of 1930 that "everybody is feeling it" and that he personally knew "people who have been completely stripped through investments in the stock market" and others "whose business has been almost ruined."[8] Rather than regard this as justification for governmental action, however, the justice expressed fear that "good people who usually adhere to correct principles of economy are losing their courage and lending a willing ear to social nostrums which you would expect them to denounce."[9]

As Van Devanter perceived, the growing Depression stimulated public support for more governmental activism. Voters increasingly elected governors who promised to initiate innovative economic measures, and the Hoover administration became more aggressive in promoting legislation to restore prosperity. For example, the Reconstruction Finance Corporation, created in 1932, loaned funds to corporations for construction of public works, and the Home Loan Bank Board

4. Harlan Fiske Stone to Felix Frankfurter, February 17, 1936, reel 3, Felix Frankfurter Papers, Manuscript Division, Library of Congress (hereafter cited as Frankfurter Papers).

5. David M. Kennedy, *Freedom from Fear: The American People in Depression and War, 1929–1945* (New York: Oxford University Press, 1999), 163–64.

6. Ibid., 163.

7. "Address of Chief Justice Hughes," *American Bar Association Journal*, June 1932, 369.

8. Willis Van Devanter to Dennis T. Flynn, October 31, 1930, box 16, Willis Van Devanter Papers, Manuscript Division, Library of Congress (hereafter cited as Van Devanter Papers).

9. Ibid.

provided money to financial institutions that offered home construction loans. The Court recognized the changes wrought by expansion of the federal government in a 1932 decision in which it filled a lacuna in the Constitution by holding that a bill signed by the president after Congress's final adjournment became a law.[10] Pointing out that Hoover received 269 bills during the last four days of the Congress that adjourned on March 4, 1931, most of which were presented to him during the final twenty-four hours, Hughes observed that the importance of providing the president with ample time to consider legislation "increases as bills multiply."[11]

With Congress and the public expanding their vision of what constituted appropriate federal and state regulation of the economy, the Court's renewed receptivity toward economic regulation was particularly significant. As the journalist Mark Sullivan remarked in 1931 in the wake of the election of a Democratic House of Representatives for the first time in a generation, "the shift . . . in the balance on the Court has much more real weight than . . . a transfer of power to Congress from Republican to Democratic, or vice versa."[12]

In several of its earliest decisions, the Hughes Court unanimously upheld state economic regulations. For example, the Court rejected due process and equal protection challenges to a controversial section of New York's worker's compensation statute.[13] In another decision, Hughes spoke for a unanimous Court in rejecting the argument that Louisiana violated due process by providing free textbooks to students who attended private schools.[14] The Court likewise rejected a cotton gin operator's contention that he was denied equal protection because Oklahoma permitted a farmers' cooperative to operate a cotton gin business that returned a portion of its net earnings to its customers.[15] The Court explained that the state did not unfairly discriminate against the operator because the state did not prevent him from returning part of his own profits to his own customers. Hughes observed that "it is to be presumed that the State in enforcing its local policies will conform its requirements to the Federal guarantees. Doubts on this point are to be resolved in favor of, and not against, the State."[16]

10. *Edwards v. United States*, 286 U.S. 482 (1932).

11. Ibid., 493.

12. "The Supreme Court's Shift to Liberalism," *Literary Digest,* June 13, 1931, 8.

13. *Staten Island Rapid Transit Railway Company v. Phoenix Indemnity Company,* 281 U.S. 98 (1930). Like its counterparts in other states, New York's workers' compensation statute relieved employers from compensating injured workers who collected more from third parties than the amount to which the workers' compensation statute would have entitled them to receive. Under this statute, employers who were thus relieved from compensation to the employee were required to contribute sums of $500 to funds to provide relief and vocational rehabilitation to certain classes of disabled employees. The challenged section of the statute required the third party to indemnify the employer for these contributions.

14. *Cochran v. Board of Education,* 281 U.S. 370 (1930).

15. *Corporation Commission of Oklahoma v. Lowe,* 281 U.S. 431 (1930).

16. Ibid., 438.

In particular, the Court continued to defer to state police power in cases involving hazardous conditions. In the 1932 decision of *Sproles v. Binford,* the Court unanimously upheld a Texas statute that limited net loads on trucks using the highways to seven thousand pounds.[17] Hughes's opinion explained that the statute did not violate due process, because the state, in exercising its police power, could properly attempt to prevent highway hazards caused by excessive loads on vehicles. Hughes declared, "When the subject lies within the police power of the State, debatable questions as to reasonableness are not for the courts but for the legislature, which is entitled to form its own judgment, and its action within its range of discretion cannot be set aside because compliance is burdensome." The Court also held that the statute did not discriminate against interstate commerce and that it did not violate the contracts clause, because "[c]ontracts which relate to the use of the highways must be deemed to have been made in contemplation of the regulatory authority of the State." Moreover, because the movement of farm vehicles was usually temporary and infrequent, exemption of farm vehicles from the law did not violate equal protection.[18]

Similarly, the Court in 1932 unanimously upheld a Cincinnati ordinance that required rental car companies to pay license fees on the vehicles and deposit insurance policies or bonds for the protection of persons and property against negligent operation of vehicles by licensees.[19] In a brief opinion, Justice Butler explained that the ordinance was a proper exercise of the police power and therefore not a violation of the due process or equal protection clauses. According to Butler, "[t]he running of automobiles necessarily is attended by danger to persons and property in the vicinity; and, when they are negligently driven upon city streets, the peril is great." The Court accepted the finding of the lower court that the operation of rental cars was "extra-hazardous to the public."[20]

In other early decisions, however, the Hughes Court sustained the constitutionality of regulatory legislation by the narrowest of margins. In a five-to-four decision in January 1931, *O'Gorman & Young v. Hartford Fire Insurance Co.,* the Court upheld a New Jersey statute that regulated fire insurance rates by prohibiting companies from allowing their agents to collect more than "a reasonable amount" as a commission on sales of policies.[21] Finding that the statute served the public interest because the compensation of agents directly affected the size of insurance premiums, the Court rejected the insurance companies' argument that the law was void under the due process clause of the Fourteenth Amendment. The brevity of the Court's two-and-a-half-page opinion upholding the legislation seemed calculated to underscore Justice Brandeis's rather impatient declaration that regulation of insurance was "a subject clearly within the scope of the police power" and that

17. 286 U.S. 374 (1932).
18. Ibid., 388, 388–89, 390.
19. *Hodge Co. v. Cincinnati,* 284 U.S. 335 (1932).
20. Ibid., 337.
21. 282 U.S. 251 (1931).

"the presumption of constitutionality must prevail in the absence of some factual foundation of record for overthrowing the statute."[22] In a much longer dissent, Justices Van Devanter, McReynolds, Sutherland, and Butler did not regard the issue as so simple. They contended that the statute could not restrict liberty of contract and "the right of insurers to control the conduct of their internal affairs" in the absence of some type of emergency or other compelling circumstance. Although the dissenters acknowledged that the contract could "ultimately affect the rate charged for policies," they pointed out that "the wages of office boys, printers, bookkeepers, actuaries [and] officers also could affect rates, as could "the price paid for pens, ink, or other supplies." Quoting the admonition of *Adkins* that "[f]reedom of contract is . . . the general rule and restraint the exception," the dissent concluded that the statute was "arbitrary, unreasonable, and beyond the power of the legislature."[23]

In another five-to-four vote, the Court in May 1931 sustained an Indiana law imposing a progressive license tax on retail stores.[24] The Court rejected a grocery chain's argument that the law violated the equal protection clause because owners of multiple stores had to pay a higher rate per store than individual proprietors. Justice Roberts declared in his opinion that "[i]t is not the function of this Court . . . to consider the propriety or justness of the tax, to seek for the motives or to criticize the public policy which prompted the adoption of the legislation. Our duty is to sustain the classification adopted by the legislature if there are substantial differences between the occupations separately classified. Such differences need not be great." The majority concluded that the tax was not unreasonable or arbitrary, because there were numerous "differences and advantages in favor of the chain store," as demonstrated by "the number of such chains established and their astonishing growth."[25] In his dissent, Justice Sutherland contended that the record demonstrated that chain stores did not enjoy any advantage that a large sole proprietorship would not have. He also echoed John Marshall's reminder that the power to tax is the power to destroy and warned that the state might later increase the tax.[26] In hailing the Court's decision, the *Nation* expressed hope that the five-to-four conservative majority that had dominated the Court during the 1920s had turned into a five-to-four liberal majority, observing that "the appointment of Mr. Roberts marks a great gain for liberalism" and that Hughes's "occasionally liberal votes are in themselves encouraging."[27]

22. Ibid., 257, 257–58.

23. Ibid., 257, 257–58, 268, 267, 270 (Van Devanter, McReynolds, Sutherland, and Butler, JJ, dissenting).

24. *State Board of Tax Commissioners of Indiana v. Jackson*, 283 U.S. 527 (1931).

25. Ibid., 537–38, 544, 541.

26. Ibid., 543–48, 552 (Sutherland, J., dissenting).

27. *Nation*, May 27, 1931, 569 (editorial). The editors also predicted that the decision would encourage enactment of similar legislation in other states, which could enable the states to limit the number of chain stores operating within their borders.

This growing deference to state economic regulation did not mean, however, that the Court would permit states to defy federal judicial authorities. In its 1932 decision in *Sterling v. Constantin,* the Court interposed its authority against the governor of Texas, who had declared martial law to circumvent a federal injunction to restrain him from infringing private property rights.[28] Like officials in many states, Governor Ross S. Sterling had feared that overproduction of petroleum depressed oil prices and threatened depletion of this important resource. Sterling also was angry that some oil operators had wastefully produced oil in defiance of state conservation laws, and he claimed that this had excited violent public emotions in the already highly charged atmosphere of the growing Depression. Accordingly, in August 1931 Sterling proclaimed "martial law" over several oil-producing counties and shut down all of the wells in those counties by military force, pursuant to his role as commander in chief of the state's militia. Production was resumed after a state commission established new production limits. Complaining that the governor had unconstitutionally deprived them of property in violation of the Fourteenth Amendment, oil producers obtained a restraining order from a federal court. In defiance of the injunction, Sterling once again seized the wells and restricted production even further.[29]

In a unanimous opinion written by Hughes, the Court found that the district court had correctly concluded that no emergency justified the imposition of martial law and that the governor lacked power under any circumstance to preclude federal judicial review of his actions. As Hughes explained, "There is no such avenue of escape from the paramount authority of the Federal Constitution. When there is a substantial showing that the exertion of state power has overridden private rights secured by that Constitution, the subject is necessarily one for judicial inquiry."[30]

Despite the many decisions in which the early Hughes Court upheld regulatory legislation, opponents of regulation prevailed in a significant number of cases. The fissures on the Court were revealed in May 1930 by the Court's four-to-three decision *Baldwin v. Missouri,* which held that Missouri violated the due process clause of the Fourteenth Amendment by imposing an inheritance tax on bonds situated in the state but owned by an Illinois decedent whose estate already had been subjected to inheritance tax by Illinois.[31] In a stinging dissent joined by Brandeis and Stone, Holmes expressed "more than anxiety" over "the ever increasing scope given to the Fourteenth Amendment in cutting down . . . the constitutional rights of the states." Holmes perceived "hardly any limit but the sky to the invalidating of those rights if they happen to strike a majority of this Court as for any reason undesirable." Echoing his 1905 dissent in *Lochner v. New York,* Holmes

28. 287 U.S. 378 (1932).
29. Ibid., 386–88.
30. Ibid., 397.
31. 281 U.S. 586 (1930).

declared, "I cannot believe that the Amendment was intended to give us *carte blanche* to embody our economic or moral beliefs in its prohibitions."[32]

Liberals were especially disappointed when Hughes and Roberts joined their more "conservative" brethren in a number of cases. These justices, however, were much too complex to fit simple and standard generalizations, and much of the apparent inconsistency about many of their liberal critics complained stemmed from their fidelity to precedent, their commitment to deciding each case on its own special facts, and their refusal to wed themselves to ideology. Invited in 1932 by a youthful correspondent to categorize himself as liberal or conservative, Hughes replied that he disdained any such labels.[33] He later explained to the Fourth Circuit that "[s]uch characterizations are not infrequently used to foster prejudices and they serve as a very poor substitute for intelligent criticism. A judge who does his work in an objective spirit, as a judge should, will address himself conscientiously to each case, and will not trouble himself about labels."[34]

In defiance of growing expectations that they were liberals, Hughes and Roberts voted in March 1933 with the Court in *Liggett v. Lee*, invoking the Fourteenth Amendment's equal protection clause to strike down a Florida statute that imposed a 25–50 percent higher tax per store on store owners whose stores were located in different counties.[35] Writing for the Court, Roberts distinguished the Indiana chain store decision on the grounds that the Florida tax was based on the location of the stores rather than upon the number of stores, a circumstance that Roberts found unduly arbitrary.[36]

In a long dissent, Brandeis declared, "There is a widespread belief that the existing unemployment is the result, in large part, of the gross inequality in the distribution of wealth and income which giant corporations have fostered" and that the Florida legislature could reasonably have concluded that only the encouragement of individual initiative could restore prosperity and protect liberty.[37] Cardozo wrote a separate dissent, joined by Stone, that avoided the larger implications of Brandeis's dissent, arguing primarily that discrimination based on location was not arbitrary.[38] In the wake of the Florida chain store decision, Stone privately remarked, "Perhaps the most astonishing manifestation of our times is the blindness of those who have the big stake in our present system to its evils. It is the story of the Bourbons all over again."[39] Although the Florida franchise tax

---

32. Ibid., 595 (Holmes, J., dissenting). Hughes and Roberts did not participate in the adjudication.

33. Charles Evans Hughes to Lillian Stover, May 9, 1932, reel 5, Papers of Charles Evans Hughes, Manuscript Division, Library of Congress.

34. "Chief Justice Hughes Addresses Judicial Conference of Fourth Circuit," *American Bar Association Journal*, July 1932, 447.

35. *Liggett v. Lee*, 288 U.S. 517 (1933).

36. Ibid., 532–33.

37. Ibid., 580 (Brandeis, J., dissenting)

38. Ibid., 580–86 (Cardozo, J., dissenting).

39. Harlan Fiske Stone to Felix Frankfurter, February 17, 1933, reel 3, Frankfurter Papers.

decision disillusioned liberals, it gave scant comfort to business corporations, which regarded the Court's reasoning as unduly narrow and Brandeis's dissent an ominous portent of growing judicial hostility toward business.[40]

Even more disillusioning to advocates of more aggressive state intervention in economic affairs was the Court's six-to-two decision in March 1932 in *New State Ice Co. v. Liebmann*,[41] in which the Court invoked substantive due process under the Fourteenth Amendment to strike down an Oklahoma statute prohibiting anyone from manufacturing, selling, or distributing ice without obtaining a permit from the state corporation commission. Although the statute, enacted in 1925, was not a response to any economic crisis and did not involve any central economic issue, its demise portended judicial hostility toward anti-Depression measures. In his opinion, Justice Sutherland concluded that the ice business was not sufficiently suffused with a "public interest" to warrant such public regulation. Distinguishing decisions in which the Court had upheld regulation of agricultural and mining activities, Sutherland explained that "[h]ere we are dealing with an ordinary business, not with a paramount industry, upon which the prosperity of the entire state in large measure depends. It is a business as essentially private in its nature as the business of the grocer, the dairyman, the butcher, the baker, the shoemaker, or the tailor." Sutherland warned that the state's regulation "does not protect against monopoly, but tends to foster it" because "[t]he aim is not to encourage competition, but to prevent it; not to regulate the business, but to preclude persons from engaging in it."[42]

Brandeis responded to the Court's opinion in a powerful dissent that crystallized the arguments that opponents of substantive due process had advanced at least since the time of Holmes's dissent in *Lochner*. Brandeis declared that "[w]hether the local conditions are such as to justify converting a private business into a public one is a matter primarily for the determination of the state legislature" and that "[w]hether the grievances are real or fancied, whether the remedies are wise or foolish, are not matters about which the Court may concern itself." Ultimately, Brandeis explicitly rejected the very "notion of a distinct category of business 'affected with a public interest,' employing property 'devoted to a public use.'" According to Brandeis, "[t]he action of the State must be held valid unless clearly arbitrary, capricious, or unreasonable." Brandeis warned that "in the exercise of this high power, we must be ever on our guard, lest we erect our prejudices into legal principles. If we would guide by the light of reason, we must let our minds be bold."[43]

In a characteristically detailed survey of economic conditions in which he relied upon a wide array of studies of the ice industry, Brandeis found that "[i]ce has come to be regarded as a household necessity, indispensable to the preservation of food and so to economical household management and the maintenance

40. "Mild Cheer for Chain Stores," *Literary Digest*, April 1, 1933, 30.
41. 285 U.S. 262 (1931). Cardozo did not participate in the case.
42. Ibid., 277, 279.
43. Ibid., 284, 285, 302, 285, 311 (Brandeis, J., dissenting).

of health," particularly in Oklahoma, where the warm climate "precludes resort to the natural product" and household refrigerators remained uncommon. Analyzing the highly competitive character of the ice industry, Brandeis also concluded that the legislature could reasonably have concluded that the ice industry lent itself to monopoly and should be treated as a public utility, particularly because the statute was the culmination of seventeen years of legislative study and regulation of the ice industry.[44]

Finally, Brandeis urged the judiciary to refrain from strangling legislative efforts at economic experimentation. Although he conceded that "[m]an is weak and his judgment is at best fallible"—an echo of Holmes's observation in his *Abrams* dissent that "all life is an experiment" and that we must wager our futures on uncertain prophecies—Brandeis insisted that the Depression cried out for experimentation: "I cannot believe that the framers of the Fourteenth Amendment, or the States which ratified it, intended to deprive us of the power to correct the evils of technological unemployment and excess productive capacity. . . . It is one of the happy incidents of the federal system that a single courageous State may, if its citizens choose, serve as a laboratory; and try novel social and economic experiments without risk to the rest of the country."[45]

In an apparent rebuke to Brandeis and other progressives for whom experimentation was a watchword, Sutherland warned that "unreasonable or arbitrary interference or restrictions cannot be saved from the condemnation of that [Fourteenth] Amendment merely by calling them experimental" and that "there are certain essentials of liberty with which the state is not entitled to dispense in the interest of experiments."[46]

The *New State Ice* case appeared to be a severe setback for progressives to the extent that Brandeis and Stone stood alone in dissent, though some predicted that Brandeis's powerful dissenting opinion would exercise considerable influence upon legislators and courts and would become the majority view.[47] Hughes, who told his biographer after his retirement that he regarded the case as a close call,[48] apparently squared his vote in *Liebmann* with his vote for regulation of the New Jersey insurance industry in *O'Gorman* because he regarded regulation as less intrusive than barriers to entry.[49] Roberts, who also had voted to uphold the regulation in *O'Gorman*, presumably made the same distinction.[50]

44. Ibid., 287, 294.

45. Ibid., 310, 311.

46. Ibid., 279.

47. "The Inalienable Right to Be an Iceman," *Literary Digest*, April 9, 1932, 13.

48. Merlo J. Pusey, *Charles Evans Hughes* (New York: MacMillan, 1951), 2:698 (based on Pusey's interview with Hughes on January 2, 1947).

49. See Richard D. Friedman, "Switching Time and Other Thought Experiments: The Hughes Court and Constitutional Transformation," 142 *University of Pennsylvania Law Review* 1891, 1911 (1994).

50. Ibid.

On the same day that it decided *New State Ice*, the Court further antagonized liberals by invoking Fifth Amendment substantive due process to strike down a federal estate tax that presumed that gifts made within two years of death were made in anticipation of death and thus taxable to the decedent's estate.[51] Although Justice Sutherland's opinion explained that the statute's presumption "excludes consideration of every fact and circumstance tending to show the real motive of the donor,"[52] Justice Stone's dissent, joined by Brandeis, urged deference to Congress and presented evidence that transfers of large wealth tended to be made much more by the old than by the young[53] and that the Court's decision would largely defeat the purpose of the estate tax.[54] "Again," the *New Republic* complained, "'due process' worked its charm on behalf of wealth."[55] Stone privately remarked that "[t]he story of the old boys from seventy to ninety who gave away their fortunes and succeeded in beating the Government was almost comical, if it were not for the tragedy which such things spell for government."[56]

The Court likewise continued to interpret narrowly the power of federal regulatory agencies. In a 1931 decision, for example, the Court unanimously held that the Federal Trade Commission (FTC) could not properly order the manufacturer of an "obesity cure" to desist from representing that its product was a scientific means of treating obesity.[57] Despite evidence that the product could endanger health when taken without medical supervision, the Court explained that the FTC had failed to demonstrate that the manufacturer's practices had interfered with competition because there was no evidence that the manufacturer had competitors.

In another 1931 decision, the Court narrowly construed the commerce power in holding that the Interstate Commerce Commission (ICC) improperly prohibited the managers of a railroad reorganization from receiving what the ICC

---

51. *Heiner v. Donnan*, 285 U.S. 312 (1932); *Handy v. Delaware Trust Co.*, 285 U.S. 352 (1932).

52. 285 U.S. 327.

53. Ibid., 343–46 (Stone, J., dissenting). Stone's statistics were a rejoinder to Sutherland's contention that "[t]he young man in abounding health, bereft of life by a stroke of lightening within two years after making a gift, is conclusively presumed to have acted under the inducement of the thought of death, equally with the old and ailing who already stands in the shadow of the inevitable end." 285 U.S. 327. Frankfurter told Stone that "perhaps your quantitative demonstration of how the aged settlers beat the government was the cruellest blow you dealt the majority, considering the deep sense of pity that Sutherland had aroused for the 'young man in abounding health . . .'—trala, la la." Felix Frankfurter to Harlan Fiske Stone, March 28, 1932, reel 3, Frankfurter Papers.

54. 285 U.S. at 342.

55. "The Supreme Court and a Balanced Budget," *New Republic*, April 27, 1932, 288. The editors alleged that "[b]y creating constitutional obstructions to effective safeguards against highly profitable evasions, the Supreme Court has put the Constitution at the disposal of evaders." Ibid., 287.

56. Harlan Fiske Stone to Felix Frankfurter, March 25, 1932, reel 3, Frankfurter Papers.

57. *Federal Trade Commission v. Raladam Co.*, 283 U.S. 643 (1931).

regarded as an exorbitant commission.[58] Justice Sutherland's opinion ruled that the ICC exceeded its statutory authority under the commerce clause because it interfered with a private contract between the railroad and its shareholders and seized property without due process of law in violation of the Fifth Amendment.[59] In a dissent joined by Holmes and Brandeis, Stone looked beyond the form of the reorganization plan to point out that the managers had almost unbridled discretion to reorganize the company in a manner that suited their self-interest rather than those of the shareholders. Stone argued that the commission had power to prevent such self-dealing because it adversely affected railroad credit, the stability of the nation's transportation system, and the public interest in low railroad rates.[60]

The Court also restricted the ICC's powers in two other 1931 decisions from which Stone, Holmes, and Brandeis dissented. In the first decision, the Court overturned an ICC rule that allowed small short-line railroads to pay lower fees for their use of freight cars owned by other railroads than larger railroads paid insofar as the smaller railroads incurred higher transaction costs in connection with the movement of such cars.[61] The Court concluded that the rule violated the Fifth Amendment's due process clause because it was inconsistent with the ICC's general rule on payments for use of freight cars. In a long and painstaking dissent, Stone explained why the ICC had adopted two different rules and pointed out the slim likelihood that the ICC intended any contradiction.

In the second case, the Court overturned an ICC order permitting a small railroad to obtain a larger proportion of the rate it shared with a larger railroad for hauling freight.[62] The Court held that the order was invalid because it did not specify the date on which it would be effective. In dissent, Stone pointed out that the Transportation Act of 1920 pursuant to which the ICC acted merely provided that commission orders could not take effect earlier than thirty days before their promulgation and that "[i]t would not . . . occur to anyone unfamiliar with legal niceties that the order failed to prescribe a time for its operation with respect to the future."[63]

These six-to-three decisions profoundly disappointed liberals, who had gathered hope from the early votes of Hughes and Roberts. The ICC cases illustrated the gap between the Court's professions of deference to Congress and administrative agencies and its actual scrutiny of their works. For example, in its decision nullifying the ICC's increase of a small railroad's share of the freight rate it shared with larger line the Court declared that "a reasonable degree of latitude must be allowed for the exercise of its [the ICC's] judgment. The mere fact that . . .

58. *United States v. Chicago, Milwaukee, St. Paul and Pacific Railroad Co.*, 282 U.S. 311 (1931).
59. Ibid., 323–31.
60. Ibid., 337 (Stone, J., dissenting). Hughes did not participate in the decision.
61. *Chicago, Rock Island & Pacific Railway Co. v. United States*, 284 U.S. 80 (1931).
62. *United States v. Baltimore & Ohio Railroad Co.*, 284 U.S. 195 (1931).
63. Ibid., 205 (Stone, J., dissenting).

mathematical accuracy . . . may not be attained is not enough to put upon the Commission's order the stamp of invalidity."[64]

In *Crowell v. Benson* in 1932, the Court unanimously agreed that findings of fact by administrative agencies must be final, but Hughes spoke only for himself and four other justices in holding that courts could determine for themselves whether they had jurisdiction in a challenge to an administrative ruling.[65] Accordingly, the Court concluded that the federal district court properly conducted a trial de novo on the issue of whether a complainant under the Longshoremen's and Harbor Workers' Compensation Act was employed by the defendant at the time of his injury. Although Hughes predicted that courts would only rarely need to conduct factual reviews for jurisdictional purposes,[66] Brandeis complained in a bitter dissent joined by Stone and Roberts that the Court's ruling would "gravely hamper the effective administration of the Act" by encouraging legal wrangling that would wear down the less wealthy litigant.[67] Writing to Frankfurter in the wake of *Crowell*, Stone remarked that his service on the Court had made him realize "what a treacherous and generally undependable instrument the human mind is."[68] Despite Stone's disappointment, *Crowell* nevertheless was an important victory for advocates of the regulatory state because it was "the first case that broadly approved transfers of trial jurisdiction from courts to agencies."[69]

The Court likewise seemed to elevate form over substance in a March 1934 decision that hobbled the FTC's power to restrain activities prohibited by the Clayton Antitrust Act. The Court held that because the Clayton Act did not explicitly prohibit mergers, the FTC had no power to prohibit a holding company's merger of two competing subsidiaries even though the merger was an apparent attempt to circumvent the commission's investigation of whether its ownership of the subsidiaries violated the statute.[70]

Even where the Court sustained the constitutionality of legislation and administrative decisions, it still presumed to carefully comb the details of regulations to determine whether they conformed to the Court's notions of due process. For example, the Court in a 1931 decision undertook a detailed factual analysis before validating the reasonableness of Nebraska's annual assessment of the deposits of banks to sustain a fund to provide relief for depositors of failed banks. The Court concluded that the assessment was not so steep that it constituted a confiscatory taking of property in violation of the Fourteenth Amendment.[71] Although the

64. *Chicago, Rock Island & Pacific Railway v. United States*, 284 U.S. 80, 92 (1931).

65. 285 U.S. 22 (1932). One seat on the Court was vacant when the case was decided.

66. Ibid., 65.

67. Ibid., 94 (Brandeis, J., dissenting).

68. Harlan Fiske Stone to Felix Frankfurter, March 2, 1932, reel 3, Frankfurter Papers. Frankfurter had told Stone that he was "in mourning" over *Crowell*. Reel 64, Frankfurter Papers.

69. Gordon G. Young, "Public Rights and the Federal Judicial Power: From *Murray's Lessee* through *Crowell* to *Schor*," 35 *Buffalo Law Review* 779 (1986), citing David Currie, *Federal Courts: Cases and Materials*, 3rd ed. (St. Paul, Minn.: West, 1982), 144.

70. *Arrow-Hart & Hegeman Electric Co. v. Federal Trade Commission*, 291 U.S. 587 (1934).

71. *Abie State Bank v. Bryan*, 282 U.S. 765 (1931).

Court had sustained the constitutionality of Nebraska's depositor protection statute in 1911,[72] Justice Holmes, in a companion case upholding a similar law in Oklahoma, had suggested that the Court revisit the constitutionality of the rates if they changed.[73] In its 1931 decision, the Court explained that the challenge to the law that the Court had rejected in 1911 "was brought immediately upon the enactment of the law, and that decision sustaining the law cannot be regarded as precluding a subsequent suit for the purpose of testing the validity of assessments in the light of the later actual experience."[74] Accordingly, the Court reviewed the statute to determine "whether the law had become so burdensome as to transcend in its operation the constitutional limits of state power."[75] The original annual assessment upheld by the Court in 1911 had been .10 percent. Although this had increased to .60 percent by the time that the second lawsuit was commenced, the Court concluded that subsequent legislation that had limited the assessment to a maximum of .20 percent for a period of ten years was not "confiscatory, or other than a reasonable method of liquidating the guaranty plan."[76]

Rather than an instinctive bias in opposition to business regulation, the Court's willingness to second-guess legislatures and administrative agencies may have been a natural response to the constitutional uncertainties created by unprecedented governmental intervention in economic affairs. William M. Wiecek aptly has explained that "[c]aution and hesitancy, rather than incoherence or contradiction, characterized the rise of the bureaucratic state."[77] As one commentary observed in 1940, the administrative agency early in the twentieth century was a new creature, one that was not mentioned in the Constitution, and one whose "rationale rests upon nothing more than sheer necessity." Accordingly, it was not surprising that "[a]s an upstart, charged with discretion in important matters, it has seemed to invade the judicial domain" and at first "inspired suspicion, aroused jealousy, [and] provoked resistance from members of the bench."[78]

Hughes was especially wary of the emergence of administrative law. Addressing the American Law Institute in 1938, he expressed dismay over "a tendency, in

72. *Shallenberger v. First State Bank,* 219 U.S. 114 (1911).

73. *Noble State Bank v. Haskell,* 219 U.S. 109 (1911). Although Holmes did not specifically say that the Court might revisit the constitutionality of the bank regulation, he wrote that "[i]t is asked whether the State could require all corporations or all grocers to help guarantee each other's solvency, and where we are going to draw the line. But the last is a futile question, and we will answer the others when they arise. With regard to the police power, as elsewhere in the law, lines are pricked out by the gradual approach and contact of decisions with the other side." 219 U.S. 112.

74. 282 U.S. at 772.

75. Ibid., 775.

76. Ibid., 784. Even the six-tenths of a percent rate appears to have been much less than the rate upheld in the Oklahoma decision. See 219 U.S. 109.

77. William M. Wiecek, *Liberty under Law: The Supreme Court in American Life* (Baltimore: Johns Hopkins University Press, 1988), 129.

78. Walton Hamilton and George Braden, "The Supreme Court Today," *New Republic,* August 5, 1940, 179.

the desire to emphasize the importance of obtaining flexibility and expertness in particular classes of cases, to depreciate the work of the courts and by comparison to exalt administrative boards and commissions." Hughes contended that "[w]hatever the shortcomings of courts, and whatever the need of administrative bodies, it is still the courts which stand out as the exemplars of the tradition of independence and impartiality. This is because judicial institutions . . . have won their place and established their standards through the historic contest against the abuses of power." He also pointed out that judges, in contrast to often faceless administrators, accepted personal responsibility for their decisions. He urged administrators to emulate judicial independence.[79]

Even though the Court invalidated only a small proportion of federal and state statutes and administrative regulations, its critics complained that these decisions had a disproportionate impact by intimidating and demoralizing citizens and public officials who sought to achieve social and economic reform. As the *New Republic* observed in the wake of the Court's 1931 decisions invalidating ICC regulations, "The Commission should be free to take such action as the meaning of the facts and its own responsible insight may dictate. Not only should the Commission be free, it should feel free. Among every group of men, no matter how high minded and able, there are always some who are unusually deferential to what is called higher authority. And nothing is more conducive to timidity than the awing authority of the Supreme Court of the United States. Men become weary of fighting, particularly when the opponent comes panoplied in the majesty of Law."[80] Similarly, Yale Law School dean Charles E. Clark pointed out in 1935 that "[i]t is the *possibility* of court action that affects the entire political, economic, and legal approach to public issues."[81]

The Court's substitution of its own judgment for the decisions of regulatory bodies likewise rankled liberals because they believed that its decisions failed to take account of economic reality. As I. F. Stone observed in 1939, the Court often had decided cases on the basis of principles "unimpeachable in themselves but bearing little relation to the facts." Stone stated,

> No one believes a rate-making agency ought to have the power to confiscate the property of a utility, but it is a far step from this general principle to the conclusion that a return of less than 7 per cent on so intangible an item as "going value" is therefore "confiscatory." "Liberty of contract" is certainly one of the basic rights in a free country, but it is a far step from this general principle to the conclusion that a minimum wage drawn up to protect a washwoman deprives her of this "liberty." The avoidance of the realistic makes the rationalization of a hidden bias easier.[82]

79. "Address by Chief Justice Hughes," *American Bar Association Journal,* June 1938, 432.

80. "Supreme Court and Interstate Commerce Commission," *New Republic,* January 20, 1932, 257.

81. Charles E. Clark, "The Supreme Court and the N.R.A.," *New Republic,* June 12, 1935, 121.

82. I. F. Stone, "The Greatest Strike-Breaker of All," *Nation,* March 25, 1939, 347.

In response to federal judicial nullification of utility rates prescribed by state commissions, a 1934 statute championed by Senator Hiram Johnson of California limited the power of federal courts to enjoin the enforcement of rates that did not affect interstate commerce and that were made after a reasonable notice and hearing and with review available in state court. As Edward A. Purcell Jr. has observed, the Johnson Act confirmed the insistence of progressives "that the federal courts served the interests of powerful corporations" and yet also "suggested the extent to which most of them were reluctant to undermine too severely the general supervisory authority of the federal courts."[83]

Despite its mixed record on regulatory agencies, the Hughes Court from the first seemed favorably disposed toward antitrust enforcement. In two 1930 decisions, the Court unanimously held that ten corporations that controlled 60 percent of the film prints used by American movie theaters violated the Sherman Act by agreeing to transact business only with theaters that used standard form contracts[84] and by refusing to distribute films to theater buyers who failed to assume sellers' contracts.[85] In 1932 the Court refused to permit modification of a 1920 antitrust consent decree between meatpackers and the federal government that barred the packers from dealing in groceries.[86] In his opinion for the majority, Cardozo explained that changes in conditions in the meatpacking and grocery businesses during the intervening dozen years were not sufficient to warrant modification of the decree, because the size of the packers and their history of "ruthless and oppressive" competition indicated that they would renew their "war of extermination" against the grocery stores if the Court ruled in their favor.[87] Butler and Van Devanter dissented, while McReynolds, ever the trustbuster, joined the majority decision. In lower-profile cases, the Court also sustained the use of the Sherman Act against practices in the dry-cleaning and paper industries.[88]

The Court also seemed deferential toward the rights of organized labor. In May 1930 Hughes wrote for the Court affirming the issuance of an injunction in favor of a labor union, to prevent a railroad from interfering with its employees' choice of a collective bargaining agent in accordance with the Railway Act of 1926.[89] In its eight-to-zero decision, the Court rejected the railroad's contention that the

83. Edward A. Purcell Jr., *Brandeis and the Progressive Constitution: Erie, the Judicial Power, and the Politics of the Federal Courts in Twentieth-Century America* (New Haven, Conn.: Yale University Press, 2000), 26. Professor Purcell has explained that "[i]n spite of its narrow scope . . . the Johnson Act was a classic victory for legal Progressivism as well as for the advocates of states' rights." Ibid., 26.

84. *Paramount Famous Lasky Corp. v. United States*, 282 U.S. 30 (1930).

85. *United States v. First National Pictures, Inc.*, 282 U.S. 44 (1930).

86. *United States v. Swift & Co.*, 286 U.S. 106 (1932).

87. Ibid., 117–19.

88. *Atlantic Cleaners & Dryers v. United States*, 286 U.S. 427 (1932); *Story Parchment Co. v. Patterson Parchment Paper Co.*, 282 U.S. 555 (1931).

89. *Texas & New Orleans Railroad Company v. Brotherhood of Railway & Steamship Clerks*, 281 U.S. 548 (1930).

statute deprived the railroad of liberty in violation of the Fifth Amendment by interfering with its right to select or discharge employees. Although the Court in 1908 and 1915 had struck down laws prohibiting employers from requiring workers to sign "yellow dog" contracts agreeing that they would not join a union,[90] the Hughes Court explained that these decisions were not applicable because the Railway Act was not directed at the right of employers to hire or fire its employees but rather "at the interference with the right of employees to have representatives of their own choosing."[91] Champions of labor recognized that the decision set an important precedent for judicial approval of collective bargaining legislation and predicted that it would encourage labor unions to protect their rights through injunctions, the very tool that the courts had used so relentlessly in the past to curtail union activity.[92] As one commentator pointed out, "For the first time in the history of labor struggles the tables were turned and the weapon which had been so effective *against* labor was being put to good use *for* labor."[93] Moreover, Barry Cushman has observed that the decision also marked the first time that the Court had resolved a conflict between liberty of contract and associational freedom in favor of the latter.[94]

The Court upheld the most controversial regulatory measure of all in February 1931, when it sustained the constitutionality of the Prohibition Amendment, rejecting the challenge that it was improperly enacted because amendments conferring new powers over individuals had to be ratified by conventions rather than state legislatures.[95] In other early decisions, the Hughes Court helped put teeth in the amendment. A May 1930 decision, for example, held that manufacturers of barrels, bottles, corks, labels, and cartons violated the Prohibition Act if they offered these commodities for sale in a manner that purposefully encouraged their purchase for illegal activity,[96] and a 1931 decision permitted federal agents to seize the furnishings of speakeasies.[97] The Court was similarly resolute in construing the Twenty-first Amendment's repeal of Prohibition. In February 1934, two months after the amendment's ratification, the Court unanimously quashed all pending prosecutions for violations of the Prohibition Enforcement Acts,[98]

---

90. *Adair v. United States*, 208 U.S. 161 (1908); *Coppage v. Kansas*, 236 U.S. 1 (1915).

91. 281 U.S. at 571.

92. See Edward Berman, "The Supreme Court Interprets the Railway Labor Act," 20 *American Economic Review* 638 (1930).

93. Joseph Percival Pollard, "Our Supreme Court Goes Liberal," *Forum*, October 1931, 199.

94. Barry Cushman, *Rethinking the New Deal Court: The Structure of a Constitutional Revolution* (New York: Oxford University Press, 1998), 125.

95. *United States v. Sprague*, 282 U.S. 716 (1931).

96. *Danovitz v. United States*, 281 U.S. 389 (1930).

97. *United States v. Ryan*, 284 U.S. 167 (1931).

98. *United States v. Chambers*, 291 U.S. 217 (1934). See also *Massey v. United States*, 291 U.S. 608 (1934) (reversing conviction when no final judgment was entered before repeal of Prohibition Act).

which provided a boon to the calendars of lower federal courts by eliminating nine thousand cases from their dockets.[99]

The Court also began to adopt a less restrictive doctrine of intergovernmental immunity. In 1931 it unanimously rejected a private investor's claim that federal taxation of the profits from sales of municipal bonds imposed an undue burden on a state's borrowing power—an argument that no state ever had made.[100] The justices, however, upheld federal taxation on profits from the sale of such bonds. The Court explained that taxes on sales, unlike taxes on interest, did not impose any direct burden on a municipal instrumentality and did not interfere with a municipality's borrowing power.[101]

The Court similarly took a relaxed view of federal immunity from state regulation in a 1931 decision upholding a state tax on domestic corporations that was measured by income that included royalties on federal copyrights.[102] Justice Stone explained that the tax did not impose any "real or direct burden on the federal government."[103] In dissent, Sutherland, Van Devanter, and Butler contended that the tax was invalid because it fell upon income that was "exempt in virtue of an implied prohibition of the federal Constitution," even though they conceded that the tax did not "impose a burden upon the exercise of a vital power of the federal government."[104] In another decision, however, the Court held that a federal tax on motorcycles to a municipal police department imposed an undue burden on the local government and was invalid under the theory of intergovernmental immunity.[105]

The continued failure of state and federal initiatives to end the worsening Depression assured the defeat of Herbert Hoover and the landslide election of Franklin D. Roosevelt in the 1932 presidential election. Although Roosevelt was careful during his campaign to deflect widespread Republican allegations that he was a dangerous radical, making no promises other than to repeal Prohibition and balance the budget, he did not discourage hopes that he would take bold initiatives to stimulate economic recovery. With a nod to progressives such as Brandeis for whom "experimentation" had long been a rallying cry, Roosevelt declared during his campaign for the nomination that "[t]he country needs and, unless I mistake its temper, the country demands bold, persistent experimentation." Roosevelt's avowed willingness to experiment, together with his promise for a "new deal for the American people" when he accepted the Democratic presidential nomination, had obvious constitutional ramifications and inspired spirited,

99. "9000 Liquor Cases Thrown from Courts," *Literary Digest*, February 17, 1934, 12.

100. *Willcuts v. Bunn*, 282 U.S. 216 (1931).

101. Ibid., 227–34.

102. *Educational Films Corp. of America v. Ward*, 282 U.S. 379 (1931).

103. Ibid., 392.

104. Ibid., 395 (Sutherland, J., dissenting).

105. *Indian Motorcycle Co. v. United States*, 283 U.S. 570 (1930). In a dissent joined by Brandeis, Stone argued that "it is not clear how a recovery by the taxpayer would benefit directly the government supposed to be burdened." Ibid., 580 (Stone, J., dissenting).

but ultimately lame, efforts by Republicans during the campaign to suggest that Roosevelt would subvert the Constitution.

One of Roosevelt's few indiscretions during the campaign was his offhand remark a few days before the election that, because most of the justices were at least nominal Republicans, the GOP controlled the Supreme Court. Although this was not part of any general attack on the Court, Republicans called widespread attention to the remark as evidence of Roosevelt's intention to subvert the Constitution. Denouncing Roosevelt's statement as "atrocious," Hoover reminded voters that he had appointed the Democratic Cardozo and insisted that any suggestion of political influence over the Court was contrary to American tradition.[106] Although the episode does not appear to have affected votes, it presaged the conflicts of the coming years.

On the eve of the election, Van Devanter confided privately that he was "praying that Roosevelt and his demagogic cohorts will not succeed."[107] Van Devanter feared that "many people are grasping at straws and ready to take chances on any proposed change without considering whither it will lead us."[108] Stone likewise had a low opinion of Roosevelt, dismissing him in April 1932 as "an utterly impossible man for President."[109] Hughes had less reason to fear Roosevelt. The two had much in common for both had been key members of the New York reform movement. Although Roosevelt had not arrived in Albany as an assemblyman until shortly after Hughes left the governorship, they had many mutual allies, including Louis Howe, who was a partisan of Hughes before he became Roosevelt's principal lieutenant. Howe remained an admirer of Hughes until his death during the fourth year of Roosevelt's presidency.[110]

Roosevelt's landslide election, bolstered by large Democratic majorities in both houses of Congress, seemed to ensure the enactment of controversial regulatory legislation that the Court would need to review. In his inaugural speech, Roosevelt promised aggressive efforts to fight the Depression and declared that such action "is feasible under the form of government which we have inherited from our ancestors. Our Constitution is so simple and practical that it is possible always to meet extraordinary needs by changes in emphasis and arrangement without loss of essential form."[111]

106. "Hoover in Direct Attack on Roosevelt Charges 'New Deal' Is Now a 'Shuffle;' Scores Remark on Supreme Court," *New York Times*, October 29, 1932, 1. See also William G. Ross, "The Role of Judicial Issues in Presidential Elections," 42 *Santa Clara Law Review* 414–15 (2002).

107. Willis Van Devanter to Mrs. John W. Lacey, October 26, 1932, box 17, Van Devanter Papers.

108. Willis Van Devanter to Thomas F. Doran, October 24, 1932, box 17, Van Devanter Papers.

109. Harlan Fiske Stone to Sterling Carr, April 9, 1832, box 8, Harlan Fiske Stone Papers, Manuscript Division, Library of Congress (hereafter cited as Stone Papers).

110. See Pusey, *Charles Evans Hughes*, 2:732.

111. *Inaugural Addresses of the Presidents of the United States from George Washington 1789 to George Bush 1989*, Senate Document 101–10, 101st Congress, 1st Session 272–73 (1989).

Immediately after his inauguration, Roosevelt carried through on his promise to take unprecedented action to restore economic stability. Taking office in the midst of an epidemic of bank failures that threatened the collapse of the nation's financial system, Roosevelt ordered all banks to close for nine days to avert panic and to permit the Treasury Department to review accounts to determine which banks were sound enough to reopen. Authority for such reviews was conferred by a hastily enacted Emergency Banking Relief Act, which also gave the president broad power to regulate banking transactions in currency, credit, bullion, and foreign exchange and authorized the Treasury to require surrender of all gold and gold certificates.[112] To stop spiraling deflation, Congress in June cancelled gold clauses in private and public contracts and made all debts payable only in currency.[113] Ten days later, Congress enacted the Glass-Steagall Act, which insured bank deposits up to five thousand dollars, separated commercial banking from investment banking, and gave the Federal Reserve Board more power to prevent banks from speculating on credit.[114]

During the epic first "One Hundred Days" of the Roosevelt administration, Congress with little debate and much enthusiasm also enacted a raft of other presidential proposals to relieve human suffering, promote economic recovery, and craft reforms that would help to stabilize capitalism. Roosevelt's "New Deal" attacked unemployment by establishing the Civil Conservation Corps, which employed a quarter million men to plant trees, drain swamps, and otherwise facilitate conservation of natural resources on federal lands.[115] Congress granted funds to states to establish similar work programs[116] and created a federal employment service that was designed to discourage exploitation of workers by private agencies.[117] To assist depression-ravaged farmers, the Agricultural Adjustment Act attempted to raise prices by giving subsidies to farmers who curtailed production. Taxes on processors of agricultural products financed the subsidies.[118] This law also provided refinancing for farm mortgages, and another statute created the Home Owners' Loan Corporation to refinance nonfarm home mortgages.[119]

The most ambitious of the administration's recovery statutes was the National Industrial Recovery Act, which attempted to comprehensively regulate most business enterprises through a complex combination of federal coercion and cooperation.[120] The statute authorized industries to develop codes of fair competition to regulate prices, labor conditions, and trade practices, which the president had power to approve. By denying licenses to businesses that violated the code of their

112. Ch. 1, 48 Stat. 1.
113. Gold Repeal Joint Resolution, Ch. 48, 48 Stat. 112.
114. Banking Act, Ch. 89, 48 Stat. 162.
115. Civilian Conservation Corps Act, Ch. 17, 48 Stat. 31.
116. Federal Emergency Relief Act, Ch. 30, 48 Stat. 55.
117. National Employment System Act, Ch. 49, 48 Stat. 113.
118. Ch. 25, 48 Stat. 31.
119. Home Owners Refinancing Act, Ch. 64, 48 Stat. 128.
120. Ch. 90, 48 Stat. 195.

industry, the president could effectively destroy such businesses. In addition to creating the National Recovery Administration (NRA) and the National Labor Board to supervise this unprecedented intrusion into private economic activity, the statute also established the Public Works Administration (PWA) to reduce unemployment and shore up the nation's infrastructure through the construction of public schools, dams, airports, roads, and hospitals. Throughout the nation, businesses displayed the ubiquitous NRA logo, with its blue eagle and motto, "We Do Our Part," a symbol of the common effort to restore the nation's prosperity.

In promoting long-term reform, Congress in May 1933 enacted the Federal Securities Act to prevent another stock market crash by requiring publicly traded companies to disclose information about their finances.[121] A year later, Congress created the Securities and Exchange Commission to regulate securities trading.[122]

In its only venture into extensive and long-range economic planning and federal control of economic enterprise, Congress in May 1933 created the Tennessee Valley Authority (TVA), vesting it with the power to undertake the economic and social transformation of the backward Tennessee Valley area through a program of flood control, power generation, and reforestation.[123]

Roosevelt's earliest measures, particularly the bank holiday, received approbation even from many conservatives, who recognized the compelling need for temporary emergency measures. Van Devanter privately observed ten days after the inauguration that "[t]he President has been taking a courageous course which has met with quite general approval. There is marked evidence that confidence is returning."[124] McReynolds also approved of some of Roosevelt's emergency measures.[125]

In a decision nine days after Roosevelt's inauguration, the Court upheld an attempt by coal producers in the wretchedly depressed Appalachian region to stabilize prices through the creation of a sales agency to fix prices among competing coal dealers.[126] Only McReynolds dissented. Rejecting the federal government's Sherman Act challenge, Hughes's opinion explained that a "cooperative enterprise, otherwise free from objection, which carries with it no monopolistic menace, is not to be condemned as an undue restraint merely because it may effect a change in market conditions, where the change would be in mitigation of recognized evils and would not impair, but rather foster, fair competitive opportunities." In a candid recognition of the economic emergency that had inspired the arrangement, Hughes declared that, "[w]hen industry is grievously hurt, when

---

121. Ch. 38, 48 Stat. 74.

122. Securities Exchange Commission Act, Ch. 404, 48 Stat. 911.

123. Ch. 32, 48 Stat. 58 (1933).

124. Willis Van Devanter to Mrs. John W. Lacey, March 14, 1933, box 17, Van Devanter Papers.

125. James E. Bond, *I Dissent: The Legacy of Chief [sic] Justice James Clark McReynolds* (Fairfax, Va.: George Mason University Press, 1992), 81.

126. *Appalachian Coals, Inc. v. United States*, 288 U.S. 344 (1933).

producing concerns fail, when unemployment mounts and communities dependent upon profitable production are prostrated, the wells of commerce go dry."[127]

Hughes's words echoed his remarks in a 1932 speech at a federal judicial conference in which he similarly seemed to recognize the need for flexibility in
responding to the national emergency, declaring, "[W]e should be faithless to our
supreme obligation if we interpreted the great generalities of the Constitution so
as to forbid flexibility in making adaptations to meet new conditions, and to prevent the correction of new abuses incident to the complexity of our life."[128] Similarly, Brandeis declared in his *Liebmann* dissent that the Depression was "an
emergency more serious than war. Misery is wide-spread, in a time, not of scarcity,
but of over-abundance. The long-continued depression has brought unprecedented unemployment, a catastrophic fall in commodity prices and a volume of
economic losses which threaten our financial institutions. Some people believe
that the existing conditions threaten even the stability of the capitalistic system."
Accordingly, Brandeis insisted that "[t]here must be power in the States and the
Nation to remould, through experimentation, our economic practices and institutions to meet changing social and economic needs."[129]

Such pronouncements by Hughes and Brandeis on and off the bench inspired
hopes—and fears—that the Court would uphold New Deal legislation. Writing in
November 1933, Yale law professor Thurmond Arnold disparaged predictions that
New Deal legislation would run afoul of the Court. Although Arnold acknowledged that both liberal and conservative thinkers were "used to assuming that
the Constitution necessarily discourages adventure in economic organization,"
Arnold averred that "[i]n reality the Supreme Court for a long period of time has
been paving the way to declare the present recovery legislation constitutional. The
emergency finds itself well supplied with the necessary formulas," particularly "the
process of curbing state legislatures and extending the power of the national government over interstate commerce."[130] Other liberals were not so confident. Also
writing in November 1933, another commentator argued that Roberts's record of
voting to sustain economic regulation was too shaky to predict "his response to
new situations" and that Hughes's moderate response to such legislation did not
ensure that he would "support the revolutionary aspects of the New Deal. With
him much depends on how well the government can sugar-coat the pill to a sem-
blance of conformity to an order that appears to be passing away."[131]

The calmness in the Court's chambers increasingly contrasted with the misery
and menace of violence that pervaded the nation. The Court met twice during
May 1932 under extra police guard in the wake of rumors of demonstrations by

127. Ibid., 373–74, 372.

128. "Hughes Stresses Flexibility of Law," *New York Times,* June 10, 1932, 4.

129. 285 U.S. at 311 (Brandeis, J., dissenting).

130. Thurmond Arnold, "The New Deal Is Constitutional," *New Republic,* November 15,
1933, 8–10.

131. Mitchell Dawson, "The Supreme Court and the New Deal," *Harper's Magazine,* November 1933, 648, 649.

Communist advocates of the Scottsboro Boys and by veterans who had come to Washington from throughout the nation to persuade the government to make early payment on their war bonus.[132] Predictions of both industrial and agrarian revolution became increasingly common. Deploring the plight of the farmers who suffered from high freight rates, Minnesota's Farmer-Labor governor Floyd B. Olson warned in October 1933 that "the sound of marching feet, unless relief is soon obtained, will not be strange. These men are not 'Reds,' nor Communists, but discriminatory legislation has made their plight increasingly clear."[133]

By early 1933 farm foreclosures in the Midwest already had provoked widespread unrest that threatened violence that was reminiscent of Shay's Rebellion, the armed attacks in 1786 by indebted farmers on Massachusetts courthouses that helped precipitate the Philadelphia constitutional convention in 1787. Throughout the winter of 1932–1933, farmers in numerous states used various forms of threats and intimidation to prevent sheriffs' sales, as when five hundred men stormed a Sioux City courthouse.[134] The most dramatic incident occurred in April 1933, when two hundred men in Le Mars, Iowa, invaded the courtroom of Judge Charles C. Bradley and threatened to hang him unless he promised to refrain from continuing to conduct farm foreclosure proceedings. When the judge refused to acquiesce to the mob's demands, rioters dragged him from his bench, abducted him into the countryside, and strung him up with a rope from a telegraph pole, choking him into unconsciousness.[135] In response to this violence, Iowa's governor temporarily declared martial law in seven counties and suspended the operation of the civil courts in two others in which military tribunals were formed.[136]

In an effort to forestall such violence and to stabilize economic conditions in agriculture, the Minnesota legislature in 1933 enacted a so-called mortgage moratorium law, which authorized local courts to grant farmers additional time to raise funds to satisfy delinquent payments on foreclosed mortgages. During the period of the moratorium, the debtor remained obligated to pay interest on the loan and a fair rental value as assessed by a court. On January 8, 1934, in a five-to-four vote the Court sustained the constitutionality of the law in *Home Building & Loan Association v. Blaisdell.*[137] In his opinion for the majority, Hughes found that the statute did not violate the contracts clause because all contracts include an

132. "High Court Is Guarded on Rumor of Red Riot," *New York Times,* May 17, 1932, 2; "Police Guard Congress and Supreme Court, on Rumors of Red and Bonus Demonstrations," *Harper's Magazine,* May 24, 1932, 5.

133. *President Pledges Support for Seaway,* New York Times, October 20, 1933, 10.

134. "When Fighting Farmers Defy Foreclosure," *Literary Digest,* January 21, 1933, 32–33; "When the Farmers' Fury Explodes," *Literary Digest,* February 4, 1933, 10.

135. "Recount Threats to Kill Iowa Judge," *New York Times,* May 4, 1933, 5; "Behind the Iowa Farm Riots," *Literary Digest,* May 13, 1933, 8.

136. "Sober Iowa Favors Resort to Militia," *New York Times,* May 7, 1933, 1; "Iowa's Agrarian Outrages," *New York Times,* May 7, 1933, IV, 4 (editorial).

137. 290 U.S. 398.

implicit reservation of power by the state "to safeguard the vital interests of its people." The contracts clause, he declared, did not create an absolute prohibition "and is not to be read with literal exactness like a mathematical formula." Explaining that the Court had long recognized that such reservations were inherent in the police power, Hughes observed that "there has been a growing appreciation of public needs and of the necessity of finding ground for a rational compromise between individual rights and public welfare." In language that seemed to presage judicial approval of other anti-Depression legislation, Hughes declared that, "[w]hile emergency does not create power, emergency may furnish the occasion for the exercise of power." Expressing frank understanding that the nation's economic catastrophe threatened political stability, Hughes remarked that "the policy of protecting contracts against impairment presupposes the maintenance of a government by virtue of which contractual relations are worthwhile." Hughes found that the mortgage crisis in Minnesota justified the stay of "immediate and literal enforcement of contractual obligations" insofar as the emergency was real and no mere legislative subterfuge; the statute was designed for the benefit of society as a whole rather than particular individuals; and the legislation was temporary and no broader than necessary to accomplish its purpose. Hughes also denied that the statute violated due process or equal protection.[138]

In a long and piercing dissent joined by Van Devanter, McReynolds, and Butler, Justice Sutherland emphasized that legislative impairment of foreclosure rights during the economic depression that followed the Revolution had motivated the Framers to write the contracts clause. As Sutherland explained, the contracts clause was "framed and adopted with the specific and studied purpose of preventing legislation designed to relieve debtors *especially* in time of financial distress." Rejecting the Court's conclusion that an emergency justified some leeway in interpreting the contracts clause, Sutherland declared that a constitutional provision cannot "mean one thing at one time and an entirely different thing at another time." Sutherland pointed out that "[t]he present exigency is nothing new," because "periods of depression, of industrial failure, of financial distress, of unpaid and unpayable indebtedness" had "alternated with years of plenty." Sutherland warned that "[t]he effect of the Minnesota legislation, though serious enough in itself, is of trivial significance compared with the far more serious and dangerous inroads upon the limitations of the Constitution which are almost certain to ensue as a consequence naturally following any step beyond the boundaries fixed by that instrument."[139]

Two months later, the Court in another landmark five-to-four decision upheld another state anti-Depression measure, New York's regulation of milk prices, in its decision in *Nebbia v. New York.*[140] To protect dairy farmers from declining milk prices that in 1932 fell below the costs of production, New York in 1933 had established a three-member milk control board to regulate prices. After the board fixed

---

138. Ibid., 434, 428, 442, 426, 435, 440, 435, 440, 448, 453.

139. Ibid., 453, 449, 471, 448 (Sutherland, J., dissenting).

140. 291 U.S. 502 (1934).

the price of milk at nine cents per quart, Leo Nebbia, the proprietor of a small Rochester grocery store, was convicted of a misdemeanor after he sold two quarts of milk and a loaf of five-cent bread for a total of eighteen cents. In rejecting Nebbia's contention that the statute violated due process, Justice Roberts declared that "neither property rights nor contract rights are absolute; for government cannot exist if the citizen may at will use his property to the detriment of his fellows, or exercise his freedom of contract to work them harm. Equally fundamental with the private right is that of the public to regulate it in the common interest." According to Roberts, "a state is free to adopt whatever economic policy may reasonably be deemed to promote public welfare, and to enforce that policy by legislation adapted to its purpose."[141] Roberts's opinion was perhaps most significant for its apparent rejection of the doctrine, affirmed so recently by the Court in *New State Ice v. Liebmann,* that the state could regulate only businesses cloaked with a public interest.

In a dissent joined by Van Devanter, Sutherland, and Butler, Justice McReynolds declared that "[i]f now liberty or property may be struck down because of difficult circumstances, we must expect that hereafter every right must yield to the voice of an impatient majority when stirred by distressful exigency." Arguing that constitutional rights are not "enjoyed in subjection to mere legislative findings," McReynolds contended that such rights do not vanish merely because a legislature concludes that their extinction or impairment suits the public interest. "The Legislature," McReynolds averred, "cannot lawfully destroy guaranteed rights of one man with the prime purpose of enriching another, even if for the moment, this may seem advantageous to the public." Flatly asserting the Court's right to inquire into "the wisdom of the enactment," McReynolds concluded that the legislation was not reasonably calculated to relieve the distress of farmers since the increase of retail prices would not discourage continued overproduction, to which McReynolds attributed falling wholesale prices.[142]

Blaisdell and *Nebbia* were widely seen as a harbinger of far-reaching approval of state and federal anti-Depression measures by a now "liberal" Court.[143] The *Nation* asserted that the two decisions made "certain that President Roosevelt can carry through his policies without having to pack the Supreme Court with new justices in order to do it."[144] Similarly, *Collier's* remarked that the decision was "fortunate for both the country and the Supreme Court" because a contrary ruling would have made the Court "an object of bitter political controversy."[145] The *New Republic* remarked that "not in this generation has the Supreme Court eaten so much crow" and predicted that "[i]t will be difficult for the Court to recapture the

141. Ibid., 523, 537.

142. Ibid., 545–46, 548, 558, 556, 556–58 (McReynolds, J., dissenting).

143. E.g., Joseph Sugarman, Note, *Boston University Law Review* 14 (April 1934): 419–20; "News and Comment from the National Capital," *Literary Digest,* January 20, 1934, 10.

144. *Nation,* March 14, 1934, 1 (editorial).

145. "Battle Lines of '36," *Collier's,* February 17, 1936, 54.

ground it has thus relinquished" because the likelihood of continued economic turmoil would not provide the auspicious "climate of opinion in which the old ideas flourished."[146] The *St. Louis Dispatch* declared that the Court "has broken chains which have bound the American people for sixty years."[147] Charles Edward Clark told the annual meeting of the New York State Bar Association that *Blaisdell* augured a "historic" turn of the Court toward approval of social and economic regulatory legislation.[148] Conservatives tended to agree, fearing that *Blaisdell* presaged dangerous experimentation and derogation of vested property rights. Van Devanter warned his sister that the decision could generate "incalculable harm and instability."[149] A former American Bar Association president privately lamented to Sutherland that the decision "throws a cloud, a doubt upon every contract executed in the future" and would inflict "deplorable" harm upon both creditors and borrowers because "[f]ew will care to loan money if the Legislature may declare an emergency and deny their remedy for one, two or three years."[150] *Blaisdell*, however, may not have been as revolutionary as its critics or admirers thought. As one scholar recently has pointed out, *Blaisdell* merely represented an application of the Court's long-standing mediation between vested contract rights and the state's power to regulate for the public interest.[151] Moreover, *Nebbia* easily could have gone the other way, because Roberts reportedly paced the floors of his home for hours late at night in indecision before casting his vote.[152]

Despite the widespread contemporary perception of *Nebbia* and *Blaisdell* as a watershed in the Court's approach toward regulatory legislation, some commentators correctly perceived that the Court's split in the decisions and the vigor of the dissents portended trouble for New Deal legislation.[153] As one law review note pointed out, much New Deal legislation, particularly the National Industrial Recovery Act, would "present totally different constitutional problems,"[154] such as the scope of the commerce power and congressional delegation issues. In particular, some observers pointed out that many New Deal measures, in contrast to the New York and Minnesota laws, were viewed as permanent reforms rather than temporary responses to emergencies.[155]

146. "The Supreme Court Eats Crow," *New Republic*, March 21, 1934, 146–47.

147. "The Supreme Court and the Emergency," *Literary Digest*, March 17, 1934, 9.

148. "High Court Backing for NRA Predicted," *New York Times*, January 27, 1934, 4.

149. Willis Van Devanter to Mrs. John W. Lacey, January 23, 1934, box 17, Van Devanter Papers.

150. F. Dumont Smith to George Sutherland, January 26, 1934, box 5, Papers of George W. Sutherland, Manuscript Division, Library of Congress.

151. Samuel R. Olken, "Charles Evans Hughes and the Blaisdell Decision: A Historical Study of Contract Clause Jurisprudence," 72 *Oregon Law Review* 600–602 (1993).

152. Edward S. Corwin, *Constituional Revolution, Ltd.*, (Westport, Conn.: Greenwood Press, repr. 1977), 75–76 (reporting the story on "first-rate authority.")

153. See, for example, note, 47 *Harvard Law Review* 668 (1934).

154. Note, 34 *Columbia Law Review* 362 (1934).

155. See T.R.B., *New Republic*, January 24, 1934, 308 ("a considerable part of the [New Deal] program is bound to be permanent, but the Court [in *Blaisdell*] did not have to face that issue and was concerned only with statutes admittedly of temporary character"); *New Republic*,

The importance of the limited duration of the Minnesota law was demonstrated four months after *Blaisdell,* when the Court unanimously invalidated an
Arkansas statute prohibiting garnishment of life insurance policies by creditors.
The Court distinguished *Blaisdell* on the ground that the Arkansas statute was not
of limited duration.[156] While advocates of robust state intervention in the economy
complained bitterly that five-to-four decisions such as *O'Gorman, Nebbia,* and *Blaisdell* demonstrated the absurdity of placing the fate of legislation in the hands of
an unelected court,[157] only 25 of the 798 cases adjudicated by the Court during
the 1930 through 1934 terms were decided by a margin of one vote. Some 85
percent of the decisions during these five terms were unanimous. The importance
of many of the closely divided decisions, however, made liberals understandably
uneasy about tight votes. Although some critics of the Court supported legislation
that would require the concurrence of more than a majority of justices to invalidate legislation, these proposals vanished into obscurity with most other Court-
curbing proposals.[158] If enacted by Congress, however, the Court might have
upheld such a measure. The Court in 1930, in the first opinion written by Hughes,
had upheld an Ohio statute that prohibited the state supreme court from nullifying a statute without the concurrence of at least all but one of the justices.[159]

In addition to expanding the scope of state police power, the early Hughes
Court also tended to expand the discretion of states in exercising power over
interstate commerce pursuant to the so-called dormant commerce clause doctrine, which permits states to enact regulations that may affect interstate commerce if Congress has not enacted contrary laws and if the state regulations would
not unduly interfere with the flow of interstate commerce. In deciding whether a
state statute conflicted with Congress's power to regulate interstate commerce
when congressional exercise of that power was unused or "dormant," the Hughes
Court began to move away from the distinction between "direct" and "indirect"
burdens on interstate commerce that the Court had crafted in its earlier decisions.
At least tacitly, the Court began to accept the more flexible analysis of Justice
Stone, who had criticized the test in a 1927 dissent as "too mechanical, too uncertain in its application, and too remote from actualities to be of value." Stone had

---

March 14, 1934, 1 (editorial) ("[a]bout the only remaining doubt is whether the Court will be
as liberal in its interpretations when and if it can be argued that the emergency is past");
"Supreme Court Makes the New Deal More Secure," *Literary Digest,* January 20, 1934, 4 (quoting
David Lawrence and Mark Sullivan).

156. *W. B. Worthen Co. v. Thomas,* 292 U.S. 426 (1934).

157. See *Nation,* March 14, 1934, 1.

158. William G. Ross, *A Muted Fury: Populists, Progressives, and Labor Unions Confront the
Courts, 1890–1937* (Princeton, N.J.: Princeton University Press, 1994), 218–32, 291, 298.

159. *Ohio v. Akron Park District* and *Ohio v. Zangerle,* 281 U.S. 74, 79–81 (1930). The Court
held that the Constitution's guarantee of a republican form of government in the states was the
responsibility of Congress rather than the courts, that the right of appeal was not essential to
due process, and that the equal protection clause was not violated even though the same statute
could be constitutional in one county and unconstitutional in another.

urged consideration of "all the facts and circumstances, such as the nature of the regulation, its function, the character of the business involved and its actual effect on the flow of commerce."[160] Although the Court did not formally adopt a more flexible test until 1938, the early Hughes Court decisions seemed more concerned with balancing the regulatory needs of the state with the potential for interstate discrimination than with applying a rigid "direct/indirect" formula. The Hughes Court's decisions therefore had the effect of encouraging more state regulation of business enterprises.

In upholding the trucking load limitation in *Sproles v. Binford,* for example, the Court had declared that states could legislate "according to the special requirements of local conditions . . . until Congress sees fit to act."[161] In another 1932 decision, the justices unanimously held that an Oklahoma statute that prohibited the waste of petroleum did not burden interstate commerce, because it applied only to production and not to sales or transportation.[162]

The Court similarly took a practical approach in cases involving state taxation of goods that were part of interstate commerce. In *Liggett v. Lee,* the Court rejected the argument that the Florida chain store tax burdened interstate commerce even though chain stores were more likely than local stores to purchase goods in interstate commerce, insofar as there was no intentional discrimination and the burden was minimal.[163] In another case, the Court held that a state could tax the generation of electricity from a water plant even though the electricity was transmitted over wires to consumers in another state to the extent that the process of production was completed prior to transmission.[164] Similarly, the Court in 1931 held that a state tax on operation of buses engaged exclusively in interstate commerce could not be sustained unless it was levied only as compensation for the use of the state's highways or to defray the costs of building the roads and regulating their traffic.[165] The Court likewise held that a state could not impose a tax on a foreign corporation that was engaged solely in interstate commerce.[166] In a dissent joined by Brandeis and Stone, Cardozo pointed out that the company was able to conduct intrastate business and might start doing so during the period of the tax.

Despite the political turmoil over the New Deal, the Court did not review any New Deal legislation until nearly a year after Roosevelt's inauguration. As one commentator observed, "During all these tumultuous months of legislative incubation and administrative initiation of new laws, nine lonely old men, who carry their noon lunches to work and munch their oranges, apples and sandwiches in a colonial chamber buried deep in the central gloom of the Capitol Building, have

160. *Di Santo v. Pennsylvania,* 273 U.S. 34, 43–44 (1927) (Stone, J., dissenting).
161. 306 U.S. at 351.
162. *Champlin Refining Co. v. Commission,* 286 U.S. 210, 234, 235 (1933).
163. 288 U.S. 538–39.
164. *Utah Power & Light Co. v. Pfost,* 286 U.S. 165 (1932).
165. *Interstate Transit, Inc. v. Lindley,* 283 U.S. 183 (1931).
166. *Anglo-Chilean Corp. v. Alabama,* 288 U.S. 218 (1933).

been sitting on the sidelines, watching and wondering."[167] The early decisions of the Hughes Court inspired much hope that the Court would generally sustain New Deal legislation or at least would examine it with eyes tempered by the nation's economic catastrophe. As Hughes stated in a 1932 address to lower federal judges, "We should be faithless to our supreme obligation if we interpreted the great generalities of the Constitution so as to forbid flexibility in making adaptations to meet new conditions, and to prevent the correction of new abuses incident to the complexity of our life, or as crystallizing our own notions of policy, our personal views of economics and our theories of moral or social improvement."[168]

During the first half of 1934, the Court finally had occasion to rule on the constitutionality of two New Deal statutes, both of which were designed to promote economy in government and achieve Roosevelt's campaign promise to balance the federal budget. Although neither case involved any significant federal legislation, the Court's invalidation of both laws augured poorly for the New Deal. Because the Court's invalidation of federal legislation generally tends to shrink the size of government, it is ironic that the effect of both of these decisions was to require increased federal expenditures.

In the first case, *Booth v. United States*,[169] the Court unanimously held that Congress's 1932 reduction of pensions for retired federal judges violated the provision of section 1 of article 3 that prohibits the diminution of the compensation of federal judges.[170] The Court reasoned that judges who retired rather than resigned "unquestionably" retained their office because they remained eligible for the assignment of judicial duties, and indeed many carried heavy workloads. The Court held that the 50 percent pay cut was unconstitutional even though Congress had not reduced the compensation of the plaintiff judges below what they earned when they first were appointed to the bench.[171] In a small but not entirely insignificant manner, this decision helped to confirm judicial independence and therefore potentially emboldened "retired" but still active lower federal judges, most of whom were Republican, to question the constitutionality of New Deal legislation.

In *Lynch v. United States*, the only other decision prior to 1935 in which the Court struck down a New Deal statute, the Court unanimously held that Congress had violated the Fifth Amendment's due process clause by abrogating the federal government's contracts with war veterans for life and disability term insurance.[172]

167. Ray Tucker, "Court of the Last Guess," *Collier's*, July 7, 1934, 32.

168. "Chief Justice Hughes Addresses Judicial Conference of Fourth Circuit," *American Bar Association Journal*, July 1932, 446.

169. 291 U.S. 339 (1934).

170. The most celebrated victim of the statute was Oliver Wendell Holmes Jr., whose pension was reduced from twenty thousand to ten thousand dollars until Congress voted to restore his full pension. Artemus Ward, *Deciding to Leave: The Politics of Retirement from the United States Supreme Court* (Albany: State University of New York Press, 2003), 137.

171. 291 U.S. at 348–52.

172. 292 U.S. 571 (1934).

In language that called into question the constitutionality of Congress's repudiation of the gold standard, the Court declared that "[p]unctilious fulfillment of contractual obligations is essential to the maintenance of the credit of public as well as private debtors." Although the Court acknowledged that "there was in March, 1933 great need of economy . . . because of lessened revenues and the heavy obligations to be issued in the hope of relieving widespread distress," it explained that abrogation of contractual obligations "would be not the practice of economy, but an act of repudiation."[173]

Contrary to widespread expectations, the New Deal won an overwhelming vote of public confidence in the 1934 congressional elections. Although the nation remained mired in the greatest depression of its history, the economy had considerably improved since Roosevelt had become president, and the new administration had done much to restore confidence in the nation's future even among Americans who continued to suffer from poverty. As Stone privately observed, however, the results may not have represented "satisfaction with the New Deal, so much as they do a realization that our Republican brethren have nothing constructive to offer."[174] Gaining seats in both the Senate and the House, Democrats now controlled approximately three-quarters of the seats in both houses of Congress. Never before had the party that controlled the White House performed so well in a midterm election. The Democratic landslide ensured the enactment of more innovative legislation that the Court would need to review.

173. Ibid., 580.
174. Stone to Sterling Carr, November 7, 1934, box 8, Stone Papers.

3

BLOCKING THE NEW DEAL, 1935–1936

Speculation and suspense about how the Court would respond to New Deal legislation finally started to abate early in 1935, when the justices began to decide the constitutionality of a raft of measures to relieve economic distress, stimulate recovery, and promote reform. The outcomes of the Court's decisions were generally even worse than Roosevelt and most New Dealers had feared. During the course of seventeen months, between January 1935 and June 1936, the Court invalidated eight federal economic regulatory statutes and limited the scope of one other, while upholding only one in its entirety and another only in part.

Many proponents of the New Deal naturally regarded the carnage as catastrophic, for the extent to which the Court exercised its power of judicial review was unprecedented, qualitatively and quantitatively. Until 1935, the Court had struck down only sixty-three federal statutes and parts of sixty-seven others of the fifty thousand federal laws enacted during the history of the Republic. Even during the previous three decades, a time of unusual judicial activism, the Court had invalidated only a couple of dozen. Never before had the Court so severely frustrated an administration's political agenda during so short a period, though no previous administration had so quickly generated laws that so fundamentally altered the nation's social and economic system. Moreover, the Court narrowly construed congressional and presidential power across a broad constitutional spectrum. In three decisions, the Court held that federal legislation violated the commerce clause, in two more it invoked substantive due process, in two others the Court reined in the president's power to delegate power to Congress, in another two it held that the Tenth Amendment protected states from federal legislation, and in one other the Court limited Congress's power to tax. As if the nullification of federal statutes were not bad enough for New Dealers and other proponents of economic regulation, the Court during this period also limited the president's power to remove federal officers and revived substantive due process as a barrier to state regulatory legislation. The New Deal's only victories were the Court's razor-thin validation of the repudiation of the gold standard, and a decision that hinted at the constitutionality of the Tennessee Valley

Authority (TVA). Meanwhile, the Court continued to strike down dozens of state regulatory laws.[1]

This strangulation of so much regulatory legislation has forever marked the second half of Roosevelt's first term as one of the most dramatic epochs in American constitutional history. The Court's decisions during this period often serve to illustrate the potential for abuse of judicial review and the perils of conflicts between the Court and the other branches of the federal government. In traditional accounts that historians only recently have challenged, the justices' presumed hostility toward the New Deal marked the last gasp of conservatism before the transformative events of the judicial revolution of 1937.

The actual holdings of the Court's 1935–1936 decisions, however, did not wreak as much devastation upon the New Deal as is often supposed. The Court invalidated only 11 of the 2,669 statutes signed by Roosevelt during his first term, albeit all of the statutes that the Court nullified were high-profile laws. The most far-reaching statute to fall victim to the Court was Title I of the National Industrial Recovery Act (NIRA), which already had become a political embarrassment to the administration and which was facing congressional termination even before the Court invalidated it. One of the statutes, the Federal Farm Bankruptcy Act, was not actually part of the New Deal, and the Municipal Bankruptcy Act had little practical significance. Moreover, several of the statutes, particularly NIRA, suffered from such serious constitutional infirmities that even those justices who were ordinarily the most receptive toward regulatory legislation joined in opinions striking them down. Only invalidation of the statutes regulating agriculture and coal mining and providing pensions to railroad workers seriously impeded recovery and reform efforts, and even these decisions were rendered moot after 1937, when the Court upheld similar statutes that remedied the constitutional infirmities about which the Court had complained. Perhaps the greatest significance of the decisions of 1935 and 1936 at the time they were rendered was not in what they actually did to the New Deal but in what they portended for other and subsequent New Deal legislation. Advocates of reform could not be confident that the Court would approve new legislation that responded to the infirmities of nullified legislation, and the Court's cramped vision of commerce and its expansive view of due process suggested that it would remain hostile toward other federal measures, particularly the critically important social security, labor relations, and securities regulation statutes.

---

1. Between 1933 and 1936, the Court upheld state regulatory measures in seventy-seven decisions and invalidated such laws in thirty-nine decisions. Although this was not a significantly greater proportion of the state legislation than the Court had disapproved during 1930 through 1933, many of the statutes during the latter period were, as one scholar has pointed out, important "New Deal–inspired legislation." Charles A. Leonard, *A Search for a Judicial Philosophy: Mr. Justice Roberts and the Constitutional Revolution of 1937* (Port Washington, N.Y.: Kennikat Press, 1971), 94.

In the first major test of New Deal regulatory legislation, *Panama Refining Co. v. Ryan,* the Court on January 6, 1935, struck down provisions of NIRA permitting the president to prohibit interstate shipment of oil produced in excess of limits established by oil-producing states that had attempted to conserve oil reserves and raise prices by curtailing production.[2] As one contemporary commentary explained, Congress enacted the legislation because oil produced in violation of the state laws "had gushed from the great oil fields of Oklahoma City and East Texas in such volume as to render the operations within those fields a nightmare of roaring gas, wild wells, burning oil, and wasteful use. All fair competition in the oil industry was demoralized by bootleg prices at which hot oil or its products were sold," driving down oil prices to a few cents a barrel.[3] Injunctions issued by federal courts prevented states from controlling the interstate shipment of the illegally produced oil.[4]

Although it did not deny that Congress could delegate power to the president to regulate interstate commerce, the Court determined that NIRA failed to provide the president with sufficient guidelines for the exercise of such authority. In his opinion, Hughes contended that the delegation was so sweeping that validation of the law would wipe out any "limitations upon the power of the Congress to delegate its law-making function."[5] Cardozo, the sole dissenter, argued that it was enough that the statute was expressly designed to conserve natural resources and to protect law-abiding petroleum dealers from unfair competition with lawbreakers. Pointing out that the "Constitution of the United States is not a code of civil practice," Cardozo declared, "There is no fear that the nation will drift from its ancient moorings as the result of the narrow declaration of power permitted by this Section."[6] Although Stone considered a less categorical dissent, he privately explained that he wished to "save my powder for where it would do more good."[7]

Even though it affected only part of NIRA and was based upon procedural defects that could be cured by statute,[8] the Court's decision in this "hot oil" case cast a pall over the rest of NIRA and other statutes under which Congress had delegated power to the president. Moreover, the case humiliated the administration because it graphically illustrated the chaotic administrative methods about which the New Deal's critics had so bitterly complained. During oral argument, Assistant Attorney General Harold M. Stephens revealed that the government had

2. 293 U.S. 388 (1935).

3. "What Does the Supreme Court Mean?" *Nation,* January 23, 1935, 87.

4. Ibid.

5. 293 U.S. at 430.

6. Ibid., 447, 443 (Cardozo, J., dissenting).

7. Alpheus Thomas Mason, *Harlan Fiske Stone: Pillar of the Law* (New York: Viking Press, 1956), 388.

8. Roberts privately assured Interior Secretary Harold Ickes that he was sympathetic toward federal efforts to control "hot oil," and that he hoped that the Administration would write new legislation to overcome the Court's objections. Harold L. Ickes, *The Secret Diary of Harold L. Ickes,* vol. 1, *The First Thousand Days, 1933–1936* (New York: Simon & Schuster, 1953), 273.

indicted and jailed violators of NIRA's petroleum code for a year before discovering that the code inadvertently lacked a penal section. Under questioning from astonished justices, Stephens also admitted that there was no general publication of executive orders prohibiting the transportation of "hot oil" and that they would be "rather difficult" to obtain, though it was possible to get certified copies from the National Recovery Administration (NRA).[9] Even Cardozo's dissent rebuked the administration for its slipshod practices, declaring, "One must deplore the administrative methods that brought about uncertainty for a time as to the terms of executive orders intended to be law."[10] Later in 1935, after the House Judiciary Committee condemned the "utter chaos" with which administrative rules were promulgated, Congress created the *Federal Register* for publication of all administrative rules having the force of law.[11]

Only one day after handing down its "hot oil" ruling, the Court began to hear oral arguments in litigation challenging Congress's repudiation of the gold standard as a violation of the Fifth Amendment's due process and takings clauses. Perhaps the most far-reaching of the legislation enacted during the first hundred days of the Roosevelt administration, the prohibition against the use of gold for satisfaction of obligations in public and private contracts was intended to conserve the nation's gold reserves, inflate prices in a deflationary economy, discourage hoarding of bullion, prevent bank failures, stimulate economic growth, and improve the nation's balance of payments by devaluing the dollar in relation to foreign currencies. Although the extent to which this measure achieved these goals was doubtful by the time that it reached the Court, even many conservatives predicted that its nullification would have devastating economic consequences because, for nearly two years, American businesses had based every contract upon the assumption that obligations were payable only in currency. By permitting any holder of paper redeemable in gold to receive an additional sixty-nine cents on each dollar, an adverse ruling could have imposed crushing financial burdens on businesses that finally had begun to lift themselves from the trough of depression. So intense was public interest in the cases that Hughes ordered the Court's clerk to reveal in advance of the first two Mondays of February that the Court was not yet ready to announce a decision.[12] When Hughes made no such statement in advance of the third Monday, Securities and Exchange Commission (SEC) commissioners seriously considered ordering the stock markets to close on that day to prevent financial panic if the Court repudiated the repudiation.[13] Meanwhile, Roosevelt, in anticipation of a decision adverse to his administration, reportedly

---

9. Merlo J. Pusey, *Charles Evans Hughes* (New York: MacMillan, 1951), 2:734.

10. 293 U.S. at 434 (Cardozo, J., dissenting).

11. H. Rept. No. 280, 74th Congress, 1st Session 1–2 (1935); 49 Stat. 500 (1935).

12. Mason, *Harlan Fiske Stone*, 389.

13. William F. Swindler, *Court and Constitution in the 20th Century: The New Legality, 1932–1968* (Indianapolis: Bobbs-Merrill, 1970), 35.

drafted a radio address announcing his refusal to enforce a ruling agaist the government.[14]

In three separate decisions written by Hughes, the Court sustained the constitutionality of the gold repeal by a parlous margin of five-to-four. In its first decision, *Norman v. Baltimore & Ohio Railroad Co.*, the Court upheld the prohibition on repayment in gold in private contracts on the ground that Congress had broad power to regulate the nation's monetary system to facilitate the national interest.[15] Hughes explained that even the most explicit contracts "cannot fetter the constitutional authority of the Congress. Contracts may create rights of property, but when contracts deal with a subject matter which lies within the control of the Congress, they have a congenital infirmity. Parties cannot remove their transactions from the reach of dominant constitutional power by making contracts about them." Hughes's opinion hinted at reservations that the chief justice might have had about the wisdom of the legislation. Hughes declared that "[t]he question before the Court is one of power, not of policy" and indicated that harshness of legislation does not invalidate its constitutionality.[16]

Congress's abrogation of the gold clauses in federal bonds was even more difficult for the Court to swallow, for this repudiation called into question the integrity of the federal government. That the subject of the litigation was a Liberty Bond issued during the First World War made the case all the more poignant. Hughes's opinion in *Perry v. United States* held that this repudiation was unconstitutional but spared the governmental financial disaster by denying relief to the claimant.[17] Although the Court found that Congress lacked power to repudiate gold clauses in public contracts because this would impugn the integrity of the federal government, it determined that the bond holder who challenged the law had incurred only nominal damages since the fall in prices during the Depression had eliminated most of the difference between repayment in gold and repayment in currency. As William F. Swindler observed, "No opinion since *Marbury v. Madison* had so astutely pronounced a rule of law and in the same instance demonstrated why the rule could not be given its literal effect."[18] Another commentary has remarked that "the government emerged with a technical victory but sustained a moral loss not seen since John Marshall had tongue-lashed Jefferson and Madison in the *Marbury* case."[19] Erwin Griswold told Justice Stone that one of his Harvard Law School colleagues remarked that "the Supreme Court has held the

14. Pusey, *Charles Evans Hughes*, 2:736; Swindler, *Court and Constitution*, 35.

15. 294 U.S. 240 (1935).

16. Ibid., 307–8, 297, 306.

17. 294 U.S. 330 (1935).

18. Swindler, *Court and Constitution*, 37.

19. Melvin I. Urofsky and Paul Finkelman, *A March of Liberty: A Constitutional History of the United States*, vol. 2, *From 1877 to the Present*, 2d ed. (New York: Oxford University Press, 2002), 677.

abrogation of the gold clause in government bonds unconstitutional, nine Justices dissenting."[20]

Stone alone among the justices refused to deny that the government could repudiate even its own obligations. In a concurring opinion, he explained that, although he deplored "this refusal to fulfill the solemn promise of bonds of the United States," the Court's decision that the government was immune from liability precluded any need for the Court to make any pronouncement about the government's power to abrogate the gold clauses in government bonds, particularly because this could limit the government's ability to respond to future economic conditions. Seeing through Hughes's sleight of hand, Stone also pointed out that the Court's denial of relief to the bondholder was an implicit recognition that the government's repudiation was "itself a constitutional exercise of the power to regulate the value of money."[21]

In another decision, *Nortz v. United States,* the Court upheld the suspension of redemption of treasury notes in gold on the ground that the note holder suffered no damages because the treasury secretary in 1933 and 1934, acting under authorization of the Emergency Banking Relief Act, had required all Americans to deliver gold coins, bullion, and certificates to the United States treasurer.[22] The bond holder therefore could not have kept his gold even if the government had redeemed his currency in gold.

In an acrimonious dissent from all three decisions, McReynolds, joined by his fellow Horsemen, declared that "[j]ust men regard repudiation and spoliation of citizens by their sovereign with abhorrence" and that "[l]oss of reputation for honorable dealing will bring us unending humiliation; the impending legal and moral chaos is appalling."[23] McReynolds's remarks in court were even more dramatic. Racked with anger, McReynolds stunned the courtroom by brushing aside his written dissent and delivering a blistering extemporaneous condemnation of the opinions. "The Constitution is gone," he began. "The guarantees heretofore supposed to protect against arbitrary action, have been swept away." After denouncing Congress for repudiating solemn financial obligations, McReynolds declared, "Shame and humiliation are upon us. Moral and financial chaos may confidently be expected."[24]

Commentators disagreed about whether the gold cases augured judicial acceptance of other New Deal legislation or whether the close division of the justices portended trouble for the New Deal. The *Nation* foresaw judicial approval of other reforms insofar as it believed that abrogation of the gold clauses was more difficult

20. Erwin N. Griswold to Harlan Fiske Stone, March 5, 1935, box 15, Harlan Fiske Stone Papers, Manuscript Division, Library of Congress (hereafter cited as Stone Papers).

21. 294 U.S. at 359, 359–60, 361 (Stone, J., concurring).

22. 294 U.S. 317 (1935).

23. Ibid., 362, 381 (McReynolds, J., dissenting).

24. James E. Bond, *I Dissent: The Legacy of Chief* [sic] *Justice James Clark McReynolds* (Fairfax, Va.: George Mason University Press, 1992), 91–92.

to defend on constitutional grounds than were other New Deal measures.[25] The *New Republic,* on the other hand, deplored the insecurity of a constitutional system "that delegates power over the highest decisions of social policy to a few politically non-responsible men."[26] Moreover, many members of the Roosevelt administration resented having had to cower in terror at the prospect of an adverse outcome, notwithstanding the result.[27]

In any event, the gold cases provided only a temporary respite for the New Deal. Ten weeks later, the Court in *Railroad Retirement Board v. Alton Railroad Co.* nullified a statute that required railroads and their employees to contribute to a federally administered pension fund.[28] In this five-to-four decision, the justices held that the statute seized property without due process of law in violation of the Fifth Amendment, and also exceeded Congress's power under the commerce clause. The decision clouded the constitutionality of the Social Security Act, enacted three months after *Alton,* which contained provisions closely resembling those in the railroad statute.

Roberts's opinion was a classic specimen of substantive due process, for it unabashedly substituted the Court's own assessment of the law's justifications for those of Congress, even though Roberts professed to eschew any inquiry into the statute's merits.[29] Roberts's due process and interstate commerce arguments were rife with a sometimes subtle but always unmistakably sarcastic dismissal of the government's central argument that railroad workers would perform more effectively if they could look forward to a pension. Roberts was particularly contemptuous of the statute's provision for pensions for 146,000 former employees who were employed by a railroad within a year of the statute's enactment. Roberts wrote, "It is arbitrary in the last degree to place upon the carriers the burden of gratuities to thousands who have been unfaithful and for that cause have been separated from the service, or who have elected to pursue some other calling, or have retired from the business, or have been for other reasons lawfully dismissed. And the claim that such largess will promote efficiency or safety in the future operation of the railroads is without support in reason or common sense."[30]

Roberts similarly scorned the statute's requirement for pension payments to any of the other million former railroad workers who returned to work for a railroad, even if temporarily and even if another railroad had dismissed the worker for cause. Roberts declared that this imposed a future burden never contemplated by either party during the earlier employment and that "[t]his onerous financial

25. *Nation,* February 27, 1935, 233.

26. "The Week," *New Republic,* February 27, 1935, 57.

27. "Washington Notes," *New Republic,* March 6, 1935, 100.

28. 295 U.S. 330 (1935).

29. As the *Nation* pointed out, "[h]aving established this point, Justice Roberts proceeds throughout his lengthy decision to discuss little else than the wisdom and desirability of the act and its separate provisions." "The Court Rules Out Security," *Nation,* May 22, 1935, 588.

30. 295 U.S. at 349.

burden cannot be justified upon the plea that it is in the interest of economy, or will promote efficiency or safety."[31]

In objecting to the statute's retroactive award of benefits to the 1.2 million workers who presently were employed by railroads, Roberts also complained that the law required "further compulsory payment" for employees whose work was "completed and compensated in full conformity with the agreement of the parties." He further pointed out that the law would permit pension payments even to those dismissed "for peculation" or "gross negligence" and that the statute could encourage early retirement by competent and experienced employees who had attained the thirty years of service required for maximum pension benefits. In response to the government's argument that the statute would improve employee morale by assuring employees that they would receive a pension even if they lost their jobs, Roberts retorted that, "if 'morale' is intended to connote efficiency, loyalty, and continuity of service, the surest way to destroy it in any privately owned business is to substitute legislative largesse for private bounty and thus transfer the drive for pensions to the halls of Congress and transmute loyalty to employer into gratitude to the legislature."[32]

Roberts also objected to the statute's provision that the railroads pool their employee contributions, alleging that this discriminated against railroads that had a smaller proportion of retired employees and required employers to cover the obligations of railroads that were insolvent or had ceased business. He explained that "[t]here is no warrant for taking the property or money of one and transferring it to another without compensation, whether the object of the transfer be to build up the equipment of the transferee or to pension its employees."[33]

Even more astringent in his denial that the statute was within the commerce power, Roberts triumphantly cited statistics demonstrating that railroad efficiency and safety for both employees and passengers had steadily increased for many years before the statute's enactment. If "the fostering of a contented mind on the part of an employee by legislation of this type" constituted a regulation of interstate commerce, Roberts cautioned, "there is no limit to the field of so-called regulation. The catalogue of means and actions which might be imposed upon an employer in any business, tending to the satisfaction and comfort of his employees, seems endless." Observing that "[p]rovision for free medical attendance and nursing, for clothing, for food, for housing, for the education of children, and a hundred other matters, might with equal propriety be proposed as tending to relieve the employee of mental strain and worry," Roberts concluded that "the social welfare of the worker [was] outside the orbit of Congressional power."[34]

In one of his most biting dissents, Hughes urged deference to Congress. Joined by Brandeis, Stone, and Cardozo, this dissent explained that the commerce power

31. Ibid., 350.
32. Ibid., 353, 351, 352, 351.
33. Ibid., 357.
34. Ibid., 364–67, 368.

did not require that its exercise by Congress "should be wise, much less that it should be perfect. The power implies a broad discretion and thus permits a wide range even of mistakes." Pointing out that pension experts disagreed about "the manner in which they should be set up," Hughes cautioned that "[i]t is not our province to enter that field." Hughes, however, was unclear about the precise standard of review that the Court should use in reviewing economic legislation. His general remark that "[t]he appropriate relation of the exercise of constitutional power to the legitimate objects of that power is always a subject of judicial scrutiny" seemed to accept a moderately active role for the Court, as did his careful review and endorsement of various justifications for the statute. In his discussion of the methods by which Congress established pension eligibility, however, Hughes appeared to anticipate the Court's post-1937 use of a "rational basis" test for evaluating legislation when he averred that the question for the Court was whether the congressional plan was "destitute of rational support."[35]

Disagreeing that the railroad industry's high level of efficiency and safety could not justify the statute, Hughes explained that this "gratifying fact does not establish that further improvement is not needed or obtainable, or that a sound pension plan would not be of considerable benefit to the carriers' operations." Hughes pointed out that the federal government already had extensively regulated the relations between railroads and their employees in legislation limiting hours, imposing a duty to furnish safe tools, providing for settlement of labor disputes, and abolishing contributory negligence, the fellow servant rule, and assumption of risk as defenses to actions for injuries. Likewise drawing a close parallel between the federal railroad pension act and state worker compensation laws that the Court had upheld, Hughes remarked that both types of laws were based on the theory "that industry should take care of its human wastage, whether that is due to accident or age." Hughes declared that this "view cannot be dismissed as arbitrary or capricious. It is a reasoned conviction based upon abundant experience." Moreover, Hughes argued that the coverage of 82 percent of railroad employees by company-sponsored pensions demonstrated "a widespread conviction that the assurance of security through a pension plan for retired employees is closely and substantially related to the proper conduct of business enterprises." Hughes observed that "[t]here has been not only the paramount consideration of safety, but also the recognition of the fact that fair treatment in other respects aids in conserving the peace and good order which are essential to the maintenance of the service without disastrous interruptions, and in promoting the efficiency which inevitably suffers from a failure to meet the reasonable demands of justice."[36]

35. Ibid., 391–92, 392, 379, 391 (Hughes, C.J., dissenting).
36. Ibid., 379, 376–77, 384, 379–80, 376–77 (Hughes, C.J., dissenting). Although Hughes considered the Court's due process argument "superfluous" since the Court's interpretation of the commerce clause was enough to nullify the statute, he also dismissed the Court's "pooling" argument on the ground that "Congress has the power to treat the transportation system of the country as a unit for the purpose of regulation in the public interest, so long as particular railroad properties are not subjected to confiscation." Accordingly, "Congress was entitled to

Although the Court's decision in *Alton* was a harsh setback for the New Deal, it was merely a warm-up exercise for what soon was to come. The worst fears and suspicions of New Dealers were confirmed on May 27, 1935, when a triad of unanimous decisions seemed to them to strike at the heart of congressional and presidential power to combat the Depression. On this day, which immediately entered the annals of constitutional history as "Black Monday," the Court invalidated key sections of NIRA, nullified the Federal Farm Bankruptcy (Frazier-Lemke) Act, and ruled that the president lacked power to remove members of independent regulatory commissions.

The decision striking down most of the remaining parts of Title I of NIRA, *Schechter Poultry Corp. v. United States*,[37] dismissed the government's case against a Brooklyn poultry producer charged with selling sick chickens and violating the wages and hours provisions of a code of conduct for the poultry industry in the New York metropolitan area, which had been approved by Roosevelt in 1934 pursuant to NIRA after recommendation by trade associations representing 90 percent of the region's poultry trade.

In reasoning foreshadowed by the "hot oil" decision, the Court held that Congress had unconstitutionally delegated power to the president. The legislation's grant of authority to the president to approve industry codes was so sweeping, and the guidelines for such authorization were so vague and so broad, that the Court declared that the president's discretion to enact laws "for the government of trade and industry throughout the country, is virtually unfettered." The justices were particularly troubled that NIRA failed to define the phase "fair competition" in authorizing the president to approve "codes of fair competition" approved by various industries.[38]

In addition to holding that the statute involved excessive delegation of congressional power, *Schechter* also restrictively interpreted the commerce clause, ruling that the Schechter poultry business was so local that it was beyond congressional regulation. Even though nearly all poultry sold in New York was sent there from other states, the Court held that the Schechters' transactions were not "in" interstate commerce because the Schechters slaughtered their chickens within a single state and sold them locally to dealers and butchers who sold them directly to consumers in New York. The Court explained that "[t]he mere fact that there may be a constant flow of commodities into a State does not mean that the flow continues after the property has arrived and has become commingled with the mass of property within the State and is there held solely for local disposition and use."[39]

Moreover, the Court held that the Schechters' transactions were so local that they did not directly "affect" interstate commerce. In rejecting the government's

---

weigh the advantages of such a system . . . and reach a conclusion as to the policy best suited to the needs of the country." Ibid., 375, 387.

37. 295 U.S. 495 (1935).

38. Ibid., 529–42, 535, 531–33.

39. Ibid., 541–43, 543.

argument that wages and hours had an interstate impact because they affected prices, the Court explained that this argument would permit Congress to regulate other factors influencing price, including rents and advertising. The Court warned that, if Congress could regulate enterprises that had only an indirect effect on commerce, "the federal authority would embrace practically all the activities of the people, and the authority of the State over its domestic concerns would exist only by sufferance of the federal government."[40]

Although the Court's interpretation of the commerce clause in *Schechter* was not inconsistent with established doctrine, proponents of the New Deal had hoped that the Court would construe the commerce clause more broadly to permit greater federal regulation during a time of crisis. Advocates of federal economic intervention likewise were disappointed that the Court brushed aside the argument that economic emergency justified the statute, which was intended to stimulate prices, employment, and markets. Although the justices acknowledged that "[e]xtraordinary conditions may call for extraordinary remedies," the majority declared that "extraordinary conditions do not create or enlarge constitutional power" and that "the recuperative efforts of the federal government must be made in a manner consistent with the authority granted by the Constitution." Critics of *Schechter,* who found the Court's refusal to consider the need for emergency legislation to be inconsistent with *Blaisdell,* overlooked the fact that *Blaisdell* involved a state's exercise of its police power rather than congressional power under the commerce clause.[41]

The *Schechter* decision particularly stung many New Dealers because the concurring opinion of Cardozo, joined by Stone, not only endorsed the general argument of the Court's opinion, but also attacked the statute in astringent language that contrasted with the generally mild tone of Hughes's opinion. Cardozo described the delegation of power as "a roving commission to inquire into evils and then, upon discovering them, correct them." Cardozo pointed out the statutory warrant for "fair competition" could require not only elimination of fraud or trickery, but also "whatever ordinances may be desirable or helpful for the well-being or prosperity of the industry." This, he declared, "is delegation running riot." With respect to interstate commerce, Cardozo contended that extension of the commerce power to the Schechters' business would "obliterate the distinction between what is national and what is local in the activities of commerce."[42]

The Court's opinion seemed to be based more on the extremity of the delegation than upon any inherent objection to delegation itself. As recently as 1932, the Court had unanimously rejected the claim that the Pure Food and Drug Act violated separation of powers by giving administrative authority to various executive departments to make rules and regulations permitting reasonable variations

40. Ibid., 544, 546.
41. Ibid., 528, 550.
42. Ibid., 551, 552–53, 553, 554 (Cardozo, J., concurring).

from the act's general requirement that the food packages be marked with the quantity of their contents.[43] Although Sutherland's opinion in that case acknowledged that "the legislative power of Congress cannot be delegated," the Court explained that "Congress may declare its will, and after fixing a primary standard, devolve upon administrative officers the 'power to fill up the details' by prescribing administrative rules and regulations."[44] Indeed, *Schechter* and *Panama Refining* remain virtually the only decisions in which the Court has struck down legislation for unconstitutional delegation of power to the president.

Schechter had little practical impact because NIRA had become such an embarrassment to the Roosevelt administration that Congress probably would not have renewed the statute when its initial term expired during the summer of 1935.[45] Designed to enable business, labor, and consumers and other competing interests to cooperate to achieve common economic goals and allocate profits more equally, NIRA and the NRA tended to discourage competition and foster a benign form of oligopoly. By permitting unprecedented governmental regulation of private businesses, even though the businesses in large measure wrote their own regulations, NIRA also seemed quasi-socialist, and there was a growing consensus that its maze of bureaucratic regulations was hindering rather than promoting economic recovery.

The *Schechter* decision also seemed consistent with the temper of the times to the extent that the partial economic recovery had removed the sense of crisis in which the NIRA was incubated. As *Commonweal* observed, "What we confront nationally is not so much the demise of the Blue Eagle—which was pretty senile anyhow—but the passing of a conception of presidential authority which was hailed in 1933 and is out of date today. . . . At present the emergency still exists, of course, if one thinks of great collective problems like unemployment and relief. But the fear of disaster has been lifted in many quarters."[46] Moreover, many New Dealers and other advocates of economic regulation of business were uncomfortable with NIRA's corporatism, distrustful of its regulation of business by business. Others, sharing Brandeis's longstanding misgivings about centralization, preferred more regulation at the state level.

Although even many liberals agreed that the Court correctly objected to the statute's broad delegation of power,[47] its restrictive interpretation of the commerce clause inspired widespread dismay. Some liberals blamed the Roosevelt administration for avoiding judicial challenges in cases that provided stronger facts and suggested that the Court might have spared NIRA if it had heard a case

---

43. *U.S. v. Shreveport Grain & Elevator Co.*, 287 U.S. 77 (1932).

44. Ibid., 85.

45. As a columnist observed, the Court's decision "private delighted" many Democratic senators. Frank R. Kent, "An Inescapable Lesson," *Wall Street Journal*, May 30, 1935, 2.

46. "Week by Week," *Commonweal*, June 14, 1935, 170–71.

47. See, for example, "Social Control vs. the Constitution," *New Republic*, June 12, 1935, 117.

that involved an industry that was more intimately involved in transstate commerce.[48]

In its second Black Monday decision, the Court unanimously invalidated the Federal Farm Bankruptcy Act of 1934, which denied banks the power to foreclose on bankrupt farms until five years after adjudication of bankruptcy.[49] The Court determined that the statute constituted a taking of the property of the mortgage holders without due process of law, in violation of the Fifth Amendment. Brushing aside the argument that a crisis of foreclosures justified this effort to prevent the growth of farm tenancy and rural economic distress, the Court declared that "the Fifth Amendment commands that, however great the Nation's need, private property shall not be thus taken even for a wholly public use without just compensation." The justices explained that eminent domain was the only proper means of taking property from mortgagees to relieve mortgagors insofar as this would permit all taxpayers to bear "the burden of the relief afforded in the public interest."[50] Although this decision was a disappointment to many liberals, it was not a defeat for the administration, which had not supported this statute, which was sponsored by two progressive Republican senators from North Dakota.

In its third decision, *Humphrey's Executor v. United States,* the Court unanimously limited the president's power to dismiss members of independent federal regulatory agencies.[51] The majority held that the president could remove members of such commissions only for good cause and not for political reasons. Accordingly, the justices held that Roosevelt had improperly dismissed William E. Humphrey as a member of the Federal Trade Commission (FTC).

Roosevelt had fired Humphrey within six months of becoming president, explaining, "I do not feel that your mind or my mind go along together on either the policies or the administering of the Federal Trade Commission." With more than five years remaining in Humphrey's term, Roosevelt regarded dismissal of the antiregulatory Humphrey as essential for restoring the FTC's effectiveness in exposing and prosecuting unfair business practices. Humphrey, a pugnacious conservative Republican, had worked as a lumber industry lobbyist before his appointment to the five-member FTC by Calvin Coolidge in 1925. To the despair of progressives in both parties, Humphrey's appointment tipped the FTC's membership in favor of laissez-faire conservatives, who promptly changed the FTC's rules to handle cases in an informal matter that shielded businesses from unfavorable publicity. During Humphrey's tenure, the FTC's investigations of unfair business practices slackened, while Humphrey often publicly proclaimed his contempt for reformers, his opposition to federal regulation of industry, and his belief that

48. See Charles E. Clark, "The Supreme Court and the N.R.A.," *New Republic,* June 12, 1935, 121. Clark indicated that the Court might have upheld the licensing of milk vendors in Chicago because 40 percent of Chicago's milk came from beyond the borders of Illinois.

49. *Louisville Joint Stock Land Bank v. Radford,* 295 U.S. 555 (1935).

50. Ibid., 602.

51. 295 U.S. 602 (1935).

the FTC should act as business's partner rather than its watchdog. When Hoover nominated him for a second term in 1931, twenty-eight senators voted against his confirmation.[52]

In his opinion for the majority, Sutherland explained that Congress intended for the FTC to act as an independent and nonpartisan agency, "free from executive control." Therefore "it must, from the very nature of its duties, act with entire impartiality. It is charged with the enforcement of no policy except the policy of the law. Its duties are neither political nor executive, but predominately quasi-judicial and quasi-legislative." Any power of the president to remove FTC commissioners would threaten their independence, for "one who holds his office only during the pleasure of another, cannot be depended upon to maintain an attitude of independence against the latter's will."[53] The Court held that there was a critical distinction between Roosevelt's dismissal of Humphrey and Wilson's removal of a postmaster, which the Court had sustained in 1926 in *Myers v. United States*[54] as an exercise of the president's broad power to dismiss executive officers without the Senate's approval. The Court explained that a postmaster, unlike an FTC commissioner, was an executive officer, "charged with no duty at all related to either the legislative or judicial power." In contrast, the FTC "cannot in any proper sense be characterized as an arm or an eye of the executive."[55] *Humphrey's Executor* therefore was a critical landmark in securing the independence of federal regulatory agencies and one of history's most important separation-of-powers decisions.

The Court's Black Monday decisions generated the most vociferous outcries against the Court heard since its *Adkins* decision a dozen years earlier. Like *Adkins*, these decisions generated a plethora of proposals to curb the Court's power, including constitutional amendments to circumvent the decisions, removal of the Court's power over social and economic questions, and a national constitutional convention.[56] Senator George W. Norris introduced legislation to prevent the Court from invalidating federal legislation without concurrence of at least two-thirds of the justices and to deprive lower federal courts of jurisdiction to decide cases involving constitutional issues.[57] The power of lower federal judges to invalidate federal regulatory legislation vexed Norris almost as much as the Supreme Court's power of judicial review. As Norris privately remarked, it was "wrong that some district judge, one of the many from Maine to California, can hold such a

52. William E. Leuchtenburg, "The Case of the Contentious Commissioner: Humphrey's Executor v. U.S.," in Harold M. Hyman and Leonard W. Levy, *Freedom and Reform: Essays in Honor of Henry Steele Commager* (New York: Harper and Row, 1967), 276–91.

53. 295 U.S. at 624, 629.

54. 272 U.S. 52 (1926).

55. 295 U.S. at 627–28, 628.

56. "Plans Offered to Solve NRA Situation Include National Constitutional Convention," *New York Times*, May 30, 1935, 13.

57. S.J.Res. 149, 74th Congress, 1st Session, 1935; "Norris Asks Ban on 5–4 Decisions," *New York Times*, June 18, 1935, 2.

law unconstitutional, and even though he may be reversed, it will take two or three years to do it, because the case must travel its weary road to the Supreme Court."[58]

In his first public criticism of the Court, Roosevelt complained at a press conference that its decisions were relics of the "horse-and-buggy definition of interstate commerce." When asked whether he had any plans for circumventing the decision, however, Roosevelt replied, "We haven't got to that yet."[59] Echoing the president's "horse-and-buggy" metaphor, critics of the Court's decision argued that its definition of interstate commerce and states' rights should take account of the vast changes in transportation and communication since the adoption of the Constitution. As the *Nation* pointed out, "the sprawling American commonwealth" of 1787 "was as vast as the whole world today. Parts of it were as distant as Washington now is from Abyssinia. In such conditions state government was not a theory but a crying necessity."[60] Privately, Roosevelt may have welcomed *Schechter,* which relieved him of much of the responsibility for a program that even many of the most ardent New Dealers regarded as a failure. In contrast, Roosevelt regarded *Humphrey's Executor* as a severe blow to his program, even a personal affront, and the desertion of even Cardozo and Brandeis left him crestfallen. "Where was Ben Cardozo?" he plaintively asked an advisor. "And what about old Isaiah?"[61]

Despite their widespread unpopularity and the plethora of Court-curbing proposals that they generated, the Black Monday decisions failed to produce any serious Court-curbing movement. A Gallup poll in September 1935 indicated that only 31 percent of persons surveyed favored limitations on the Court's power to invalidate congressional legislation, whereas 53 percent opposed such a curb.[62] Norris acknowledged privately that "it would only be a waste of time" to work for his bill.[63] The Court's Black Monday decisions produced some of the earliest signs that many liberals who had blasted the Court in earlier years for its invalidation of economic regulatory legislation now hoped that the Court would protect the nation from the New Deal's tendency to aggrandize presidential power and disrupt federalism. Idaho Republican senator William E. Borah, one of the Court's most vociferous critics during the 1920s and one of the chief critics of Hughes's nomination, delivered a radio speech praising the Court for its fidelity to the Constitution in *Schechter* and warning that any contrary interpretation would create the type of "judicial oligarchy" about which he had so often warned.[64]

58. George W. Norris to Layton Spicher, March 29, 1935, box 118, George W. Norris Papers, Manuscript Division, Library of Congress (hereafter Norris Papers).

59. Leuchtenburg, *The Supreme Court Reborn,* 90–91.

60. "A Constitutional Plutocracy," *Nation,* June 12, 1935, 672.

61. Eugene C. Gerhart, *America's Advocate: Robert H. Jackson* (Indianapolis: Bobbs-Merrill, 1958), 99.

62. George H. Gallup, William P. Hansen, and Fred L. Israel, eds., *The Gallup Poll: Public Opinion, 1935–1971,* vol. 1 (New York: Random House, 1972), 2.

63. Norris to Frank J. Heney, September 6, 1935, MS 3298, box 1, George W. Norris Papers, State Archives, Nebraska State Historical Society, Lincoln, Nebraska.

64. "Senator Borah's Radio Address Supporting Court's Decision on NRA," *New York Times,* June 3, 1935, 2.

Black Monday occurred during the midst of the so-called Second New Deal, while Congress was approving a new raft of reform legislation that was even more sweeping than the laws enacted during the first hundred days of Roosevelt's presidency. In contrast to the "First New Deal," which sought to enlist cooperation between big businesses and government in restricting production and generally did not require massive federal expenditures, the Second New Deal was unabashedly populistic and was based on a theory that substantial federal spending could help revive the economy. In April 1935 Congress approved the Emergency Relief Appropriation Act, allocating five billion dollars to increase funding for the Civilian Conservation Corps (CCC) and the Public Works Administration (PWA) and providing additional jobs for the unemployed by creating a Works Progress Administration (WPA).[65] Acting on the statute's authorization to create new administrative agencies, Roosevelt issued executive orders five weeks later establishing the Rural Electrification Administration and the National Youth Administration.[66]

Notwithstanding the Court's decisions, Congress during the months immediately following Black Monday enacted two of the most important and enduring New Deal statutes, the National Labor Relations Act and the Social Security Act. The former, also known as the Wagner Act, provided for regular and comprehensive federal involvement in labor-management disputes. The statute established a National Labor Relations Board to define bargaining units, supervise union elections, certify union representatives, and order management to cease and desist from actions that the board found to be unfair.[67] The Social Security Act created federal systems of unemployment compensation and old-age pensions.[68]

Meanwhile, Congress applied the principles of NIRA to the Depression-ridden coal industry, enacting the Bituminous Coal Conservation Act, which regulated production, prices, and labor practices.[69] This statute, also known as the Guffey Act, imposed a 15 percent levy on coal producers, 90 percent of which was remitted for compliance with the legislation. The statute attempted to circumvent *Schechter* insofar as coal production clearly seemed an interstate enterprise, and Congress kept a tight rein over the regulations. Similarly, Congress responded to *Radford* with a new Farm Mortgage Moratorium Act that provided farmers with extended credit, allowed repurchase of foreclosed properties at appraisals that reflected deflation, and authorized suspension of foreclosures for five years with the consent of creditors.[70] Meanwhile, Congress increased the top tax bracket on individuals from 59 percent to 75 percent, strengthened the Federal Reserve Board's power over member banks, and enacted the Public Utility Holding Company Act, which had the effect of breaking up the nation's largest utility companies.[71]

65. Ch. 48, 49 Stat. 115.
66. Swindler, *Court and Constitution*, 405.
67. Ch. 372, 49 Stat. 449.
68. Ch. 531, 49 Stat. 620.
69. Ch. 824, 49 Stat. 991.
70. Ch. 792, 49 Stat. 942.
71. Ch. 687, 49 Stat. 803.

The Court renewed its onslaught against New Deal legislation during the first week of 1936, when *United States v. Butler* narrowly construed the taxing power to invalidate the Agricultural Adjustment Act (AAA).[72] In its six-to-three decision, the Court held that a federal tax on processors of agricultural products to finance price supports for farmers who limited production was not a valid tax because it was designed to promote social and economic policies rather than generate revenue for general federal purposes. Justice Roberts's opinion for the Court concluded that the processing tax was not a true tax because it expropriated "money from one group for the benefit of another."[73]

The Court similarly rejected the argument that the tax was valid as an exercise of Congress's constitutional power to tax and spend for the benefit of the general welfare. Although Justice Roberts's opinion conceded that Congress has broad power under the Constitution to promote the general welfare, the Court held that the statute "invades the reserved rights of the states. It is a statutory plan to regulate and control agricultural production, a matter beyond the powers delegated to the federal government." Rejecting the argument that the tax was constitutional because it was voluntary, the Court explained that "the power to confer or withhold unlimited benefits is the power to coerce or destroy," resulting in likely "financial ruin" for noncooperating farmers who could be undersold by farmers who accepted federal payments. But even if it were voluntary it would still be unconstitutional because "[a]t best it is a scheme for purchasing with federal funds submission to federal regulation of a subject reserved to the states." The Court stated that "[i]t does not help to declare that local conditions throughout the nation have created a situation of national concern; for this is but to say that whenever there is a widespread similarity of local conditions, Congress may ignore constitutional limitations upon its own powers and usurp those reserved to the states." The Court denied that the Framers, who had "intended sedulously to limit and define" federal powers, "so as to reserve to the states and the people sovereign power," would not by a single clause have granted Congress power to "tear down the barriers, to invade the states' jurisdiction, and to become a parliament of the whole people, subject to no restrictions save such as are self-imposed." In a parade of horribles, the Court provided various examples of how Congress could employ the taxing power to impose regulations upon all sorts of industris in response to demands from "every business group which thought itself under-privileged" and demanded "that a tax be laid on its vendors or vendees, the proceeds to be appropriated for redress of its deficiency of income."[74]

Despite the Court's conclusion that the statute was beyond the scope of congressional power, Roberts at the behest of Hughes wrote dicta endorsing the proposition that the general welfare clause provides an independent source of

72. 297 U.S. 1 (1936).
73. Ibid., 61.
74. Ibid., 67, 68, 71, 72, 74–75, 78, 76.

congressional power to tax and spend.[75] Hughes believed that "the most impor-tant ruling in the *Butler* case was the adoption of the view of Hamilton and Story, in preference to that of Madison, as to the scope of the taxing power."[76]

In an apparent effort to shield the institution from allegations of judicial activ-ism, Roberts stated that the Court "neither approves nor condemns any legislative policy. Its delicate and difficult office is to ascertain and declare whether the legis-lation is in accordance with, or in contravention of, the provisions of the Constitu-tion; and, having done that, its duty ends." In explaining how the Court makes such a determination, Roberts advanced a theory that came to be mocked as the "T-square rule": "When an act of Congress is appropriately challenged in the courts as not conforming to the constitutional mandate the judicial branch of the Government has only one duty,—to lay the article of the Constitution which is invoked beside the statute which is challenged and to decide whether the latter squares with the former."[77]

In a dissent joined by Brandeis and Cardozo, Stone argued that "[i]t is a contra-diction in terms to say that there is power to spend for the national welfare, while rejecting any power to impose conditions reasonably adapted to the attainment of the end which alone would justify the expenditure." Opposing the Court's sug-gestion that congressional power "must now be curtailed by judicial fiat because it may be abused," Stone pointed out that the power of judicial review is subject to the guiding principles that "courts are concerned only with the power to enact statutes, not with their wisdom" and that, "while unconstitutional exercise of power by the executive and legislative branches . . . is subject to judicial restraint, the only check upon our own exercise of power is our sense of self-restraint." Disparaging the notions that "it is the business of courts to sit in judgment on the wisdom of legislative action" and that "the responsibility for the preservation of our institutions is the exclusive concern of any one of the three branches of gov-ernment," Stone concluded, "the power to tax and spend includes the power to relieve a nationwide economic maladjustment by conditional gifts of money."[78] Even though he dissented, Stone privately questioned the wisdom of the legisla-tion and praised Herbert Hoover for his public criticisms of it.[79]

The Court's invalidation of the AAA produced even more consternation among New Deal supporters than had the Black Monday decisions. Unlike the NIRA, the AAA was based on economic theories that had germinated over a long

75. Ibid., 65–67. See Richard D. Friedman, "Switching Time and Other Thought Experi-ments: The Hughes Court and Constitutional Transformation," 142 *University of Pennsylvania Law Review* 1955 (1994).

76. David J. Danelski and Joseph S. Tulchin, eds., *The Autobiographical Notes of Charles Evans Hughes* (Cambridge, Mass.: Harvard University Press, 1973), 309–10.

77. 297 U.S. at 63, 62.

78. Ibid., 85, 87, 78, 78–79, 87, 87–88 (Stone, J., dissenting).

79. Harlan Fiske Stone to Herbert Hoover, November 19, 1935 and January 22, 1936, box 17, Stone Papers.

period of time and was drafted with considerable care and precision.[80] Secretary of Agriculture Henry A. Wallace had taken pains to structure the statute in a manner that would avoid constitutional objections,[81] and the statute had received the votes of all but eight Republican senators. The American Federation of Labor's executive council, which claimed that the decision created an "emergency" by impeding the organization of workers and encouraged child labor, called for a constitutional amendment to meet the Court's objections to regulatory legislation in *Schechter* and the railroad retirement decision.[82] Regarding the Court's reasoning as disingenuous, Wallace declared that "[w]ere agriculture truly a local matter . . . half the people in the United States would quickly starve."[83] Some critics of the "Court's Dred Scotting of the AAA" direly predicted that *Butler* would produce a revolution, just as *Dred Scott* had precipitated a civil war.[84] One commentator observed that extreme radicals regarded the Court "as their chief ally" in promoting a revolution because the Court's invalidation of New Deal legislation seemed to demonstrate the impracticability of moderate and incremental reform.[85]

Although the Court's decision did not foreclose state legislation, comprehensive local responses to the agricultural crisis seemed impracticable because agriculture had national dimensions. Many liberals also believed that powerful interests would block state agricultural legislation. *Butler* therefore highlighted the frustration of liberals over what they regarded as the Court's cramped definitions of federal power and the Court's growing tendency to invalidate federal legislation. As an FTC attorney privately complained to Senator Norris, "The present division of authority between states and nation has become the bulwark behind which entrenched greed so successfully hides. . . . The great corporations do not want one government in these United States. They want at least forty nine."[86]

Despite the widespread criticism, however, *Butler* appears to have been broadly acceptable to the American people insofar as a Gallup poll shortly before the Court's decision indicated that 59 percent of the public disapproved of the AAA.[87] For many farmers and opponents of federal regulation, the Court's invalidation of a law that imposed significant federal restrictions upon agriculture came as a relief. In 1934, for example, an Iowa attorney reported to Van Devanter that a

80. Edward L. Schapsmeier and Frederick H. Schapsmeier, *Henry A. Wallace of Iowa: The Agrarian Years, 1910–1940* (Ames: Iowa State University Press, 1968), 174–76.

81. Ibid., 212–13.

82. Philip Taft, *The A.F. of L. from the Death of Gompers to the Merger* (New York: Harper & Brothers, 1959), 49.

83. Henry A. Wallace, *Whose Constitution? An Inquiry into the General Welfare* (New York: Reynal & Hitchcock, 1936), 93.

84. Samuel Lubell, "Agriculture and the Constitution," *North American Review*, March 1936, 57, 70.

85. Morton Taylor, "The Middle West Answers the Court," *New Republic*, February 26, 1936, 72.

86. Thomas Hart Kennedy to George Norris, January 15, 1936, box 118, Norris Papers.

87. Gallup, Hensen, and Israel, *The Gallup Poll*, 1:9.

client who operated a chick hatchery with forty-two employees had received a telegram from an AAA official warning him that he would need to raise his prices or risk an investigation that "will probably ruin your business." The attorney complained that "[i]t seems almost intolerable to me that a citizen engaged in a legitimate business entirely satisfactory to him and to his customers can be threatened by Federal Agents with ruin of his business unless he raises his price to his customers."[88]

For many other farmers, however, the Court's decision undercut hopes for recovery in a devastated industry. The Court's invalidation of the AAA also left countless farmers wondering how to compensate for canceled benefit payments for crop controls, and it jeopardized the employment of more than six thousand AAA employees, many of whom were stranded in remote rural areas. The decision also disrupted the federal budget by leaving the government pledged to pay more than $600 million in benefits to farmers while eliminating as much as $700 million in current processing taxes that the government had expected to collect during the coming year.[89] To the degree that the decision was expected to depress farm prices, it intensified hostility toward the Court among farmers and business owners who relied on agricultural prosperity. Yet the decision was not popular among many city dwellers because it did not seem to produce any reduction in consumer prices.[90] A journalist who traveled through the Middle West in the winter of 1936 found that "[t]he belief is current in most farming communities that the decision was induced by judicial sympathy with the wealthy class."[91] Wallace called the Court's refund of processing taxes "the greatest legalized steal in American history."[92] Rather than sulking, however, Wallace almost immediately began to formulate new farm relief legislation,[93] which Congress enacted only seven weeks after *Butler* in amendments to the Soil Conservation and Domestic Allotment Act of the previous year.[94]

Four months after *Butler,* the Court struck down another important New Deal statute, the Bituminous Coal Conservation Act.[95] Ignoring evidence that the devastation of the coal industry greatly exacerbated the national depression, the Court in its decision in *Carter v. Carter Coal Co.* held that coal mines were beyond the reach of the congressional power to regulate interstate commerce because they

88. Frederick F. Faville to Willis Van Devanter, March 12, 1934, box 37, Willis Van Devanter Papers, Manuscript Division, Library of Congress (hereafter cited as Van Devanter Papers).

89. "AAA, New Deal Pillar, Smashed," *Literary Digest,* January 11, 1936, 7; "Seething Vacuum of the AAA," *Literary Digest,* January 18, 1936, 6.

90. Morton Taylor, "The Middle West Answers the Court," *New Republic,* February 26, 1936, 72.

91. Ibid.

92. "Tariff Aid to Farmers," *Literary Digest,* February 8, 1936, 8.

93. John C. Culver and John Hyde, *American Dreamer: The Life and Times of Henry A. Wallace* (New York: W. W. Norton, 2000), 160–61.

94. 49 Stat. 1148, amending 49 Stat. 163.

95. *Carter v. Carter Coal Co.,* 298 U.S. 238 (1936).

were essentially local operations. Justice Sutherland's opinion, joined by his fellow Horsemen and Roberts, reiterated the distinction between commerce and manufacturing that had led the Court in its 1918 decision in *Hammer v. Dagenhart* to strike down the first federal child labor law. The Court also revitalized its old distinction between direct and indirect effects on commerce. Similarly, in holding that the imposition of additional excise taxes on noncomplying mines was an unconstitutional penalty, the Court reiterated the doctrine that Congress could tax only to raise revenue and not to induce compliance with regulation. Finally, the Court held that the statute's delegation of power to the industry to prescribe its own regulations violated due process because it exceeded Congress's power of delegation. The Court found this delegation even more obnoxious than the NIRA delegation because Congress had delegated power to private producers and their employees rather than to the president.

Sutherland's opinion echoed the warnings of countless conservatives who warned that the New Deal was the primrose path to federal tyranny: "Every journey to a forbidden end begins with the first step; and the danger of such a step by the federal government in the direction of taking over the powers of the states is that the end of the journey may find the states so despoiled of their powers, or— what may amount to the same thing—so relieved of the responsibilities which possession of the powers necessarily enjoins, as to reduce them to little more than geographical subdivisions of the national domain."[96]

In a dissent joined by Brandeis and Stone, Cardozo vigorously argued that the devastation of the coal industry had such profound national implications that Congress clearly had power to enact price regulations pursuant to the commerce clause. "Congress was not condemned to inaction in the face of price wars and wage wars so pregnant with disaster," Cardozo declared. "Commerce had been choked and burdened; its normal flow had been diverted from one state to another; there had been bankruptcy and waste and ruin alike for capital and for labor. The liberty protected by the Fifth Amendment does not include the right to persist in this anarchic riot." Cardozo further argued that Congress could regulate even intrastate prices because they affected interstate commerce, and he concluded that there was no unconstitutional delegation of power because the statute prescribed detailed standards.[97] The dissenters did not address the constitutionality of the statute's provisions concerning labor provisions, regarding the challenge as premature.

In a separate opinion, Hughes adopted a middle position. He agreed with the Court that mining was not commerce, that the tax was a penalty, and that the labor provisions unconstitutionally delegated power to private industry and exceeded the commerce power. Hughes therefore agreed that federal regulation of local wages were unconstitutional, but he approved the constitutionality of the

96. Ibid., 295–96.
97. Ibid., 331, 326–32, 332–34 (Cardozo, J., dissenting).

statute's regulation of prices of coal sold in interstate commerce and its prohibition of unfair competition in interstate transactions. Hughes suggested that the people might wish to enact a constitutional amendment to "give Congress the power to regulate industries within the State."[98]

Meanwhile, the Court in April 1936 adopted a cramped view of the powers of the SEC, which had won widespread plaudits even among many conservatives for its effectiveness in helping to stabilize the securities industry through strict enforcement of the new securities laws. In its decision in *Jones v. SEC,* the Court sidestepped the constitutionality of the Securities Act of 1933, but struck down an SEC rule that compelled an applicant for securities registration to testify about its plan for selling securities even after withdrawal of an application.[99] Justice Sutherland's opinion reasoned that the SEC lacked any legitimate interest in the plan insofar as it could not prejudice investors once it was withdrawn. Although the Court based its decision upon statutory interpretation and common-law principles rather than any specific constitutional provision, the decision's implications for constitutional law were obvious. Condemning the SEC's action as "wholly unreasonable and arbitrary," Sutherland declared that it violated "the cardinal precept upon which the constitutional safeguards of personal liberty ultimately rest—that this shall be a government of laws." In words that cast a pall over the New Deal's expansion of the administrative state, Sutherland explained that "[t]o escape assumptions of such power on the part of the three primary departments of the government, is not enough. Our institutions must be kept free from the appropriation of unauthorized power by lesser agencies as well." Warning that the substitution of the "mere will of an official or an official body" for the rule of law could transform the government into an autocracy, although perhaps not "a supreme autocracy," Sutherland warned, "Arbitrary power and the rule of the Constitution cannot both exist. They are antagonistic and incompatible forces; and one or the other must of necessity perish whenever they are brought into conflict."[100]

In an acerbic dissent joined by Brandeis and Stone, Cardozo declared that "[r]ecklessness and deceit do not automatically excuse themselves by notice of repentance." Although Cardozo acknowledged the timelessness of Sutherland's reminder of the dangers of misuse of governmental power, Cardozo pointed out that securities traders had abused countless investors by circulating falsehoods and half-truths. Rather than indulging such wrongs "as peccadilloes, or even perhaps as the part of the amenities of business," Cardozo argued that they "must be dragged to light and pilloried." He further cautioned that "[t]o permit an offending registrant to stifle an inquiry by precipitate retreat on the eve of his exposure is to give immunity to guilt; to encourage falsehood and evasion; to invite the cunning and unscrupulous to gamble with detection." Cardozo feared that the decision could make the statute "the sport of clever knaves."[101] Similarly, the *New*

98. Ibid., 317–24, 318 (separate opinion of Hughes, C.J.).
99. 298 U.S. 1 (1936).
100. Ibid., 23, 24, 25, 24.
101. Ibid., 30, 32.

Republic wryly remarked, "We wish Mr. Justice Sutherland . . . would not use liberty as a blanket for quite so many sins."[102] Frankfurter complained to Stone that "Sutherland writes as though he were still a United States senator, making a partisan speech, but surely the Chief knows better."[103] Stone told the constitutional historian Charles A. Beard that he did not regard the immediate issue in the case as especially important but that "the Court's setting aside the plain command of Congress, without reference to any identifiable prohibition of the Constitution, is a matter of transcendent importance."[104] To Frankfurter, Stone vented that the Court's decision "was written for morons . . . [b]ut I can hardly believe that intelligent people . . . will swallow such buncombe."[105]

On May 25, 1936, the Court in a five-to-four vote continued its assault on the New Deal by nullifying the Municipal Bankruptcy Act of 1934 on the grounds that Congress had invaded the sovereignty of the states by permitting local governments to declare bankruptcy.[106] The Court reasoned that, if the congressional taxing power could not reach the states or their political subdivisions, neither could congressional power arising from the bankruptcy clause. In dissent, Cardozo, Hughes, Brandeis, and Stone pointed out that no municipality could invoke the law unless the law of its state authorized its operation. Cardozo observed that to judicially nullify the statute "because of a supposed affront to the dignity of a state, though the state disclaims the affront and is doing all it can to keep the law alive, is to make dignity a doubtful blessing."[107] Stone complained privately that the Court's decision was so transparently political that it constituted "a form of indecent exposure."[108] Although the *New Republic* observed that the Court's decision was relatively unimportant because the statute had not been widely invoked, it complained that the decision evinced a "menacing" tendency "since it envisages the nation as a congeries of separate and independent states, tied together only by a government that in many important respects cannot govern."[109]

The growing polarization of the Court in its bitterly divided decisions vexed many liberals, who particularly deplored Hughes's agreement with the Four Horsemen in so many of the controversial 1936 decisions. Taking apparent delight in the Court's blows to the administration, Hughes tacitly taunted Roosevelt and the New Deal in his May 1936 address to the American Law Institute, when he

102. *The New Republic*, April 15, 1936, 262 (unsigned editorial).

103. Felix Frankfurter to Harlan Fiske Stone, April 7, 1936, box 13, Stone Papers.

104. Harlan Fiske Stone to Charles Beard, April 16, 1936, box 6, Stone Papers.

105. Harlan Fiske Stone to Felix Frankfurter, April 7, 1936, box 13, Stone Papers.

106. *Ashton v. Cameron County Water Improvement District*, 298 U.S. 513 (1936). Congressional authorization for municipal bankruptcies was necessary because the contracts clause precluded municipalities from taking the initiative to declare bankruptcy.

107. Ibid., 532, 541.

108. Harlan Fiske Stone to Felix Frankfurter, May 30, 1936, reel 3, Felix Frankfurter Papers, Manuscript Division, Library of Congress (hereafter cited as Frankfurter Papers).

109. *The New Republic*, June 3, 1936, 86.

declared, "I am happy to report that the Supreme Court is still functioning," provoking two minutes of applause from the predominately conservative legal scholars.[110] Meanwhile, progressive Republicans who admired Stone's moderation tried
to promote Stone as their party's 1936 presidential nominee. Stone's lack of interest quickly squelched the movement. As he explained to a friend, justices "should
keep out of politics."[111] Some Republicans also considered drafting Roberts,[112]
who was no more willing than Stone to leave the Court for politics.

In addition to curbing the expansion of federal power during 1935–1936, the
Court also protected states' rights, this time in a unanimous decision specifically
invoking the Tenth Amendment, when it nullified a provision of the Federal
Home Owners' Loan Act that permitted state building and loan associations to
convert themselves into a Federal Savings and Loan Association upon the vote of
a bare majority of its members, without consent of the state.[113] Justice Cardozo's
opinion decried the statute as an "invasion of the sovereignty or quasi-sovereignty
of Wisconsin and an impairment of its public policy" of establishing savings and
loan corporations for the promotion of the common good.[114]

Aside from the decisions in the Gold Clause cases, the New Deal's only important judicial victory during the Roosevelt administration's first term was the
Court's approval of one limited feature of the TVA. In *Ashwander v. Tennessee Valley
Authority* in February 1936, the Court sustained the validity of a contract between
the TVA and a private power company for the sale of excess power generated by
the TVA-owned Muscles Shoals Dam in Alabama.[115] The Court explained that the
TVA constructed the dam to provide power for national defense and improve the
navigability of interstate waterways, both of which were within Congress's power
to regulate interstate commerce. The Court also reasoned that the federal government had power to dispose of property that it had lawfully acquired.[116]

The Court's decision left the TVA on sandy legal soil because the decision
expressly refrained from ruling on the TVA's massive programs of soil reclama-
tion, flood control, electric power development, and other activities designed to
transform the depressed economy of the Tennessee Valley. Moreover, several justices objected to the Court's consideration of any constitutional issue. In a concurring opinion joined by Stone, Roberts, and Cardozo, Justice Brandeis contended
that stockholders lacked standing to challenge the company's contract with the
TVA.[117] McReynolds, the sole dissenter, attacked the TVA at its roots, arguing that

---

110. Alpheus Thomas Mason, "Charles Evans Hughes: An Appeal to the Bar of History," 6
Vanderbilt Law Review 8 (1952).

111. Harlan Fiske Stone to Sterling Carr, May 29, 1934, box 8, Stone Papers. See also Carr
to Stone, March 14, 1936; Carr to Stone, November 26, 1935, box 8, Stone Papers.

112. Sterling Carr to Harlan Fiske Stone, June 4, 1936, box 8, Stone Papers.

113. *Hopkins Federal Savings & Loan Association v. Cleary*, 296 U.S. 315 (1935).

114. Ibid., 337.

115. 297 U.S. 288 (1936).

116. Ibid., 324–40.

117. Ibid., 342–44, 347–56 (Brandeis, J., concurring).

the federal government lacked the power to enter the business of generating, transmitting and selling power, particularly because these activities displaced private companies that had expended great sums of money to acquire and develop electric power systems that had adequately responded to the needs of their customers.[118]

The New Deal's constitutional victory in the TVA case was not as isolated as it seemed, for many New Deal measures prior to 1937 survived constitutional scrutiny by default because they were not subjected to lawsuits contesting their legality. In recounting the Court's exacting scrutiny and frequent invalidation of New Deal programs, historians often overlook the fact that the Court never reviewed the constitutionality of several important New Deal measures because they were so clearly within congressional power to appropriate funds for the general welfare that even diehard conservatives shrunk from challenging them. In particular, no significant legal opposition was mounted against the PWA and the WPA, which provided jobs for millions of Americans in a vast array of projects ranging from the construction of public buildings to the preparation of travel guides and oral histories. Also escaping legal challenge were the CCC, which employed hundreds of thousands of youths on soil conservation projects, and the Home Owners' Loan Corporation, which helped refinance home mortgages. The immunity of such legislation, however, offered little consolation to liberals, who feared for the constitutionality of so many other New Deal measures.

The Court's decisions restricting federal power particularly demoralized New Dealers because the states often were not free to fill the void left in areas in which the Court had prohibited congressional legislation. The Court's imposition of restrictions on state legislation often blocked this path, while competition among states tended to discourage regulatory experiments in less industrialized states that were seeking to lure business from sister states. Alleging that the Court had "created a great No Man's Land where neither Congress nor state legislature has any effective power to legislate," one commentator in 1936 concluded that "[t]he issue is not between regulation by the federal government and regulation by the states. It is rather between regulation by the federal government and no regulation at all."[119]

Meanwhile, the Court likewise continued to attenuate the power of federal administrative agencies. The Court reasserted a broad power to review the decisions of administrative agencies in April 1936 in *St. Joseph Stock Yards Co. v. United States,* holding that federal courts could review the constitutionality of rates established by regulatory agencies.[120] Although the Court unanimously agreed that Secretary of Agriculture Henry A. Wallace's order fixing stockyard prices was not confiscatory, the justices sharply divided on whether courts could review the order. In his opinion for the Court, Hughes insisted that abnegation of the power

118. Ibid., 356–72 (McReynolds, J., dissenting).

119. Louis P. Eisner, "Constitution vs. New Deal," *Review of Reviews,* January 1936, 62.

120. 298 U.S. 38 (1936).

of judicial review when "the evidence clearly establishes that the findings are wrong and constitutional rights have been invaded, is to place those rights at the mercy of administrative officials and seriously to impair the security inherent in our judicial safeguards. That prospect, with our multiplication of administrative agencies, is not one to be lightly regarded." Hughes cautioned, however, that "this judicial duty to exercise an independent judgment does not require or justify disregard of the weight which may properly attach to findings upon hearing and evidence."[121]

In a dissent joined by Stone and Cardozo, Brandeis argued that "Congress concluded that a wealthy and litigious utility might practically nullify rate regulation if the correctness of findings by the regulating body of the facts as to value and income were made subject to judicial review." Anticipating a doctrine that the Court would accept within only a few years, Brandeis also drew a distinction between personal and property rights, contending that courts should review the factual record of agency decisions impinging on personal freedom but that "when dealing with property a much more liberal rule applies" and "due process of law does not always entitle an owner to have the correctness of findings of fact reviewed by a court."[122] Hughes explicitly rejected this dichotomy.[123]

Similarly, the Court circumscribed the scope of the Interstate Commerce Act when it held that a railroad could transport goods produced by a manufacturer owned by the same holding company as the railroad, notwithstanding the statute's "commodities clause" prohibition against a railroad's transportation of goods produced by the railroad or a business under its authority.[124] Stone's dissent, joined by Brandeis and Cardozo, pointed out that the commodities clause was intended to prevent the favoritism and abuse of power that had occurred when "a single business interest occupies the inconsistent position of carrier and shipper" and that the decision emasculated the clause by enabling the holding company, which closely controlled both the railroad and the manufacturer, to commit the abuses that the statute was intended to prevent.[125]

The Court exercised similarly exacting scrutiny of the actions of state regulatory agencies. In the February 1936 *Great Northern Railway v. Weeks* decision, for example, the Court held that North Dakota's tax commissioner had deprived a railroad of due process of law by assessing a tax on a railroad that the Court found to exceed by $10 million the true market value of the railroad's property in the state because the commissioner had failed to take account of depressed prices.[126] In a dissent joined by Brandeis and Cardozo, Stone insisted that the Court should defer to the discretion of state authorities in the absence of any showing of discrimination among taxpayers. Stone expressed special concern "that for the first

---

121. Ibid., 52, 53.
122. Ibid., 93, 77 (Brandeis, J., dissenting).
123. Ibid., 53.
124. *United States v. Elgin, Joliet and Eastern Railway Co.*, 298 U.S. 492 (1936).
125. Ibid., 504, 512, 508–12 (Stone, J., dissenting).
126. 297 U.S. 135 (1936).

time this Court is setting aside a tax as a violation of the Fourteenth Amendment on the ground that the assessment on which it is computed is too high, without any showing that the assessment is discriminatory or that petitioner is in any way bearing an undue share of the tax burden imposed on all property owners in the state."[127]

In a six-to-three decision in June 1935, the Court held that the Public Service Commission of Maryland had deprived a telephone company of due process by using a method of valuation that translated an earlier valuation into the present price index.[128] Roberts's opinion objected that the price index had not been prepared for purposes of the valuation and that prices levels were an unreliable and hence arbitrary method of calculating valuations because they were subject to "sudden shifts."[129] Stone's dissent argued that the commission's rate of valuation left the company with a return of 4.5 percent, which was not confiscatory and therefore not a denial of due process. Stone complained that, "[i]n assuming the task of determining judicially the present fair replacement value of the vast properties of public utilities, courts have been projected into the most speculative undertaking imposed upon them in the entire history of English jurisprudence." He also accused the Court of hypocrisy insofar as it had not objected to the use of price indexes in establishing valuations when prices were rising.[130] Coming only one week after Black Monday, the decision seemed to many contemporary observers to signal intensified judicial hostility toward public regulation of utility rates.[131] In a unanimous decision earlier in 1935, the Court held that a commission denied due process to a utility by setting its rates at only 4.53 percent.[132]

At the same time that the Court was taking a dim view of New Deal legislation, its reactions to state regulatory legislation remained mixed. The Court's validation of some state laws even while it wreaked carnage on the New Deal suggests that the Court's adverse reactions to the New Deal laws were based on adherence to well-established legal doctrines rather than on implacable hostility toward regulation. The continuity between the Court's decisions on state legislation before 1935 and its decisions during 1935 and 1936 likewise indicate that the Court's antipathy toward New Deal legislation did not represent any sudden lurch to the political Right.

The Court's general deference toward state legislation was illustrated in its unanimous rejection of a due process challenge to California's regulation of sardine processing.[133] Although Justice Sutherland's opinion cited *Adkins* in support of its declaration that the due process clause protected liberty of contract, the Court held that the statute did not interfere with liberty of contract merely

127. Ibid., 155, 154 (Stone. J., dissenting).

128. *West v. Chesapeake & Potomac Telephone Co. of Baltimore*, 295 U.S. 662 (1935).

129. Ibid., 669–672.

130. Ibid., 689, 692 (Stone, J., dissenting).

131. See "Another Supreme Court Fiasco," *New Republic*, July 3, 1935, 211.

132. *West Ohio Gas Co. v. Public Utilities Commission of Ohio*, 294 U.S. 63 (1935).

133. *Bayside Fish Co. v. Gentry*, 297 U.S. 423 (1936).

because it deterred a processor from entering into a contract for the purchase of sardines. Sutherland explained that a "statute does not become unconstitutional merely because it has created a condition of affairs which renders the making of a related contract, lawful in itself, ineffective." Moreover, because the statute, which was intended to conserve the state's fish supply, was a valid exercise of the police power, the Court could not invalidate it merely because the Court objected to the state's policy or because it would inflict hardship on some persons. The Court also ruled that the statute did not violate equal protection by imposing regulations only on processing of sardines that were not prepared for human consumption. Emphasizing that equal protection was not denied merely because some inequality resulted, Sutherland explained that the law would not be invalid unless the inequality were "actually and palpably unreasonable and arbitrary."[134]

In a May 1935 decision, the Court unanimously upheld an Oregon statute that prohibited dentists from various advertising practices, including advertisement of prices or free dental work, claims of professional superiority, or use of "glaring light signs."[135] In rejecting a dentist's due process challenge, Hughes emphasized that the Court should defer to legislative determinations of what was needed to protect the public from injurious practices. In a tacit reiteration of the "public interest" test, Hughes pointed out that "[t]he legislature was not dealing with traders in commodities, but with the vital interests of public health, and with a profession treating bodily ills and demanding different standards of conduct from those which are traditional in the competition of the market place."[136]

Similarly, the Court unanimously sustained a state vehicle tax that exempted vehicles engaged in hauling passengers or farm products between points or through towns lacking railroad facilities.[137] Cardozo's opinion explained that a classification "designed to ameliorate the lot of the producers of farm and dairy products is not an arbitrary preference." Diminution of the plight of the Depression-era Georgia farmer by relieving "him of fresh burdens might seem to a wise statecraft to be a means whereby to foster agriculture and promote the common good."[138]

In other decisions, the Court continued to closely divide in favor of regulatory legislation. In a five-to-four decision in March 1935, *Metropolitan Casualty Insurance Co. v. Brownell,* the Court upheld an Indiana statute that discriminated between domestic and foreign insurance corporations in establishing limitations on the time during which lawsuits could be commenced.[139] In his opinion for the Court, Stone declared that "courts may not declare a legislative discrimination invalid unless, viewed in the light of facts made known or generally assumed, it is of such

---

134. Ibid., 427, 427–28, 428–30, 429.
135. *Semler v. Oregon State Board of Dental Examiners,* 294 U.S. 608 (1935).
136. Ibid., 612.
137. *Aero Mayflower Transit Co. v. Georgia Public Service Commission.* 295 U.S. 285 (1935).
138. Ibid., 290–91, 291.
139. 294 U.S. 580 (1935).

a character as to preclude the assumption that the classification rests upon some rational basis within the knowledge and experience of the legislators." Accordingly, Stone explained that a "statutory discrimination will not be set aside as the denial of equal protection of the laws if any state of facts reasonably may be conceived to justify it."[140] Because Stone's statement of the Court's standard of review was essentially the same as what the Court had enunciated in its 1931 decision in the Indiana chain store case and other decisions, its reiteration at this time in a decision upholding regulatory legislation indicates that the Court had changed neither its doctrine nor its application of that doctrine.

The continuity of the Court's mixed responses toward regulatory decision was likewise manifest in two February 1936 decisions in which the Court upheld one part of a New York milk price statute while striking down another part. In the first decision, from which the Four Horsemen dissented, the Court held that New York could permit milk dealers who lacked well-advertised trade names to sell milk for a penny a quart less than the price charged by dealers who were better known in the market.[141] In his opinion, Roberts found that the legislature had rationally discriminated between the two types of dealers in order to try to replicate so far as possible the price structure that had existed before price regulation. "To attempt the maintenance of that balance," Roberts explained, "was to strive for equality of treatment, equality of burden, not to create inequality. To adapt the law to the existing trade practice was neither unreasonable nor arbitrary."[142]

In the second decision, the Court held that the statute violated equal protection to the extent that dealers who lacked well-advertised trade names were not given the benefit of the one-cent price reduction if they entered into business after the enactment of the milk price regulation.[143] In his opinion, Roberts explained that the state had failed to offer any justification for the discrimination. In a stinging dissent joined by Brandeis and Stone, Cardozo summoned many reasons to justify the discrimination, particularly the significant investment that dealers in less-advertised brands had made in their businesses by the time of the statute's enactment. In addition to citing *Brownell*'s statement that the Court should not nullify legislation "if any state of facts reasonably may be conceived to justify it," Cardozo declared that "[t]he judicial function is discharged when it appears from a survey of the scene that the lawmakers did not play the part of arbitrary despots in choosing as they did." Chiding the Court for inconsistency with an opinion "announced a minute or so earlier," Cardozo alleged that the Court had made "a choice between competing considerations of policy and fairness, however emphatic its professions that it applies a rule of law."[144] The Court's failure to discern the justifications for the discrimination that the three dissenters

140. Ibid., 584.
141. *Borden's Farm Products Co., Inc. v. Ten Eyck*, 297 U.S. 251 (1936)
142. Ibid., 262.
143. *Mayflower Farms, Inc. v. Ten Eyck*, 297 U.S. 266 (1936).
144. Ibid., 278, 276, 274, 276.

so clearly perceived indicates that the Court continued in practice, at least in some cases, to subject economic regulatory legislation to a more exacting standard of review than its professed "rational basis" standard would suggest.

The Court's division over the extent to which it owed deference to state legislatures was particularly manifest in cases involving taxation. In *Stewart Dry Goods Co. v. Lewis,* for example, a March 1935 decision, the Court split six to three over the question of whether a Kentucky statute imposing graduated taxes on the retail sales of merchants violated the equal protection clause.[145] Justice Roberts's opinion for the Court explained that the tax, with rates ranging from .05 percent on sales less than $400,000 to 1 percent on sales greater than $1 million, was "unjustifiably unequal, whimsical and arbitrary" because "the gross sales of a merchant do not bear a constant relation to his net profits." It therefore violated the Fourteenth Amendment's equal protection clause. Roberts pointed out that a merchant with gross receipts of $1 million and a net loss had to pay more tax than a merchant with receipts of $400,000 and a net profit. Dismissing the argument that the receipts tax was easier to administer than an income tax, Roberts explained that "[g]ross inequalities may not be ignored for the sake of ease of collection" and that "it is difficult to be just, and easy to be arbitrary." Roberts found that "[t]he record fails to show that an income tax or a flat tax on sales would not accomplish the desired end." He observed that the adoption of income taxes by many states "is a practical confirmation of the view that they are effective."[146]

Cardozo's dissent, joined by Brandeis and Stone, declared that "[i]t is not the function of a court to make itself the arbiter between competing economic theories professed by honest men on grounds not wholly frivolous. . . . Responsibility for economic wisdom has been laid upon the legislature. There is finality in its choice, even though wisdom may be lacking, unless [its] choice can be found to be so void of rationality as to be the expression of a whim rather than an exercise of judgment." Cardozo drew upon statistics compiled by economists in trying to demonstrate that there was a reasonably close correlation between business receipts and profits. Although he acknowledged that the correlation between receipts and profits was not perfect, he remarked that "[t]he law builds upon the probable, and shapes the measure of the tax accordingly." Cardozo also pointed out that in its recent decisions in the Indiana chain store and *Liggett* decisions the Court had permitted classifications that "ran athwart the lines of profit."[147]

Sharply disagreeing with the majority's contention that an income tax could be more easily administered, Cardozo argued that calculation of profits "are subject to possible inaccuracies, almost without number." Accordingly, Cardozo found that "[t]here is nothing arbitrary in rescuing a vast body of taxpayers from the labor and expense of preparing elaborate reports, at best approximately accurate. There is nothing arbitrary in rescuing a government from the labor and

145. 294 U.S. 550 (1935).
146. Ibid., 557, 558, 560, 563.
147. Ibid., 569–70, 571, 579 (Cardozo, J., dissenting).

expense of setting up the huge and unwieldy machinery of an income tax department with a swarm of investigators and accountants and legal and financial
experts." Cardozo therefore contended that Kentucky's legislation to avoid the
problems of an income tax was "no act of sheer oppression, no abandonment of
reason, no exercise of the general will in a perverse or vengeful spirit," but rather
"a pursuit of legitimate ends by methods honestly conceived and rationally cho-
sen." Cardozo observed that no more should be required of legislatures by judges
"who have learned from experience and history that government is at best a make-
shift, that the attainment of one good may involve the sacrifice of others, and that
compromise will be inevitable until the coming of Utopia."[148]

In another example of its close scrutiny of state taxation, the Court in *Colgate
v. Harvey* in December 1935 invalidated a Vermont income tax law on the ground
that its exemption of unsecured loans made within the state violated the Fourteenth Amendment's privileges and immunities clause because it discriminated
against loans made out of the state.[149] In a dissent joined by Cardozo and Brandeis,
Stone complained that the statute could not violate the privileges and immunities
clause if it failed to transgress the equal protection clause.[150] Privately, Stone bitterly accused the Court of hypocrisy in circumscribing state power in this manner
in the wake of so many decisions nullifying federal statutes as invasions of state
power.[151] The *New Republic* likewise pointed out the same inconsistency and
expressed alarm that this "egregious mutation" of the privileges and immunities
doctrine would protect "a seemingly vast and indeterminate range of private property rights," providing a basis for striking down legislation even when the prohibitions of the doctrines of interstate commerce, due process, and equal protection
were unavailable.[152]

In some cases, the Court was united in its disapproval of state legislation. For
example, the Court unanimously held that a Kansas statute violated the takings
clause by permitting the state highway commission to order a pipeline company,
at its own expense, to relocate to conform to plans adopted for new highways.[153]
McReynolds explained that "[t]he police power of a State, while not susceptible
of definition with circumstantial precision, must be exercised within a limited
ambit and is subordinate to constitutional limitations. . . . Under it there is no
unrestricted authority to accomplish whatever the public may presently desire. It
is the governmental power of self protection, and permits reasonable regulation
of rights and property in particulars essential to the preservation of the community from injury."[154]

148. Ibid., 576, 577.
149. 296 U.S. 404 (1935).
150. Ibid., 443–50 (Stone, J., dissenting).
151. Mason, *Harlan Fiske Stone,* 400.
152. "The Supreme Court Improvises," *New Republic,* January 1, 1936, 214.
153. *Panhandle Eastern Pipe Line Co. v. State Highway Commission,* 294 U.S. 613 (1935). Justices
Stone and Cardozo concurred without opinion.
154. Ibid., 622.

Meanwhile, the Court continued its tendency to take a more relaxed response toward state regulation under the doctrine of the so-called dormant commerce clause. In several of these decisions, the Court found that proper exercises of the police power justified incidental burdens upon interstate commerce. In upholding the Georgia statutes that imposed fees for the privilege of transporting motor vehicles through the state for sale in other states, for example, the Court found that the fees were justified because the movement of car caravans created special hazards that required additional policing.[155] In a similar case, the Court upheld a statute that imposed a license fee upon private carriers transporting persons or property for hire over public highways.[156] Similarly, the Court in another case unanimously held that state licensing and bonding of commission merchants who solicited and sold intrastate consignments of farm products did not unduly interfere with interstate commerce even though some of the products came from out of state and a federal statute provided similar regulations for interstate consignments of farm products.[157] The Court reasoned that the state law was a proper exercise of the police power, designed to encourage "proper accounting, honest dealing, and prompt remittance," and that it did not unduly burden interstate commerce or interfere with the operation of the federal statute.[158]

In a number of other decisions, the Court likewise found that various state regulations that affected interstate commerce did not improperly discriminate against interstate commerce. For example, the Court unanimously held that an Oregon administrative order prescribing containers for packers of raspberries and strawberries did not unduly burden interstate commerce because it was nondiscriminatory and operated only intrastate, after the original package had been broken.[159] The Court also unanimously rejected a commerce clause challenge to the California statute that regulated the processing of sardines insofar as the court found that the regulation was purely local and did not discriminate—and was not intended to discriminate—against the interstate movement of sardines.[160]

The Court likewise rejected commerce clause challenges to various taxes. For example, the Court upheld a Pennsylvania tax on fuel that was brought into Pennsylvania from other states. In their decision, the justices explained that the tax did not discriminate against interstate commerce.[161] Similarly, the Court unanimously held that a state could impose a tax on the intrastate income of a telecommunications corporation that was engaged in interstate commerce, even though the company's intrastate and interstate operations were inseparable, where there was no showing that the tax imposed a burden on interstate commerce.[162]

155. *Morf v. Bingaman*, 298 U.S. 407 (1936).
156. *Aero Mayflower Transit Co. v. Georgia Public Service Commission*, 295 U.S. 285, 289 (1935).
157. *Hartford Accident & Indemnity Co. v. Illinois*, 298 U.S. 155 (1936).
158. Ibid., 159, 158–59.
159. *Pacific States Box & Basket Co. v. White*, 296 U.S. 176 (1935).
160. *Bayside Fish Flour Co. v. Gentry*, 297 U.S. 422 (1936).
161. *Wiloil Corp. v. Pennsylvania*, 294 U.S. 169 (1935).
162. *Pacific Telephone & Telegraph Co. v. Tax Commission of Washington*, 297 U.S. 403 (1936).

In *Baldwin v. Seelig,* one of the few decisions in which the Court determined that a state regulation improperly interfered with interstate commerce, the Court unanimously held that New York unconstitutionally burdened interstate commerce by prohibiting the sale of milk imported from another state unless the price paid to the producer in the other state was at least the minimum that New York prescribed for purchasers from local producers.[163] In his opinion for the Court, Cardozo explained that the statute "set a barrier to traffic" between states as effective "as if customs duties, equal to the price differential, had been laid upon the thing transported." Cardozo vigorously rejected the argument that this law, like the milk price control that the Court sustained in *Nebbia,* was a constitutional effort to protect consumers. A public-welfare exception to dormant commerce clause, Cardozo argued, would swallow the rule and would "invite a speedy end to our national solidarity. The Constitution . . . was framed upon the theory that the peoples of the several states must sink or swim together, and that in the long run prosperity and salvation are in union and not division."[164] The Court also struck down a state tax upon a telephone company for each phone in the state, finding that the statute imposed a direct burden on interstate commerce by failing to discriminate between intrastate and interstate uses.[165]

The Court's hostility toward state regulatory legislation seemed even less defensible than its nullification of federal measures because, as Frankfurter observed, "one can't say that the emotional undertow of New Deal legislation was operating."[166] As Michael E. Parrish has observed, decisions such as *Colgate, Great Northern,* and *Mayflower Farms* "betrayed more than a fleeting hostility to legislative interference with property rights. They clearly exposed the desire of six justices to fashion new weapons with which to check the advance of state economic regulations that impinged on those rights."[167]

Most of the Court's decisions on state regulation of business received scant public attention, regardless of whether they sustained a law or struck it down. But on June 1, 1936, only two weeks after the Court left liberals reeling from *Carter Coal,* its decision nullifying New York's minimum wage law for women generated more indignation than any other state law decision of the Hughes Court. The decision in *Morehead v. New York ex rel. Tipaldo*[168] confirmed the worst suspicions of the Court's critics by revitalizing the supposedly moribund doctrine of "liberty of contract" and contravening the public's general acceptance of legislation to protect workers.

163. *Baldwin v. Seelig,* 294 U.S. 499 (1935).

164. Ibid., 521, 523.

165. *Cooney v. Mountain States Telephone & Telegraph Co.,* 294 U.S. 384 (1935).

166. Felix Frankfurter to Stanley Reed, February 15, 1936, box 170, Frankfurter Papers, cited in Michael E. Parrish, "The Hughes Court, the Great Depression, and the Historians," 40 *Historian* 299 (1978).

167. Parrish, "The Hughes Court," 300.

168. 298 U.S. 587 (1936).

The five-to-four *Tipaldo* decision breathed new life into substantive due process by holding that the statute violated the Fourteenth Amendment's due process clause by depriving employers and workers of their liberty to make contracts without undue governmental interference. Justice Butler's opinion relied heavily upon the 1923 decision in *Adkins*, striking down the District of Columbia's provisions for minimum wages for women. Espousing a normative view that ignored the harsh realities of the marketplace that many and probably most Americans had long since rejected, Butler declared that "[i]n making contracts of employment, generally speaking, the parties have equal right to obtain from each other the best terms they can by private bargaining." Accordingly, he explained, "legislative abridgement of that freedom can only be justified by the existence of exceptional circumstances."[169]

In a dissenting opinion joined by Brandeis, Stone, and Cardozo, Hughes distinguished *Adkins* on the ground that the New York statute prescribed wages on the basis of the reasonable value of employees' services, in contrast to the District of Columbia law, which had required wages adequate to provide a standard of living that would protect the health and morals of women. Hughes also pointed out that the Court often had said that "liberty of contract is a qualified and not an absolute right," particularly in cases involving women.[170]

In a separate dissent joined by Brandeis and Cardozo, Stone rejected *Adkins* altogether. "There is grim irony in speaking of the freedom of contract of those who, because of their economic necessities, give their services for less than is needful to keep body and soul together," Stone observed. Economic studies since *Adkins*, he explained, had demonstrated "that a wage is not always the resultant of free bargaining between employers and employees; that it may be one forced upon employees by their economic necessities and upon employers by the most ruthless of their competitors." He warned that unfair wages not only harmed workers, but also "may affect profoundly the entire economic structure of society" and cast on taxpayers and government "the burden of solving the problems of poverty, subsistence, health and morals of large numbers in the community." Stone declared, "It is difficult to imagine any grounds, other than our own personal economic predilections, for saying that the contract of employment is any the less an appropriate subject of legislation" than the scores of other economic regulatory statutes the Court had upheld. "The legislature must be free to choose, unless government is to be rendered impotent."[171] Privately, Stone expressed puzzlement that Hughes had written such a limited opinion. "It is a pity," he remarked to Frankfurter, "that such an imposing facade rests, at times, upon such a meager foundation."[172]

Stone was irritated that many persons thought that his dissent expressed his "own economic predilections, whereas quite the contrary is the fact." He privately

169. Ibid., 610.
170. Ibid., 623–24, 628 (Hughes, C.J., dissenting).
171. Ibid., 632, 635, 633, 636 (Stone. J., dissenting).
172. Harlan Fiske Stone to Felix Frankfurter, June 3, 1936, box 13, Stone Papers.

explained to the journalist Irving Brant, "I have a good deal of skepticism about the satisfactory operation of price fixing schemes, but in my mind that is something with which the courts have nothing to do. Unless legislatures are free to deal with such questions, we are clutched in the dead hand of the economic theories of a century ago." He continued, "Judicial labors would be intolerable to me if I felt they placed on me the responsibility of choice of economic theories about which reasonable men may differ, and the choice of which with changing experience might be very different at one time than that at another." Although he believed that judges should not read their economic views into the Constitution, Stone contended that they had a duty of "seeking to ascertain objectively the *mores* of the time."[173]

The Court's decision in *Tipaldo* had implications far beyond New York, because it implicitly impugned the constitutionality of all but three of the sixteen state minimum wage statutes.[174] The *Tipaldo* decision was a particularly extreme exercise of judicial review because state minimum wage laws, which involved an exercise of the police power, were a far less controversial exercise of governmental regulation than were the New Deal experiments the Court had invalidated during the preceding year, many of which altered the contours of federalism. Having hamstrung congressional power on principles of federalism, the Court now hindered the states from exercising their police powers. Denouncing the decision as "a blunder of magnitude" that would "do more to undermine the prestige of the Court" than any decision of the previous four years, *Commonweal* declared, "Our very blood is tainted by the grasping miserliness of operatives who know they are dealing with persons compelled to accept work at almost any figure. No concept of competition that is in any way defensible would involve the right of employers under existing conditions to hire labor for what are starvation dollars and cents."[175] Fearing that the decision played into the hands of radicals, Frankfurter remarked to Stone that "millions of people and precious social institutions may ultimately pay the price for the recklessness of a few men."[176]

Even many conservative Republicans denounced the decision. Some who had ardently defended the Court against the ever-swelling ranks of its critics regarded *Tipaldo* almost as a betrayal because it belied their argument that the Court was trying only to protect federalism from the depredations of the New Deal.[177] Hamilton Fish, the New York Republican who represented Roosevelt's own congressional district and was an especially strident critic of the administration, warned that the decision would win a million votes for the Democrats in the upcoming

173. Harlan Fiske Stone to Irving Brant, June 13, 1936, box 7, Stone Papers.

174. "31c. an Hour: Minimum Pay of New York Laundresses National Issue by Court Decision," *Literary Digest*, June 13, 1936, 6.

175. "A Deplorable Decision," *Commonweal*, June 19, 1936, 199.

176. Felix Frankfurter to Harlan Fiske Stone, June 2, 1936, box 13, Stone Papers.

177. William Lasser, *The Limits of Judicial Power: The Supreme Court in American Politics* (Chapel Hill: University of North Carolina Press), 1988, 142.

presidential election.[178] Decided on the eve of the Republican National Convention, the decision acutely embarrassed the GOP. Alfred M. Landon, the Republican presidential nominee, advocated a constitutional amendment to permit states to impose maximum working hours, while the Republican platform called for minimum wage laws, which it somehow contended could be enacted "within the Constitution as it now stands."[179] In the wake of the furor over *Tipaldo*, Cardozo privately remarked to Stone that "we should be less than human if we failed to sit back in our chairs with a grin on our face as we watch the response to the minimum wage decision."[180]

Despite its general unpopularity, *Tipaldo* generated praise from some women's rights advocates, including the National Woman's Party, who believed that the statutory discrimination in favor of women hindered the movement for gender equality.[181] Writing to thank Van Devanter for his vote, a Maryland woman declared, "You did my sex the honor of regarding women as persons and citizens, in the eyes of the law."[182] During recent years, some feminist scholars, many of whom generally favor regulatory economic regulatory legislation, have commended the decision for the same reason. Women who actively supported regulatory legislation, however, generally deplored *Tipaldo* as ardently as men.[183]

Coming in the wake of so many recent decisions striking down New Deal legislation, *Tipaldo* confirmed the opinion of many of the Court's critics that some type of measure was needed to curb the Court. Although many liberals had hoped that time would solve the problem by inducing at least one of the more conservative justices to resign, no one left the Court during Roosevelt's first term even though the average age of the justices by the end of 1936 was 71.2 years. Not since Monroe's first administration had a president served out a full term without making an appointment to the Supreme Court. Justices were understandably reluctant to resign at a time of critical ferment in constitutional law, when so much was at stake. As one commentator observed, "With historic decisions in their making, they would no more quit than a fireman would drop a hose in the midst of a blaze."[184] More pragmatically, several of the aged justices may have been loath to surrender their comfortable salaries because of the1932 federal statute limiting the pensions of federal judges to ten thousand dollars, only half of what they earned on the bench.

178. "31c. an Hour," *Literary Digest,* June 13, 1936, 6.

179. Donald Bruce Johnson, comp., *National Party Platforms,* Vol. 1 (Urbana: University of Illinois Press, 1978), 367.

180. Benjamin N. Cardozo to Harlan Fiske Stone, June 9, 1936, box 74, Stone Papers.

181. See, for example, Ruth G. Williams to George Sutherland, June 3, 1936, box 5, Papers of George W. Sutherland, Manuscript Division, Library of Congress.

182. Edith Houghton Hooker to Willis Van Devanter, April 2, 1937, box 38, Van Devanter Papers..

183. See Mary R. Beard to Harlan Fiske Stone, June 2, 1936, box 6, Stone Papers.

184. Ray Tucker, "Court of the Last Guess," 32.

In the absence of resignations, many critics of the Court—at least since *Schechter*—had been considering Court-curbing measures. In conversations with Harold Ickes near the beginning and end of 1935, Roosevelt had mentioned the possibility of adding more justices, though Ickes reported that Roosevelt found this possibility "distasteful."[185] On several occasions during 1935 and 1936, the president confided in Ickes that he preferred a constitutional amendment or statute that would recognize the Court's power of judicial review but permit the next succeeding Congress to reenact any federal statute that the Court had found to be unconstitutional and forbid the Court to pass again upon its constitutionality. The intervening congressional election would function as a public referendum on the statute.[186] Meanwhile, members of Congress and various commentators once again dusted off a wide array of measures to curtail the Court's power, including abrogation of judicial review, limitations on judicial tenure, and requirement of a concurrence of more than a majority of justices to invalidate legislation.[187]

In the wake of growing public impatience with the Court and increasing demands for curbs on its power, many voters and political advisors urged Roosevelt to make the Court an issue in the 1936 election campaign.[188] Others, however, worried that any attack on the Court would play into Republican hands by lending credibility to allegations that the New Deal was revolutionary and that Roosevelt was dictatorial. Senator Robert M. La Follette's third-party presidential bid in 1924 had suffered incalculable harm from relentless Republican charges that the Wisconsin Progressive's proposal to permit Congress to overturn Supreme Court decisions threatened economic stability, the rights of minorities, and democracy itself.[189] Republicans in 1936 seemed particularly likely to take refuge in the Marble Palace and drape themselves in the Constitution because the burgeoning economical revival deprived Republicans of the opportunity to claim that the New Deal was ineffective.[190] Even before the 1936 campaign began, there were signs that Republicans relished the opportunity to use Democratic criticism of the Court as a prime example of Roosevelt's contempt for the Constitution and the rule of law.[191]

185. Ickes, *Secret Diary*, 1:274, 495.

186. Ibid., 467, 495, 529.

187. William G. Ross, *A Muted Fury: Populists, Progressives, and Labor Unions Confront the Courts, 1890–1937* (Princeton, N.J.: Princeton University Press, 1994), 296–98.

188. William G. Ross, "The Role of Judicial Issues in Presidential Campaigns," 42 *Santa Clara Law Review* 415 (2002) (citing letters on file in the Franklin D. Roosevelt Library).

189. Ross, *A Muted Fury*, 254–84.

190. William E. Leuchtenburg, "When the People Spoke, What Did They Say? The Election of 1936 and Ackerman Thesis," 108 *Yale Law Journal* 2082 (1999).

191. Early in 1936, for example, Senator William E. Borah of Idaho attempted to make judicial independence and constitutional integrity an issue in his campaign for the Republican presidential nomination. See "Text of Senator William E. Borah's Address to Brooklyn Republicans," *New York Times*, January 29, 1936, 13; "Text of Senator Borah's Address on 'The Constitution and Entangling Alliances,' " *New York Times*, February 23, 1936, 32; "Text of Senator Borah's Address Opening Campaign in His Native State of Illinois," *New York Times*, March 22, 1936, 40.

Although the *Tipaldo* decision hindered Republican efforts to portray Democrats as a threat to the Court, because *Tipaldo* was too much even for many Republicans to swallow, Republicans did not abandon all efforts to stigmatize the Democrats for their criticism of the Court. The Republican platform pledged to "resist all attempts to impair the authority of the Supreme Court" and warned that "[t]here can be no individual liberty without an independent judiciary."[192] Meanwhile, Landon and his running mate, Frank Knox, accused Roosevelt of threatening the Court's independence. On the eve of the election, former President Hoover presciently warned that Roosevelt might try to "stuff the Court."[193] Even those Republicans who did not accuse Roosevelt of harboring plans for assaulting the Court warned that his judicial appointments during a second term would imperil basic constitutional doctrines.[194]

Recognizing the risks of public attacks on what remained a largely sacrosanct institution, Roosevelt prudently refrained from criticizing the Court or proposing any form of judicial reform during his reelection campaign. This low-risk strategy seemed particularly appropriate because Roosevelt already had the solid support of voters whom the Court had antagonized. As William E. Leuchtenburg has pointed out, Roosevelt preferred to bide his time until the Court wreaked "enough additional mischief to create a popular demand for action."[195] The Democratic platform was nearly as circumspect as the president, limiting itself to an enigmatic pledge to seek a constitutional amendment to clarify the power of Congress and the state legislatures to enact laws to safeguard economic security if the nation's economic problems could not effectively be solved "through legislation within the Constitution."[196] The risk of attacking the Court was particularly acute because not even the most optimistic Democrats foresaw the size of Roosevelt's landslide, whereas many political analysts predicted a close election. A July Gallup poll showed Roosevelt and Landon in a very tight race, and the final *Literary Digest* poll forecast a Landon landslide.[197] Uncertain of his reelection, Roosevelt may have feared that criticism of the Court could cost him so many votes that he would not have any mandate for judicial reform even if he won.[198] Moreover, as Leuchtenburg has pointed out, Roosevelt did not need to make the Court an issue "because the dissenting Justices, along with others, were making it for him."[199]

Despite widespread uncertainty about the election's outcome, the Democrats won an unprecedented landslide at the polls. Roosevelt won 61 percent of the

192. *National Party Platforms,* 366.

193. Herbert Hoover, "Text of Hoover's Denver Address Warning of New Deal 'Shackles on Liberty,'" *New York Times,* October 31, 1936, 4.

194. Robert A. Taft, "Sidestepping the Constitution," *Review of Reviews,* September 1936, 37.

195. Leuchtenburg, "When the People Spoke," 2082.

196. *National Party Platforms,* 367.

197. "Final Returns in the Digest's Poll of Ten Million Voters," *Literary Digest,* October 31, 1936, 5.

198. Michael Nelson, "The President and the Court: Reinterpreting the Court-packing Episode of 1937," 103 *Political Science Quarterly* 288 (1988).

199. Leuchtenburg, "When the People Spoke," 2107.

popular vote and carried every state except Maine and Vermont. The Democratic Party emerged from the election with approximately four-fifths of the seats in both the House and the Senate. The stunning Democratic victory emboldened the Court's critics, who became even more vocal and prolific in proposing Court-curbing measures. Although, as Thomas Reed Powell observed, the election did not necessarily provide "any clear mandate to curb the Court," the election "yielded a roar in which cheers for the Supreme Court were pretty thoroughly drowned out."[200] Despite Roosevelt's discreet silence about the Court during the election campaign, the Democratic landslide likewise generated widespread expectations that Roosevelt would propose some type of measure to circumvent the judicial impasse. Only the form of the measure remained uncertain.

    200. Thomas Reed Powell, "The Next Four Years: The Constitution," *New Republic*, January 13, 1937, 319.

The 1930–1932 Hughes Court. By Harris & Ewing. Collection of the Supreme Court of the United States

Chief Justice Charles Evans Hughes. By Harris & Ewing. Collection of the Supreme Court of the United States

The 1940–1941 Hughes Court. By Harris & Ewing Photographic Services.
Collection of the Supreme Court of the United States

Supreme Court Building under construction. By Commercial Photo Company.
Collection of the Supreme Court of the United States

Justice Benjamin Nathan
Cardozo. By Eben
Farrington Comins.
Collection of the
Supreme Court of the
United States

Justice James Clark
McReynolds. By Bjorn Egeli.
Collection of the Supreme
Court of the United States

Justice Owen J.
Roberts. By Alfred
Jonniaux. Collection of
the Supreme Court of
the United States

Chief Justice Harlan Fiske
Stone. By Charles J. Fox.
Collection of the Supreme
Court of the United States

4

EVOLUTION AND REVOLUTION, 1937

While the Court's critics formulated Court-curbing plans in the wake of the 1936 election, the justices rendered several decisions that in a different political atmosphere could have gone far toward ameliorating antagonism against the Court. The Court's opinions during the two months after the election seemed to give credence to the fictional Mr. Dooley's famous observation that the Court "follows the 'liction returns." During this period, the Court sustained a major state insurance unemployment law, expanded the scope of the commerce clause, broadened the reach of civil liberties, upheld a key provision of the federal bankruptcy law, construed the federal taxing power in a manner that facilitated the Roosevelt administration's fiscal policy, and broadly construed the president's power over foreign relations. Hughes, ever eager to bear glad judicial tidings, wrote most of the opinions. In their totality, these decisions seemed to many Americans to signal a change of direction by the Court, but they were too little and too late to stem the momentum of the Court-curbing movement that the spectacular Democratic victory had invigorated.[1]

In the first of these actions, the Court on November 23 took a major stride toward approving the Social Security Act when it affirmed a New York Court of Appeals decision upholding the constitutionality of the unemployment insurance law that New York had enacted in response to the federal statute.[2] Although the Court divided four to four and issued no opinion, the decision constituted a major victory for the Roosevelt administration because the justices almost certainly would have approved the statute by a five-to-four vote if Stone had not been too ill to vote. The statute's apparent approval by Roberts and Hughes suggested to some commentators that they would vote to sustain the constitutionality of the federal statute,[3] though more restrained observers pointed out that there were

1. See William G. Ross, "When Did the 'Switch in Time' Actually Occur? Re-evaluating the Supreme Court's 'Forgotten' Decisions of 1936–1937," 37 *Arizona State Law Journal* 1153–1220 (2005).

2. *Chamberlin v. Andrews*, 299 U.S. 515 (1936) (per curiam).

3. As the *Survey* explained, "Friends of social security are greatly heartened by the outcome of the New York cases. Knowing the usual position of Justice Stone on social measures, they see an excellent chance for at least a five to four decision in favor of the Social Security Act if and when it comes before the Supreme Court." *Survey*, December 1936, 368.

important differences between the state and federal laws.[4] Hailing this "great victory for labor," American Federation of Labor president William Green declared that the Court's decision "encourages labor to believe that the National Social Security act will be held constitutional," while Senator Joseph C. O'Mahoney, a Democrat from Wyoming, remarked that "Mr. Dooley seems to be right."[5]

In its landmark decision four weeks later in *United States v. Curtiss-Wright Export Corp.*, the Court broadly construed the power of both Congress and the president in upholding a joint resolution that authorized the president to prohibit the sale of arms to nations engaged in conflict in the Chaco, a region claimed by Bolivia and Paraguay.[6] In his opinion for the majority, Sutherland explained, "It is quite apparent that if, in the maintenance of our international relations, embarrassment—perhaps serious embarrassment—is to be avoided and success for our aims achieved, congressional legislation which is to be made effective through negotiation and inquiry within the international field must often accord to the president a degree of discretion and freedom from statutory restriction which would not be admissible were domestic affairs alone involved." The Court likewise declared that "he, not Congress, has the better opportunity of knowing the conditions which prevail in foreign countries, and especially is this true in time of war."[7] Only McReynolds dissented. *Curtiss-Wright* should have helped to placate Roosevelt because the Court's limitations on executive power appear to have frustrated him even more than its decisions limiting legislative power.[8] Because, however, it conceded nothing to the president's power over domestic affairs, it probably had little effect, except to the extent that the decision demonstrated that the Court was not implacably hostile to Roosevelt.

In a unanimous decision during the first week of 1937, the Court upheld the Ashurst-Sumners Act of 1934, which prohibited the transportation of convict-made goods into states that banned the sale of products manufactured by convicts.[9] In this decision, *Kentucky Whip and Collar Co. v. Illinois Central Railroad Co.*, Hughes explained that Congress had power to prevent interstate commerce from being used to impede a state policy or law. Moreover, the chief justice implicitly rejected the doctrine that the Court could prevent the interstate movement only of inherently harmful goods, which earlier had convinced the Court in *Hammer v.*

4. See, for example, "A Notable Ruling," *St. Louis Post-Dispatch*, November 24, 1936, 2C (editorial).

5. "Supreme Court Upholds New Deal and Capital Is Cheered by Swing," *Boston Globe*, November 24, 1936, 1.

6. 299 U.S. 304 (1936).

7. Ibid., 320.

8. See William E. Luechtenburg, *The Supreme Court Reborn: The Constitutional Revolution in the Age of Roosevelt* (New York: Oxford University Press, 1995), 78–80.

9. *Kentucky Whip & Collar Co. v. Illinois Central Railroad Co.*, 299 U.S. 334 (1937). In a decision during the previous year, the Court had upheld the constitutionality under the commerce power of the Hawes-Cooper Act of 1929, which provided that convict-made goods were subject to the laws of any state to which they were transported. *Whitfield v. Ohio*, 297 U.S. 431 (1936).

Dagenhart (1918) that Congress could not prohibit interstate shipment of goods made by child labor. The decision therefore appeared to overrule *Hammer* because the harnesses manufactured by the convicts for the company that challenged the law were not inherently harmful products. Hughes characteristically denied making any doctrinal innovation, claiming that his opinion was not inconsistent with *Hammer* insofar as the child labor law had placed local production under federal control. But while the child labor law had more quantitative impact insofar as it banned the interstate transportation of all child-made goods and therefore may have done more to discourage local production, the exercise of the commerce power in the two statutes was qualitatively much the same. Moreover, the decision appeared to be inconsistent with *Carter Coal*, a decision that Hughes's opinion ignored, to the extent it permitted Congress to regulate interstate commerce that had a significant intrastate component. The Court also held that the statute did not violate the Fifth Amendment's due process clause.[10]

As Samuel Hendel has observed, *Kentucky Whip* "struck a devastating blow at the doctrine of dual federalism," which had limited the congressional commerce power to protect the power of the states over local production.[11] Although the decision tacitly recognized that Congress could prohibit interstate shipment of nonharmful goods even without state consent, the context in which *Kentucky Whip* arose permitted the Court to expand congressional power even while paying obeisance to states' rights. *Kentucky Whip* was widely hailed by the Court's critics. It immediately encouraged opponents of child labor to seek legislation to prohibit the sale of goods made by children in other states,[12] and it was popular with the labor movement, which had suffered from the competition of convict labor.[13] The decision also pleased conservatives, who expected it to dampen support for expansion of federal economic regulation because it enhanced the viability of state regulations. Observing that *Kentucky Whip* contained "possibilities of enormous importance," the *Wall Street Journal* expressed hope that it would discourage efforts to enact federal child labor and wages and hours legislation.[14]

On the same day the Court decided *Kentucky Whip*, it unanimously rendered a landmark civil liberties decision, *DeJonge v. Oregon*, which overturned the criminal

10. Ibid., 351, 350, 352.

11. Samuel Hendel, *Charles Evans Hughes and the Supreme Court* (repr., New York: Russell and Russell, 1968), 257.

12. "A Way to Attack Child Labor," *St. Louis Post-Dispatch*, January 6, 1937, 2C (editorial); *New Republic*, January 13, 1937, 312.

13. *Nation*, January 9, 1937, 30.

14. "This May Be the Way," *Wall Street Journal*, January 7, 1937, 4 (editorial). The *Journal* pointed out that *Kentucky Whip* did not expand the scope of constitutionally permissible state legislation: "This decision opens the door wide to Congress to cooperate in enforcing state laws; it does not of itself affect legislation which may be passed by the state." This editorial maintained that the decision would not, for example, permit a state to forbid sale or possession of goods manufactured in a non-union shop.

conviction of a labor organizer who had been prosecuted under a state syndical-ism statute.[15] Hughes's opinion declared that the First Amendment permitted the defendant to organize and participate in a public meeting at which no unlawful action was advocated, even though the defendant was a Communist and the meet-ing was conducted under the auspices of the Communist Party, which advocated overthrow of the government. In addition to reaffirming the broad reach of the free-speech clause, the Court for the first time incorporated freedom of assembly into state law. The Court's defense of human freedom inspired widespread appro-bation.[16]

In another decision on January 4, 1937, the Court unanimously upheld the constitutionality of a provision of the federal bankruptcy law that had in effect subordinated claims of landlords of bankrupt corporations to those of sharehold-ers.[17] Hughes's opinion for the Court held that the Fifth Amendment's due pro-cess clause does not bar bankruptcy legislation affecting a creditor's remedy for enforcement of a contract right or affecting the extent of the creditor's participa-tion in the bankruptcy proceeding. Although the decision was squarely based upon Congress's constitutional power to make bankruptcy laws, the justices' refusal to engraft any "ifs" or "buts" on this power once again demonstrated that the Court did not blindly oppose legislation that had the effect of altering contrac-tual obligations.

One week later, the Court sustained the constitutionality of the Silver Purchase Act of 1934, which imposed a 50 percent tax on profits on the transfer of any interest in silver bullion, including a provision that made the statute retroactive by more than a month.[18] The U.S. Court of Claims had unanimously invalidated the statute, which was designed to discourage speculation in silver futures at a time when the federal treasury was trying to increase its silver reserves. In a brief unanimous opinion, Van Devanter held that the tax represented a valid exercise of the taxing power and that its retroactivity did not violate due process. As Robert H. Jackson later pointed out, the decision was significant because the Silver Pur-chase Act "represented a frank use of the taxing power for non-revenue purposes." It also seemed to offer continuing protection to "the Government against those who would gain from manipulating markets while public policy was being set-tled."[19]

15. 299 U.S. 353 (1937).

16. See, for example, "Liberty under Law," *Christian Science Monitor,* January 6, 1937, 16. The *New York Times* commented on the irony that "this splendid vindication of a fundamental American right" was rendered by judges "who so often have been described as narrow-minded reactionaries." *New York Times,* January 6, 1937, 22 (editorial), and the *St. Louis Post-Dispatch* declared that the decision "shows most tellingly how necessary is an independent judicial authority to protect the guarantees of the Constitution." "Protector of Human Rights," *St. Louis Post-Dispatch,* January 5, 1937, 2C (editorial).

17. *Kuehner v. Irving Trust,* 299 U.S. 445 (1937).

18. *United States v. Hudson,* 299 U.S. 498 (1937).

19. Robert H. Jackson, *The Struggle for Judicial Supremacy: A Study of a Crisis in American Power Politics* (New York: Alfred A. Knopf, 1941), 203, 205.

The Court's validation of economic regulations during the winter of 1936–1937 was perceived by some as indications that at least Hughes and Roberts feared that Roosevelt's landslide would embolden the president to curb the Court.[20] Commenting on *Kentucky Whip* and *DeJonge*, the *Nation* observed that "the judges are trying very hard to present a united front to a hostile public opinion."[21] It would, however, take more than a spate of "liberal" decisions to alter the perception that the Court threatened significant New Deal measures and the new reform legislation that was expected to follow in the wake of the Democratic landslides. Although Roosevelt naturally hoped that his landslide victory would make the Court more reluctant to nullify economic legislation, a "wait-and-see" strategy may have seemed too risky. Judicial invalidation of the Social Security and National Labor Relations Acts would gut the very core of the New Deal and would impede the enactment of new legislation even if Roosevelt had the opportunity to appoint new justices, because liberal justices, too, might be loath to reject recent precedents. Moreover, Roosevelt could not rely on Congress to reenact major reform measures, particularly because judicial nullification of major New Deal legislation might demoralize the reform movement and embolden antiregulatory forces.[22] An aggressive move against the Court would therefore be not so much an act of hubris by a power-drunk president as a sober recognition by Roosevelt, a student of history, that even the mandates of landslides are evanescent.

Breaking his long silence on the Court in his State of the Union address on January 6, Roosevelt tacitly chided the institution for its obstruction of legislation and urged it to interpret the Constitution more broadly. Without mentioning the Court by name, Roosevelt expressed hope that "we can meet new national needs with new laws consistent with an historic constitutional framework clearly intended to receive liberal and not narrow interpretation" and that "there will not be prolonged failure to bring legislative and judicial action into closer harmony." Although Roosevelt seemed to reject the need to amend the Constitution, he also appeared to warn the Court that he would not continue to tolerate its invalidation of key legislation. "The vital need is not an alteration of our fundamental law, but an increasingly enlightened view with reference to it," Roosevelt declared, averring that "[m]eans must be found to adapt our legal forms and our judicial interpretation to the actual present national needs of the largest progressive democracy in the world."[23]

Although many observers astutely perceived that Roosevelt was presaging some type of measure to circumvent the Court's obstruction of New Deal legislation,[24]

---

20. See, for example, "Supreme Court Upholds New Deal and Capital Is Cheered by Swing," *Boston Globe*, November 24, 1936, 1.

21. *Nation*, January 9, 1937, 30.

22. William E. Leuchtenburg, *The Supreme Court Reborn: The Constitutional Revolution in the Age of Roosevelt* (New York: Oxford University Press, 1995), 381–82.

23. Samuel I. Rosenman, ed., *The Public Papers and Addresses of Franklin Roosevelt*, 13 vols. (New York, 1938–1950), 5:639.

24. Marian C. McKenna, *Franklin Roosevelt and the Court-Packing Crisis of 1937* (New York: Fordham University Press, 2002), 266–67.

some were disappointed that he had failed to propose a constitutional amendment to enhance congressional power over the economy, or some type of legislation to curtail judicial power. Interpreting the speech as an effort to "underline
for Chief Justice Hughes and Justice Roberts the lessons of the last election," the
New Republic complained that Roosevelt should understand that "the American
people did not reelect him so that he might conduct in public the education of
either of the justices." Advocating legislation to permit Congress to override the
Court and amendments to expand congressional power, the editors asked, "Do
we . . . dare to make our way in the future on the resolute legs of the people
themselves, or do we prefer to cut them off and hobble along on crutches provided by the Supreme Court?"[25]

Amid rife speculation about the president's intentions, Roosevelt explored his
options. As early as 1933, Roosevelt had instructed Attorney General Homer S.
Cummings to investigate methods for removing or ameliorating the Court's
obstruction of federal legislation. Working in secret, Cummings and a few close
associates focused on two strategies favored by countless antagonists of the Court
for more than a century. One was to abolish or limit the Court's power to review
the constitutionality of statutes, perhaps by permitting Congress to reenact legislation, as Senator Robert M. La Follette Sr. had proposed in 1922. Another possibility
was to restrict the Court's jurisdiction over certain types of cases.[26] Neither measure
would necessarily have required a constitutional amendment. The Constitution
does not mention judicial review, and article 3 permits Congress to prescribe the
Court's appellate jurisdiction "with such Exceptions and under such Regulations
as the Congress shall make." The Court's power of judicial review and its appellate
jurisdiction over major constitutional questions, however, were so deeply embedded in the nation's constitutional structure that many legal experts believed that
Congress could not remove these without a constitutional amendment.

Roosevelt also considered the possibility of various constitutional amendments
that would help to ensure the safety of New Deal legislation, particularly one that
would grant broad power to Congress to regulate interstate commerce and enact
economic regulatory legislation.[27] Although such amendments were superficially
attractive because they seemed to ensure congressional power regardless of the
Court's composition, these, too, had disadvantages. Walter Lippmann warned that
proposals for an amendment to redefine congressional power to regulate the
economy were irresponsible since such an amendment would either mandate "an
intolerable centralization of power" or constitute "a meaningless jumble of weasel
words."[28] Similarly, as the journalist Frederick Lewis Allen observed in 1936, it
would be difficult to frame a constitutional amendment that "would not open

25. "A Program for Judicial Power," *New Republic*, January 23, 1937, 89–90.

26. McKenna, *Franklin Roosevelt*, 158–68.

27. Leuchtenburg, *The Supreme Court Reborn*, 92.

28. "Supreme Court Decisions Elect Next President?," *Literary Digest*, July 27, 1935, 3 (quoting column from *Today*).

the door wide enough to prevent unwarranted political interference with private affairs." Recognizing the difficulty of making "even the most scrupulously drawn amendment look like anything but a grant of tyrannical power," Democrats were naturally "reluctant to get off the fence, uncomfortable as it is to sit upon."[29]

The major objection to these and all other proposals for constitutional amendments, however, was that the amendment process was unduly protracted and parlous. It would be difficult for two-thirds of both houses of Congress to agree on the wording,[30] and any amendment approved by Congress would be vulnerable to attacks from business interests as it ran the gauntlet of ratification by three-quarters of the state legislatures. Ultimately rejecting use of an amendment for these reasons, Roosevelt recalled how manufacturers had permanently stalled a child labor amendment that had sailed through Congress by wide margins during 1924 in the wake of the Supreme Court's invalidation of the second federal child labor law.[31] The child labor amendment's failure likewise haunted many other liberals. Harvard law professor Thomas Reed Powell expressed doubt about the success of an amendment to overturn *Tipaldo*, much less an amendment to "grant Congress unlimited power over agriculture, finance, industry and labor."[32] Other commentators, however, contended that Roosevelt could obtain needed amendments by having Congress call constitutional conventions in the states, which presumably would not be controlled by the special interests that dominated state legislatures.[33] Because the use of such conventions had facilitated the 1933 repeal of Prohibition with the Twenty-first Amendment, Roosevelt's fear of the constitutional amendment process may have been excessive.[34]

Even if enacted, however, an amendment might be vulnerable to judicial review.[35] Moreover, Roosevelt's proposal for an amendment tacitly would have conceded that much of the New Deal was constitutionally infirm, if not unconstitutional.[36] Roosevelt's advisors also believed that the constitutional amendment process, even if successful, would squander precious time. As Harold L. Ickes

29. Frederick Lewis Allen, "Behind the Campaign," *Harper's Monthly*, October 1936, 476.

30. Harold Ickes to William Allen White, February 25, 1937 and March 23, 1937, series C, box 269, William Allen White Papers, Manuscript Division, Library of Congress (hereafter cited as White Papers).

31. David E. Kyvig, *Explicit and Authentic Acts: Amending the U.S. Constitution, 1776–1995* (Lawrence: University Press of Kansas, 1996), 257–61, 303, 307–10.

32. Thomas Reed Powell, "The Next Four Years: The Constitution," *New Republic*, January 13, 1937, 320.

33. *See* Henry Goddard Leach, "The Supreme Court," *Forum and Century*, June 1937, 322 (signed editorial).

34. Kyvig, *Explicit and Authentic Acts*, 305.

35. Thomas Reed Powell, "The Next Four Years: The Constitution," *New Republic*, January 13, 1937, 320. As Harold Ickes observed, when "Hughes said that the Constitution is what the courts say it is, he meant amendments also." Harold Ickes to William Allen White, series C, box 269, White Papers.

36. McKenna, *Franklin Roosevelt*, 221.

observed, voters "want the New Deal now, not twenty years from now."[37] In addition to these concerns, some New Dealers were loath to impose any institutional constraints upon the Court because the close division of the Court in many cases and the Court's approval of at least some New Deal legislation demonstrated that judicial review did not necessarily threaten Roosevelt's programs. Others, however, pointed out that the unanimity of the Court in *Schechter* and *Humphrey's Executor* demonstrated the need for an amendment by underscoring the unreliability of even the most liberal justices.

Rejecting the arduous amendment process, Roosevelt finally settled in January 1937 on a plan to increase the number of justices. Because the Constitution does not prescribe the Court's size, the constitutionality of Court packing seemed clear. The Court's membership had fluctuated from seven to ten, remaining at nine since 1869. As recently as 1921, the American Bar Association had adopted a report suggesting that the addition of three justices could help the Court better dispose of its workload.[38] And, to Roosevelt's delight, McReynolds as attorney general in 1913 had proposed legislation to permit the appointment of one lower federal judge for every one past the age of seventy who had served ten years and was eligible for retirement.[39]

Roosevelt kept his plan secret until two weeks after his second inauguration and three days after his annual reception for the justices and their wives. On February 5, 1937, he finally unveiled it, announcing that he would seek legislation to permit him to appoint as many as fifty new federal judges to supplement the services of any judge who had served for ten years and had failed to resign within six months of attaining the age of seventy. The legislation would have enabled Roosevelt to appoint six new Supreme Court justices. In his message to Congress, Roosevelt alleged that geriatric judges staggered under the burden of an intolerable workload. Pointing out that the Supreme Court had denied certiorari in 717 of the 867 petitions it had received during the past year, Roosevelt suggested without evidence that the Court's refusal to hear cases was at least sometimes motivated by overwork.[40]

Although Roosevelt did not directly complain about the Court's invalidation of economic legislation, he contended that "modern complexities" called "for a constant infusion of new blood in the courts" because a "lowered physical or mental vigor leads men to avoid an examination of complicated and changed conditions. Little by little, new facts become blurred through old glasses fitted . . . for the needs of another generation." Roosevelt likewise linked his proposal to his broader program of economic justice by contending that lowered physical capacities of elderly jurists produced delays in adjudication that harmed the poor and

37. Harold Ickes to William Allen White, February 25, 1937, series C, box 269, White Papers.
38. *Nation*, June 26, 1937, 719.
39. McKenna, *Franklin Roosevelt*, 269.
40. Rosenman, *Public Papers*, 55.

contributed to "the growing impression that the courts are chiefly a haven for the well-to-do."[41]

Roosevelt perhaps fatally diminished support for his proposal through the covert and arrogant manner with which he introduced it. Flouting the traditional wisdom of consulting with political leaders before advocating legislation, Roosevelt concocted the bill with the assistance of Cummings and a tight coterie of personal advisors. Less than half an hour before he publicly unveiled the bill at a press conference, Roosevelt imperiously revealed it to cabinet members and congressional leaders at a brief White House conference, soliciting no discussion from the astonished and mute solons. Smiling triumphantly throughout the press conference, Roosevelt conveyed the impression that he was convinced he had found an invincible means of outmaneuvering the recalcitrant Court.[42] Even so understated a commentator as Richard Strout complained that Roosevelt's means of submitting the plan involved "an abruptness and seeming levity that we commonly associate with Hitler or Mussolini."[43]

Smarting from such high-handedness, many of Roosevelt's erstwhile political allies opposed the proposal from the start. As House leaders grimly rode from the White House to the Capitol for the reading of the bill, Hatton W. Sumners, the chairman of the House Judiciary Committee whose support was critical to the bill's success, famously remarked, "Boys, here's where I cash in my chips." Meanwhile, Vice President John Nance Garner publicly held his nose and pointed thumbs down after leaving the Senate rostrum.[44] Although Roosevelt, like most presidents, normally promoted legislation first in the House, Sumners's adamant opposition presaged such rough treatment by the House Judiciary Committee that Roosevelt's forces initiated their fight in the Senate.[45] Consideration of the bill by the more conservative, independent, and leisurely Senate helped to ensure its defeat. Senate Judiciary Committee chairman Henry F. Ashurst of Arizona formally supported the bill, but his profound misgivings found expression in the committee's protracted deliberations, which permitted opposition to Court packing to galvanize and the march of events, including the Court's own decisions, to discredit the measure.[46]

Roosevelt's hubris was particularly harmful to his proposal, because the plan itself appeared arrogant. To countless Americans, it threatened judicial independence and the delicate constitutional separation of powers by permitting an already doughty president to manipulate the Court's size for apparently partisan

41. Ibid., 59.

42. Joseph Alsop and Turner Catledge, *The 168 Days* (Garden City, N.Y.: Doubleday, Doran, 1938), 66–67.

43. T.R.B., "Washington Notes," *New Republic*, September 8, 1937, 130.

44. Alsop and Catledge, 69.

45. McKenna, *Franklin Roosevelt*, 317.

46. Leonard Baker, *Back to Back: The Duel between FDR and the Supreme Court* (New York: Macmillan, 1967) 8, 68.

purposes. In addition to pointing out the threat to economic freedom, critics also emphasized that interference with the Court could diminish personal liberties.

Within a day of Roosevelt's announcement, blistering attacks on the proposal were heard from a broad spectrum of prominent Americans, including lawyers, editors, academics, and even a surprisingly large number of normally discreet judges. "Roosevelt's mandate was to function as the President, not as *Der Fuehrer*," thundered William Allen White, the Kansan whose editorials had national circulation. Similarly, the social reformer Louis Untermeyer denounced Roosevelt's proposal as "well nigh revolutionary." William Mitchell, a former attorney general, wondered "what kind of men will take appointments when they know they must listen to their master's voice." And New York Court of Appeals judge Frank H. Hiscock, one of the nation's most respected jurists, denounced the proposal as "a major disaster."[47]

Critics of the proposals asked why such a radical measure was needed to respond to an apparently temporary crisis. The *Saturday Evening Post*, for example, disparaged the notion that "because cotton is now worth fifteen cents in Texas Mr. Roosevelt has been mandated to abolish constitutional government."[48] Such a substantial increase in the Court's membership also seemed to threaten the Court's integrity by diluting the power of the individual justices. Critics of the proposal alleged that Roosevelt, despite his recent landslide reelection, lacked a mandate for such a radical measure because he had so studiously avoided any mention of the Court during the campaign.[49]

The proposal attracted widespread opposition even among many fierce critics of the Court. Gutzon Borglum, the Mount Rushmore sculptor, told Senator Norris that he was so furious over the Court's decisions that he "would like to hand Mr. Hughes a few punches on the jaw," but that he opposed Roosevelt's plan because the Court itself was "being discredited." Borglum urged Norris to help defeat the plan because he believed that it mocked the democratic ideals of the presidents whose faces appeared in his mammoth stone carvings.[50]

Opposition to Court packing also included many Americans who had voted for Roosevelt only months earlier and who generally favored New Deal legislation. Several polls conducted by George Gallup between February and May 1937 indicated that most Americans opposed Roosevelt's plan, at least without its modification. Asked whether they favored or opposed the plan, opposition ranged from 51 to 54 percent. In response to a more detailed question in late February, 38

47. "The New Deal versus the Old Courts: Storm of Criticism Greets President's Judiciary Proposals," *Literary Digest*, February 13, 1937, 5–6.

48. "How Right Is Might?," *Saturday Evening Post*, May 15, 1937, 26 (editorial).

49. See, for example, William Allen White to Harold Laski, March 2, 1937, series C, box 269, White Papers; James Truslow Adams to George W. Norris, box 118, George W. Norris Papers, Manuscript Division, Library of Congress (hereafter cited as Norris Papers); William E. Borah to Mary A. Smith, March 6, 1937, box 484, William E. Borah Papers, Manuscript Division, Library of Congress.

50. Gutzon Borglum to George Norris, February 24, 1937, box 117, Norris Papers.

percent favored enactment of the Court-packing bill, 23 percent wanted modification, and 39 percent supported its defeat.[51] In a Gallup poll in April, however, nearly two-thirds of respondents expressed support for a constitutional amendment to require Supreme Court justices to retire at some time between the ages of seventy and seventy-five.[52]

To his chagrin, Roosevelt was not able even to rely upon the steadfast support of farmers, despite the Court's nullification of the Agricultural Adjustment Act (AAA). Even more disappointing was the reaction of organized labor, which failed to embrace the plan and in many instances actively opposed it. This particularly surprised Roosevelt and his advisors because labor unions, which had complained for decades that the federal courts were hostile toward labor, now faced possible judicial nullification of the National Labor Relations Act. The American Federation of Labor's executive council endorsed the plan by the underwhelming vote of nine to three, with two abstentions.[53]

The proposal also attracted hostility from many liberal Democrats and progressive Republicans. Indeed, the fight against the plan in the Senate was led by Montana Democrat Burton K. Wheeler, who, as Robert M. La Follette's running mate on the third-party Progressive ticket in 1924, had vigorously supported the Wisconsin senator's proposal to permit Congress to override Supreme Court decisions by a two-thirds vote. Some liberals of both parties complained that the proposal did not go far enough because it did not itself diminish the Court's power or increase congressional power. To many of these liberals, Roosevelt's legislative program was too timid and was paving the way for future economic dislocation and political unrest even if the president succeeded in removing judicial obstructionism.[54] Many liberals, however, defended the proposal on the ground that it was only a prelude to an amendment to curb the Court or enable Congress to enact more expansive economic legislation.[55]

The plan attracted particularly intense hostility among progressive Republican leaders in Congress, who for decades had blasted the Court's conservatism and proposed a plethora of measures for curbing its powers. Despite their antipathy toward many of the Court's decisions and their reservations about judicial review, progressive senators correctly pointed out that the measure did not curb the Court's institutional powers. Deeply distressed about the growth of presidential power under a chief executive whose political coalition was dependent upon the urban Catholic political machines that these Protestants from small towns found so repugnant, many progressives also complained that the Court-packing plan

51. George H. Gallup, William P. Hansen, and Fred L. Israel, eds., *The Gallup Poll: Public Opinion, 1935–1971*, vol. 1 (New York: Random House, 1972), 50, 51–52, 53, 55, 57, 58, 69.

52. Ibid., 56.

53. Philip Taft, *The A.F. of L. from the Death of Gompers to the Merger* (New York: Harper & Brothers, 1959), 454.

54. *Nation*, March 6, 1937, 255

55. *Nation*, March 27, 1937, 339; *Nation*, April 17, 1937, 424; Harold Ickes to William Allen White, February 13, 1937, series C, box 269, White Papers.

aggrandized the president at the expense of Congress, the branch of government to which most of their own Court-curbing measures would have transferred power. Progressive opposition to the Court-packing plan also reflected misgivings about many aspects of the New Deal. In addition to their anxiety about the growth of executive power, progressives were troubled by its cooperation with large corporate interests, its creation of a permanent welfare state, and its erosion of federalism.[56]

Unable to unite behind Roosevelt's bill, progressives proposed a bewildering array of their own Court reform measures. Norris, the most prolific proponent of substitutes, reintroduced his bill to prohibit the Court from nullifying federal legislation without the concurrence of a two-thirds majority.[57] He also sponsored measures to limit judicial tenure[58] and to permit a direct popular vote on constitutional amendments.[59] Norris also reiterated his support for legislation to restrict further the power of lower federal courts to issue injunctions, and he continued to urge legislation to allow Congress to invalidate Supreme Court decisions.[60] Meanwhile, Republican senator William E. Borah proposed an amendment to abolish substantive due process restraints on state legislation,[61] and Democratic representative Jerry Voorhis of California proposed amendments to deprive the lower federal courts of jurisdiction over cases concerning the constitutionality of legislation involving taxation, the general welfare, or interstate commerce.[62]

Although hostility toward Court packing was naturally intense among mainstream Republicans, GOP leaders recognized that their aggressive opposition would encourage Democrats to unite in favor of the plan and that Democrats could more effectively lead the fight against it. Wisely resisting the temptation to exploit the issue for immediate partisan gain, Republicans muted their voices and worked quietly with Democrats to defeat the measure.[63]

---

56. Ronald L. Feinman, *Twilight of Progressivism: The Western Republican Senators and the New Deal* (Baltimore: Johns Hopkins University Press, 1981), 68–90, 117–35. The plan was vocally opposed by progressive Republican senators William E. Borah of Idaho, Arthur Capper of Kansas, Gerald P. Nye of North Dakota, Lynn Frazier and Henrik Shipstead of Minnesota, and Hiram W. Johnson of California, all of whom had been harsh critics of the Court and proponents of measures to curb judicial power. Senator George W. Norris of Nebraska provided only equivocal support. Robert M. La Follette Jr. of Wisconsin was the only progressive Republican senator who unambiguously advocated Court packing.

57. S. 1890, 75th Congress, 1st Session, 1937.

58. S.J. Res. 103, 75th Congress, 1st Session, 1937.

59. S.J. Res. 134, 75th Congress, 1st Session, 1937.

60. 81 *Congressional Record*, 75th Congress, 1st Session, March 12, 1937, 2142–44; "Roosevelt Drives for Court Reform as Congress Waits," *New York Times*, February 12, 1937, 1; "Robinson Cordial to an Amendment," *New York Times*, March 16, 1937, 1; "Norris for Popular Vote," *New York Times*, April 3, 1937, 2.

61. S.J. Res. 92, 75th Congress, 1st Session (1937).

62. H.R. 4900, 75th Congress, 1st Session (1937).

63. McKenna, *Franklin Roosevelt*, 321–23; Leuchtenburg, *The Supreme Court Reborn*, 140.

Although some liberal Democrats such as Wheeler opposed the plan, its defeat ultimately depended upon the opposition of more moderate Democrats. Increasingly alarmed about the growing deficit and the expansion of federal power at the expense of the states, conservative Democrats such as Sumners found that Court packing provided a convenient occasion to begin to rebel against the New Deal and Roosevelt's increasingly imperious leadership. In one of the most overt examples of conservative revolt, Democratic senator Carter Glass of Virginia on March 29 delivered an hour-long nationwide radio address in which he blasted the "abominable" bill as an invasion of judicial independence, denying that Roosevelt enjoyed any "mandate from the people to rape the Supreme Court or tamper with the Constitution."[64] The virulent opposition of Glass, a long-serving and highly respected senator who had sponsored the landmark Glass-Steagall Act, demonstrated the bill's weakness among conservative southern Democrats, one of the key elements of Roosevelt's political coalition.

Court packing likewise encountered formidable opposition among critical interest groups. Among the most prominent was the organized bar, particularly the American Bar Association. The ABA's opposition was predictable inasmuch as it reflected the conservatism of the elite bar during the 1930s. As Thomas Reed Powell sardonically observed in 1937, "One who attends a meeting of the American Bar Association or who hears talk about constitutional law from professional colleagues intelligently expert in private law must be amazed that the Supreme Court has been as happily unrepresentative of the bar as it has."[65] Four-fifths of the seventy thousand lawyers who responded to an ABA poll expressed opposition to Court packing.[66] Many less elite attorneys, however, also opposed the plan.[67]

Court packing also generated considerable opposition among ethnic Americans, particularly Roman Catholics, who feared that political subjugation of the Court would threaten the rights of minorities. Even though they were overwhelming Democratic, many Roman Catholics opposed the plan because they feared that any erosion of judicial independence would compromise their religious freedom. Both Catholics and Lutherans remained grateful to the Court for its 1925 decision in *Pierce v. Society of Sisters,* which quelled a nationwide nativistic antiparochial school movement by striking down an Oregon law that required all children to attend public school. German-American Lutherans likewise recalled that the Court in *Meyer v. Nebraska* had struck down laws that restricted the teaching of German.[68]

64. Rixey Smith and Norman Beasley, *Carter Glass: A Biography* (New York: Longman, Green and Co., 1939), 374–79, 496–510.

65. Thomas Reed Powell, "The Next Four Years: The Constitution," *New Republic,* January 13, 1937, 319.

66. William L. Ransom, "Members and Non-Members of American Bar Association Take Same Stand on Court Issues," *American Bar Association Journal,* May 1937, 338.

67. Some 77 percent of the lawyers polled by Gallup in February expressed opposition to the plan. Gallup, Hansen, and Israel, *The Gallup Poll,* 1:51.

68. James J. Kenneally, "Catholicism and the Supreme Court Reorganization Proposal of 1937," 25 *Journal of Church and State* 469–89 (1983); *Reorganization of the Federal Judiciary: Hearings before the Committee on the Judiciary of the United States Senate Seventy-fifth Congress First Session*

The ABA likewise based its vigorous opposition to the plan upon threats to personal liberties, though this may have been more tactical than principled because the ABA of the 1930s remained more concerned with protection of property rights than with civil liberties. In opposing the plan, the *American Bar Association Journal* warned that executive and legislative supremacy would threaten individual rights and that "[m]inorities should ask themselves whether they are willing to trust their interests to the changing results of popular elections at which the electorate may be particularly inflamed on some issue affecting them. The Supreme Court has many times stood between them and excess of power. Will they never need such protection again?" The editorial contended that the "Supreme Court does not stand in the way of necessary reforms. It stands in the way of headlong haste which disregards constitutional limitations as it construes the Constitution."[69]

Many other opponents of the plan took up the cry, particularly because the Court's personal liberties decisions enjoyed more widespread popularity than its decisions striking down economic regulations. In a radio address that Borah delivered four days before Roosevelt announced his plan, the senator declared that the Court had "thrown its shield of liberty about the rights of the citizen when all other appeals to relief have failed him. When war, passion, or mob passion, or political zeal, or selfish schemes have carried men beyond reason or justice, the Court, when called upon, has interposed to avert great wrong."[70] Similarly, a liberal journalist warned Senator La Follette that "when the reactionary swing which inevitably follows liberal administrations gets well under way, the same power which the present Executive might handle benevolently would be used to crush labor and destroy civil rights of citizens."[71]

In contrast to adversaries of the numerous Court-curbing measures of the early 1920s, who had defended the Court as a champion of personal liberties but could scarcely point to any decision in which the Court had protected human rights, opponents of Court packing could provide many examples of such decisions. In addition to *Meyer* and *Pierce,* the Court during the 1920s had begun to incorporate into state law key provisions of the Bill of Rights. As is explained more fully in chapter 6, the Hughes Court in landmark decisions had reviewed state legislation that infringed on freedom of speech, freedom of the press, and the rights of criminal defendants.

---

on S. 1392, a Bill to Reorganize the Judicial Branch of the Government (New York: DeCapo Press, 1970), 684 (testimony of Theodore Graebner).

69. "The Supreme Court Issue," *American Bar Association Journal,* April 1937, 268, 270 (editorial).

70. 81 *Congressional Record,* 75th Congress, 1st Session 132 (1937) (extension of remarks of Tom Connelly)

71. Walter G. Parkes to Robert M. La Follette Jr., March 31, 1937, series C, box 366, La Follette Family Papers, Manuscript Division, Library of Congress (hereafter cited as La Follette Papers).

In disparaging the argument that the Court was a bastion of protection for personal liberties, advocates of the Court plan pointed out that most civil liberties pronouncements had been in dissent or in decisions defending the liberties of conservatives. As one liberal observed early in 1937, "That the court has always—or almost always—been ready to defend the liberties of conservatives will remain of merely academic importance until police begin beating up members of the Union League for criticizing the government. . . . The Bill of Rights is prominent in the official portrait of the court, but plays an inglorious role in its actual history."[72] A study by an ACLU official found that the Court had ruled against civil liberties in forty-five important cases during its history and had supported civil liberties in only thirty-eight such cases.[73] Proponents of Court packing also derided the Supreme Court's ability to protect personal liberties. Ignoring the danger that tyranny could result from incremental assaults on civil liberties rather than a sudden dictatorship, the *New Republic* argued that "[t]he idea that a rude and ruthless movement could be held in check by nine elderly gentlemen in black robes is absurd."[74]

In addition to fears about threats to separation of powers and personal liberties, opposition to Court packing also reflected misgivings, even among many Americans who had voted for Roosevelt, about much of the legislation that the Court invalidated. As one commentator observed with some exaggeration during the Court-packing struggle, the "N.R.A. and the A.A.A. . . . had been completely discredited in the court of common sense, before the Supreme Court buried their carcasses to avoid further pollution."[75] By use of public opinion polls, Barry Cushman has demonstrated that the New Deal's relief and public works programs, the constitutionality of which the Court never reviewed, were much more popular among the public than was federal economic regulation, such as the AAA, which the Hughes Court had sometimes nullified or curtailed. These polls likewise indicate that many Americans who voted Democratic may have been more conservative than Roosevelt and Congress on issues of wealth redistribution and fiscal policy. Because most Americans were not clamoring for a social or economic revolution, it is not surprising that they welcomed or at least tolerated the constitutional limitations that the Court had placed upon the New Deal.[76]

The Court-packing proposal also suffered from Roosevelt's lack of honesty about his motives. Although Roosevelt may have feared that a blatant attack on the Court's conservatism would offend Americans, one of the president's worst tactical blunders was to contend that the justices were tired old men who were unable to shoulder their workload. Despite the advanced age of the justices, they

72. Isador Feinstein, "The Supreme Court and Civil Liberties," *Nation,* February 6, 1937, 151, 152.

73. *New Republic,* June 23, 1937, 170.

74. "The Court as Guardian of Liberty," *New Republic,* March 10, 1937, 125.

75. Albert Shaw, "Politics and the Supreme Court," *Review of Reviews,* May 1937, 34.

76. Barry Cushman, "Mr. Dooley and Mr. Gallup: Public Opinion and Constitutional Change in the 1930s," 50 *Buffalo Law Review* 25–76 passim (2002).

generally seemed energetic and healthy. In particular, the seventy-four-year-old Hughes publicly belied Roosevelt's argument every day when he was seen jauntily walking the streets of Washington, more often twirling his cane than leaning on it. Moreover, Roosevelt's argument offended many liberals who revered Brandeis, the oldest justice and one of the most reliable supporters of the New Deal. The disparagement of the abilities of aged judges also suggested a lack of respect for wisdom and experience. As one commentator observed, "White hairs are a symbol of the stability of American tradition."[77] There was no statistical evidence that the Court was behind in its work. Indeed, as Roosevelt knew, the Judiciary Act of 1925 had enabled the Court to maintain careful control over its docket. Similarly, the lower federal courts were increasingly efficient. In fiscal year 1937, the work of the district courts was current in sixty-eight of the eighty-four districts exclusive of the District of Columbia, compared with only thirty-one in 1934, forty-six in 1935, and fifty-one in 1936.[78]

Even though the infirmity of geriatric judges was widely regarded as a mere pretext for Roosevelt's Court-packing proposal, Congress recognized that at least some federal judges had remained on the bench too long past their prime. Less than a month after Roosevelt announced his plan, Congress revised the federal judicial retirement statute to encourage elderly Supreme Court justices to vacate their cherished seats.[79] The new legislation, which Roosevelt supported but did not propose, gave Supreme Court justices the option of retiring rather than resigning, a choice available to lower federal judges since 1919. The advantages of this option were manifold. Retired justices retained their status as federal judges and thus did not need to relinquish the prestige of judicial office. Eligible for temporary assignments on the lower federal bench, they could even continue to adjudicate cases. Moreover, by remaining judges, retired justices were protected from pension cuts pursuant to article 1, section 1, of the Constitution, which prohibits the diminution of judicial compensation. Justices who resigned, by contrast, were subject to the misfortune of Holmes, whose pension was briefly cut in half due to Depression cost-cutting.[80] In 1939 Congress further reformed judicial retirement by enacting the first judicial disability statute, which permits permanently disabled judges to retire regardless of their age.[81]

Recognizing that his specious arguments allegations about the infirmity of the justices discredited his proposal, Roosevelt more forthrightly alleged in an address to Democratic activists on March 4 that the Court had failed to sufficiently cooperate with the other two branches of government. He reiterated this theme several

77. Henry Goddard Leach, "The Supreme Court" *Forum and Century,* June 1937, 322 (signed editorial).

78. *American Bar Association Journal,* June 1938, 432.

79. Supreme Court Retirement Act, Ch. 754, 50 Stat. 751.

80. Artemus Ward, *Deciding to Leave: The Politics of Retirement from the United States Supreme Court* (Albany: State University of New York Press, 2003), 137.

81. Ibid., 129. Justices who have served less than ten years as a federal judge may retire at half pay and other retired judges receive their full annual salary.

days later in a fireside chat in which he accused the Court of "acting not as a judicial body, but as a policy-making body." Denying that he wished to appoint "spineless puppets," Roosevelt explained that he sought "to bring to the decision of social and economic problems younger men who have had personal experience and contact with modern facts and circumstances under which average men have to live and work." Analogizing the president, Congress, and Supreme Court to a three-horse team plowing the field of the American people, Roosevelt complained that the Court was not plowing in unison with its partners. Roosevelt's speeches failed to turn the tide against the plan. As an Idaho farmer wrote to Roosevelt, the Supreme Court "is a judicial body . . . and is not a plow horse for or with anyone."[82]

Many advocates of Court curbing shared the president's contention that the justices had only themselves to blame for a proposal that would increase the degree of political control over the Court and ruffle its cozy autonomy. Ickes confided to his diary that the proposal would tarnish Hughes's prestige, for it demonstrated that the chief justice had squandered an opportunity to rank among the greatest of the chiefs insofar as he failed to demonstrate "either the strength or the adroitness to control his court and make it an instrument for social and political progress."[83]

The outcome of the Court-packing plan at first was genuinely uncertain because it pitted Roosevelt's immense political muscle against the resilience of judicial power, which had survived so many attacks for more than a century. Five days after Roosevelt announced the plan, Van Devanter privately remarked that "the outcome cannot yet be foretold with any certainty."[84] Although 99 percent of the hundreds of letters he had received were "pronouncedly against the plan," Van Devanter acknowledged in a family letter that opponents naturally wrote to him in disproportionate numbers.[85]

Notwithstanding widespread opposition to the proposal, many commentators doubted at the outset that public respect for the Court would defeat the plan. As the journalist Paul W. Ward remarked, judges had always "been suspect with the men and women who labor for a living," who had learned from "personal experience . . . that the courts are 'with the corporations.' " He contended that conservatives were no less cynical about the judiciary insofar as they looked to the judiciary to do their bidding.[86] Even though Gallup polls indicated that a majority of Americans favored the bill's defeat, 61 percent of respondents as late as the end of April predicted that Roosevelt would win his fight to enlarge the Court.[87]

---

82. Earl O. Wolfe to Franklin D. Roosevelt, March 10, 1937, box 438, Borah Papers.

83. Harold L. Ickes, *The Secret Diary of Harold L. Ickes,* vol. 2, *The Inside Struggle, 1936–1939* (New York: Simon & Schuster, 1954), 66–67.

84. Willis Van Devanter to Robert H. Kelley, February 10, 1937, box 19, Willis Van Devanter Papers, Manuscript Division, Library of Congress (hereafter cited as Van Devanter papers).

85. Willis Van Devanter to Bradon Vandeventer, March 2, 1937, ibid.

86. Paul W. Ward, "Roosevelt Will Win," *Nation,* February 20, 1937, 202.

87. Gallup, Hansen, and Israel, *The Gallup Poll,* 1:57.

All of the justices opposed Court packing. Hughes reportedly told Senator Wheeler that it would destroy the Court as an institution,[88] and he wrote in his memoirs that the proposal "was justly regarded as an assault upon the independence of the Court."[89] Brandeis, who was one of the handful of persons informed of it in advance, told Roosevelt's advisor Thomas Corcoran that it was a major mistake and that he was unalterably opposed to it.[90] Although at least one justice, Roberts, planned to resign if the bill were approved, the chief justice was determined to make the best of any situation. "If they want me to preside over a convention," he reportedly told a confidante, "I can do it."[91]

After Brandeis arranged an entree, Wheeler, along with Democratic senator William H. King of Utah and Republican senator Warren R. Austin of Vermont, called upon Hughes at his home in mid-March and invited him to testify personally before the Judiciary Committee, presumably on the narrow but critical issue of whether the Court was able to keep abreast of its work. There was precedent for a personal appearance before the committee, because Hughes, accompanied by Van Devanter and Brandeis, had in 1935 testified in opposition to a bill, introduced by Senator Hugo L. Black of Alabama, for direct appeal to the Court from district court decrees enjoining enforcement of federal statutes.[92]

Even though Hughes later recalled that he was "entirely willing to do so for the purpose of giving the facts as to the work of the Court," he felt "it inadvisable, in view of the delicacy of the situation, that I should appear alone. It seemed to me that at least one other member of the Court should accompany me—preferably Justice Brandeis—because of his standing as a Democrat and his reputation as a liberal judge." Since Brandeis expressed strong opposition to the personal appearance of any justice before the committee, either he or Hughes proposed the alternative of a letter to the committee. After Hughes informed Wheeler of his willingness to write such a letter, Wheeler on March 20 asked him to have a letter ready two days later for the commencement of hearings on behalf of the bill's opponents.[93] Approaching his task with relish, Hughes completed his letter by late

88. Burton K. Wheeler, with Paul F. Healy, *Yankee from the West* (Garden City, N.Y.: Doubleday, 1962), 329.

89. David J. Danelski and Joseph S. Tulchin, eds., *The Autobiographical Notes of Charles Evans Hughes* (Cambridge, Mass.: Harvard University Press, 1973), 304.

90. Robert Sherwood, *Roosevelt and Hopkins* (New York: Harper and Brothers, 1949), 90 (based on a conversation between Corcoran and presidential advisor Harry Hopkins).

91. Merlo J. Pusey, *Charles Evans Hughes* (New York: MacMillan, 1951), 2:753 (based on confidential source).

92. Paul A. Freund, "Charles Evans Hughes as Chief Justice," 81 *Harvard Law Review* 28 (1967).

93. Danelski and Tulchin, *Autobiographical Notes*, 304–5; Wheeler, *Yankee from the West*, 327–30. The accounts of Hughes and Wheeler, both written long after the actual event, differ in some details but are essentially the same. In contrast with Hughes, Wheeler recalled that Brandeis expressed opposition to personal testimony by any member of the Court even before Wheeler called on Hughes, assuring Wheeler only that Hughes would provide a letter. Wheeler, *Yankee from the West*, 328. Hughes did not explain how Wheeler happened to call upon Hughes. In Wheeler's account, Wheeler visited his friend Brandeis to seek testimony from Brandeis

the following afternoon, proclaiming with a smile at his home as he personally placed the letter into the senator's hands, "The baby is born."[94]

At the outset of his letter, Hughes flatly declared, "The Supreme Court is fully abreast of its work" and that "[t]here is no congestion of cases upon our calendar." He further averred, "This gratifying condition has obtained for several years. We have been able for several Terms to adjourn after disposing of all cases which are ready to be heard." In a direct repudiation of Roosevelt's plan, Hughes declared that "[a]n increase in the number of Justices . . . , apart from any question of policy, which I do not discuss, would not promote the efficiency of the Court. It is believed that it would impair that efficiency, so long as the Court acts as a unit. There would be more judges to hear, more judges to confer, more judges to discuss, more judges to be convinced and to decide. The present number of justices is thought to be large enough so far as the prompt, adequate, and efficient conduct of the work of the Court is concerned."[95]

Hughes also dismissed as "impracticable" the argument that an increase in justices would permit the Court to hear cases in division. Hughes explained that a "large proportion of the cases we hear are important and a decision by a part of the Court would be unsatisfactory." He also contended that the provision in article 3 for "one supreme court" meant that "[t]he Constitution does not appear to authorize two or more Supreme Courts or two or more parts of a supreme court functioning as separate courts."[96]

Wheeler's presentation of Hughes's letter to the Judiciary Committee on March 22 was calculated to have maximum impact, for Wheeler was the first witness to testify in opposition to the Court bill, following nearly two weeks of testimony in favor of it. Seeing Wheeler's triumphant expression when he arrived at the hearing, Ashurst remarked to a colleague, "I don't know what he's going to spring, but it'll blow us out of the water." Before unveiling the letter, Wheeler hushed the clatter of the crowded committee room by announcing that he had

---

and Hughes after Brandeis's wife, Alice Goldmark Brandeis, had told Wheeler's daughter that Brandeis approved of opposition to the Court bill. Wheeler explained that he "interpreted this as a tipoff that Brandeis was strongly against the bill—and that I should do something about it." According to Wheeler, Brandeis told Wheeler that neither he nor Hughes would appear before the committee, but that Hughes would provide a letter. When Wheeler refused to call Hughes because he did not know him and feared a chilly reception because of his outspoken opposition to Hughes's confirmation as Chief Justice, Brandeis led Wheeler to the telephone and called Hughes himself to arrange the meeting. Ibid.

94. Pusey, *Charles Evans Hughes*, 2:755.

95. Charles Evans Hughes to Burton K. Wheeler, March 21, 1937, in *Senate Judiciary Committee, Reorganization of the Federal Judiciary, Hearings on S. 1392 before the Senate Committee on the Judiciary*, 75th Congress, 1st Session, I: Part 3, 488, 491.

96. Ibid., 491. Frankfurter privately challenged Hughes's article 3 argument, telling Stone that "I am opposed to sitting in divisions, but that is a very different thing from saying that Article III forbids it." Frankfurter to Stone, April 8, 1937, box 13, Harlan Fiske Stone Papers, Manuscript Division, Library of Congress (hereafter cited as Stone Papers).

consulted "the only source in this country that could know exactly what the facts were."[97]

Proponents of the Court-packing plan sputtered with indignation over the chief justice's public comment on a political issue. Denouncing Hughes's comments on the constitutionality of judicial panels as "an advisory opinion run riot" that "violates every tradition of our judicial process," the *New Republic* complained that Hughes had delivered his opinion "without any case before him, at the request of an opponent of the administration, to be used as an argument in a political controversy." On the merits, the *New Republic* argued that "[t]he idea that even a majority of the cases are of sufficient public importance to require all the Court to sit at once is obviously absurd" and that in many cases "three men whose exclusive attention was centered on those problems would be infinitely better than nine," provided that the entire Court reviewed the general tenor of opinions rendered by a panel.[98] Hughes's comment on the panels appeared to contradict his own expression of disapproval of advisory opinions in his 1927 Columbia lectures.[99] In correspondence to Roosevelt, Frankfurter derogated the letter as "a characteristic Hughes performance—part and parcel of that pretended withdrawal from considerations of policy, while trying to shape them, which is the core of the mischief of which the majority have so long been guilty."[100]

Even Hughes's critics could hardly deny, however, that the letter effectively belied the central premise upon Roosevelt had originally based his proposal. Ickes confided to his journal that the letter was "good tactics" and "proves again the mistake in going to court with a weak case."[101] Wheeler claimed that Vice President Garner telephoned Roosevelt at Warm Springs after hearing the letter to inform the president, "[W]e're licked."[102]

Hughes perhaps exaggerated the effect of his letter when he wrote in his memoirs that it "had a devastating effect by destroying the specious contention as to the need of additional justices to expedite the work of the Court. It had the effect of focusing attention on the real purpose of the bill."[103] The speciousness of Roosevelt's original argument was so transparent that Roosevelt himself had largely

97. Baker, *Back to Back,* 156–57.

98. "The Chief Justice's Letter," *New Republic,* April 7, 1937, 254 (editorial).

99. Hughes, *The Supreme Court of the United States* (1928), 30–31. Hughes explained that "[t]he Court from the outset has confined itself to its judicial duty of deciding actual cases" (30). Although Hughes acknowledged that the Court had accepted President Monroe's invitation to comment on the constitutionality of internal improvements, Hughes averred that "[t]his, of course, was extra-official, but it is safe to say that nothing of the sort could happen today." Ibid., 31.

100. Felix Frankfurter to Franklin D. Roosevelt, March 30, 1937, box 28, Felix Frankfurter Papers, Manuscript Division, Library of Congress (hereafter cited as Frankfurter Papers).

101. Ickes, *Secret Diary,* 2:103. Although Ickes pointed out that the Administration already had retreated from its argument that the Court was behind in its work, Hughes "shrewdly . . . chose to fight his skirmish where we were the weakest." Ibid., 2:104.

102. Baker, *Back to Back,* 159.

103. Danelski and Tulchin, *Autobiographical Notes,* 306.

abandoned it in his speeches during the first week of March. Attention already had shifted to Roosevelt's more nakedly political defenses of his legislation, though Cummings in his testimony in favor of the bill during March had emphasized that the Court needed help with its workload.[104] As one newspaper editorial observed, Hughes's "letter brought out little that was new" and "was almost an anti-climax."[105] The letter, however, at least delivered the coup de grace to the docket argument. Although the Court's ability to sustain its workload was a documented and well-known fact even before Hughes released his letter to the committee, the emphatic authority with which Hughes personally refuted the president's arguments had far more political impact than the Court's public release of dry statistics ever could have had.[106] Moreover, the letter had symbolic significance since it registered the justices' opposition to Court packing, regardless of any reason that the proposal's advocates advanced in its favor. The opposition of the justices was hardly any surprise, but Hughes's willingness to break the magisterial silence that normally characterized the Court's response to political issues underscored the gravity of congressional efforts to tamper with the judiciary.

The chief justice's letter was especially potent because it appeared to bear the unanimous approval of the justices. In closing the letter, Hughes had declared himself "confident that it is in accord with the view of the Justices," even though, "[o]n account of the shortness of time," he had been able to personally confer only with Van Devanter and Brandeis.[107] Hughes's contention that he lacked time to consult more than two of his brethren seems disingenuous. Stone, who learned of the letter from the newspapers,[108] pointed out two years later in a letter to Frankfurter that, "[a]lthough the Court was then in recess, all its members were in the city. They could have been brought together for a conference on an hour's telephone notice, or less."[109] Stone told Frankfurter shortly after Hughes released the letter that he would not have joined in its discussion of the constitutionality of the proposed legislation.[110]

Hughes probably failed to consult brethren other than Brandeis because he feared disagreements about the content of the letter, particularly its opposition to

104. *Hearings on S. 1392 before the Senate Committee on the Judiciary,* 75th Congress, 1st Session, I: Part 1, 4–12.

105. "The Chief Justice Reports," *Birmingham (Ala.) Age-Herald,* March 24, 1937, 6 (editorial).

106. As the *Herald Tribune* observed, "the whole country knew that its President had made a misleading argument in his original message" and that Court packing "could only cause delay and confusion," but "[t]hese points the Chief Justice now made crystal clear, with a judicial calm and reticence that spoke volumes for the force and integrity of the court." *New York Herald-Tribune,* March 23, 1937, 18 (editorial).

107. *Hearings on S. 1392 before the Senate Committee on the Judiciary,* 75th Congress, 1st Session, I: Part 3, 491–92.

108. Harlan Fiske Stone to Felix Frankfurter, April 8, 1937, box 13, Stone Papers.

109. Harlan Fiske Stone to Felix Frankfurter, December 21, 1939, reel 3, Frankfurter Papers.

110. Harlan Fiske Stone to Felix Frankfurter, April 8, 1937, box 13, Stone Papers.

splitting the Court into panels.[111] Though ethically dubious, Hughes's denial of his ability to consult his colleagues was eminently practical because it permitted him to strike an unambiguous blow against the Court-packing plan.[112] According to Stone, dissenting justices were loath to subject the Court "to any additional publicity."[113] The explicit assent of the venerable Brandeis, who had a long political and judicial record of supporting economic regulation, made the letter a particularly potent weapon in the arsenal of the plan's opponents.[114]

Moreover, there is no doubt that all of the justices opposed the Court bill, despite any quibbles they may have had with the language of Hughes's letter or its manner of presentation. Indeed, other justices expressed overt or covert public opposition to the bill, departing from a tradition of judicial discretion about public controversies that is never so strongly observed in practice as in theory. Speaking on March 16 at a fraternity dinner at which reporters were present, McReynolds suggested that Roosevelt was not "a good sport" because he failed to accept the Court's decisions.[115] Throughout the spring of 1937, Stone communicated privately with both proponents and opponents of Court packing in an effort to discourage the legislation.[116] Through the journalist Irving Brant, he urged the administration to consider a constitutional amendment to require retirement of justices at age seventy-five, and he hinted to prominent supporters of the plan that imminent retirements would make the legislation unnecessary.[117] To Young B. Smith, the dean of Columbia Law School, he expressed frustration that "a great many people, because they are impatient with some decisions of the Supreme Court, should be quite ready to ruin an institution which has contributed so much to the stability and success of our federated government."[118] Meanwhile, former justice John Hessin Clarke publicly announced his belief that the Court-packing bill was constitutional, though he refrained from commenting on its wisdom.[119]

111. Alpheus Thomas Mason, *Harlan Fiske Stone: Pillar of the Law* (New York: Viking Press, 1956), 451.

112. Although Pusey described Hughes's failure to consult colleagues as "a tactical error" (Pusey, *Charles Evans Hughes*, 2:756), Professor Mason concluded that "his strategem was perfect. . . . If Hughes had consulted all his colleagues . . . there would have been a far different letter or no letter at all." Alpheus Thomas Mason, "Charles Evans Hughes: An Appeal to the Bar of History," 6 *Vanderbilt Law Review* 9 (1952).

113. Harlan Fiske Stone to Felix Frankfurter, December 21, 1939, box 13, Stone Papers.

114. Freund, "Hughes as Chief Justice," 29.

115. *Literary Digest*, March 18, 1937, 4.

116. In private correspondence with the journalist Irving Brant, Stone expressed fear that "there would be a loss of efficiency in the work of the Court. The intimate conference, which ought to be carried on . . . would be increasingly difficult with increasing size. It would be a serious loss to the continuity and thoroughness of the work if every member of the Court did not participate in a case." Harlan Fiske Stone to Irving Brant, February 26, 1937, box 15, Stone Papers.

117. Mason, *Harlan Fiske Stone*, 454.

118. Harlan Fiske Stone to Young B. Smith, February 12, 1937, box 27, Stone Papers.

119. "Clarke's Speech on the Court," *New York Times*, March 23, 1937, 1, 18.

Hughes himself publicly addressed the issue only once more. Speaking before the American Law Institute early in May, Hughes reiterated that the Court was "fully up with its work" and that "[t]here are no inordinate or unjustified delays in the Supreme Court." Going beyond the technical issues addressed in his letter to Wheeler, Hughes also tacitly criticized Roosevelt's proposal on the point on which it was most vulnerable, declaring,

> The success of democratic institutions lies in the success of the processes of reason as opposed to the tyranny of force. Between these society must choose. If society chooses the processes of reason, it must maintain the institutions which embody those processes. Institutions for the exercise of the law-making power must have their fitting complement in institutions for the interpretation and application of laws, for the safeguarding of individual rights, through a competent and independent judiciary. The firm and true administration of justice is thus the primary concern of civilized society. That administration must find its ultimate assurance, not in statutes or forms, but in the sentiment of a free people,—themselves tolerant and keenly alive to the necessity of maintaining the instrumentalities for the impartial determination of controversies.[120]

On March 29, exactly one week after Wheeler triumphantly presented Hughes's letter to the Judiciary Committee, the Court discredited the plan in a different and probably even more effective manner when it upheld the constitutionality of three federal and two state economic regulatory statutes. In the decision that most clearly signaled a break with the past, the Court upheld in a five-to-four vote the constitutionality of a Washington state minimum wage law that was virtually indistinguishable from the New York minimum wage statute that the Court had struck down in a five-to-four vote in *Tipaldo* the previous June.[121] The only justice who switched sides was Roberts. Hailed as the "switch in time that saved the Nine," the Court's decision in *West Coast Hotel Co. v. Parrish* signaled what turned out to be the Court's permanent rejection of substantive due process in economic regulatory cases.

Hughes's opinion for the Court in *West Coast Hotel* was not itself revolutionary. Because the Court had so often zigzagged in applying substantive due process to regulatory legislation, he had no paucity of precedents upon which to justify the Washington statute as an appropriate exercise of the police power. Moreover, his heavy reliance upon the state's interest in protecting the health of women did not foreclose the Court from invoking liberty of contract in other cases.

The opinion was nevertheless a watershed because its explicit rejection of *Adkins* and its implicit rejection of *Tipaldo* wiped out two precedents that had immense practical and symbolic significance. Hughes's opinion also hinted that the Court would lighten its hand in all regulatory cases. Pointing out that the

---

120. "Chief Justice Hughes Pays a Tribute to Elihu Root—The Supreme Court's Work—Measures for Improving Procedure—'The Success of Democratic Institutions,'" *American Bar Association Journal,* June 1937, 431.

121. *West Coast Hotel Co. v. Parrish,* 300 U.S. 379 (1937).

"Constitution does not speak of freedom of contract," the chief justice declared that the liberty safeguarded by due process "is liberty in a social organization which requires the protection of law against the evils which menace the health, safety, morals and welfare of the people. Liberty under the Constitution is thus necessarily subject to the restraints of due process, and regulation which is reasonable in relation to its subject and is adopted in the interests of the community is due process." Hughes likewise averred that "[e]ven if the wisdom of the policy be regarded as debatable and its effects uncertain, still the legislature is entitled to its judgment." Taking "judicial notice of the unparalleled demands for relief which arose during the recent period of depression and still continue to an alarming extent despite the degree of economic recovery which has been achieved," Hughes explained that economic exploitation of workers "casts a direct burden for their support upon the community" and that the state could correct abuses arising from employers' "selfish disregard of the public interest."[122] Although these expressions of deference toward the legislature were similar to what the Hughes Court had asserted in *Jackson* and *O'Gorman* in 1931 and in *Nebbia* in 1934, Hughes's language offered reassurance that the Court continued to adhere to these principles, notwithstanding its recent invalidation of so much regulatory legislation.

In his dissent, Sutherland countered that "the meaning of the Constitution does not change with the ebb and flow of economic events," and he denied that women had less bargaining power than men. Moreover, Sutherland contended that the state could not prescribe a wage based upon the employee's economic need rather than the value of her services.[123]

In private correspondence, Stone complained that Hughes's opinion arguing that due process did not ordinarily preclude wage regulation was indistinguishable from Stone's dissent in *Tipaldo* and was broader than Hughes's own dissent in that case, thereby undermining Hughes's contention that he was simply following his own dissent in *Tipaldo*.[124] Stone expressed satisfaction that he, unlike Hughes and Roberts, did "not have to explain or take back anything" he said in *Tipaldo*.[125]

In another significant decision on March 29, the Court likewise appeared to reverse itself in unanimously sustaining the constitutionality of the second Federal Farm Bankruptcy (Frazier-Lemke) Act, which was nearly identical to the legislation that the Court unanimously had struck down two years earlier on Black Monday in *Radford*. The Court reasoned that the new statute responded to the Court's objections in *Radford* to the extent that the new statute made clear that creditors retained their right to future settlement of claims.[126]

---

122. Ibid., 400, 391, 399, 400.
123. Ibid., 402, 411–13 (Sutherland, J., dissenting).
124. Mason, *Harlan Fiske Stone,* 457–58.
125. Harlan Fiske Stone to Sterling Carr, April 1, 1937, box 8, Stone Papers.
126. *Wright v. Vinton Branch of the Mountain Trust Bank of Roanoke,* 300 U.S. 440 (1937).

In other decisions, the Court unanimously sustained the constitutionality of the regulatory tax feature of the National Firearms Act as a proper exercise of the congressional tax power[127] and upheld an amendment to the Railway Labor Act permitting collective bargaining and mediation in interstate transportation.[128] And, in its other five-to-four decision sustaining state legislation, the Court relied upon *Nebbia* in upholding a Virginia statute regulating dairy prices.[129]

Liberals greeted the five decisions with caution. Although they seemed to auger a transformation of the Court, none except *West Coast Hotel* had any great intrinsic importance, and even that decision had the potential for undermining support for federal wages and hours legislation.[130] The constitutionality of two cornerstones of the New Deal, the National Labor Relations Act and the Social Security Act, remained uncertain. As the *Nation* pointed out, the two federal decisions were not especially remarkable because "railroads come so clearly within the scope of the commerce power" and Congress in redrafting the Frazier-Lemke Act had worked so "laboriously to meet the court's objections" in its 1935 decision. With regard to the decisions on state power, the same editorial observed that "[t]he liberal margin of advantage is the margin of Justice Roberts's very changeable mind. That is not a sturdy peg on which to hang the garment of one's hopes."[131]

During the next several weeks, however, the Court demonstrated that this "liberal margin" was not so tenuous when it sustained the constitutionality of both of the National Labor Relations and Social Security Acts. It is ironic that the victories that the Court awarded to the Roosevelt administration in upholding these key statutes sealed the doom of the Court-packing plan.

In five separate decisions on April 12, the Court sustained the constitutionality of the National Labor Relations Act, holding that Congress had properly exercised its power over interstate commerce and that the statute did not violate due process. The Court found that the employers in the cases had violated the act by discriminating against union members and interfering with unionization efforts. Every justice agreed that the commerce power extended to an interstate motor bus company and the Associated Press because these enterprises were engaged in activities that clearly involved interstate commerce.[132] Five justices, however, also were willing to extend the commerce power to three manufacturing enterprises,

---

127. *Sonzinsky v. United States,* 300 U.S. 506 (1937).

128. *Virginia Railway Co. v. System Federation No. 40,* 300 U.S. 515 (1937).

129. *Highland Farms Dairy v. Agnew,* 300 U.S. 608 (1937).

130. The *Wall Street Journal* expressed satisfaction that the decision deprived proponents of federal wage legislation of "one of their main supports." "The Minimum Wage Decision," *Wall Street Journal,* March 30, 1937, 4 (editorial).

131. "Is the Supreme Court Going Liberal?," *Nation,* April 3, 1937, 368.

132. *Associated Press v. National Labor Relations Board,* 301 U.S. 103 (1937); *Washington, Virginia & Maryland Coach Co. v. National Labor Relations Board,* 301 U.S. 142 (1937). Four dissenters contended that the statute's application to the Associated Press would violate freedom of the press under the First Amendment. This issue is discussed in greater detail in chapter 6.

the Jones & Laughlin Steel Co., and the producers of trailers and clothes.[133] Rejecting the distinction between direct and indirect effects on commerce that so often had led the Court to conclude that manufacturing was not commerce, the Court held that the manufacturing enterprises were engaged in interstate commerce because they were part of what Hughes described as a "stream of commerce."[134] As one commentator has noted, *Jones* and its progeny were "of tremendous importance" because they "repudiated the doctrine of dual federalism as a limitation upon federal delegated power" and "placed the regulation of the relationships between labor and capital clearly within the province of governmental power, national and state, and thereby struck another blow at the *laissez-faire* conception of liberty under due process which for so long had held dominance in the Court."[135]

In his opinion for the Court in *Jones & Laughlin Steel*, Hughes read the commerce and general welfare clauses expansively to permit Congress to regulate labor-management relations in an industry that often had been riven by strife. Insofar as "[r]efusal to confer and negotiate" had "been one of the most prolific causes of strife" in steel manufacturing, Hughes explained that "recognition of the right of employees to self-organization and to have representatives of their own choosing for the purpose of collective bargaining is often an essential condition of industrial peace." Because Jones was the nation's fourth-largest manufacturer of steel and employed half a million persons, the interstate effects of labor discord within even isolated parts of the company "would be immediate and it might be catastrophic." Explaining that "interference with . . . commerce must be appraised by a judgment that does not ignore actual experience," the Court affirmed that Congress had the power "to protect interstate commerce from the paralyzing consequences of industrial war." The justices explained that "congressional authority to protect interstate commerce from burdens and obstructions is not limited to transactions which can be deemed to be an essential part of a 'flow' of interstate or foreign commerce. Burdens and obstructions may be due to injurious action springing from other sources."[136]

The Court found that the trailer and clothes manufacturers likewise were part of interstate commerce even though their operations were smaller and more localized than those of Jones and Laughlin. Both obtained substantial amounts of raw materials from other states and shipped most of their products across state lines for sale in other states.[137]

In rejecting a due process challenge, Hughes explained in *Jones* that the statute did not interfere with "the normal exercise of the right of the employer to select

133. *NLRB v. Jones & Laughlin Steel Corp.*, 301 U.S. 1 (1937); *National Labor Relations Board v. Freuhauf Trailer Co.*, 301 U.S. 49 (1937); *National Labor Relations Board v. Friedman-Harry Marks Clothing*, 301 U.S. 58 (1937).

134. 301 U.S. at 41.

135. Hendel, *Hughes and the Supreme Court*, 268.

136. 301 U.S. at 42, 41, 42, 41, 36.

137. Ibid., at 53–57; 301 U.S. at 72–75.

its employees or to discharge them" and that the statute was designed to provide employees with the correlative "right to organize for the purpose of securing the redress of grievances and to promote agreements with employers relating to rates of pay and conditions of work." The Court found that "the statute goes no further than to safeguard the right of employees to self-organization and to select representatives of their own choosing for collective bargaining or other mutual protection without restraint or coercion by their employer."[138]

McReynolds's dissenting opinion, joined by Van Devanter, Butler, and Sutherland, insisted that manufacturing was "distinct from commerce and subject to the authority of the state" and that the distinction between commerce and manufacturing "may not be abridged because of some vague possibility of distant interference with commerce." Although McReynolds acknowledged that the alleged wrongful discharge of the employees in the cases could create discontent and perhaps a strike that might reduce production and "reduce the volume of goods moving in interstate commerce," he could hardly imagine a "more remote and indirect interference with interstate commerce or a more definite invasion of the powers reserved to the states" under the Tenth Amendment. McReynolds observed that "[a]lmost anything—marriage, birth, death—may in some fashion affect commerce." The dissenters also contended that the statute violated substantive due process under the Fifth Amendment. Citing the Court's decisions in *Adair* and *Coppage* striking down prohibitions on yellow-dog contracts, McReynolds declared that the statute deprived a private business owner of "power to manage his own property by freely selecting those to whom his manufacturing operations are to be entrusted."[139] The Four Horsemen presumably did not regard the statute's application to the Associated Press and the bus company as a violation of due process because they regarded them as businesses that were affected with a public interest.[140]

The National Labor Relations Board decisions surprised and elated many liberals. The *Nation* described them as "nothing short of a miracle."[141] The same publication observed that the Court acted as "a stabilizing force in our national life" because the board "had been so bitterly fought and sabotaged by big business that it was almost a dead letter. Yet when five out of nine justices of the court placed their imprimatur upon it, big business accepted it."[142]

These decisions naturally diminished support for Court packing, particularly among labor unions, which became even more perfunctory in their advocacy of Roosevelt's proposal.[143] The Court's decisions, however, did not immediately convince proponents of Court packing that Roosevelt's measure was not needed. As

138. Ibid., 45, 43–44, 33.

139. Ibid., 101, 97, 99, 103 (McReynolds, J., dissenting).

140. Barry Cushman, *Rethinking the New Deal Court: The Structure of a Constitutional Revolution* (New York: Oxford University Press, 1998), 137.

141. "The Wagner Decisions," *Nation*, April 17, 1937 (editorial).

142. "Judges Are Human," *Nation*, April 24, 1937, 452.

143. Baker, *Back to Back*, 203.

the *New Republic* asked, "Who knows when Mr. Justice Roberts will do another flop?"[144] Despite the victory for labor, John L. Lewis, president of the Congress of Industrial Organizations (CIO), complained that the "Court is as variable as the winds, and the people wonder how long they are to be victims of its instability."[145] In disgust, Frankfurter privately remarked that he felt "like finding some honest profession to enter."[146] Although the Court's about-face may have restored the Court's credibility among many liberals, some proponents of Court packing predicted that it would further diminish the institution's prestige by lending credence to their argument that the Court was unabashedly political.[147] Relishing the Court's "complete somersault" in *West Coast Hotel,* Ickes predicted that the decision would undermine the Court's prestige because it had "run to cover" under fire. Ickes, who "would have had more respect for the Court if it had gone down fighting and snarling after the manner of Justice McReynolds," believed that "Hughes and Roberts ought to realize that the mob is always ready to tear and rend at any sign of weakness."[148]

Hughes himself dismissed as "utterly baseless" the allegation that the Court's decisions in *West Coast Hotel* or *Jones & Laughlin Steel* "were influenced in the slightest degree by the president's attitude, or his proposal to reorganize the Court." In his autobiographical notes, Hughes pointed out that five members of the Court had decided to sustain the Washington minimum wage law "before the President's attack upon the Court had been made or anyone had any notion that it was coming."[149] Hughes also pointed out that the decision was consistent with his own rejection of the "liberty of contract" doctrine in the *McGuire* decision in 1911,[150] and that he had expressed his views in support of Oregon's minimum wage law in conference in 1916 shortly before resigning from the Court in a case in which the Court eventually voted to sustain the law.[151] Hughes contended that his opinion in *Jones & Laughlin Steel* was consistent with views that he had expressed as early as his opinion in the *Minnesota Rate Cases.*[152] Hughes similarly denied that the Court-packing plan had influenced his brethren, declaring that "[t]he Court acted with complete independence."[153] Similarly, Paul Freund pointed out that

144. "Labor Wins in Court," *New Republic,* April 21, 1937, 307 (editorial).

145. Richard C. Cortner, *The Jones & Laughlin Case* (New York: Alfred A. Knopf, 1970), 171–72. .

146. Nelson Lloyd Dawson, *Louis D. Brandeis, Felix Frankfurter, and the New Deal* (Hamden, Conn.: Archon Books, 1980), 148–49 (quoting letter from Frankfurter to Roosevelt, April 12, 1937, box 98, Frankfurter Papers).

147. *Nation,* April 17, 1937, 424.

148. Ickes, *Secret Diary,* 2:107.

149. Danelski and Tulchin, *Autobiographical Notes,* 311–12.

150. Ibid., at 312, citing *Chicago, Burlington & Quincy R.R. Co. v. McGuire,* 219 U.S. 549 (1911) (sustaining Iowa statute which denied validity of contracts between railroads and employees limiting liability for personal injuries).

151. Ibid., citing *Stettler v. O'Hara,* 243 U.S. 629 (1917).

152. Ibid., referring to 230 U.S. 352 (1913).

153. Ibid., 313.

the comprehensive guarantee of collective bargaining to prevent strikes seems more related to protection of interstate commerce than did the establishment of wages and hours for coal miners that the Court struck down in *Carter Coal*, and that the gargantuan Jones and Laughlin Steel Company obviously was more related to interstate commerce than was the Schechter poultry business.[154] Other scholars have argued, however, that Roberts's categorical opposition to the railroad retirement plan in his opinion *Alton* is difficult to square with his vote in *Jones & Laughlin Steel*, and that the vision of the taxing power he espoused in *Butler* is not easily recoiled with his vote in the social security cases.[155]

Even more difficult to explain as the product of legal logic was Justice Roberts's apparent inconsistency in voting to sustain the Washington minimum wage law in *West Coast Hotel* in March 1937 after he had voted only nine months earlier in *Tipaldo* to strike down a virtually indistinguishable law. Although historians have taken pains to explain Roberts's "switch" in *West Coast Hotel*, they have rarely asked why he voted so conservatively in *Tipaldo*. Irving Brant believed that Roberts's vote in the earlier case was partly emotional, based on "a fear to make the least concession lest if an inch is given [a]ll will be lost."[156] In 1937 and for many years thereafter, Roberts's "switch" was widely regarded as a response to the threat of Court packing.[157] In 1955 Frankfurter challenged this received wisdom in an article claiming that Roberts informed Frankfurter in a 1945 memorandum that he had changed his vote because Washington state, unlike New York, had specifically asked the Court to overrule *Adkins*.[158] Frankfurter also contended that the Court-packing plan could not have influenced Roberts because the Court had voted on *West Coast Hotel* on December 19, 1936, nearly seven weeks before FDR announced his proposal, a fact that Hughes already had pointed out in his autobiographical notes.[159]

154. Freund, "Hughes as Chief Justice," 34, 36.

155. See, for example, William Lasser, "Justice Roberts and the Constitutional Revolution of 1937—Was There a 'Switch in Time'?," 78 *Texas Law Review* 1354–61 (2000).

156. Irving Brant to Harlan Fiske Stone, June 2, 1936, box 7, Stone Papers.

157. See, for example, Edward S. Corwin, *Constitutional Revolution, Ltd.* (1941; repr., Westport, Conn.: Greenwood Press, 1977), 73; Benjamin F. Wright, *The Growth of American Constitutional Law* (New York: Reynal & Hitchcock, 1942); Leo Pfeffer, *This Honorable Court: A History of the United States Supreme Court* (Boston, Beacon Press, 1965), 317–24.

158. Felix Frankfurter, "Mr. Justice Roberts," 104 *University of Pennsylvania Law Review* 311 (1955). For divergent opinions concerning the authenticity of this memorandum and Frankfurter's reasons for publishing it, compare Michael Ariens, "A Thrice-Told Tale, or Felix the Cat," 107 *Harvard Law Review* 620 (1994), and Richard D. Friedman, "A Reaffirmation: The Authenticity of the Roberts Memorandum, or Felix the Non-Forger," 142 *University of Pennsylvania Law Review* 1985 (1994). Roberts's memorandum to Frankfurter is consistent with what Roberts told Hughes's biographer in a 1946 interview. Merlo J. Pusey, "Justice Roberts's 1937 Turnaround," *1983 Yearbook Supreme Court Historical Society*, 105–6.

159. Danelski and Tulchin, *Autobiographical Notes*, 312. Accordingly, Hughes declared that "[t]he President's proposal had not the slightest effect on our decision." Ibid., 312.

The obvious problems with these interpretations is that Roberts was free to overrule *Adkins* without invitation from counsel and that the November 1936 election had made some type of Court-curbing legislation almost certain, even though the form that it took generated widespread surprise. Indeed, many commentators have attributed the Court's "revolution" more to the election than to the specific threat of Roosevelt's proposal. Scholars likewise have pointed out that there were differences between the New York and District of Columbia statutes upon which Roberts could have relied to uphold the New York legislation;[160] that the attorneys for the state in *Tipaldo* asked the Court to reconsider *Adkins;*[161] that Roberts incorrectly stated that Washington State had requested that the Court overturn *Adkins;*[162] and that Roberts was willing to overturn an even more venerable precedent without invitation from counsel the following year in *Erie Railroad v. Tompkins.*[163] Roberts himself recalled after his retirement from the bench "the tremendous strain, and the threat to the existing Court, of which I was fully conscious."[164]

Although Frankfurter's account received much credence in legal academia at the time of its publication and some prominent scholars have more recently made cogent arguments that Roberts had principled reasons for his votes in the two decisions,[165] many legal realists, historians, and political scientists continue to

160. John W. Chambers, "The Big Switch: Justice Roberts and the Minimum-Wage Cases," 10 *Labor History* 65 (1969).

161. Lasser, "Justice Roberts and the Constitutional Revolution," 1362.

162. Richard D. Freidman, "Switching Time and Other Thought Experiments: The Hughes Court and Constitutional Transformation," 142 *University of Pennsylvania Law Review* 1949–53 (1994).

163. Edward A. Purcell Jr., "Rethinking Constitutional Change," 80 *Virginia Law Review* 290 (1994), discussing 304 U.S. 64 (1938).

164. Ibid., at 279, quoting *Composition and Jurisdiction of the Supreme Court: Hearings on S.J. Res. 44 before the Subcomm. on Constitutional Amendments of the Senate Comm. on the Judiciary,* 83rd Congress, 2d Session 9 (1954) (statement of Owen J. Roberts).

165. Cushman, *Rethinking the New Deal Court,* 94–104; Friedman, "Switching Time and Other Thought Experiments," 1940–53; Charles A. Leonard, *A Search for a Judicial Philosophy: Mr. Justice Roberts and the Constitutional Revolution of 1937* (Port Washington, N.Y.: Kennikat Press, 1971), 89–92, 179–80 (reaffirming the Frankfurter thesis). Professor Cushman has argued that Roberts's opinion in *Nebbia* demonstrates that Roberts believed that *Adkins* should be overruled, but that Roberts refused to vote to uphold the constitutionality of the New York minimum wage law in *Tipaldo* because Hughes would not concede that *Adkins* was wrongly decided. Unwilling to tolerate the inconsistency of upholding both the New York law and *Adkins,* Roberts was willing to join the Four Horsemen in an opinion that was narrowly based on the *Adkins* precedent. Cushman, *Rethinking the New Deal Court.* Professor Friedman has concluded, "There is no reason to believe that the presidential election had any significant impact on Roberts's vote. . . . The short-term political factors seem likely to have affected Roberts only in inducing him to confront the issue whether Adkins should be overruled, not in leading him to believe a minimum wage law was constitutional; his prior conduct, in Nebbia and other cases, makes this result one would most likely expect him to reach." Friedman, "Switching Time and Other Thought Experiments," 1952–53.

regard Roberts's vote in *West Coast Hotel* as a prime example of how politics influences the Court.[166] Daniel A. Farber has aptly concluded that "[u]nless new evidence is discovered, it is unlikely that we will ever have a definitive answer."[167]

Even if the threat of Court packing did not affect the Court's decisions, some scholars have suggested that the Court was influenced, if not pressured, by contemporary political events to the extent that the acrimonious sit-down strikes that swept the nation early in 1937 may have helped convince the Court in the National Labor Relations Act cases that labor relations affected interstate commerce.[168]

Three weeks after the National Labor Relations Act decisions, the Court gave Roosevelt an even more personal victory when it upheld the constitutionality of his 1933 diplomatic recognition of the Soviet government.[169] In *Belmont v. United States,* the Court amplified the broad presidential discretion in foreign relations it had enunciated three months earlier in *Curtiss-Wright* and explained that Roosevelt's agreement with the Soviet Union did not require Senate approval because it was not a treaty. *Belmont* also was consistent with the Court's growing solicitude for federal power by rejecting the argument that the transfer to the United States of Soviet claims against property nationalized by the Soviet government was void because the nationalization of such property contravened New York's public policy. The decision likewise was consistent with the Court's expanding view of federal power because it held that the bank with which the nationalized property was

---

166. See Roger Corley, "Was There a Constitutional Revolution in 1937?" in *Franklin Roosevelt and the Transformation of the Supreme Court,* ed. Stephen Shaw, William Pederson, and Frank Williams, 26–59 (Armonk, N.Y.: M.E. Sharpe, 2004); Conrad Black, *Franklin Delano Roosevelt: Champion of Freedom* (New York: Public Affairs, 2003), 413. For a survey of literature, see, for example, Michael E. Parrish, "The Hughes Court, the Great Depression, and the Historians," 40 *Historian* 296–97 (1978). At least three Justices of the U.S. Supreme Court appear similarly to have believed that external factors influenced the Court. In explaining why the Court may be justified in overturning its precedent in certain situations, Justices O'Connor, Kennedy, and Souter in their opinion in *Planned Parenthood v. Casey* suggested that the Court overturned *Adkins* because "the Depression had come and, with it, the lesson that seemed unmistakable to most people by 1937, that the interpretation of contractual freedom protected in *Adkins* rested on fundamentally false assumptions about the capacity of a relatively unregulated market to satisfy minimal levels of human welfare." 505 U.S. at 861–62 (1992).

167. Daniel A. Farber, "Who Killed Lochner?" (book review), 90 *Georgetown Law Review* 1001 (2002).

168. Drew D. Hansen, "The Sit-Down Strikes and the Switch in Time," 46 *Wayne Law Review* 49 (2000); Richard C. Cortner, *The Wagner Act Cases* (Knoxville: University of Tennessee Press, 1964), 175. Jim Pope has argued that the Court "plainly and simply" yielded to the pressure of the sit-down strikers in *Fruehauf* and *Friedman-Marks* because "anything short of a Board sweep would have defeated Congress's attempt to resolve the labor crisis and, conversely, only a sweep could have deflated the pressure for court-packing as a means of freeing Congress to resolve that crisis." Jim Pope, "Worker Lawmaking, Sit-Down Strikes, and the Shaping of American Industrial Relations, 1935–1958," 24 *Law and History Review* 97 (2006).

169. 301 U.S. 324 (1937).

deposited could not invoke the takings clause of the Fifth Amendment to challenge transfer of the property to the United States.

The prospects for the Court-packing plan's success were further diminished when Van Devanter announced on May 18 that he would retire two weeks later. At last, after more than four years, Roosevelt could appoint a justice, and the likelihood that the new justice presumably would help tilt the Court in favor of regulatory legislation made the case for Court packing much less compelling. Because Van Devanter had postponed his retirement for financial reasons until Congress enacted the new statute permitting federal judges to retire after age seventy at full pay, the pension law bore fruit even while the Court-packing plan withered. Van Devanter's retirement and the retirement of Sutherland the following December, suggest that Roosevelt could have reconstituted the Court through pension legislation alone, avoiding the politically costly fight over Court packing.

On May 24, 1937, the Court gave the Roosevelt administration another major victory in two decisions sustaining the constitutionality of the Social Security Act, the most far-reaching New Deal legislation.[170] In upholding the act's provision for unemployment compensation, the Court in *Steward Machine Co. v. Davis* held that Congress's power of taxation was broad enough to permit Congress to tax employers to fund a program to protect unemployed workers from poverty. Adopting an expansive view of Congress's power to tax to promote the general welfare of the nation, Cardozo's opinion for the Court bristled with impatience at the plaintiff's contention that the Constitution precluded bold measures to address the nation's economic emergency. "It is too late today for the argument to be heard with tolerance that in a crisis so extreme the use of the moneys of the nation to relieve the unemployed and their dependents is a use for any purpose narrower than the promotion of the general welfare," he declared. Cardozo pointed out that unemployment between 1929 and 1936 regularly exceeded ten million people and reached a peak of sixteen million. Moreover, this "was only a partial roll of the destitute or needy" because "[d]isaster to the breadwinner meant disaster to dependents." Because states lacked the ability to provide sufficient relief, "[t]he problem had become national in area and dimensions. There was need for help from the nation if the people were not to starve."[171]

The Court likewise held that the statute did not improperly coerce the states or contravene the Tenth Amendment in encouraging the states to establish their own unemployment compensation funds by allowing employers a credit of as much as 90 percent of their federal tax for contributions to a state unemployment compensation fund. Cardozo explained that federal legislation enabled states to enact unemployment compensation laws without fearing that this would place

170. *Steward Machine Co. v. Davis*, 301 U.S. 548 (1937); *Helvering v. Davis*, 301 U.S. 619 (1937).

171. Ibid., 586–87, 586.

them at a competitive disadvantage against other states and that such state legisla-tion relieved the federal government of a "mountainous" burden in assisting the unemployed.[172]

Although the Four Horsemen dissented, Sutherland and Van Devanter did so on surprisingly narrow grounds. While they agreed that Congress had the power to levy the tax and that the tax did not unduly coerce the states, they objected to the statute only to the extent that it interfered with the states' power to administer its own unemployment compensation fund.

In sustaining the old-age provisions of the Social Security Act by a vote of seven to two in the companion case of *Helvering v. Davis,* the Court reiterated its broad interpretation of the federal power to tax in promotion of the general welfare. In what could serve as an appropriate epigram for the judicial revolution of 1937, Cardozo declared that the Court's concern was "with power, not with wisdom." In holding that the Tenth Amendment did not bar the statute, Cardozo explained that unemployment was a national problem to which Congress had discretion to commit "the resources of the Nation." Moreover, Congress reasonably concluded that state and local governments lacked the resources to "finance an adequate program of security for the aged." Echoing an argument he had made in *Steward Machine Co.,* Cardozo pointed out that states also were understandably reluctant to institute their own programs because "[t]he existence of such a system is bait to the needy and dependant elsewhere, encouraging them to migrate and seek a haven of repose. Only a power that is national can serve the interests of all." Observing that Congress did not improvise the statute, Cardozo pointed to the "great mass of evidence" upon which Congress relied in finding that approxi-mately three-quarters of persons older than sixty-five were dependent upon others for support. "The hope behind this statute," Cardozo observed, "is to save men and women from the rigors of the poor house as well as from the haunting fear that such a lot awaits them when journey's end is near." In rejecting the argument that the statute could invade the rights of the states by generating a paternalism that might conflict with a state's policy of promoting self-reliance, Cardozo remarked that any national legislation, such as a tariff, could offend a state and that the "issue is a closed one" because state nullification of federal law no longer was sound constitutional doctrine.[173] McReynolds and Butler wrote in their one-line dissent that the pension provisions were "repugnant to the Tenth Amend-ment."[174]

In a related decision on May 24, the Court by a vote of five to four upheld the constitutionality of the unemployment compensation statute that Alabama had enacted pursuant to the federal Social Security Act.[175] Rejecting due process and equal protection challenges, Justice Stone's opinion declared that "relief of the

172. Ibid., 585–93, 588.
173. Ibid., 644, 641, 644, 642–43, 641, 645–46.
174. Ibid., 646.
175. *Carmichael v. Southern Coal & Coke Co.,* 301 U.S. 495 (1937).

unemployed . . . is a permissible use of state funds" and a proper basis for exercise of the state's power of taxation. In considering the other side of the *Steward* coin, Stone explained that the state had not unconstitutionally delegated power to the federal government by enacting legislation pursuant to the Social Security Act insofar as the federal and state governments had a "common concern" with unemployment and could undertake a "cooperative legislative effort" to ameliorate it. In dissent, even Sutherland, Butler, and Van Devanter agreed that the state's objective was constitutional, objecting only on technical grounds to the statute's provision for pooling of the funds of different industries.[176] Only McReynolds entered a general dissent.

On May 24, the Court in another five-to-four vote sustained the constitutionality of a Wisconsin statute prohibiting the use of injunctions to restrain nonviolent picketing.[177] The Court's refusal to limit the statute was particularly striking because the facts of the case provided a strong argument for curtailing its scope. The plaintiff, a tile contractor who provided the manual labor for nearly half his business, refused to unionize his shop only because unionization would prevent him from personally laying tiles and thereby presumably would render him unable to continue his business. Union members who picketed his place of business, which also was his home, condemned him as antiunion and advertised the services of unionized businesses. Although Brandeis's majority opinion assumed that the pickets were truthful and that the pickets were merely incident to the ordinary give and take of economic competition, Butler's dissenting opinion made a powerful argument that the pickets untruthfully maligned the tile layer as antiunion and unfairly sought to drive him out of business. The Court's willingness to defer to the statute even in the face of such extreme facts—and in a case in which a contrary ruling would have upheld the claim of a manual laborer—demonstrated how far the Court would go in deferring to legislation, including prounion legislation.

Although the Social Security cases further eroded support for Court packing, many of the more ardent liberals were unconvinced that the Court's decisions marked any permanent constitutional shift and expressed fear that the Court would revert to stricter scrutiny of economic legislation once the pressure of the Court-packing plan disappeared.[178] Many liberals were convinced that the Court's decisions were directly influenced by the threat of Court packing and thus constituted what one editorial called "shotgun liberalism."[179] Constitutional scholar Edward S. Corwin observed that "the lesson of the November election could have been lost only on members of the Bench with a messianic complex of some sort; and the CIO 'sit-down strikes' must also have had a profound effect in the demonstration which they afforded that the country is not to be governed by the simple expedient of tossing acts of Congress out of the window."[180]

176. Ibid., 515, 526, 527–31.
177. *Senn v. Tile Layers Protective Union*, 301 U.S. 468 (1937).
178. "The Court Bitter-Enders," *New Republic*, July 14, 1937, 265 (editorial).
179. "Is the Supreme Court Going Liberal?" *Nation*, April 3, 1937, 368.
180. Edward S. Corwin, "The Court Sees a New Light," *New Republic*, August 4, 1937, 357.

Similarly, Roosevelt and his advisors continued to push the Court plan because they regarded the new majority as tenuous, particularly because they believed that Roberts had turned "liberal" only in order to subvert the plan.[181] Having complained for so long that the New Deal faced a constitutional "no man's land," Roosevelt now worried that his program was adrift in what he called "Roberts' land."[182] Meanwhile, Irving Brant warned Roosevelt that even decisions that sustained New Deal legislation would not necessarily protect Roosevelt's long-term goals because Hughes was likely to write "narrow and grudging" opinions.[183]

Roosevelt likewise may have pressed ahead, even after Van Devanter's retirement, because he feared that he could not necessarily rely upon all of his appointees to support New Deal legislation. Roosevelt and his advisors were keenly aware that many justices had defied the expectations of the presidents who placed them on the Court.[184] Roosevelt had special reason to worry because he had at least tacitly promised to give one seat to Senate Majority Leader Joseph T. Robinson, who had fought valiantly for the Court-packing bill despite personal misgivings. With good reason, Roosevelt doubted whether Robinson, a conservative Arkansan, would feel the constraints of partisan loyalty so keenly as a justice. Although Roosevelt was not bound to appoint Robinson, Roosevelt recognized that bypassing Robinson would further antagonize Senate Democrats, whom the popular Robinson had led for fifteen years.[185]

Two weeks after the Court's Social Security decisions, the Senate Judiciary Committee delivered a staggering blow to the Court bill when it rejected every provision of the bill on June 7 by a vote of ten to eight, with several Democrats joining the majority. The astringent tone of the report was widely interpreted as a personal rebuke to Roosevelt and a portent of an open rupture between conservative and liberal Democrats that could divide the party on issues far beyond the Court plan.[186]

The report ridiculed Roosevelt's contention that it would promote judicial efficiency and warned that it would in fact imperil judicial independence and personal liberties. Denouncing the bill as "an invasion of judicial power such as has never before been attempted in this country," the committee declared that "we would rather have an independent Court, a fearless Court . . . that will . . . be the defense of the liberties of the people, than a Court that out of fear or sense of obligation to the appointing power . . . approves any measure we may enact. We are not the judges of the judges. We are not above the Constitution." Praising

181. Baker, *Back to Back*, 180.

182. Ibid., 181.

183. Ibid., 172.

184. Indeed, some critics of the FDR plan feared that the difficulty of predicting judicial performance would cause Roosevelt to nominate only persons who pledged in advance to support the Administration. See Mary Allen Wright to Robert M. La Follette Jr., March 31, 1937, series C, box 366, La Follette Family Papers.

185. Leuchtenburg, *The Supreme Court Reborn*, 145; McKenna, *Franklin Roosevelt*, 469–70.

186. Baker, *Back to Back*, 230.

the Court for its "vigilant, able, and faithful" defense of human rights in various decisions, many of which the Hughes Court had decided, the committee declared that the bill "violates every sacred tradition of American democracy" and would "destroy the independence of the judiciary, the only certain shield of individual rights."[187]

The committee's adverse vote left Roosevelt with no choice but to compromise. Almost immediately, Roosevelt acceded to a measure that would have permitted him to appoint one justice each year for each one who was more than seventy-five years old. Even this measure faced fierce opposition, for it still permitted the president to manipulate the Court's size for political purposes.[188] Critics pointed out that making annual appointments optional actually increased the president's ability to influence or coerce the Court.[189] Galvanized by their success in defeating the original plan, opponents of Court packing fought the compromise measure with no less tenacity. Uncertain that they could defeat the compromise in a formal vote, its opponents threatened a filibuster that Robinson tried to ward off by conducting continuous debate on the Senate floor. Stretching through many stifling July days, the acrimonious debate strained the health of Robinson and many of his colleagues.[190]

Beset from the start with misfortune, the Court-packing plan suffered yet another dramatic blow on July 14, when Robinson, alone in his Capitol Hill apartment on a steamy Friday night, died of a heart attack. Without vigorous leadership, the compromise bill seemed doomed to fail, and many senators who accompanied Robinson's bier to Little Rock grumbled during the long train journey that Roosevelt had callously encouraged the ailing Robinson to sacrifice his life for the Court-packing measure.[191]

Roosevelt suffered further political embarrassment the following week when half the Democratic senators opposed Roosevelt's choice for Robinson's successor as majority leader, Senator Alben W. Barkley of Kentucky, who was selected only after Vice President Garner broke the tie. Meeting with Roosevelt on July 21, Garner, never a supporter of Court packing, undertook the grim task of informing the president that the proposal had no realistic hope of passing the Senate. Roosevelt instructed Barkley to obtain the best compromise possible. Wheeler rejected Garner's proposal to limit Court packing to two additional justices, and neither side wished to take the risk of scheduling a vote on the bill's merits. Garner preferred simply to have the Senate discontinue its consideration of the bill. But Wheeler,

---

187. *Reorganization of the Judiciary, Adverse Report,* 75th Congress, 1st Session, Rpt. No. 711, 11, 14, 23.

188. Baker, *Back to Back,* 235.

189. See, for example, *Report of the Committee on Federal Legislation of the Association of the Bar of the City of New York on the Amendment (in the nature of a substitute) to Senate Bill 1392 to Reorganize the Judicial Branch of the Government,* July 16, 1937, 6.

190. McKenna, *Franklin Roosevelt,* 498–500; Leuchtenburg, *The Supreme Court Reborn,* 151–52.

191. Leuchtenburg, *The Supreme Court Reborn,* 152; McKenna, *Franklin Roosevelt,* 505–6.

wanting to deliver a direct rebuke to the administration, insisted upon a vote to recommit the bill to the Judiciary Committee. On July 22, the Senate recommitted the bill by a vote of seventy to twenty-two, with fifty-three Democrats helping to sound the bill's death knell.[192]

Defeat of Roosevelt's plan and the Court's transformational decisions also chilled support for constitutional amendments. Supporters of the plan complained that liberal opponents who had favored amendments as alternatives failed to carry through with such proposals after the plan's defeat.[193] Although Corwin expressed agreement with those who asked why one should "follow up a successful shotgun wedding by shooting the bridegroom," he suggested that it might be prudent to take "precautions to make it reasonably probable that the bridegroom will now turn to and support the family."[194]

The defeat of the Court-packing plan also diminished support for new initiatives in social and regulatory legislation, for it emboldened opponents of the New Deal by demonstrating that Roosevelt was not invulnerable. It also cost the president much precious goodwill among many members of Congress, revitalizing the conservative wing of the Democratic Party.[195] With considerable exaggeration, Henry A. Wallace recalled that "[t]he whole New Deal really went up in smoke as a result of the Supreme Court fight."[196] It is ironic that the Court-packing battle, which may have made the Court more receptive to regulatory legislation, reduced the inclination of Congress to enact such laws.

The only parts of Roosevelt's proposal to survive the firestorm were his recommendations for noncontroversial procedural reforms. A month after shelving the Court-packing plan, Congress approved the president's recommendations to make the federal government a party to federal lawsuits challenging the constitutionality of federal legislation, to provide for direct appeal to the Supreme Court in cases in which a lower federal court had invalidated a federal statute, and to facilitate the more efficient deployment of federal judges.[197]

The Court-packing plan was the victim of many forces, including Roosevelt's furtiveness, disingenuousness, overconfidence, and arrogance. Roosevelt's failure to offer a more permanent solution to judicial obstruction of legislation also drove away many potential supporters. Even if Roosevelt had not for once lost his political grip, the proposal might have been doomed, for it ran afoul of the deep and abiding respect of the American people for the Court as the guardian of the rule of law. Ashurst believed that Roosevelt "could not overcome an 'imponderable' which for generations has emotionally and mystically invested the Supreme Court . . . with symbolism as the power which protects the security and personal liberty of

---

192. Baker, *Back to Back*, 259–67

193. *Nation,* June 19, 1937, 689; *Nation,* June 26, 1937, 730.

194. Edward S. Corwin, "The Court Sees a New Light," *New Republic,* August 4, 1937, 357.

195. See William E. Leuchtenburg, *Franklin Roosevelt and the New Deal, 1932–1940* (New York: Harper & Row, 1963), 239.

196. Leuchtenburg, *The Supreme Court Reborn,* 158.

197. Judicial Procedure Reform Act, Ch 754, 50 Stat. 751.

the citizens." As Senator Ashurst aptly observed, even many Roosevelt supporters opposed the bill "because they were haunted with the terrible fear that some future President might, by suddenly enlarging the Supreme Court, suppress free-speech, free assembly, and invade other Constitutional guaranties of citizens."[198] Similarly, the journalist Max Lerner wrote in the wake of Roosevelt's defeat that "the cult of the Supreme Court is the characteristic emotional cement by which American capitalism and American democracy are held together."[199]

Even the prevalence of respect for the Court might not, however, have defeated Court packing if the Court had not appeared to change its course so suddenly and so thoroughly. As Corwin observed in August 1937, no revolution in American constitutional law was "so radical, so swift, so altogether dramatic" as that of the Court's most recent term.[200] The reasons for the Court's apparent transformation remain controversial, and some scholars have argued that 1937 was a year of evolution rather than revolution.

The transformation did not involve all of the justices; the Four Horsemen continued to oppose regulatory legislation with undiminished fervor. The traditional view was summarized in a 1940 commentary: "On his way to Damascus, Mr. Justice Roberts . . . saw a great light, shifted sides and touched off a legal revolution."[201] The reality, of course, is more complex. Neither Roberts nor Hughes—nor even any of the Four Horsemen—ever categorically opposed economic regulatory legislation. As Cushman has demonstrated, the Court even before 1937 frequently voted, often unanimously, to sustain economic regulatory legislation.[202] Although both Roberts and Hughes in 1937 began to vote regularly to sustain economic regulatory legislation, they remained more restrained in their doctrinal positions than did their more liberal brethren.

The Court's "revolution" may in part have resulted from the character of the legislation that the justices reviewed beginning in 1937. In recent years, scholars have increasingly contended that the poor craftsmanship of many early New Deal statutes and the mediocrity of government lawyers who defended these laws before the Court go far toward explaining the Court's nullification of many statutes, particularly those that even the Court's most liberal justices voted to strike down,[203] Hughes told Wheeler when he met with him to discuss his letter to the Judiciary Committee that the outcome of many of the Court's decisions might

---

198. George F. Sparks, ed., *A Many-Colored Toga: The Diary of Henry Fountain Ashurst* (Tucson: University of Arizona Press, 1962), 375.

199. Max Lerner, "Constitution and Court as Symbols," 46 *Yale Law Journal* 1312 (1937).

200. Edward S. Corwin, "The Court Sees a New Light," *New Republic*, August 4, 1937, 334.

201. Walton Hamilton and George Braden, "The Supreme Court Today," *New Republic*, August 5, 1940, 178.

202. Generally see Barry Cushman, "The Secret Lives of the Four Horsemen," 83 *Virginia Law Review* 559 (1997).

203. Neal Devins, "Government Lawyers and the New Deal" (book review), 96 *Columbia Law Review* 240, 251–52, 257, 259–60, 266 (1996); Peter H. Irons, *The New Deal Lawyers* (Princeton, N.J.: Princeton University Press, 1982), 4–6, 10–13.

have been different if the laws had not been so poorly drafted and if Cummings had not presented such weak briefs and oral arguments.[204] Similarly, the better drafting and more able legal defenses of later federal legislation, particularly the National Labor Relations Act, may help to explain why the Court was more receptive to these laws.[205]

However, although the voting patterns and doctrinal beliefs of the justices did not change as much during 1937 as the actual outcome of the Court's decisions might suggest, it is clear that the Court's 1936–1937 term represented a watershed in the Court's history, for it marked the end of the Court's half-century role as the self-appointed arbiter of the constitutionality of economic regulatory legislation. Never again would the Court strike down such legislation as a violation of due process or equal protection, and it would be more than a half century before the Court would again invoke the commerce clause to strike down federal legislation.

Although it is possible that Roberts, and perhaps even Hughes, allowed the threat of Court packing to influence at least one or some of their votes in 1937— Robert's vote in *Parrish* is the most obvious possibility—it is more likely that public antagonism toward the Court's decisions influenced these and perhaps other justices in a more subtle and less overtly political manner.

As one study of the Court has explained, "[G]iven the institutional restraints imposed on the Court, the Justices cannot effectuate their own policy and institutional goals without taking account of the goals and likely actions of the members of the other branches."[206] Similarly, another study has concluded that "public opinion can and does influence the decisions of individual justices whether by stimulating changes in judicial attitudes or by shaping their subjective norms."[207] The Court particularly needs to be responsive to public opinion because it relies "on political leaders for the implementation of its decisions."[208] The Supreme Court has an institutional stake in remaining attentive to public opinion, particularly congressional opinion, insofar as criticism of its decisions and movements to curtail its powers "can diminish the public respect which is so critical to the maintenance of its powers."[209]

As one commentator presciently, albeit prematurely, observed early in 1935 in predicting that the Court would sustain most New Deal legislation, "[T]he habit

204. Wheeler, *Yankee from the West,* 329. Wheeler reported that Hughes complained that "we've had to do the work that should have been done by the Attorney General." Hughes believed that Wall Street lawyers could have drafted better legislation because they better understood the abuses committed by their clients. Ibid.

205. See Devins, "Government Lawyers and the New Deal."

206. Lee Epstein et al., "The Supreme Court as a Strategic National Policymaker," 50 *Emory Law Journal* 83–84 (2001).

207. William Mishler and Reginald S. Sheehan, "Public Opinion, the Attitudinal Model and Supreme Court Decision Making: A Micro-Analytic Perspective," 58 *Journal of Politics* 198 (1996).

208. Gerald N. Rosenberg, "Judicial Indpendence and the Reality of Political Power," 54 *Review of Politics* 382 (1992).

209. William G. Ross, "The Resilience of *Marbury v. Madison:* Why Judicial Review Has Survived So Many Attacks," 38 *Wake Forest Law Review* 711 (2002).

of the Court is to act affirmatively rather than negatively, constantly broadening the interpretation of the Constitution rather than narrowing it, making it grow as the country grows, responsive to the changing times, meeting and overcoming every crisis, no matter how nerve-racking, so that the great instrument devised by the fathers remains ever as great as the nation is and as the people want it to be."[210] Similarly, Hughes observed in a 1939 address to a joint session of Congress that "what the people really want, they generally get."[211]

Many contemporaries attributed the Court's shift to the personal statesman-ship of Hughes. Senator Thomas T. Connally of Texas told Ickes that Hughes "had played a bad hand perfectly" while Roosevelt's forces had "played a good hand badly."[212] The journalist Robert S. Allen remarked at the end of May that "Hughes has played high politics . . . and played it with boldness and agility" and "consum-mate deftness and finesse." Allen asserted that Hughes alone was "responsible for the three five-to-four decisions . . . that have so heavily undermined public and Congressional support for the president's bill" insofar as "[n]ot only did he reverse himself, but he accomplished the much more difficult feat of persuading Justice Roberts to stop nesting with the four diehards and loop the loop with him."[213] Although Hughes's influence on Roberts is problematical, there is no doubt that the political acumen that Hughes acquired as New York's governor, as secretary of state, and as a presidential nominee served him well during the Court-packing crisis.

Ultimately, however, New Deal legislation survived judicial review not because of the threat of Court packing, but because death and resignations produced numerous vacancies that Roosevelt was able to fill with justices who did not disap-point him. Between the spring of 1937 and the time that Hughes retired in June 1941, all four Horsemen left the Court, along with Cardozo and Brandeis. Roose-velt was singularly shrewd and fortunate in his selection of justices, because, as Stone once pointed out, "such appointments are often a lottery, for it is very diffi-cult to predict from a man's past experience just what he will do as a Supreme Court Judge."[214]

Roosevelt's first appointment was Senator Hugo L. Black of Alabama, whose nomination Roosevelt announced on August 12, 1937, nearly three months after Van Devanter's resignation and only three weeks after the Senate shelved the Court-packing proposal. Black, an outspoken populist and ardent advocate of New Deal legislation, including the Court-packing proposal, seemed likely to provide reliable votes in favor of sustaining regulatory legislation. Although liberals could hardly complain about Black's commitment to economic reform, they expressed widespread objections about his qualifications and character. The son of a rural

210. John Lorance, "Law and Supreme Court," *Commonweal*, March 1, 1935, 501.
211. "Address of Chief Justice Hughes," *American Bar Association Journal*, April 1939, 289.
212. Ickes, *Secret Diary*, 2:145.
213. Robert S. Allen, "Hughes Checkmates the President," *Nation*, May 29, 1937, 610.
214. Harlan Fiske Stone to Sterling Carr, December 6, 1932, box 8, Stone Papers.

shopkeeper, the fifty-one-year-old Black had graduated from the University of Alabama Law School and practiced law in Birmingham, where he served as a police court judge and county prosecutor, before his election to the Senate in 1926. The rustic and folksy manner that had served Black so well in Alabama politics grated upon fashionable liberals, who underestimated Black's erudition and ability. An autodidact, Black had compensated for his lack of a college education through a comprehensive and highly disciplined regimen of reading that included the ancient classics and works as diverse as those of Gibbon, Montesquieu, Rousseau, Locke, and Veblen.[215]

Many liberals likewise underestimated Black's commitment to personal liberties. They particularly doubted that an Alabamian would provide justice for racial minorities. Rumors that Black was a Klansman plagued him after his nomination and helped to generate sixteen votes against his confirmation.[216] While Black traveled in Europe before taking his judicial oath, a Pittsburgh newspaper reporter confirmed that Black had joined the Klan during his first Senate race in 1926.[217] After returning to the United States four weeks later, Black admitted during a terse radio address that he had joined the Klan but explained that he had resigned his membership and that he harbored no racial or religious prejudices. Black offered no apology for his Klan membership and never again spoke of it in public. Despite widespread calls for his resignation, Black took his seat three days later as liberals throughout the United States continued to express outrage.[218] One political cartoon depicted a white-robed, hooded Black posing for the Court's official portrait among his black-robed brethren. Once again, Black's critics underestimated this complex man, for Black became one of the most steadfast and eloquent defenders of human rights in the Court's history.

Roosevelt had an opportunity to make a second appointment following Sutherland's retirement in January 1938. As one editorial remarked, "If the proposal for the reconstitution of the court was already dead, this buries it."[219] Sutherland, who had turned seventy-five early in 1937, continued to relish his work and had no major ailment, but he feared that the advancing infirmities of age unduly limited his energies.[220] He probably would have resigned nearly a year earlier, after

215. Gerald S. Dunne, *Hugo Black and the Judicial Revolution* (New York: Simon & Schuster, 1977), 128–29; Howard Ball and Phillip J. Cooper, *Of Power and Right: Hugo Black, William O. Douglas, and America's Constitutional Revolution* (New York: Oxford University Press, 1992), 24.

216. Dunne, *Hugo Black*, 56–59.

217. Roger K. Newman, *Hugo Black: A Biography* (New York: Pantheon Books, 1994), 247–49.

218. Ball and Cooper, *Of Power and Right*, 28–30; Newman, *Hugo Black*, 256–63.

219. "Justice Sutherland Retires from Supreme Court," *Christian Century*, January 19, 1938, 69.

220. George W. Sutherland to Richard R. Lyman, January 21, 1938, box 6, Papers of George W. Sutherland, Manuscript Division, Library of Congress (hereafter cited as Sutherland Papers); Sutherland to Joane Tunbridge, January 18, 1938, box 6, Sutherland Papers; Sutherland to Fred O.D. Meakin, February 13, 1938, box 6, Sutherland Papers; Sutherland to Chief Justice Hughes and Justices McReynolds, Brandeis, Butler, Stone, Roberts, Cardozo, and Black, box 6, Sutherland Papers.

the enactment of the retirement statute, if had he not feared that his resignation during the pendency of the Court-packing bill would appear as a capitulation to political pressure.[221] To replace Sutherland, Roosevelt named Solicitor General Stanley F. Reed, who had successfully argued so many recent cases before the Court on behalf of the administration. Reed's sincere advocacy of New Deal legislation helped to convince Roosevelt of his reliability as a justice, while his respected legal talents, reputation for personal probity, and bland personality spared Roosevelt the controversies and embarrassments of Black's appointment. Nominated only eight days after Sutherland's resignation, Reed was unanimously approved by the Senate ten days later.

Born and raised in a small Kentucky town in 1884, the son of a physician, Reed graduated from Yale College and studied law at Columbia and the Sorbonne before returning to Kentucky to practice in the town of Maysville. Reed went to Washington in 1929 as general counsel of the Federal Farm Board and later served in both the Hoover and Roosevelt administrations as general counsel for the Reconstruction Finance Corporation before becoming solicitor general on March 18, 1935. Although his appointment came after the arguments of the Court's Black Monday decisions of May 1935, Reed unsuccessfully argued in favor of the AAA later that year before going on to win a string of victories during 1937 and 1938.[222] During his nineteen years on the Court, he more than fulfilled Roosevelt's expectations. Reed demonstrated a high level of deference to both Congress and the president in cases involving economic regulation. He was also in step with the post-1937 Court in his frequent championship of First Amendment liberties and the rights of racial minorities, though his deference toward federal antisubversive measures during the McCarthy era and his reluctance to declare school segregation unconstitutional in *Brown* tarnished his reputation as a liberal.

Roosevelt was able to fill the seat of a third Horseman after Butler died suddenly in November 1939. The president reached into his own Cabinet to nominate Attorney General Francis W. Murphy, a former mayor of Detroit, governor of Michigan, and governor-general of the Philippines. Like Butler, Murphy was a midwesterner, an Irish American, and a devout Roman Catholic, but Murphy's political views were poles apart from Butler's. As Peter H. Irons has aptly observed, Murphy was "arguably the most liberal—even radical—justice ever to sit on the Supreme Court."[223] Throughout his life, Murphy strove to promote social and economic justice, particularly for blacks and blue-collar workers. He established generous welfare programs as Detroit's mayor during the depth of the Depression, attempted as governor to mediate the bitter strikes in Michigan's automotive industry, and instituted his own version of the New Deal in the Philippines. As attorney general, Murphy created

---

221. See George W. Sutherland to Lyman, January 21, 1938, box 6, Sutherland Papers.

222. John D. Fassett, *New Deal Justice: The Life of Stanley Reed of Kentucky* (New York: Vantage Press, 1994), 7, 14–15, 33–35, 49–58, 82–195.

223. Peter Irons, "Francis (Frank) William Murphy," in Melvin I. Urofsky, ed., *The Supreme Court Justices: A Biographical Dictionary* (New York: Garland, 1994), 331.

the Civil Rights Division and aggressively prosecuted local officials for corruption and for denial of rights to blacks and labor organizers. Despite Murphy's ardent liberalism, Murphy's nomination to the Court encountered virtually no active opposition and was confirmed by a voice vote.

Murphy probably fulfilled the hopes and expectations of Roosevelt more than any of the other eight justices he appointed. In addition to defending the rights of racial and political minorities and criminal defendants, Murphy wrote many important opinions interpreting the Fair Labors Standards Act in a manner that favored workers. Liberal even by the standards of the "Roosevelt Court," Murphy frequently dissented in civil liberties cases in which the Court sided with the government. More of a politician than a lawyer, Murphy unabashedly allowed his heart to guide his head and did not seem to care whether his judicial opinions crossed the line between law and public policy. A bachelor whose flair for theatrical gestures and rhetoric found expression in his frequent and often strident dissents, he was always something of a misfit on the Court. Wags remarked that justice was "tempered with Murphy" and that Murphy was "the McReynolds of the left."[224] His emotionalism and disregard for judicial craftsmanship have blighted his reputation even among scholars who might be expected to admire his humane constitutionalism, and the shortness of his tenure has further contributed to his relative obscurity. Suffering a fatal heart attack at age fifty-nine, Murphy served only nine years as a justice, contributing little during his final two years, when he was racked with illness.

In addition to filling the seats of the four Horsemen, Roosevelt also appointed successors to Cardozo, who died of a heart attack on July 9, 1938, and Brandeis, who retired on February 13, 1939. Roosevelt replaced Cardozo with another scholar, Harvard law professor Felix Frankfurter, who had served as one of Roosevelt's principal legal and political advisors. Born in Vienna in 1882, Frankfurter arrived in New York at age fourteen. After graduating first in his class at Harvard Law School, Frankfurter worked at a major New York law firm and served as an aide to Secretary of War Henry L. Stimson before accepting a law professorship at Harvard in 1914. Like his friend Brandeis, Frankfurter immersed himself in civil liberties causes, particularly the defense of political radicals such as the alleged Communists that Attorney General Mitchell Palmer sought to deport during the "red scare" of 1919 and the anarchists Nicola Sacco and Bartolomeo Vanzetti, for whom Frankfurter attempted to obtain a new trial after their murder convictions. An outspoken critic of judicial nullification of economic reform legislation, Frankfurter called in 1924 for the abolition of the Fourteenth Amendment, contending that its occasional usefulness on behalf of personal liberties did not outweigh its harm as a weapon against state economic regulation. While Frankfurter privately seems to have opposed Roosevelt's Court-packing plan, he maintained a discreet

<hr>

224. J. Woodford Howard Jr., *Mr. Justice Murphy: A Political Biography* (Princeton, N.J.: Princeton University Press, 1968), 340, 470.

public silence and advised the president on law and strategy during the legislative battle.

Although Frankfurter's nomination encountered vocal opposition among critics of the New Deal and raised the hackles of nativists and anti-Semites,[225] the Senate unanimously confirmed his nomination. During his twenty-three years on the Court, Frankfurter remained committed to judicial restraint even as the Court's activism shifted from economic regulatory legislation to restraints upon civil liberties. While his consistency may have represented a principled theory of judicial power, it placed him increasingly at odds with the liberals whose political views he continued to share and has caused his reputation to suffer. Frankfurter's reputation also is tarnished by his abrasiveness, arrogance, and condescension toward many of his judicial brethren, most of whom he openly regarded as his intellectual inferiors. Frankfurter was, however, steadfast in his respect for Hughes.

Roosevelt replaced Brandeis in 1939 with another liberal activist, William O. Douglas, the chairman of the Securities and Exchange Commission (SEC). An ardent New Dealer, Douglas was a personal friend of Roosevelt's and had taught law at Columbia and Yale before moving in 1934 to the newly established SEC, where he became a commissioner in 1936 and chair in 1937. The son of a Presbyterian minister who died when Douglas was six, he was raised by his mother in penurious circumstances that left him with a lifelong empathy for the poor and the dispossessed. During his thirty-six years on the Court, the longest tenure in the Court's history, Douglas was in the forefront of its defenses of civil liberties in numerous decisions involving speech, religion, race, and criminal procedure. A result-oriented jurist, Douglas was impatient with legal technicalities, and his hastily crafted opinions receive little respect even from scholars who admire his dedication to liberal ideals. Restless on the bench, Douglas was not too reticent to proclaim his views publicly on a wide spectrum of nonjudicial issues, and he became involved in many extrajudicial causes, particularly environmentalism. With the possible exceptions of Black and Murphy, Douglas probably conformed more closely to Roosevelt's expectations than any other justice he appointed. Douglas nearly succeeded Roosevelt as president, for Roosevelt during the 1944 Democratic convention informed party leaders that he wanted his running mate to be either Douglas or Harry Truman.[226]

When Hughes resigned in 1941, every remaining justice except Roberts and Stone had been appointed by Roosevelt, who named more justices than any other president except Washington. Although many justices have disappointed the presidents who have appointed them, every justice appointed by Roosevelt was deferential toward economic regulatory legislation and protective of personal liberties. Roosevelt therefore won his confrontation with the Court through the appointment process even though his Court-packing plan failed.

225. *Hearings before the Senate Committee on the Judiciary on the Nomination of Felix Frankfurter to Be Associate Justice of the Supreme Court of the United States,* 76th Congress, 1st Session (1939), 29, 65, 74–75, 95, 96.

226. Bruce Allen Murphy, *Wild Bill: The Legend and Life of William O. Douglas* (New York: Random House, 2003), 212–232.

5

AFTER THE "REVOLUTION"

Economic Decisions, 1937–1941

The Hughes Court's unwavering deference to Congress in a long line of important decisions during the spring of 1937 provided powerful evidence of a profound shift in the Court's direction. By March 1938 the Court was so restrained in its review of economic legislation that the *Nation* remarked with only partial hyperbole that business interests would attack the Court but for its long previous history of sympathy for economic privilege.[1] The prospect of additional Roosevelt appointments made likely the further consolidation of the Court's new liberal majority. Many contemporaries, however, regarded the Court's future course with much uncertainty. Liberals could not forget past false springs, particularly the periods from 1912 to 1918, and 1930 to 1934. Any number of unforeseen events could tilt the Court back to decisions that stymied regulatory legislation. A shift toward Republicanism among the electorate, a new justice or two who defied Roosevelt's expectations, backsliding by Hughes or Roberts, or bold new activism in the wake of the defeat of Roosevelt's Court-packing plan—these and other circumstances could reverse the "revolution." Despite the continued anxiety of liberals, though, the Court by the time of Hughes's retirement in 1941 had established so powerful a constitutional foundation for the federal regulatory and welfare state that only another "revolution" could reverse its work. Between 1937 and 1941, the Court firmly rejected the doctrine of economic due process in state and federal cases, liberally interpreted federal labor statutes, committed itself to a broad interpretation of the federal commerce power, removed significant impediments to state regulation of commerce, broadly construed the power of the federal and state governments to tax and spend for the public welfare, and sanctioned the expanded power of administrative agencies.

The Court's decision in *West Coast Hotel* signaled the Court's abandonment after 1937 of the Fifth and Fourteenth Amendments as grounds for nullifying economic regulatory legislation. Although the Court invoked substantive due process early in 1938 to strike down a California tax on a Connecticut insurance contract,[2] a few months later the Court, in *United States v. Carolene Products Co.,*

1. "The Court Writes a Labor Code," *Nation*, March 12, 1938, 290.
2. *Connecticut General Life Ins. Co. v. Johnson*, 303 U.S. 77 (1938).

enunciated a broad theory of deference to Congress in rejecting a Fifth Amendment challenge to a federal statute prohibiting interstate shipment of skimmed milk compounded with any fat or oil other than milk fat.[3] As the Court explained, "[T]he existence of facts supporting the legislative judgment is to be presumed, for regulatory legislation affecting ordinary commercial transactions is not to be pronounced unconstitutional unless in the light of the facts made known or generally assumed it is of such a character as to preclude the assumption that it rests upon some rational basis within the knowledge and experience of the legislators."[4] This so-called rational basis standard has remained the Court's foundation for review of economic legislation. As applied by the Court, the test is so deferential that the Court never has invoked it to strike down any state or federal economic regulation. Hughes and Roberts, however, do not appear to have interpreted the test so expansively, for they continued in some cases to deny the constitutionality of economic legislation.[5]

Toward the very end of Hughes's tenure, the Court delivered the coup de grace to the doctrine by which due process had protected liberty of contract. In their unanimous decision in *Olsen v. Nebraska,* the justices sustained the constitutionality of a Nebraska statute permitting an employment agency to obtain no more than 10 percent of the first month's wages of a person for whom the agency had found employment.[6] In expressly rejecting the Taft Court's 1928 decision in *Ribnik v. McBride,*[7] Justice Douglas's opinion explained that later decisions—including *O'Gorman, Nebbia, West Coast Hotel,* and *Darby*—had made clear that the constitutionality of price-fixing legislation did not depend upon whether a public emergency existed or whether the business was "affected with a public interest." Douglas also brushed aside various public policy arguments in opposition to the statute, including the contention that economic forces of competition prevented the agencies from exploiting their clients. The Court was not concerned, Douglas explained, "with the wisdom, need, or appropriateness of the legislation." Such "notions of public policy," he declared, "should not be read into the Constitution."[8]

The Court's deference to state legislatures also manifested itself in cases involving equal protection. In the 1940 decision of *Madden v. Kentucky,* the Court overruled its controversial decision in *Colgate v. Harvey* (1935) by holding that a state did not violate the equal protection clause by imposing a tax of fifty cents per hundred dollars on out-of-state bank deposits while taxing local accounts at only

---

3. 304 U.S. 144 (1938).

4. Ibid., 152.

5. Barry Cushman, "Lost Fidelities," 41 *William and Mary Bill of Rights Law Review* 95 (1999), passim.

6. 313 U.S. 236 (1941).

7. 277 U.S. 350 (1928).

8. 313 U.S. at 245, 246, 246–47.

ten cents per hundred dollars.[9] In a forceful expression of its new attitude of deference toward legislatures, Reed's opinion declared that "in taxation, even more than in most other fields, legislatures possess the greatest freedom in classification. Since the members of a legislature necessarily enjoy a familiarity with local conditions which this Court cannot have, the presumption of constitutionality can be overcome only by the most explicit demonstration that a classification is a hostile and oppressive discrimination against particular persons and classes."[10] Hughes concurred on the grounds that the classification was reasonable, whereas Roberts entered a dissent, joined by McReynolds, in which he relied upon the reasoning of *Colgate.*

The post-1937 Court also demonstrated increased solicitude for the rights of labor in decisions involving the National Labor Relations Act, the Fair Labor Standards Act of 1938, and the Norris–La Guardia Anti-injunction Act of 1932. The Court after 1937 likewise removed antitrust impediments to labor organization and eliminated obstacles to prohibitions against yellow dog contracts. In addition to regularly sustaining the constitutionality of labor legislation during the last years of the Hughes Court, the Court sometimes construed these statutes more broadly than their texts might have required. The Court's growing deference to the rights of labor unions was particularly significant, because union leaders during the early twentieth century so often had complained of judicial antagonism. Although the Court had sustained much labor legislation, it had struck down or limited a number of significant state and federal statutes, while lower federal judges often had enjoined various union activities. Indeed, some scholars have argued that the "Lochner Era" was more a period of judicial antipathy toward labor unions than one of hostility toward state or federal measures designed to protect the public health, safety, welfare, or morals.

The Court upheld the constitutionality of the Norris–La Guardia Act early in 1938 in *Lauf v. E. F. Shinner & Co.,*[11] which confirmed the power of Congress to effectively eliminate the use of the long-feared injunction as a weapon against unionization and other labor activity. Disposing of the constitutional issue in only one sentence, Justice Roberts declared that Congress had the power to define and limit the jurisdiction of the federal courts over injunctions. Roberts's opinion held that a federal judge who had enjoined picketing by a labor union had failed to make the findings required by the statute as a prerequisite for the issuance of an injunction. The judge, who had found only irreparable injury and lack of a legal remedy, had failed to balance the equities or to consider whether law enforcement officials were able and willing to provide adequate protection for the threatened property. Accordingly, the Court remanded the case for additional consideration.[12]

9. 309 U.S. 83 (1940). The Court likewise rejected a privileges and immunities challenge, explaining that "the right to carry out an incident to a trade, business or calling such as the deposit of money in banks is not a privilege of national citizenship." Ibid., 92–93.

10. Ibid., 88.

11. 303 U.S. 323 (1938).

12. Ibid., 329–31.

In a dissent joined by McReynolds, Butler argued that the Norris–La Guardia Act did not apply to picketing of a business whose employees were not members of a union and that the statute would violate the Fifth Amendment's due process clause if it did.[13] The Court's summary disposition of the constitutional issues in *Lauf* masked a considerable controversy over the statute's legality. As Edward A. Purcell Jr. has pointed out, several lower decisions, "stunning in their recalcitrance," had threatened to make the statute a dead letter.[14]

One month after *Lauf,* the Court invoked the Norris–La Guardia Act to over-turn an injunction prohibiting picketing of a grocery store.[15] The pickets alleged that the store, located in a predominately black area of the District of Columbia, deliberately refused to hire African American clerks. In a decision that combined the Court's newfound solicitude for labor with its burgeoning concern for the rights of racial minorities, the Court held there was a labor dispute within the meaning of the statute even though the dispute arose from racial discrimination. Justice Roberts's opinion explained that "[r]ace discrimination by an employer may reasonably be deemed more unfair and less excusable than discrimination against workers on the ground of union affiliation."[16] In a dissent joined by Butler, McReynolds denied that Congress intended to "encourage mobbish interference with the individual's liberty of action."[17]

The scope of the Court's shift in its approach to labor cases also was amply manifest in its decisions liberating labor from the restrictions of the antitrust laws. In its landmark decision in *Apex Hosiery Co. v. Leader* (1940), the Court held that a union could not be liable for damages under the Sherman Antitrust Act where its activities were intended to improve working conditions rather than interfere with free competition in the marketplace.[18] The Court therefore affirmed a reversal of damages against sit-down strikers who had destroyed machinery in the plant they had occupied and forced the suspension of their employer's business. In his opin-ion for the Court, Stone stopped short of overruling earlier precedents, including *Duplex Printing,* which had restricted the Clayton Antitrust Act's labor activity exemption to union activities directed against an employer by its own employees. Hughes dissented in an opinion joined by Roberts and McReynolds, arguing that

13. Ibid., 333–337, 340 (Butler, J., dissenting).

14. Edward A. Purcell Jr., *Brandeis and the Progressive Constitution: Erie, the Judicial Power, and the Politics of the Federal Courts in Twentieth-Century America* (New Haven, Conn.: Yale University Press, 2000), 148. As Purcell has explained, "For six years the fate of the Norris–LaGuardia Act hung in doubt. Its careful draftsmanship and its form as a restriction on jurisdiction, over which Congress admittedly had complete control, seemed to place it on solid constitutional ground. Nevertheless, the fact that it denied equitable relief to persons suffering legal wrong shrouded the status of the act in uncertainty," particularly in view of such decisions as *Truax v. Corrigan* and *Duplex Printing Press Co. v. Deering.* Ibid.

15. *New Negro Grocery Alliance v. Grocery Co.,* 303 U.S. 552 (1938).

16. Ibid., 561.

17. Ibid., 563 (McReynolds, J., dissenting).

18. 310 U.S. 434 (1940).

the Sherman Act should apply to activities that directly interfered with the interstate movement of goods. In response to Stone's warning that the Sherman Act's
application to the case would bring every strike within the act's purview, Hughes
contended that there was a sharp difference between strikes and other legitimate
union activities, as opposed to an effort to block the channels of interstate commerce.[19]

A year later, in *United States v. Hutcheson*, a case involving a secondary boycott,
the Court finally held that labor unions could not be criminally prosecuted for
violations of the Sherman Act.[20] In his opinion for the Court, Frankfurter found
that the Norris–La Guardia Act was intended to reject *Duplex Printing* by removing
labor union activity entirely from the scope of the antitrust laws. In a concurring
opinion, Stone relied upon *Apex* in concluding that the union had not restrained
trade, but he refused to endorse Frankfurter's sweeping construction of Norris–
LaGuardia,[21] preferring what Stone's biographer described as "a more cautious,
empirical approach" that kept "the old line of precedents behind the door—just
in case."[22] In a dissent joined by Hughes, Roberts argued even more forcefully
than Stone that Norris–La Guardia had not removed union activity from the antitrust laws, and he contended that the secondary boycott clearly restrained interstate commerce.[23]

A week after *Hutcheson*, the Court held that a state could not enjoin picketing
in secondary boycotts.[24] Frankfurter's opinion for the Court declared, "A state
cannot exclude workingmen from peacefully exercising the right of free communication by drawing the circle of economic competition between employers and
workers so small as to contain only an employer and those directly employed by
him. The interdependence of economic interest of all engaged in the same industry has become a commonplace."[25] Roberts and Hughes dissented on technical
grounds.

In a companion case, however, the Court sustained a state's right to enjoin
union picketing that tended to promote violence.[26] Rejecting the union's free
speech claim, Frankfurter declared in his opinion that "the Fourteenth Amendment still leaves the state ample discretion in dealing with manifestations of force
in the settlement of industrial conflicts," particularly because the National Labor
Relations Board had power to enjoin picketing in the face of violence. Frankfurter
declared that "nothing in the Fourteenth Amendment . . . prevents a state . . .
from placing confidence in a chancellor's decree and compels it to rely exclusively

19. Ibid., 529 (Hughes, C.J., dissenting).

20. 312 U.S. 219 (1941).

21. Ibid., 237 (Stone, J., concurring).

22. Alpheus Thomas Mason, *Harlan Fiske Stone: Pillar of the Law* (New York: Viking,
1956), 500.

23. 312 U.S. 243–46 (Roberts, J., dissenting).

24. *A.F. of L. v. Swing*, 312 U.S. 321 (1941).

25. Ibid., 326.

26. *Milk Drivers Union v. Meadowmoor Dairies*, 312 U.S. 287 (1941).

on a policeman's club."[27] Frankfurter, who had fiercely criticized the labor injunction in a book that he had coauthored in 1930,[28] went out of his way to praise principles of free speech and express opposition to unfettered use of injunctions in labor disputes. He emphasized, however, that violence undermines freedom of speech. Expressing his general philosophy of judicial deference to legislatures, Frankfurter pointed out that if Illinois citizens wished "to withdraw the use of the injunction in labor controversies, the democratic process for legislative reform is at their disposal."[29] In dissent, Black, Douglas, and Reed conceded the state's power to enjoin violence, but contended that in this case the threat of violence was insufficient to justify the injunction.[30]

In one of its final decisions, the Hughes Court overturned whatever remained of its decisions striking down state and federal prohibitions against yellow dog contracts. In *Phelps Dodge v. National Labor Relations Board*,[31] the Court held that an employer subject to the National Labor Relations Act could not refuse to hire an employee solely because he or she was affiliated with a labor union. Frankfurter declared that *Coppage* and *Adair* were "completely sapped . . . of their authority,"[32] whereas Stone and Hughes disagreed with the Court's conclusion that the National Labor Relations Act authorized a court to reinstate an employee who had found other employment or to order an employer to hire persons whom he never had employed. Roberts took no part in the decision.

The dissents of Hughes and Roberts in so many of these labor cases provides support for the thesis that they did not "switch" sides or undergo any metamorphosis in 1937 or afterward. Labor's victories in the Court appear to have resulted more from changes in the Court's personnel than from any "revolution."

In decisions following its 1937 *Jones & Laughlin Steel* decision sustaining the constitutionality of the National Labor Relations Act, the Court continued to interpret that statute broadly. In a 1938 decision, for example, the Court held that the statute's prohibition on company unions permitted the National Labor Relations Board to require an employer to withdraw recognition of a company union.[33]

The Court's National Labor Relations Board decisions were particularly significant because so many of them involved expansive interpretations of congressional power under the commerce clause. In *Jones & Laughlin Steel*, the Court had declared, "We are asked to shut our eyes to the plainest facts of our national life

27. Ibid., 295.

28. Felix Frankfurter and Nathan Greene, *The Labor Injunction* (New York: MacMillan, 1930).

29. 312 U.S. at 299.

30. Ibid., 299–317 (Black, J., dissenting); ibid., 317–21 (Reed, J., dissenting). Justice Douglas joined Black's dissent.

31. 313 U.S. 177 (1941).

32. Ibid., 187.

33. *NLRB v. Pennsylvania Greyhound Lines*, 303 U.S. 261 (1938).

and to deal with the question of direct and indirect effects in an intellectual vacuum . . . We have often said that interstate commerce itself is a practical conception. It is equally true that interference with that commerce must be appraised by a judgement that does not ignore actual experience."[34] In the same decision, however, Hughes warned that the scope of the commerce power "must be considered in the light of our dual system of government and may not be so extended as to embrace effects upon interstate commerce so indirect and remote that to embrace them . . . would effectually obliterate the distinction between what is national and what is local and create a completely centralized government."[35] The Court's labor decisions after *Jones* demonstrated the Court's willingness to continue to acknowledge the practical realities of a national labor market while remaining sensitive to the exigencies of federalism.

The Court reiterated and clarified the commerce clause doctrine of *Jones & Laughlin Steel* in 1938 in *Santa Cruz Fruit Packing Co. v. Labor Board,* applying the National Labor Relations Act to a fruit-canning company that shipped only about 37 percent of its products out of state.[36] Hughes explained that the issue was "whether the unfair labor practices involved have such a close and substantial relation to the freedom of interstate commerce from injurious restraint that these practices may constitutionally be made the subject of federal cognizance through provisions looking to the peaceable adjustment of labor disputes." Although Hughes's opinion disdained "mathematical or rigid formulas," the chief justice concluded that "[i]t would be difficult to find a case in which unfair labor practices had a more direct effect upon interstate and foreign commerce."[37] The Court's finding that the labor activities involved interstate commerce may have been influenced by the fact that the employees were engaged not in production but rather in the initial stages of interstate marketing and transportation. Hughes again claimed that the Court was not overruling *Carter Coal* since some intrastate activities remained beyond the scope of federal regulation, but Butler and McReynolds dissented on the ground that the Court's ruling was inconsistent with that decision.[38] Many contemporary observers likewise had difficulty reconciling the two decisions.[39]

The Court interpreted the commerce clause even more expansively in two later NLRA cases in which the employers sold all of their products within a single state. As in *Jones* and *Santa Cruz*, the Court emphasized the interstate implications of industrial strife. In upholding the act's application to an electric company in *Consolidated Edison v. National Labor Relations Board,* Hughes's opinion for the Court explained that the criterion for application of the statute was "the effect upon

34. 301 U.S. at 41–42.

35. Ibid., 37.

36. 303 U.S. 453 (1938).

37. Ibid., 467, 469.

38. Ibid., 469–70 (Butler, J., dissenting).

39. See, for example, Note, "Interstate Commerce Jurisdiction of NLRB," 47 *Yale Law Journal* 1221, 1222 (May 1938).

interstate or foreign commerce, not the source of the injury."[40] Disruption of electrical power, the justices found, would affect radio and telegraph services, lighthouses, an airport, federal buildings, interstate railroads and other interstate operations to which the company sold power. "[I]t cannot be maintained," Hughes explained, "that the exertion of federal power must await the disruption of that commerce."[41] In a dissent joined by McReynolds, Butler relied upon *Schechter* and *Carter Coal* in arguing that "the activities of the employers and their employees were exclusively local."[42]

The following year, in *NLRB v. Fainblatt,* the Court applied the NLRA to a women's sports garment manufacturer that made all of its clothes in New Jersey.[43] Stone's opinion explained that "interstate commerce was involved in the transportation of the materials to be processed across state lines to the factory . . . and in the transportation of the finished product to points outside the state for distribution to purchasers and ultimate consumers." In a possible effort to exorcise *Schechter,* Stone rejected the factory's argument that the statute was inapplicable because the volume of commerce was small. "The power of Congress to regulate interstate commerce," Stone observed, "is plenary and extends to all such commerce be it great or small." Noting the "long and tragic history of industrial strife" in the garment industry, Stone pointed out that Congress presumably intended to include even small factories within the statute's scope.[44] The six-to-two margin by which the Court decided *Fainblatt* masked divisions within the Court concerning the scope of federal power under the commerce clause. Stone's opinion represented an elaborate compromise to accommodate a spectrum of views ranging from Roberts's relatively narrow interpretation of the commerce clause to Black's highly expansive vision.[45] In a dissent joined by Butler, McReynolds contended that the Court's interpretation of commerce would permit Congress to regulate any economic activity, and he warned that "curtailment of the independence reserved to the states and the tremendous enlargement of federal power denote the serious impairment of the very foundation of our federated system."[46]

The post-1937 Court did not always interpret the National Labor Relations Act in a manner that pleased organized labor. Early in 1939, the Court ruled in favor of employers in three decisions that involved issues of statutory interpretation or evidence rather than the scope of the commerce clause. In *NLRB v. Fansteel Metallurgical Corp.,* the Court held that the National Labor Relations Board had no power to order reinstatement of employees who were fired for engaging in

---

40. 305 U.S. 197, 222 (1938).

41. Ibid., 220–21, 222.

42. Ibid., 241 (Butler, J., dissenting).

43. 306 U.S. 601 (1939).

44. Ibid., 605, 606, 607–8.

45. Barry Cushman, *Rethinking the New Deal Court: The Structure of a Constitutional Revolution* (New York: Oxford University Press, 1998), 186–90.

46. 306 U.S. 614 (McReynolds, J., dissenting).

illegal acts by seizing factory buildings during a sit-down strike.[47] Although the
Wagner Act stated that nothing in it "shall be construed so as to interfere with or
impede or diminish in any way the right to strike," Hughes's opinion for the Court
in *Fansteel* declared that "this recognition of 'the right to strike' plainly contemplates a lawful strike," the "unquestioned right to quit work." The policy behind
the National Labor Relations Act was to promote industrial peace and "not a line
in the statute" encouraged employees "to resort to force and violence in defiance
of the law of the land."[48] In a dissent joined by Black, Reed argued that the board
could reinstate the employees because their lawlessness was a response to unlawful
antiunion activities by their employer.[49]

The Court likewise refused to defer to the evidentiary findings of judges in
National Labor Relations Act cases. On the same day that the Court decided *Fansteel*, it also held that the National Labor Relations Board lacked sufficient evidence to conclude that an employer had to reinstate employees because it had
failed to bargain with their union.[50] The Court concluded that the employer could
properly refuse to bargain with labor conciliators because they did not represent
the employees. Although the statute stated that the board's findings of fact, "if
supported by the evidence, shall be conclusive," Stone's opinion for the Court
explained that "[s]ubstantial evidence is more than a scintilla, and must do more
than create a suspicion of the existence of the fact to be established."[51] The
Court's opinion therefore suggested that the Court would begin to undertake
more aggressive reviews of the decisions of administrative agencies. In dissent,
Black and Reed contended that the Board could reasonably have concluded that
the conciliators were acting at the behest of the union.[52] In another decision, the
Court held that the National Labor Relations Board lacked evidence to support
its conclusion that an employer had improperly interfered with labor organizations and collective bargaining when it terminated union members in response
to a union demand that the company abandon its seniority policy.[53] The Court
concluded that the discharges were proper because the union demands violated
their contract, which gave the employer the right to operate its plant on the basis
of seniority. Black and Reed dissented without opinion.

Liberals and union leaders decried these decisions and expressed fear that the
Court was reverting to its old conservatism. The journalist I. F. Stone alleged that

47. 306 U.S. 240 (1939).

48. Ibid., 256, 257–58.

49. Ibid., 265–68 (Reed, J., dissenting).

50. *NLRB v. Columbian Enameling & Stamping Co.*, 306 U.S. 292 (1939).

51. Ibid., 300.

52. Ibid., 303–4 (Black, J., dissenting).

53. *NLRB v. Sands Manufacturing Co.*, 306 U.S. 332 (1939). The *Nation* warned that "[i]f
breaches of contract can be so easily established, labor must prepare itself for a terrific
onslaught in the courts," and lamented that "these three decisions plainly imply that it is
the courts which will decide when a strike is lawful." "The Court Reverts," *Nation*, March 11,
1939, 281.

"[t]he court, which follows liberal election returns only at a great distance and most unwillingly, set off at a gallop at the first whiff of reaction in the hope that the 1940 election returns will follow the court."[54] Similarly, the *Nation* worried that "the liberal phase which began under the impact of the president's court plan was merely a strategic retreat. The court has been encouraged by the revival of reaction to serve again as the chief instrument of propertied interests in combating progressive legislation."[55] Such fears ultimately were misplaced, of course, but it is understandable that organized labor and liberals during the years immediately following 1937 were unconvinced that the Court had indeed altered its approach toward labor and regulatory legislation.

Despite such misgivings among many advocates of organized labor, the Court's willingness to interpret broadly the National Labor Relations Act emboldened Congress to enact the Fair Labor Standards Act of 1938, the last major New Deal legislation, which established a federal minimum wage and prescribed uniform national limitations on working hours.[56] In its landmark February 1941 decision in *United States v. Darby*, the Court without dissent upheld provisions of the Fair Labor Standards Act of 1938 that prohibited the interstate shipment of goods produced by employees who earned less than twenty-five cents per hour or who worked more than forty-four hours per week.[57]

Darby offered an even more expansive scope for federal regulation of interstate commerce than the Court had provided in decisions such as *Carolene Products*, upholding restrictions on interstate shipment of harmful products, and its 1937 *Kentucky Whip* decision, permitting Congress to prohibit interstate shipment of products in aid of state regulation. In his opinion for the Court in *Darby*, Stone stated that the commerce power extended not only to regulation of commerce among the states, but also to intrastate commerce that affects interstate commerce. Because Congress could regulate interstate commerce in the same manner in which the states exercised the police power, Congress could properly as a matter of public policy regulate "interstate commerce competition in the distribution

54. I. F. Stone, "The Greatest Strike-Breaker of All," *Nation*, March 25, 1939, 346. Stone complained that the decisions played into the hands of Marxists who taught that "the state is the instrument of a ruling class and that government instrumentalities—whatever the good intentions of those who set them up—must ultimately become new means of exploiting and oppressing the less privileged orders of our society, whether workers, farmers, consumers, small investors, or little business men." Ibid., 347.

55. "The Court Reverts," *Nation*, March 11, 1939, 280. The *Nation* declared that "[t]he court, in accordance with a pattern all too familiar . . . has entered on the task of transforming a law meant to aid the less powerful into a means of oppressing them. The judicial veto is more spectacular, but what one might term the process of judicial erosion is as effective in destroying legislation that does not meet with the court's approval," as when the Court narrowly construed the antitrust laws and utility regulations. Ibid., 281.

56. Melvin I. Urofsky and Paul Finkelman, *A March of Liberty: A Constitutional History of the United States*, vol. 2, *From 1877 to the Present*, 2d ed. (New York: Oxford University Press, 2002), 702.

57. *United States v. Darby*, 312 U.S. 100 (1941).

of goods produced under substandard labor conditions." Stone explained that "[t]he motive and purpose of a regulation of interstate commerce are matters for the legislative judgment upon . . . which the Constitution places no restriction and over which the courts are given no control."[58] Although Hughes regarded the statute as "borderline," he refrained from expressing his reservations in a concurring or dissenting opinion.[59]

In rejecting a Tenth Amendment challenge to the Fair Labor Standards Act, the Court in *Darby* made clear that it would not regard the enigmatic Tenth Amendment as providing any independent limitation upon federal power. Reducing the Tenth Amendment to a virtual redundancy, Stone declared that it "states but a truism that all is retained which has not been surrendered. There is nothing in the history of its adoption to suggest that it was more than declaratory of the relationship between the national and state governments as it had been established by the Constitution before the amendment or that its purpose was other than to allay fears that the new national government might seek to exercise powers not granted, and that the states might not be able to exercise fully their reserved powers."[60]

Darby also provided a belated but welcome victory for opponents of child labor, for the Court's decision upholding the wages and hours provisions of the NLRA implicitly sustained the statute's prohibition on the interstate movement of goods produced by children. More specifically, Stone declared that the Court's notorious 1918 decision in *Hammer v. Dagenhart* striking down a child labor law "was a departure from the principles which have prevailed in the interpretation of the commerce clause both before and since the decision. . . . It should be and now is overruled."[61] Liberals warned, however, that *Darby* should not diminish support for the Child Labor Amendment, which they believed was still needed to eliminate child labor in intrastate businesses.[62]

In addition to its broad interpretation of the commerce clause in labor cases, the Court likewise expansively defined interstate commerce in cases involving other forms of economic regulation. In a 1941 decision, for example, the Court held that federal construction of a dam on the Red River in Texas and Oklahoma was within the commerce power and did not invade the sovereignty of any state in contravention of the Tenth Amendment.[63] Espousing the Court's newfound deference to Congress, Justice Douglas in his unanimous opinion for the Court

58. Ibid., 114–15, 115.

59. Mason, *Harlan Fiske Stone,* 551. For contrasting interpretations of Hughes's reservations, see Richard D. Friedman, "The Sometimes-Bumpy Stream of Commerce," 55 *Arkansas Law Review* 981, 999–1000 (2003); Barry Cushman, "Small Differences?" 55 *Arkansas Law Review* 1097, 1138–42 (2003).

60. 312 U.S. at 124.

61. Ibid., 116–17.

62. *Nation,* February 15, 1941, 170.

63. *Oklahoma v. Atkinson Co.,* 313 U.S. 509 (1941).

explained that, although the extent to which the project would ameliorate flooding was conjectural, "such matters raise not constitutional issues but questions of policy. They relate to the wisdom, need, and effectiveness of a particular project. They are therefore questions for the Congress, not the courts." Douglas similarly explained that the Court must abstain from considering "whether the resulting benefits to commerce as a result of this particular exercise . . . of the commerce power outweigh the costs of the undertaking."[64]

The Court likewise propounded an expansive definition of interstate commerce in cases involving agriculture. In its 1939 decision in *Currin v. Wallace,* the Court upheld the Tobacco Inspection Act of 1935, which required federal inspection and certification of tobacco sold at auctions for interstate sale.[65] In his opinion for the Court, Hughes explained that "[t]he fact that intrastate and interstate transactions are commingled on the tobacco market does not frustrate or restrict the congressional power,"[66] an echo of Hughes's opinion in the *Shreveport Rate Cases* in 1914 that the Interstate Commerce Commission could regulate intrastate rates that directly affected interstate commerce. Butler and McReynolds dissented without opinion.

In a brief opinion two months later, in *Mulford v. Smith,* the Court sustained the constitutionality of the Agricultural Adjustment Act of 1938, another law enacted by a Congress emboldened by the judicial revolution of the previous year.[67] With the Court in *Butler* having disapproved of the use of the taxing power as a means of regulating agriculture, Congress in enacting the second AAA had relied upon the commerce power. The Court rejected the contention of tobacco farmers that Congress lacked power to stimulate price increases by imposing penalties on farmers whose marketing exceeded quotas set by the secretary of agriculture. Auction warehouses deducted the penalty from the proceeds of tobacco marketed in excess of the quota and remitted the penalty to the federal government. Roberts, who had written the opinion striking down the first AAA in *Butler,* concluded in his brief opinion for the Court that the statute regulated interstate commerce rather than production, which the Court regarded as a local activity beyond Congress's competency to regulate.

Roberts explained that the statute did "not purport to control production," setting "no limit upon the acreage which may be planted or produced" and imposing "no penalty for the planting and producing of tobacco in excess of the marketing quota." Moreover, farmers remained free to store and sell in a later year tobacco that exceeded the marketing quota. Instead, Roberts found that the statute "purports to be solely a regulation of interstate commerce, which it reaches and affects at the throat where tobacco enters the stream of commerce—the marketing warehouse." Congress, Roberts explained, had the power to "foster, protect

64. Ibid., 526–27, 527, 528.
65. 306 U.S. 1 (1939).
66. Ibid., 11.
67. 307 U.S. 38 (1939).

and conserve" interstate commerce "or to prevent the flow of commerce from working harm to the people of the nation." Although Roberts acknowledged that some of the tobacco on which the quota was imposed was marketed only intrastate, he pointed out that "at least two-thirds of all flue-cured tobacco sold at auction warehouses is sold for immediate shipment to an interstate or foreign destination." "Regulation to be effective," he averred, "must . . . apply to all sales." Circumventing the problem that Congress had regulated commerce in tobacco for the obvious purpose of limiting its production, Roberts declared that the "motive of Congress in exerting the power is irrelevant to the validity of the legislation." In a dissent joined by McReynolds, Butler asserted that "[i]t is wholly fallacious to say that the penalty is not imposed upon production. The farmer raises tobacco only for sale. Punishment for selling is the exact equivalent of punishment for raising the tobacco."[68]

The Court's expansive interpretation of interstate commerce was especially manifest in two decisions in which the Court upheld minimum milk prices set by the secretary of agriculture pursuant to the Agricultural Marketing Act of 1937, which Congress had enacted in response to *Butler*'s invalidation of the Agricultural Adjustment Act.[69] Rejecting the argument that sales by dairy farmers to rural plants was a local transaction that was completed before any interstate commerce commenced, Justice Reed's opinion for the Court in *United States v. Royal Rock Co-op* explained that "where commodities are bought for use beyond state lines, the sale is a part of interstate commerce," which may be dependent upon activities "conducted within state lines." Reed declared that "Where local and foreign milk alike are drawn into a general plan for protecting the interstate commerce in the commodity from the interferences, burdens and obstructions, arising from excessive surplus and the social and sanitary evils of low values, the power of the Congress extends also to the local sales." Echoing the Court's landmark decisions in *Gibbons v. Ogden* and the *Minnesota Rate Cases*, Reed observed, "This power over commerce when it exists is complete and perfect."[70] The decision also represented an application of the *Shreveport* doctrine beyond businesses affected with a public interest. Invoking substantive due process, Roberts and Hughes dissented on the ground that the regulations violated the Fifth Amendment by causing "disastrous" harm to small milk handlers who sold milk only within the regulated market area.[71]

The distinction between production and pricing likewise was critical to the Court's 1940 decision sustaining the constitutionality of the Bituminous Coal Conservation Act, which Congress had reenacted in 1937 in the wake of *Carter Coal*.[72]

68. Ibid., 47, 51, 48, 47, 48, 53.

69. *United States v. Rock Royal Co-operative, Inc.*, 307 U.S. 533 (1939); *H. P. Hood & Sons, Inc. v. United States*, 307 U.S. 588 (1939).

70. Ibid., 569.

71. Ibid., 583–87 (Roberts, J., dissenting).

72. *Sunshine Anthracite Coal Co. v. Adkins*, 310 U.S. 381 (1940).

To circumvent *Carter Coal*'s ruling that the statute's labor regulations affected production that did not involve interstate commerce, Congress had limited the new statute to regulation of prices, unfair trade practices, and marketing rules, the constitutionality of which *Carter Coal* had not considered. In upholding the new statute in *Sunshine Anthracite Coal Co. v. Adkins,* the Court quoted with approval Cardozo's statement in his dissenting opinion in *Carter Coal* that "[t]o regulate the price for such transactions is to regulate commerce itself, and not alone its antecedent conditions or its ultimate consequences."[73] *Darby* later effectively overturned whatever part of *Carter Coal* might have survived *Sunshine Coal.*

As in *Jones, Royal Rock,* and so many of its other recent commerce clause decisions, the Court in *Sunshine Coal* found that the history of economic turmoil warranted federal regulation of an industry that once only the states had regulated. Although Douglas's opinion for the Court averred that policy issues and "the wisdom of the legislation" were "matters which are not our concern," Douglas found that federal intervention in the coal industry was justified by "[o]verproduction and savage, competitive warfare" that "wasted the industry" at the expense of both labor and capital. "Financial distress among operators and acute poverty among miners prevailed even during periods of general prosperity. This history of the bituminous coal industry is written in blood as well as in ink." Citing *Rock Royal,* Douglas explained that the commerce clause empowered Congress "to undertake stabilization of an interstate industry through a process of price-fixing which safeguards the public interest by placing price control in the hands of its administrative representative." Summarizing the Court's post-1937 philosophy in cases involving economic regulation, Douglas warned that the Court should refrain from "trespassing on the legislative domain."[74] Only McReynolds dissented. Perhaps recognizing that he was fighting a lost cause and having expressed his objections to similar legislation in earlier dissents, McReynolds wrote no opinion.

Although congressional legislation regulating agriculture encouraged producers and distributors to enter into agreements to conform to federal regulations, such businesses remained subject to the restrictions of the antitrust laws. In a 1939 decision, the Court held that the Agricultural Marketing Act did not displace the Sherman Antitrust Act with respect to agreements among producers and distributors restricting interstate commerce in milk to which the Department of Agriculture had not given its approval. The Court similarly held that the Capper-Volstead Act's provisions for agricultural producers to act collectively in preparing, handling, and marketing their products remained subject to the Sherman Act.[75]

The Court likewise sustained congressional regulation pursuant to the commerce power in the 1938 decision of *Electric Bond and Share Company v. S.E.C.,* sustaining the registration provisions of the Public Utility Holding Company Act of 1935.[76] Writing for the majority, Hughes found that large holding companies

73. Ibid., 394, quoting 298 U.S. at 326.
74. Ibid., 395, 396, 394.
75. *United States v. Borden,* 308 U.S. 188 (1939).
76. 303 U.S. 419 (1938).

were engaged in interstate commerce and he declared that "from these defendants, with their highly important relation to interstate commerce and the
national economy, Congress was entitled to demand the fullest information as to
organization, financial structure and all the activities which could have any bearing upon the exercise of congressional authority."[77] The justices refrained from
considering the constitutionality of other provisions of the statute, which the Securities and Exchange Commission had not yet enforced. McReynolds dissented
alone without opinion, with Butler joining the majority.

In addition to its expansive definition of congressional power over commerce,
the Hughes Court during its final years likewise provided an expansive view of the
power of the dormant commerce clause, permitting states more leeway to enact
legislation affecting interstate commerce in the absence of federal regulation. In
contrast with its decisions on the scope of federal legislation, most of these decisions were unanimous. Some of these decisions were easy and could have been
decided the same way before the judicial revolution. As McReynolds observed in
a decision in which the Court unanimously held that Indiana did not violate the
commerce clause by providing regulations for the prompt disposal of animal carcasses, "The mere power of the Federal Government to regulate interstate commerce does not disable the States from adopting reasonable measures designed
to secure the health and comfort of their people."[78] Other decisions, however,
departed from earlier Hughes Court decisions that had more restrictively interpreted the power of the states.

The Court's approach to the scope of the so-called dormant commerce clause
was exemplified by *South Carolina Highway Department v. Barnwell Brothers,* in which
the justices sustained a statute that barred from South Carolina's highways trucks
wider than ninety inches and weighing more than ten tons.[79] Even though 85–90
percent of the trucks in interstate commerce were ninety-six inches wide and
weighed more than ten tons, the justices found that the statute did not unduly
intrude upon interstate commerce in the absence of any federal regulation. The
statute, moreover, was a proper exercise of the police power insofar as South Carolina's highways were so narrow that the prohibited vehicles could cause safety
problems. In his opinion, from which no justice dissented, Stone emphasized that
states financed their own highways, and he explained that regulation of state highways was "peculiarly of local concern," even though such regulation inevitably
affected interstate commerce. Stone also emphasized that the statute did not "discriminate against" interstate commerce.[80]

As Stephen Gardbaum has explained, the *Barnwell* decision commenced a
phase during which the Court rejected its earlier "nationalist concept of the Commerce Clause as mandating a common market . . . in favor of one that effectively

77. Ibid., 441.
78. *Clason v. Indiana,* 306 U.S. 442, 444 (1939).
79. 303 U.S. 177 (1938).
80. Ibid., 187, 189–96.

understood the clause as establishing only a customs union among the states, so that the only limitation it placed on their sovereignty was the duty of nondiscrimination against out-of-state goods. This represented a very significant enhancement of state power."[81] From 1938 until 1945, the Court rejected most dormant commerce clause challenges to state regulations. Although it has retreated somewhat from *Barnwell* since 1945 in decisions that attempt to balance state and federal interests, the Court has continued to cleave more closely to *Barnwell*'s nondiscrimination standard than to the nationalism that characterized decisions prior to the Hughes Court.[82]

The Court reaffirmed *Barnwell* in a unanimous 1939 decision that upheld a Kentucky law permitting transportation of intoxicating liquors only by licensed carriers. The justices determined that the Twenty-first Amendment, which permits states to legislate regulation of intoxicating liquors, constituted an independent source of authority[83] within the meaning of *Barnwell's* conclusion that a state could impose some burden on interstate commerce pursuant to "an inseparable incident of the exercise of a legislative authority which, under the Constitution, has been left to the states."[84]

Similarly, the Court in a 1940 decision, *Milk Board v. Eisenberg Co.*, upheld a Pennsylvania statute requiring milk dealers to obtain licenses, post bonds, and pay minimum prices prescribed by an administrative agency.[85] The Court concluded that the law did not run afoul of the commerce clause, because only a small share of the state's milk production was exported and the statute's effect on interstate commerce was incidental. As Roberts explained in his opinion, "Every state police statute necessarily will affect interstate commerce in some degree, but such a statute does not run counter to the grant of Congressional power merely because it incidentally or indirectly involves or burdens interstate commerce." Roberts distinguished *Baldwin v. Seeling* on the grounds that the statute in that case attempted to regulate out-of-state prices and thus constituted a tariff.[86] Butler and McReynolds dissented.

In a unanimous decision during its final weeks, *California v. Thompson,* the Hughes Court rejected a commerce clause challenge to a state statute requiring highway travel agents, who arranged for both intrastate and interstate transportation, to obtain a license and file a bond.[87] In his opinion for the Court, Stone at last was free to write into law the substance of his 1927 dissent in *DiSanto,* which had struck down a state law requiring licenses to sell steamship tickets. Stone

81. Stephen Gardbaum, "New Deal Nationalism and the Unshackling of the States," 64 *University of Chicago Law Review* 520–21 (1997).

82. Ibid., 521. The Court began to apply its balancing test in *Southern Pacific Railroad Co. v. Arizona*, 325 U.S. 761 (1945).

83. *Ziffrin, Inc. v. Reeves*, 308 U.S., 138–41 (1939)

84. Ibid., at 141, quoting 303 U.S., 189.

85. 306 U.S. 346 (1939).

86. Ibid., 351, 353.

87. 313 U.S. 109 (1941).

explained that during the years "[s]ince the decision in that case this Court has been repeatedly called upon to examine the constitutionality of numerous local regulations affecting interstate motor vehicle traffic. It has uniformly held that in the absence of pertinent Congressional legislation there is constitutional power in the states to regulate interstate commerce by motor vehicle wherever it affects the safety of the public or the safety and convenient use of its highways, provided only that the regulation does not in any other respect unnecessarily obstruct interstate commerce." As Stone declared, "[T]he Commerce Clause, in conferring on Congress power to regulate commerce, did not wholly withdraw from the states the power to regulate matters of local concern with respect to which Congress has not exercised its power, even though the regulation affects interstate commerce." The type of fraud that the statute in question was designed to prevent was "peculiarly a subject of local concern and the appropriate subject of local regulation" because "[i]n every practical sense regulation of such conduct is beyond the effective reach of Congressional action."[88]

The Hughes Court during its later years also began to adopt a less restrictive view of the commerce clause in cases involving the power of states to impose taxes. These decisions served as the foundation for the contemporary doctrine, more fully developed in post–Hughes Court decisions, that states generally may tax interstate commerce related to activities in their states unless there is a threat of double taxation or discrimination against interstate commerce. As one commentary remarked in 1940, the Court during the past three years had upheld a "veritable catalogue of state taxes, with peculiarities of assessment, unique schemes of classification, [and] out-of-state complications . . . against claims of 'deprivation of property,' 'denial of equal protection,' [and] 'burden upon interstate commerce.'"[89]

The Court in 1938, for example, held that New Mexico's 2 percent tax on the advertising revenue of newspapers and magazines published within the state was valid even when such publications were circulated in other states and derived revenue from out-of-state advertisers.[90] Stone's opinion emphasized that the tax did not burden interstate commerce because other states could not impose a cumulative tax, and because the business of preparing and publishing the advertising was essentially local. Stone observed that "[i]t was not the purpose of the commerce clause to relieve those engaged in interstate commerce from their just share of state tax burden even though it increases the cost of doing the business."[91]

The Court also unanimously sustained a Virginia tax on vehicles operated by peddlers because the tax was imposed equally upon local and out-of-state peddlers.[92] Although local businesses tended to be exempt from the tax because they

88. Ibid., 115–16, 113, 115.

89. Walton Hamilton and George Braden, "The Supreme Court Today," *New Republic,* August 5, 1940, 179.

90. *Western Live Stock v. Bureau of Revenue,* 303 U.S. 250 (1938).

91. Ibid., 260, 254.

92. *Caskey Baking Co. v. Virginia,* 313 U.S. 117 (1941).

paid other state taxes, the Court pointed out that invalidation of the tax would make "peddlers the only vendors in Virginia to escape some form of taxation."[93] Similarly, the Court held that a Louisiana tax on production of natural gas that was transported in interstate commerce did not burden interstate commerce because no other state could tax its production.[94] Although Reed's opinion acknowledged that the tax added to the cost of interstate commerce, this alone did not constitute an undue interference.[95] The Court again applied this "multiple burden" rule in sustaining New York City's 2 percent sales tax in a case involving the sale of coal mined in Pennsylvania. Stone's decision explained that the tax did not impose an undue burden on interstate commerce insofar as the tax "was conditioned upon a local activity" and neither discriminated against or obstructed interstate commerce.[96] In a dissent joined by Roberts and McReynolds, Hughes contended that the interstate transportation of the coal into New York was an integral part of the transaction and that the tax therefore was similar to a tariff.[97]

Despite these decisions, the Court continued to invalidate state taxation of interstate transactions that threatened multiple taxation, in the absence of apportionment between or among the affected states.[98] As Michael E. Parrish has observed, "Hughes and his brethren failed to articulate a magic formula capable of subsuming the myriad taxation schemes generated by the Great Depression. Their use of such of such concepts as 'multiple burdens' or 'local incidents' to justify some state taxes while overturning others failed to convince many critics."[99] Their principal critic was Black, who urged the Court to defer to Congress. As Black wrote in one of his dissents, "Only a comprehensive survey and investigation of the entire national economy—which Congress alone has powers and facilities to make—can indicate the need for, as well as justify, restricting the taxing power of a State so as to provide against conjectural taxation by more than one State on identical income."[100]

In 1939, for example, the Court unanimously struck down a Florida statute imposing an inspection fee on cement from out of state, while requiring no inspection of local cement.[101] In his opinion for the majority, Frankfurter

93. Ibid., 121 (Hughes, C.J., dissenting).

94. *Coverdale v. Arkansas-Louisiana Pipe Line Co.*, 303 U.S. 604 (1938). Only McReynolds dissented.

95. Ibid., 612.

96. *McGoldrick v. Berwind-White Coal Mining Co.*, 309 U.S. 33, 58 (1940).

97. Ibid., 59–70.

98. *Adams Manufacturing Co. v. Storen*, 304 U.S. 307 (1938); *Gwin, White & Prince, Inc. v. Henneford*, 305 U.S. 434 (1939).

99. Michael E. Parrish, *The Hughes Court: Justices, Rulings, and Legacy* (Santa Barbara, Calif.: ABC-CLIO, 2002), 157.

100. *Gwin*, 305 U.S. at 449 (Black, J., dissenting). Black feared that the Court's decisions created a "tax exempt refuge" that provided interstate business with an advantage over intrastate commerce. Ibid., 450.

101. *Hale v. Bimco Trading, Inc.*, 306 U.S. 375 (1939).

explained that it was unrealistic to suppose that all foreign cement, which was 30 percent of cement sold in Florida, needed inspection while no domestic cement needed any inspection. He remarked that the "other justification—the competitive effect of foreign cement in the Florida market—is rather a candid admission that the very purpose of the statute is to keep out foreign goods."[102] Similarly, the Court unanimously invalidated a North Carolina statute that levied an annual tax of $250 for display of samples of goods in hotels or homes by anyone who did not conduct a retail business within the state.[103] Observing that most businesses that sold by sample were located outside the state and that the tax was levied regardless of "how small the sales turn out to be," Reed declared in his opinion that a fee imposed only on foreign businesses "can operate only to discourage and hinder" interstate commerce, which could "hardly survive in so hostile an atmosphere."[104]

During the following year, in *McCarroll v. Dixie Greyhound Lines, Co.*, the Court struck down an Arkansas tax on gasoline brought into the state by a motor vehicle for use as fuel in such vehicle.[105] McReynolds's opinion, and Stone's concurrence, found that the tax did not represent fair compensation to the state for use of its roads by out-of-state vehicles.[106] In dissent, Black, Frankfurter, and Douglas argued that Arkansas reasonably could have concluded that its law defrayed the cost of "serious wear and tear upon roads" and that "[i]t is not for us to approve or disapprove." The dissenters argued that "Congress alone" could properly evaluate the constitutionality of such a tax because courts could only "treat the subject by the hit-and-miss method" of litigation. "Spasmodic and unrelated instances of litigation cannot afford an adequate basis for the creation of integrated national rules which alone can afford that full protection for interstate commerce intended by the Constitution."[107]

During its final years, the Hughes Court similarly deferred to state taxation in cases involving due process. In a five-to-four decision in late 1940, the Court upheld a state's power to impose a tax on corporate dividends, in proportion to the amount of income attributable to the state, regardless of where the dividend was paid.[108] The Court rejected the argument that the due process clause of the Fourteenth Amendment imposed any substantive limitation upon a state's taxing power. In an opinion urging judicial deference to legislatures, Frankfurter declared, "Nothing can be less helpful than for courts to go beyond the extremely limited restrictions that the Constitution places upon the states and to inject themselves in a merely negative way into the delicate processes of fiscal policy-making."

102. Ibid., 380.

103. *Best & Co. v. Maxwell*, 311 U.S. 454 (1940).

104. Ibid., 456, 456–57, 456.

105. 309 U.S. 176 (1940).

106. Ibid., 180; ibid., 180–83 (Stone, J., concurring). Hughes, Roberts, and Reed joined the concurring opinion.

107. Ibid., 184, 186, 189.

108. *Wisconsin v. J. C. Penney Co.*, 311 U.S. 435 (1940).

Unimpressed by the argument that dividends declared out of state were unreachable, Frankfurter explained that "[t]he simple but controlling question is whether the state has given anything for which it can ask return." Frankfurter declared that a "state is free to pursue its own fiscal policies, unembarrassed by the Constitution, if by the practical operation of a tax the state has exerted its power in relation to opportunities which it has given, to protection which it has afforded, to benefits which it has conferred by the fact of being an orderly, civilized society." Endorsing an expansive view of state taxing power, Frankfurter emphasized that "the limits on the otherwise autonomous powers of the states are those in the Constitution and not verbal weapons imported into it."[109] A dissent by Roberts—joined by Hughes, McReynolds, and Reed—argued that a state could tax the income of a foreign corporation but could not touch the residue of the income after it leaves the state.[110] Rejoicing in the decision, the *New Republic* remarked that "the states will not now be as helpless as they were in catching each other's escaping tax fleas" and that the decision was thus "one of the great steps toward creating a bill of social duties for big property as a bill of legal rights."[111]

During its final years, the Hughes Court also broadly interpreted congressional taxing and spending powers. During the first week of 1938, the Court unanimously rejected challenges by private utility companies to loans made by the Public Works Administration to municipalities for use in developing electric power projects.[112] Sutherland's opinion for the Court declared that a utility company had no "right to be immune from lawful municipal competition" and therefore no standing to challenge federal funding of municipal utility projects.[113] Sutherland's approval of the PWA loans was consistent with his authorship of 1923 opinions rejecting challenges to a federal grant-in-aid program and his vote to sustain the grant-in-aid concept of the Social Security Act.[114] As Parrish has observed, "With his consistent endorsement of Congress's spending power via the grant-in-aid, soon to become the most powerful engine of expanding federal authority, Justice Sutherland, otherwise the nemesis of big government, could lay claim to sponsoring the luxurious growth of the post–World War II welfare state."[115]

The Court likewise turned aside a challenge to the constitutionality of the Tennessee Valley Authority (TVA) in January 1939, holding that private utility companies had no standing to object to competition by the TVA as constituting a violation of the Fifth, Ninth, and Tenth Amendments.[116] In his opinion for the Court, Roberts explained that "neither their charters nor their local franchises

109. Ibid., 445, 444.
110. Ibid., 446–52 (Roberts, J., dissenting).
111. "New Tax Powers for the States," *New Republic,* January 6, 1941, 8.
112. *Alabama Power Co. v. Ickes,* 302 U.S. 464 (1938).
113. Ibid., 480, 480–83.
114. Parrish, *The Hughes Court,* 77, citing *Massachusetts v. Mellon,* 262 U.S. 447 (1923) and *Frothingham v. Mellon,* 262 U.S. 447 (1923).
115. Parrish, *The Hughes Court,* 77.
116. *Tennessee Electric Power Co. v. TVA,* 306 U.S. 118 (1939).

involve the grant of a monopoly or render competition illegal." Although Roberts did not address the question of whether Congress had the power to establish the TVA, he declared that "[t]he sale of government property in competition with others is not a violation of the Tenth Amendment" and that the utilities lacked standing to challenge the statute as a violation of either the Ninth or Tenth Amendments in the absence of any objections by the states in which the TVA conducted its operations. The Court likewise upheld the trial court's determination that the TVA had not procured contracts through coercion, duress, or fraud.[117] Butler and McReynolds dissented on the grounds that the utilities had standing to challenge the law because they suffered the loss of valuable property rights as a result of competition from the TVA. In the wake of the Court's decision, private utility interests sold many of their facilities in the Tennessee Valley.[118]

In addition to its broad interpretation of the federal taxing and spending powers, the later Hughes Court also expressed more deference toward the federal government in income tax decisions. As a 1940 commentary observed, the Hughes Court's recent federal income tax decisions had "erased fine distinctions, demolished esoteric dialectic, torn away corporate veils, [and] looked to the realities of transactions."[119] For example, in a 1938 decision construing the federal tax code to circumscribe the deductibility of capital losses upon liquidation of a corporation, Justice Stone's opinion rejected the argument that doubts in a tax case should always be resolved in favor of the taxpayer.[120] Roberts and the two remaining Horsemen dissented without opinion. Stone told his former law clerk Louis Lusky, "I have waited a long time to say this when it would stick and count for something."[121]

The Court similarly espoused a broad view of federal power in sustaining the constitutionality of a Municipal Bankruptcy Act that Congress had enacted in the wake of *Ashton*. In its decision in *United States v. Bekins* (1938),[122] the Court upheld a statute that was virtually identical to the one that the Court had invalidated by a five-to-four vote in *Ashton*, except that it was even more scrupulous in making clear that a municipality could not declare bankruptcy without the consent of its state. Hughes's opinion for the Court in *Bekins* essentially was the same as his dissenting opinion in *Ashton*. He explained that the statute was "carefully drawn so as not to impinge upon the sovereignty of the State," which retained "control of its fiscal affairs." Indeed, Hughes observed that the statute promoted the state's sovereignty insofar as it enabled the state to exercise its will in facilitating the bankruptcies of its municipalities. Citing *Steward Machine Co.*, Hughes pointed out that "the

117. Ibid., 139, 144, 143–44, 145, 152.

118. Robert H. Jackson, *The Struggle for Judicial Supremacy: A Study of a Crisis in American Power Politics* (New York: Alfred A. Knopf, 1941), 260.

119. Hamilton and Braden, "The Supreme Court Today," *New Republic*, August 5, 1940, 179.

120. *White v. United States*, 305 U.S. 281 (1938).

121. Harlan Fiske Stone to Louis Lusky, February 17, 1939, box 24, Harlan Fiske Stone Papers, Manuscript Division, Library of Congress (hereafter cited as Stone Papers).

122. *United States v. Bekins*, 304 U.S. 27 (1938).

formation of an indestructible Union of indestructible States" did not preclude "coöperation between the Nation and the States through the exercise of the power of each to the advantage of the people who are citizens of both." Once again, the post-1937 Court took cognizance of the exigencies of the Great Depression, explaining that municipal agencies "were in distress. Economic disaster had made it impossible for them to meet their obligations." The Constitution, in the interest of state sovereignty, did not reduce "both sovereigns to helplessness in such a case."[123]

Bekins provides a useful test case for considering the causes of the "judicial revolution." Making no effort to distinguish the Court's 1936 decision striking down the Municipal Bankruptcy Act of 1934, Hughes made no pretense of denying that the Court had reversed itself. Although one could argue that the statutes were disinguishable because the second statute made clearer that the municipality needed the state's consent, Roberts was the only justice who could have found this distinction persuasive, because he was the only justice who switched his vote. Butler and McReynolds, who had voted to strike down the original statute in *Ashton,* wrote a one-line dissent arguing that *Ashton* controlled the case.[124] Van Devanter and Sutherland, who also had voted with the majority in *Ashton,* were no longer members of the Court. Chief Justice Hughes and Justices Stone and Brandeis, who voted in favor of the constitutionality of both the statutes, were joined in the second decision by the new justices, Black and Reed. Cardozo, who voted to sustain the constitutionality of the first statute, was too ill to participate in the second decision. *Bekins* therefore serves as another example of how the "judicial revolution" was not the product of any wholesale philosophical migration by a group of justices, but rather the result of occasional "switches" by Roberts and more rarely Hughes, combined with the addition of new justices who steadfastly supported the constitutionality of regulatory legislation.

After 1937 the Hughes Court also was more tolerant of delegation of congressional power to executive agencies. Indeed, the Court's 1935 decisions in *Panama Refining* and *Schechter* remain virtually the only decisions in which the Court ever has disapproved congressional delegations of power. In a companion case to *Darby,* the Court without dissent held that the Fair Labor Standards Act did not unconstitutionally delegate congressional legislative power to the administrator of the Wage and Hour Division of the Department of Labor.[125] Stone's opinion observed that "[i]n an increasingly complex society Congress obviously could not perform its functions if it were obliged to find all the facts subsidiary to the basic conclusions which support the defined legislative policy in fixing, for example, a tariff rate, a railroad rate or the rate of wages to be applied in particular industries by a minimum wage law." Declaring that the Constitution "is not to be interpreted as demanding the impossible or the impracticable," Stone explained that "[t]he

---

123. Ibid., 52, 53, 54.
124. Ibid., 54 (McReynolds and Butler, J.J., dissenting).
125. *Opp Cotton Mills v. Administrator,* 312 U.S. 126 (1941).

essentials of the legislative function are the determination of the legislative policy and its formulation as a rule of conduct." The Court explained that Congress satisfies these functions when it permits an agency to reach a conclusion based upon relevant data that conform to guidelines prescribed by Congress. In this case, Congress had provided sufficient guidance to the administrator by directing him to raise minimum wages to forty cents per hour "as rapidly as is economically feasible without substantially curtailing employment."[126]

Similarly, the Court in *Currin* held that Congress could permit the secretary of agriculture to establish standards for the inspection of tobacco and to inspect tobacco and certify it for sale. Hughes explained, "We have always recognized that legislation must often be adapted to conditions involving details with which it is impracticable for the legislature to deal directly."[127]

Likewise, in *Rock Royal* the Court sustained delegation to the secretary of agriculture to work with food industries to establish minimum prices because Congress had provided clear guidelines for the exercise of the secretary's power.[128] The Court specifically contrasted this delegation with the more general one that the Court disapproved in *Schechter*. The Court pointed out that the it had never denied that Congress could delegate "broad powers to executives to determine the details of any legislative scheme."[129] In a joint dissent, McReynolds and Butler denounced the delegation as government "by caprice."[130] In a related case, Roberts wrote a dissent joined by McReynolds and Butler in which Roberts relied upon *Panama Refining* and *Schechter* in arguing that Congress had failed to prescribe a standard under which the secretary could act.[131]

Again the Court in *Mulford* found that Congress had not violated separation of powers by authorizing the secretary of agriculture to establish quotas on the supply and marketing of tobacco and to allot the quota among states and farms.[132] Similarly, the Court in *Sunshine Coal* found that Congress had not improperly delegated power to the National Bituminous Coal Commission, an executive branch agency; to coal producers, who helped to administer the law but were subordinate to the commission's authority; or to the courts, whose jurisdiction was not infringed by the commission's administrative powers.[133]

The Court's tolerant opinions on delegation were a corollary of the justices' growing deference to the work of administrative agencies. As a commentary observed in 1940, "Where the Court once strove to become overlord to all the agencies of government, it is now concerned to ensure to each independence in the performance of its specified task." Indeed, in some cases, the Court chided

126. Ibid., 145, 145–46, 135.
127. 306 U.S. at 15.
128. 307 U.S. at 574–77.
129. Ibid., 574, 574–75, 574.
130. Ibid., 582.
131. *H. P. Hood & Sons v. U.S.*, 307 U.S. at 603–8 (Roberts, J., dissenting).
132. 307 U.S. at 48–49.
133. 310 U.S. at 397–401.

lower courts for interfering with the work of agencies.[134] The constitutionality of administrative decision making became accepted during the late 1930s, one scholar has observed, "even if administrators tended to function free from governmental constraints. The central question became not *when* administrators could decide matters, but *how* they should decide matters."[135]

The Court's growing deference to administrative agencies was most keenly demonstrated in a 1940 decision, *Railroad Commission v. Rowan & Nichols Oil Co.,* holding that due process did not require a court to undertake an independent determination of fact even when an agency allegedly confiscated private property.[136] Accordingly, the Court reversed a decision of the court of appeals affirming the district court's de novo review of an oil proration order by the Texas Railroad Commission that had the potential to permit neighboring wells to drain away the plaintiff's oil reserves. In his opinion for the Court, Frankfurter declared that "courts must not substitute their notions of expediency and fairness for those which have guided the agencies to whom the formulation and execution of policy have been entrusted." He explained that "in a domain of knowledge still shifting and growing . . . it would be presumptuous for courts, on the basis of conflicting expert testimony, to deem the view of the administrative tribunal, acting under legislative authority, offensive to the Fourteenth Amendment." Indeed, Frankfurter denied that courts should "supplant the Commission's judgment even in the face of convincing proof that a different result would have been better."[137]

In another important series of decisions, the Hughes Court substantially restricted the scope of intergovernmental tax immunity. In two decisions from which only Butler and McReynolds dissented, it eroded the theory of such immunity involving both federal and state governments. In *Helvering v. Gerhardt* in 1938, the Court sustained a federal income tax on employees of the Port of New York Authority, rejecting the argument that taxation of these public workers imposed an undue burden on the states of New York and New Jersey, which owned and operated the port authority.[138] The Court's decision was inconsistent with a March 1937 decision that a New York City employee was exempt from federal taxation.[139] Stone declared that the employees had a duty to support the federal government whose benefits they enjoyed and that the effects of the tax were not passed along to the states in a manner that obstructed their operation of the Port Authority. Echoing one of the theories that he had advanced a month earlier in *Carolene Products,* Stone pointed out that the Court should defer to Congress's imposition of the tax insofar as the Port Authority employees could adequately guard against abuse of the taxing power because they were represented in Congress. Stone

134. Hamilton and Braden, "The Supreme Court Today," *New Republic,* August 5, 1940, 179.
135. Ronald A. Cass, "Models of Administrative Action," 72 *Virginia Law Review* 364 (1986).
136. 310 U.S. 573 (1940).
137. Ibid., 581, 581–82, 584.
138. 304 U.S. 405 (1938).
139. *Brush v. Commissioner,* 300 U.S. 352 (1937).

observed that "the possibility of resort to the usual processes of political action . . . provides a readier and more adaptable means than any courts can afford, for securing accommodation of the competing demands for national revenue, on the one hand, and for reasonable scope for the independence of state action, on the other." Stone also explained that immunity from taxation could unduly "interfere with the sovereign power of the nation to tax." Again taking account of the dynamics of the political system, Stone observed that state legislatures could not be relied upon to grant their citizens immunity in a manner that did not seriously impede "the taxing power of the nation."[140]

The following year, in *Graves v. New York ex rel. O'Keefe*, the Court reciprocally applied *Gerhardt* in holding that New York did not impose an unconstitutional burden on the federal government by taxing income of an employee of the Home Owners' Loan Corporation.[141] Stone's opinion explained that the theory "that a tax on income is legally or economically a tax on its source, is no longer tenable." Immunity of the employee, Stone declared, would unduly interfere with "the taxing power which the Constitution has reserved to the state governments."[142] As one scholar has observed, Hughes's concurrence without opinion appears to have "reflected the painful dilemma of the Chief Justice," who "deemed it desirable to go along with the change but found himself either disturbed by some expressions of the Court or by the necessity of overturning one very old and one very recent precedent of the Court."[143] Privately, Stone expressed "discomfort" at overturning doctrine supported by old precedents, but he derived "some comfort from the fact that the books are barren of any reasoning to support it."[144]

The influence and effects of these decisions were demonstrated in a 1939 decision based upon statutory construction in which the Court held that the federal Home Owners' Loan Corporation's immunity from state taxation was so broad that a state could not impose a small mortgage recordation fee, even though the fee did not appear discriminatory or burdensome.[145]

The Hughes Court's later economic decisions attracted no vocal protest and may have bolstered public respect for the Court, overcoming earlier perceptions that the justices often read their own personal predilections into law. Public faith that the justices were disinterested may have been especially enhanced by a 1939 decision upholding a 1932 federal statute imposing taxes on the income of federal judges.[146] The Court explicitly rejected its 1920 decision[147] that a federal tax on judicial income violated article 3, section 1 of the Constitution, which provides

140. 304 U.S. at 416, 417.

141. 306 U.S. 466 (1939).

142. Ibid., 480, 487.

143. Samuel Hendel, *Charles Evans Hughes and the Supreme Court* (New York: Russell and Russell, reissue, 1968), 194.

144. Harlan Fiske Stone to Louis Lusky, April 13, 1939, box 24, Stone Papers.

145. *Pittman v. Home Owners' Corp.*, 308 U.S. 21 (1939).

146. *O'Malley v. Woodrough*, 307 U.S. 277 (1939).

147. *Evans v. Gore*, 253 U.S. 245 (1920).

that the "Compensation" of "Judges" "shall not be diminished during their Continuance in Office." In a short and simple decision, Frankfurter brushed aside the argument that taxation threatened judicial independence. He explained that taxation recognizes "that judges are also citizens, and that their particular function in government does not generate an immunity from sharing with their fellow citizens the material burden of the government whose Constitution and laws they are charged with administering."[148] Frankfurter's decision was notable for its references to law review articles and judicial opinions from other countries, an example of the Court's growing tendency to base its decisions upon a broad range of sources. Butler based a lengthy dissent on the need to protect judicial independence.[149]

The tendency of Black, Murphy, and Douglas to read their political predilections into the Constitution bothered some of their brethren, particularly Stone, who was no more tolerant of ideological jurisprudence among liberals than among the Horsemen. Stone complained privately that Black was "frittering away his opportunity for judicial effectiveness by lack of a good technique."[150] Toward the end of Black's first term, the columnist Marquis Childs caused a flap by reporting in the *St. Louis Post-Dispatch* and *Harper's* that Stone had complained about deficiencies in Black's legal knowledge, writing skills, and ability to carry his share of the Court's workload. Although Stone denied having disparaged Black, he may at least have expressed concern to confidantes that Black was squandering his talents by advocating hopeless positions.[151] Black particularly isolated himself in a 1938 dissent in which he flatly rejected the well-established doctrine that the word "person" in the Fourteenth Amendment includes corporations. As the journalist Max Lerner admiringly remarked, Black's challenge "sweeps away fifty years of Supreme Court history and strikes at one of the props of corporate power."[152] Black's dissent led the *Nation* to remark that "Black, whom many liberals expected to turn bourbon when he was safely on the court, has startled even his supporters by the uncompromising quality of his recent dissents."[153]

On the whole, however, the Court during the late 1930s was more united on economic issues than it had been before 1937; the departures of Van Devanter, Sutherland, and Butler in 1937 and 1938 had left McReynolds as the sole remaining Horseman. McReynolds dissented thirty-two times during 1939 and 1940. As is evident from the foregoing discussion, however, Hughes and Roberts were found in dissent in some important cases, too, for they never were willing to defer

148. 307 U.S. at 282.
149. Ibid., 283–99 (Butler, J., dissenting).
150. Mason, *Harlan Fiske Stone,* 469. At Stone's request, Frankfurter, still a Harvard law professor, wrote a memorandum to Black acknowledging that judges make law but that "they cannot decide things by invoking a major premise out of cloth," as a legislature could. Ibid., 470.
151. Irving Brant to Hugo L. Black, May 10, 1938, box 7, Stone Papers.
152. 303 U.S. at 85; Max Lerner, "Justice Black, Dissenting," *Nation,* March 5, 1938, 265.
153. "The Shape of Things," *Nation,* February 12, 1938, 169 (editorial).

to Congress so thoroughly as some of their brethren. As Barry Cushman has explained,

> Theirs was a jurisprudence that rejected the principal categorical restraints of substantive due process while at the same time insisting on a rationality standard with some teeth. They were willing to embrace broader notions of public purpose and thus more relaxed standards of government neutrality than were the Four Horsemen. But they were not prepared to abandon entirely the Court's traditional role of preserving state neutrality—particularly in instances that implicated the right to pursue a lawful calling on terms of equality with all others.[154]

The Court's newfound restraint in constitutional law cases involving economic issues also manifest itself in private law disputes. In 1938, for example, the Court rejected a claim by the National Biscuit Company, which had purchased the Shredded Wheat Company in 1930, that the Kellogg Company committed unfair competition by marketing a "pillow-shaped biscuit" similar to the one produced by the Shredded Wheat Company and calling it "shredded wheat."[155] The Court concluded that the name and form of the product was dedicated to the public after the expiration of patents and that Kellogg had made no effort to confuse its product with that of its competitor.[156] McReynolds and Butler dissented. Contending that the decision was consistent with the Court's newfound liberalism on constitutional issues, one commentator proclaimed that "Human Rights have again prevailed over Property Rights" and that "shredded wheat belongs to the ages, and the Bill of Rights takes a long deferred front seat in the cereal-products business."[157]

The Court's commitment to judicial restraint was especially evident in the context of private law in one of the Hughes Court's most significant rulings, *Erie Railroad Co. v. Tompkins,* decided in 1938.[158] In *Erie,* the Court held that federal courts must apply the common law of the state in which they sit in cases in which the court's jurisdiction is based upon diversity of citizenship between the parties to the lawsuit. The Court's decision stunned attorneys because, in overturning the Court's 1842 precedent in *Swift v. Tyson,*[159] *Erie* swept away at one stroke the vast body of federal general common law that federal courts had constructed over nearly a century.[160]

Like other "revolutionary" Hughes Court decisions, however, the Court's change of course was not nearly as abrupt as it appeared. In a decision ten years

154. Cushman, "Lost Fidelities," 142–43.

155. *Kellogg Co. v. National Biscuit Co.,* 305 U.S. 111 (1938).

156. Ibid., 122.

157. Frederic Nelson, "Human Rights with Cream," *New Republic,* February 1, 1939, 366.

158. 304 U.S. 64 (1938).

159. 16 Pet. 1 (1842).

160. Although *Erie* sometimes is supposed to have wiped out all federal common law, it did not affect the large body of common law interpreting federal statutes. Nor did it alter federal common law involving the legal and proprietary interests of the United States, international disputes, disputes between states, and admiralty and maritime issues.

earlier, the Court had sustained *Swift* by a vote of only six to three, with Holmes registering a vigorous dissent in which Brandeis and Stone joined.[161] In that case, the Court upheld federal diversity jurisdiction over a lawsuit between taxicab companies incorporated in Kentucky and Tennessee, even though the Tennessee company had moved its corporate citizenship from Kentucky to Tennessee to obtain the benefit of federal law in a dispute over whether a railroad could confer upon it the exclusive right to solicit passengers at the train station in Bowling Green, Kentucky. Arguing that the dispute "was a purely local question, on which . . . the State should have its own way," Holmes denied that there was "a transcendental body of law outside of any particular State."[162] This decision exacerbated widespread opposition toward diversity jurisdiction among progressives, who complained that federal courts all too often provided a refuge in which business corporations could obtain more favorable judgments. In 1930 and 1931 Senator Norris introduced bills to abolish diversity jurisdiction, which were approved by the Senate Judiciary Committee.[163]

In *Erie,* a Pennsylvania citizen named Harry Tompkins had lost his right arm, while trespassing on railroad property, when an object protruding from a passing train struck him. Tompkins won a verdict of thirty thousand dollars in a lawsuit against a New York railroad in a federal court in New York. In contrast with state law, which would have denied Tompkins recovery as a trespasser, federal common law required the railroad to exercise a duty of care because the public had long made use of the path along the tracks without objection from the railroad. The Court's decision in *Erie* required the district court on remand to rule in favor of the railroad because it had to apply the law of New York state, which would follow the law of Pennsylvania, where the accident occurred.[164]

Brandeis's opinion for the Court in *Erie* first reinterpreted section 34 of the Judiciary Act of 1789, the so-called Rules of Decision Act, which provided that "[t]he laws of the several states . . . shall be regarded as the rules of decision in trials at common law, in the courts of the United States." In contrast to *Swift,* which had interpreted "laws" as including both statutory law and common law, *Erie* held that "laws" referred solely to statutory law.[165] The Court next concluded that *Swift* suffered from "defects, political and social" because continued divergence between state and federal law had "developed a new well of uncertainties."

---

161. *Black & White Taxicab Co v. Brown and Yellow Taxicab Co.,* 276 U.S. 518 (1928).

162. Ibid., 533 (Holmes, J., dissenting).

163. S. 4357, 71st Congress, 2d Session, 1930, Report 691; S. 939, 72d Congress, 1st Session 1931, report 530.

164. Three years later, in its unanimous decision in *Klaxon v. Stentor Electric Manufacturing Co.,* 313 U.S. 487 (1941), the Hughes Court explicitly held that federal courts under the *Erie* doctrine are obligated to follow the conflict-of-laws rules of the state in which they sit.

165. 304 U.S. 72–73. The Court based its decision upon Charles Warren's article, "New Light on the History of the Federal Judiciary Act of 1789," 37 *Harvard Law Review* 51–52, 81–88, 108 (1923).

The Court also pointed to "mischievous results" of *Swift*, particularly the prevention of "uniformity in the administration of the law of the State." Although diversity jurisdiction was intended to prevent discrimination against noncitizens of a state by providing a supposedly more neutral federal forum, *Swift* had permitted discrimination against citizens by noncitizens, who could avoid application of the law of the citizen's state by removing a case to federal court.[166]

At the urging of Stone, however, who threatened to write a concurring opinion,[167] Brandeis ultimately rested the decision on the constitutional ground that "Congress has no power to declare substantive rules of common law applicable in a state." "There is," Brandeis averred, "no federal general common law."[168] In expounding this theory of federalism and congressional power, Brandeis implicitly rejected the possibility that the commerce clause might permit Congress to authorize the federal courts to craft rules of common law in diversity litigation. Brandeis also might have relied more explicitly upon a theory of federalism to reach his conclusion that federal courts must defer to state common law when diversity of citizenship was the sole basis for federal jurisdiction. Moreover, Brandeis could have rejected *Swift* on the constitutional grounds that judicial development of federal common law without congressional authorization violated separation of powers.

In addition to resting on a constitutional theory of congressional power, *Erie* also implicitly invoked the Tenth Amendment by alleging that *Swift* permitted federal courts to invade rights that "are reserved by the Constitution to the several States." Brandeis presumably avoided direct reference to the Tenth Amendment because opponents of economic regulation had so often attempted to use the Tenth Amendment as a substantive restriction on the exercise of federal power, particularly the congressional regulation of interstate commerce.[169]

Although *Erie* has affected the outcome of countless individual cases, it has had little practical effect upon the development of American law. Contrary to Brandeis's assertions, the growing uniformity of state law and the increasing congruence between state and federal law meant by 1938 that most cases would be decided the same way under either state law or the old federal common law. *Swift*, which had helped to foster economic development by creating a uniform and predictable body of federal commercial law at a time when the crazy quilt of state law produced troubling uncertainties for enterprises that conducted interstate business, had outlived its usefulness by the time of *Erie*.

Although *Erie* may have devolved power to the states at a time when the Court was helping Congress and the president to expand federal power, *Erie* was consistent with the Hughes Court's renewed devotion to federal judicial restraint. As

---

166. 304 U.S. at 74, 75–78.

167. Harlan Fiske Stone to Louis D. Brandeis, March 25, 1938, box 73, Stone Papers.

168. 304 U.S. at 78.

169. Purcell, *Brandeis and the Progressive Constitution,* 178. Professor Purcell has pointed out that "Justice Stone, too, was flatly opposed to a substantive Tenth Amendment, and any direct reliance on its independent mandate would surely have lost his vote." Ibid.

Purcell has explained, *Swift* "stood for the idea that the federal courts had authority to impose substantive rules of law free from legislative alteration, and it exemplified the Supreme Court's willingness to use its power to ordain its own institutional primacy." Accordingly, as Purcell points out, "*Swift* was the private law counterpart of the public law doctrine of substantive due process—twin pillars of the activist federal judiciary that had crimped and barred Progressive reform for half a century." *Swift*'s demise therefore "affirmed the fundamental constitutional principle of legislative primacy."[170]

Erie was one of the Hughes Court's two most important decisions affecting private law. The other was *Aetna Life Insurance Co. v. Haworth*,[171] decided in March 1937 during the Court-packing controversy, in which the Court sustained the constitutionality of the federal Declaratory Judgment Act of 1934. This statute, like its counterparts in numerous states, permitted courts to declare the rights and obligations of parties to a controversy without awarding any monetary damages, injunction, or other coercive relief. As the Senate report on the legislation explained, the declaratory judgment would be "useful in avoiding the necessity, now so often present, of having to act at one's peril or to act on one's interpretation of his rights, or abandon one's rights because of a fear of incurring damages. . . . In jurisdictions having the declaratory judgment procedure, it is not necessary to bring about such social and economic waste and destruction in order to obtain a declaration of one's rights."[172] Critics of the procedure alleged, however, that it authorized courts to render advisory opinions, in contravention of the constitutional requirement that federal courts may adjudicate only "[c]ases and [c]ontroversies." Although many progressives favored the declaratory judgment device as a means of making litigation more expeditious, others feared that it would provide yet another weapon in the arsenal of antiregulatory judges. During the 1920s and early 1930s, Frankfurter publicly opposed federal declaratory judgments, and Brandeis helped derail federal declaratory judgment legislation for five years by denouncing the concept in a 1928 decision.[173]

In *Haworth*, Hughes's opinion for a unanimous Court held that the statute, which explicitly limited federal declaratory judgment jurisdiction to "cases of actual controversy," did not violate article 3's limitation of federal jurisdiction to cases and controversies. Hughes explained that Congress, in prescribing procedural rules, was "not confined to traditional forms or traditional remedies. . . . In dealing with methods within its sphere of remedial action the Congress may create and improve as well as abolish or restrict." Accordingly, Congress could authorize the Court to render judgments that did not award the traditional coercive remedies of money damages or injunctions, so long as the dispute was not "hypothetical

---

170. Purcell, *Brandeis and the Progressive Constitution*, 190–91.

171. 300 U.S. 227 (1937).

172. *Senate Report No. 1005*, 73rd Congress, 2d Session 5 (1934).

173. See Purcell, *Brandeis and the Progressive Constitution*, 124–32. The decision was *Willing v. Chicago Auditorium Association*, 277 U.S. 274 (1928).

or abstract" or "academic or moot." The controversy, Hughes explained, need only "be definite and concrete, touching the legal relations of parties having adverse legal interests."[174]

Applying these principles to the case, Hughes ruled that an insurance company could obtain a declaration from a court concerning its obligation to pay benefits under insurance policies insofar as the insured was demanding payment under the policies, and the company contended that no payment was due because the insured was not disabled and the policies had lapsed. Hughes explained that "[s]uch a dispute is manifestly susceptible of judicial determination. It calls, not for an advisory opinion upon a hypothetical basis, but for an adjudication of present right upon established facts."[175] By permitting the insurer to obtain a declaration of its duty to pay without having to wait for a lawsuit by the insured or make a hasty settlement in anticipation of litigation, *Haworth* nicely illustrated the manner in which the Declaratory Judgment Act enables a party to a controversy to obtain an expeditious adjudication of its rights and obligations. The declaratory judgment procedure, at both the state and federal levels, remains an important and useful device.

The Court's decisions on economic issues during the final years of the Hughes Court eventually convinced even many skeptics that a lasting revolution had indeed occurred. As one commentary observed in 1940, "The Court will brook no act that strikes at the heart of the federal system; but it will tolerate no conceptual rigmarole invented to escape responsibility to government. Nor will it allow either 'states rights' or 'interstate commerce' to become judicial rhetoric for 'laissez faire.'"[176]

174. 300 U.S. at 240, 240–41.
175. Ibid., 242.
176. Hamilton and Braden, "The Supreme Court Today," *New Republic*, August 5, 1940, 180.

6

EXPANDING CIVIL LIBERTIES

The Due Process Revolution

Although the Hughes Court is best remembered for its decisions on economic regulation, the Court decided so many landmark civil liberties cases that scholars have begun to believe that its record on personal liberties transformed the law as profoundly as its "revolution" in economic cases. During Hughes's chief justiceship, the Court incorporated into state law the First Amendment's guarantees of freedom of speech, press, assembly, and religion, and it enhanced the due process rights of criminal defendants. The Court also handed down landmark equal protection decisions that provided the foundation for the Court's desegregation rulings of the 1940s and 1950s. Although the Taft Court deserves credit for commencing the Court's modern role as the guardian of personal liberties, the Hughes Court consolidated that role and placed it on a durable doctrinal foundation. Because the Hughes Court was expanding personal freedoms at the same time it had begun to defer to legislative judgments about economic legislation, this marked the beginning of a long period, not yet ended, in which individual rights occupied a prominent and often central place on the Court's docket.

Hughes became chief justice at a critical time of ferment in civil liberties law. Nearly seven years earlier, in June 1923, the Court in *Meyer v. Nebraska* for the first time invoked the Fourteenth Amendment's due process clause in striking down a law that infringed noneconomic liberties.[1] In *Meyer* and its companion cases, the Court held that Nebraska, Iowa, and Ohio could not prohibit the teaching of the German language in nonpublic schools. Although the Court based its holding at least in part upon economic due process to the extent it held that the statute violated the liberty of parents and teachers to enter into contracts, the Court's opinion also presented a striking vision of the personal liberties guaranteed by the Fourteenth Amendment. Although the Court explained that it was not necessary "to define with exactness" the liberty guaranteed by the Fourteenth Amendment, it declared "without doubt" that the amendment "denotes not merely freedom from bodily restraint but also the right of the individual to contract, to engage in any of the common occupations of life, to acquire useful knowledge, to

1. 262 U.S. 390 (1923).

marry, establish a home and bring up children, to worship God according to the dictates of his own conscience, and generally to enjoy those privileges long recognized at common law as essential to the orderly pursuit of happiness by free men."[2]

Two years later, the Court relied upon *Meyer* in *Pierce v. Society of Sisters,* which struck down a nativist-inspired Oregon law that required all children to attend public schools.[3] Although the decision was based partly on the economic rights of nonpublic schools, whose property the statute would have destroyed, the Court also emphasized that parents have the right to control the education of their children unless the state has a strong interest in abridging that right.[4]

The Taft Court's defense of noneconomic liberties in *Meyer* and *Pierce* helped to deflect growing criticism of the Court among progressives and labor leaders, who complained that the Court was more interested in protecting property than people from undue governmental regulation. Attacks on the Court and congressional proposals for curbing the Court's power had reached a new pitch of intensity in 1923 after the justices in *Adkins* struck down the District of Columbia's minimum wage law for women. Chief Justice Taft was acutely aware of the public relations value of *Meyer* and *Pierce*, and he shrewdly engineered attempts to publicize the decisions among the Court's antagonists.[5]

The Court could have decided both *Meyer* and *Pierce* on the First Amendment grounds of freedom of religion, because the parents who challenged the statutes objected primarily to manner in which the laws interfered with religious instruction. Both cases also might have been decided under the First Amendment's free speech clause.[6] The Court presumably avoided reliance upon the First Amendment, however, because settled law, dating back to 1833, maintained that the Bill of Rights was not applicable to the states.[7] Although the Fourteenth Amendment in 1868 had engrafted the Fifth Amendment's due process clause on the states, the Waite Court held in *Hurtado v. California* in 1884 that the Fourteenth Amendment's due process clause did not incorporate into state law the provisions of the Bill of Rights.[8] Invoking the ancient doctrine of statutory interpretation that maintains that no part of a document is superfluous, *Hurtado* reasoned that the specific liberties prescribed by the Bill of Rights would be redundant if they were embraced by the "due process" clause of the Fifth Amendment. Because another doctrine of statutory construction holds that words and phrases have the same meaning throughout a document, the Court found that "due process" had the

2. Ibid., 399.

3. 268 U.S. 510 (1925).

4. Ibid., 534, 535.

5. William G. Ross, *A Muted Fury: Populists, Progressives and Labor Unions Confront the Courts, 1890–1937* (Princeton, N.J.: Princeton University Press, 1994), 27–31, 246–49, 250, 265, 286.

6. William G. Ross, *Forging New Freedoms: Nativism, Education and the Constitution, 1917–1927* (Lincoln: University of Nebraska Press, 1994), 190–91.

7. *Barron v. Baltimore,* 7 Pet. 243 (1833).

8. 110 U.S. 516, 534, 535 (1884).

same meaning in both the Fifth and Fourteenth Amendments and that inclusion of the liberties of the Bill of Rights within the Fourteenth Amendment's due process clause would likewise make them redundant under the nonsuperfluousness doctrine.[9]

Although the Court in its 1908 decision in *Twining v. New Jersey* had indicated that there could be a congruence between Fourteenth Amendment due process and the guarantees of the Bill of Rights,[10] it was not until 1925 that the Taft Court began to incorporate the Bill of Rights into state law. In *Gitlow v. New York*, decided only one week after *Pierce*, the Court declared in dictum that it assumed that "freedom of speech and of the press . . . are among the fundamental personal rights and 'liberties' protected by the due process clause of the Fourteenth Amendment from impairment by the States."[11] In subsequent decisions, however, the Court seemed to back away from the full implications of its dictum in *Gitlow*. In the 1927 decision of *Whitney v. California*, sustaining a conviction under California's syndicalism statute, the Court referred only in passing to "the freedom of speech which is secured by the Constitution," concluding that it did not confer an absolute right to speak.[12] On the same day, the Court in *Fiske v. Kansas* overturned a conviction under Kansas's syndicalism statute as a violation of due process under the Fourteenth Amendment, without mentioning freedom of speech or the press.[13]

The status of the incorporation doctrine therefore remained uncertain when Hughes became chief justice. It did not remain unclear for long. The Court formally endorsed the application of the First Amendment's free speech and free press guarantees in two landmark decisions during the spring of 1931, *Stromberg v. California*[14] and *Near v. Minnesota*.[15]

In *Stromberg*, the Court reversed the conviction of Yetta Stromberg, a nineteen-year-old member of the Young Communist League and summer camp supervisor, for displaying at camp a red flag representing both the Soviet government and the Communist Party in the United States. The California statute under which she was convicted prohibited as a felony the display of a red flag in public "as a sign,

---

9. Ibid., 534–35. The Court in *Hurtado* held that states were not required to follow the Fifth Amendment's requirement that a grand jury indictment precede a trial for a capital crime. For a discussion of the incorporation aspects of *Hurtado*, see Richard C. Cortner, *The Supreme Court and the Second Bill of Rights: The Fourteenth Amendment and the Nationalization of Civil Liberties* (Madison: University of Wisconsin Press, 1981), 12–24.

10. In this decision, *Twining v. New Jersey*, 211 U.S. 78 (1908), the Court rejected the argument that the Fourteenth Amendment's due process clause incorporated the Fifth Amendment's privilege against self-incrimination, but stated that some rights protected by the due process clause were similar to those enumerated in the Bill of Rights.

11. 268 U.S. 652, 666 (1925).

12. 274 U.S. 357, 371 (1927).

13. 274 U.S. 380 (1927).

14. 283 U.S. 359 (1931).

15. 283 U.S. 697 (1931).

symbol or emblem of opposition to organized government or as an invitation or stimulus to anarchistic action or as an aid to propaganda that is of a seditious character." Although the Court sustained the constitutionality of the parts of the statute that prohibited the display of a red flag for purposes of provoking anarchy or facilitating seditious propaganda, it held that a section barring display as an expression of "opposition to organized government" violated the Fourteenth Amendment. Because the trial court had not specified the precise section under which it convicted Stromberg, the Court held that the conviction could not stand. Making clear that it was linking the Fourteenth Amendment with the First Amendment, Chief Justice Hughes cited *Gitlow, Whitney,* and *Fiske* in declaring that the Court had determined "that the conception of liberty under the due process clause of the Fourteenth Amendment embraces freedom of speech."[16]

In his opinion for the Court, Hughes stated that "a fundamental principle of our constitutional system" is "[t]he maintenance of the opportunity for free political discussion to the end that government may be responsive to the will of the people and that changes may be obtained by lawful means, an opportunity essential to the security of the Republic." Accordingly, Hughes explained that "[a] statute which upon its face, and as authoritatively construed, is so vague and indefinite as to permit the punishment of the fair use of this opportunity is repugnant to the guaranty of liberty contained in the Fourteenth Amendment."[17]

McReynolds and Butler dissented on technical grounds, neither endorsing nor opposing the Court's disposition of the constitutional issue. McReynolds argued that the statute was divisible and that the conviction was therefore valid even if one of the three sections was unconstitutional because the Court did not deny the constitutionality of the other two sections. Butler contended that Stromberg was not convicted under the clause of the statute prohibiting display of the red flag for "opposition to organized government" and that her attorney had not at trial objected to the constitutionality of that clause.[18]

Two weeks after *Stromberg,* the Court in *Near v. Minnesota* formally incorporated into state law the First Amendment's guaranty of freedom of the press. Going beyond the dictum of *Gitlow,* the Court used the free press clause as the basis for invalidating a "gag law" under which a court had enjoined a newspaper from publishing articles accusing Minneapolis officials of corruption. In *Near,* Hennepin County district attorney Floyd B. Olson, later Minnesota's crusading Farmer-Labor governor, had obtained an injunction against Jay Near's publication of the *Saturday Press* under a 1925 statute that defined any "malicious, scandalous and defamatory newspaper, magazine, or other periodical" as a public nuisance and permitted a court to enjoin its publication. The statute allowed the publisher "the defense that the truth was published with good motives and for justifiable ends." Olson had procured the injunction after eight issues of the *Press* during the

16. Ibid., 362, 361, 369, 370, 369–70, 368.
17. Ibid., 369.
18. Ibid., 371, 372–73.

autumn of 1927 had accused various persons—including Olson, the mayor and police chief of Minneapolis, and a sitting grand jury—of complicity with gangsters who allegedly controlled local gambling, bootlegging, and racketeering.[19]

Hughes wrote in his opinion for the Court that "[t]he object of the statute is not punishment . . . but suppression of the offending newspaper or periodical" and that the statute "put the publisher under an effective censorship." He also pointed out that the prohibition on previous restraints on publication had deep roots in Anglo-American law and had received the approbation of William Blackstone, James Madison, Joseph Story, and many decisions arising under state constitutions. Although the Court acknowledged that prior restraints could validly issue to enjoin publication of threats to national security, obscenity, or incitements to violence, it determined that these exigencies were not applicable in *Near*. Describing the Minnesota law as "unusual, if not unique," Hughes remarked that the virtual absence of any previous attempts to impose prior restraints upon publications alleging malfeasance by public officers demonstrated "the deep-seated conviction that such restraints would violate constitutional right." Citing *Gitlow, Whitney, Fiske,* and *Stromberg,* Hughes declared that "[i]t is no longer open to doubt that the liberty of the press, and of speech, is within the liberty safeguarded by the due process clause of the Fourteenth Amendment from invasion by state action."[20]

Although Hughes acknowledged that newspapers could abuse their freedom, he denied that the statute was needed in order to redress individual wrongs insofar as "[r]emedies for libel remain available and unaffected." Hughes contended that such abuse was less common than during the early days of the Republic and that the growing complexity of government and the proliferation of opportunities for official malfeasance and corruption demonstrated the need for "a vigilant and courageous press, especially in great cities." Hughes further observed that "[c]harges of reprehensible conduct, and in particular of official malfeasance, unquestionably create a public scandal, but the theory of the constitutional guaranty is that even a more serious public evil would be caused by authority to prevent publication."[21]

Even though the Four Horsemen dissented from the Court's ruling that the injunction was improper, they did not disagree that the free speech clause was binding upon the states. In a long dissent joined by his fellow Horsemen, Butler demonstrated a deference to state authority that he more rarely demonstrated in decisions involving economic regulation. Butler quoted long scurrilous passages from the *Saturday Press,* particularly those accusing Jews of dominating the city's underworld, in support of his contention that the newspaper constituted a public nuisance. He likewise emphasized that the *Saturday Press* had accused a local newspaper with which Near formerly was associated of using its power to blackmail and

---

19. Ibid., 703–704, 701.
20. Ibid., 711, 712, 713–14, 716, 718, 707.
21. Ibid., 709, 719–20, 722.

otherwise corrupt public officials. Butler declared, "It is of the greatest importance that the States shall be untrammeled and free to employ all just and appropriate measures to prevent abuses of the liberty of the press." He also pointed out
that Story's commentary that "every man shall be at liberty to publish what is true,
with good motives and for justifiable ends" closely paralleled the language of the
Minnesota statute.[22]

Moreover, Butler contended that the statute did not operate as a "previous
restraint" in the traditional sense of that term because it did "not authorize administrative control in advance such as was formerly exercised by the licensors and
censors but prescribes a remedy to be enforced by a suit in equity" to prevent the
further and continuing "business" of publication of scandalous articles.[23] Butler
also alleged that existing libel laws were "inadequate effectively to suppress evils
resulting from the kind of business and publications that are shown in this case."[24]

Eighteen months after *Near*, the Court in *Powell v. Alabama* once again safeguarded basic liberties against state intrusion and continued to grapple with the
issue of nationalization of the Bill of Rights in a decision holding that the Fourteenth Amendment's due process clause required states to provide attorneys at
no cost to criminal defendants who faced the death penalty.[25] Finding that the
defendants failed to receive meaningful legal representation, the Court in *Powell*
reversed the convictions of seven of the "Scottsboro Boys," young black drifters
who were accused of raping two white women hobos on a freight train near Scottsboro, Alabama, in a case that attracted international attention as a test of justice
in the American South.[26] Because most sensational cases do not raise novel legal
issues, *Powell* was a rare case in which the Court found itself involved in a cause
célèbre.

Although the local court had appointed two attorneys to represent the defendants, the justices held that the record demonstrated that the defendants were
denied adequate representation because their attorneys were appointed on the
eve of trial and lacked time for adequate preparation. Speaking for the Court,
Sutherland explained that "in a capital case, where the defendant is unable to
employ counsel, and is incapable adequately of making his own defense because
of ignorance, feeble mindedness, illiteracy, or the like, it is the duty of the court,
whether requested or not, to assign counsel for him as a necessary requisite of
due process of law." The denial of such a right, the Court indicated, "would be

22. Ibid., 724, 731–32, 732, 733.

23. Addressing this argument, Hughes declared that if "the publisher has a constitutional
right to publish, without previous restraint, an edition of his newspaper charging official dere-
lictions, it cannot be denied that he may publish subsequent editions for the same purpose. He
does not lose his right by exercising it." Ibid., 720.

24. Ibid., 735, 737.

25. 287 U.S. 45 (1932).

26. For detailed discussions of the case, see Dan T. Carter, *Scottsboro: A Tragedy of the American
South*, rev. ed. (Baton Rouge: Louisiana State University Press, 1979); James Goodwin, *Stories of
Scottsboro* (New York: Pantheon Books, 1994).

little short of judicial murder." Moreover, the justices observed that "[e]ven the intelligent and educated layman has small and sometimes no skill in the science of law. If charged with a crime, he is incapable, generally, of determining for himself whether the indictment is good or bad. He is unfamiliar with the rules of evidence. . . . He lacks both the skill and knowledge adequately to prepare his defense, even though he have a perfect one. He requires the guiding hand of counsel at every step in the proceedings against him." Accordingly, the Court declared that the "right to be heard would be, in many cases, of little avail if it did not comprehend the right to be heard by counsel." Sutherland also observed that the goal of prompt disposition of criminal cases could not justify denial of the right to counsel, for "[t]o do that is not to proceed promptly in the calm spirit of regulated justice but to go forward with the haste of the mob."

In its first explicit discussion of the incorporation doctrine, the Court explained that *Gitlow, Stromberg,* and *Near* established "that notwithstanding the sweeping character of the language in the *Hurtado* case, the [nonsuperfluousness] rule laid down is not without exceptions." The Court concluded, "The rule is an aid to construction, and in some instances may be conclusive; but it must yield to more compelling considerations whenever such considerations exist." Accordingly, the Court explained that "it is possible that some of the personal rights safeguarded by the first eight Amendments against National action may be safeguarded against state action, because a denial of them would be a denial of due process. If this is so, it is not because those rights are enumerated in the first eight Amendments, but because they are of such a nature that they are included in the conception of due process of law."[27] As Richard C. Cortner has written, "What had been implicit in the Court's decisions since *Twining v. New Jersey* was now made explicit. The doctrine of nonsuperfluousness was subject to major qualifications, and those qualifications would be made by the Court when a right listed in the Bill of Rights was asserted under the Due Process Clause."[28] Even though *Powell* did not actually incorporate the Sixth Amendment's right to counsel into state law, Sutherland's dicta helped to lay the doctrinal foundations for expansion of nationalization of the Bill of Rights.

In a dissent joined by McReynolds, Butler argued that there was no need for the Court to reach the issue of incorporation since any failure of the trial court to permit the defendants the time and opportunity to secure counsel would constitute a general denial of due process sufficient to overturn the convictions. Noting that the issue of incorporation had not been raised by the attorneys, Butler complained that "[t]he Court, without being called upon to consider it, adjudges without a hearing an important constitutional question concerning criminal procedure in state court." Butler concluded, moreover, that the Alabama court had not denied due process to the defendants because the record demonstrated that

27. 287 U.S. 67–68; 211 U.S. at 99.
28. Cortner, *Supreme Court and the Second Bill of Rights,* 125.

their attorneys had represented them with sufficient competence and zeal.[29]

Powell marked the first time that the Court had suggested that any of the numerous criminal procedure provisions of the Bill of Rights were binding upon the states. The decision therefore commenced the revolution in criminal procedure that eventually led during the 1960s to the incorporation of nearly all of the procedural protections contained in the Fourth, Sixth, and Eighth Amendments.

Because most states already had their own bills of rights that were similar to the federal guarantees, incorporation of the Bill of Rights into state law through the Fourteenth Amendment and the closer scrutiny of civil liberties under the due process clause did not for the most part impose significant new formal restraints on the powers of state officials. The nationalization process, however, profoundly altered state law by making the interpretation of civil liberties subject to interpretation by federal judges, who generally have accorded broader scope to freedom of speech, freedom of the press, and the rights of the criminally accused than have state judges.

At the time of *Powell*, for example, Alabama law technically provided more "due process" for criminal defendants in capital cases than did the Sixth Amendment because an Alabama statute specifically required courts to appoint counsel for criminal defendants facing capital charges who were unable to hire a lawyer.[30] The U.S. Supreme Court, however, interpreted the due process clause of the Fourteenth Amendment more broadly than the Alabama Supreme Court had interpreted the state statute. Whereas the Alabama court found that the minimal representation provided to the defendants satisfied the more stringent letter of state law, the U.S. Supreme Court determined that such hasty and slipshod lawyering violated the Fourteenth Amendment.

It is not clear why the Court chose to begin the nationalization of the Bill of Rights rather than continue to invoke substantive due process in its civil liberties decisions. After a careful study of the justices' private papers, Klaus H. Heberle concluded that the Court undertook this step with so little internal debate and perhaps so little thought that it resulted from "absent-minded incrementalism."[31] The Court's "incrementalism" may in part be explained by the relative novelty of civil liberties issues. Until the federal government curtailed personal liberties during World War I, the Court had few occasions to consider the contours of free speech under the First Amendment. The war and the fear of Bolshevism during the war's aftermath also produced a spate of state legislation imposing significant curbs on personal liberties that was challenged before the Court. It is hardly surprising that a Court that was presented so suddenly with a major new sphere of constitutional issues would improvise in its selection of doctrines.

The use of incorporation rather than substantive due process may have represented an effort by the Court to confine civil liberties law within the boundaries

29. 287 U.S. at 76, 75–76 (Butler, J., dissenting).

30. Ala. Code, sec. 5567 (1928).

31. Klaus H. Heberle, "From Gitlow to Near: Judicial 'Amendment' by Absent-Minded Incrementalism," 34 *Journal of Politics* 458–83 (1972).

of the Bill of Rights rather than permitting it to continue to roam more freely through substantive due process. Although the attorney whose clients won the *Meyer* case rejoiced that *Meyer* had produced "a fenceless land of liberty,"[32] the Court may have preferred a more determinate law of civil liberties. Critics of judicial activism, both liberal and conservative, likewise may have preferred constitutional fences, particularly if the Court was to be the surveyor of liberty's terrain. The use of the Bill of Rights also placated the Court's critics by disassociating the emerging law of civil liberties from the detested doctrine of substantive due process. The Court's use of substantive due process in civil liberties decisions in *Meyer* and *Pierce* had dampened the enthusiasm of liberals for those decisions insofar as the Court's use of substantive due process in defense of personal liberties helped to legitimize the Court's use of the same theory to nullify economic regulations.[33] As Felix Frankfurter observed after *Pierce,* "a heavy price must be paid for these occasional services to liberalism."[34]

Because *Stromberg, Near,* and *Powell* had solid roots in constitutional and common law and were consistent with the growing line of cases in which the Court protected personal liberties, these decisions may be explained largely without reference to external events, particularly the Great Depression and the concomitant spread of political radicalism. The justices certainly must have been aware, however, that these decisions would help to shore up public faith in American political institutions, especially the Court. Just as the Court had decided *Meyer* and *Pierce* at a time when the Court was under attack for opposing economic regulations, the Court's decisions in *Stromberg, Near,* and *Powell* were handed down at a time when the Court had reason to fear a new onslaught of efforts to curtail its powers.

Powell was decided on the day before the 1932 election, in the wake of recent aspersions directed against the Court by Democratic presidential candidate Franklin D. Roosevelt, who pointed out that eight of the nine justices were Republican. Even though this was not part of any general attack on the Court, Republican leaders seized on the remark as evidence of a Democratic plot to strip the Court of its powers.[35] With memories of the Court-curbing proposals of the early 1920s and the firestorm over the Hughes and Parker nominations still fresh in their minds, the justices could hardly help but wonder whether the growing economic misery and political unrest would exacerbate hostility against the Court. Although the justices could not have foreseen the full scope of the New Deal, they surely supposed that the Court would need to review the constitutionality of state and federal economic reform legislation that was being enacted even before Roosevelt's election, that the Court probably would nullify some of this legislation, and

32. Arthur F. Mullen, *Western Democrat* (New York: Funk, 1940), 226.

33. See the *Survey,* April 15, 1925, 77 (editorial).

34. Felix Frankfurter, "Can the Supreme Court Guarantee Toleration?" *New Republic,* June 17, 1925, 85–87 (unsigned editorial).

35. William G. Ross, "The Role of Judicial Issues in Presidential Campaigns," 35 *Santa Clara Law Review* 414 (2002).

that such decisions would renew and perhaps intensify demands for curtailment of federal judicial power.

While the Court had emerged from previous periods of criticism with its power intact, the justices in November 1932, at the time of *Powell*, must have recognized that the unprecedented economic cataclysm of the Depression called into question the future of all American institutions. Speaking at a cornerstone-laying ceremony at the unfinished Supreme Court building only three weeks before *Powell*, Hughes had declared that the Marble Palace would be a memorial to judges whose decisions had ensured that "the fundamental conception of limited governmental powers and of individual liberty have persisted despite crises . . . and still remain triumphant and unyielding."[36] Deliberating on *Powell* in the old quarters in the Capitol at the same time that the steel frame girders of the lavish new Supreme Court building were rising across the street, the justices might have wondered whether the Court would retain a power worthy of the new building's grandeur. A chief justice with the acute political instincts of Hughes must have recognized that the Court's civil liberties decisions would ameliorate hostility against the Court. As Hughes dryly observed in an address to Fourth Circuit judges in 1932, "Even those who appear to be disposed to decry" judicial limitations on economic legislation "are not slow in invoking the aid of the courts to enforce their constitutional rights if freedom of speech or of the press is endangered."[37] In the wake of *Powell*, the *New York Times* remarked that the decision "ought to abate the rancor of extreme radicals, while confirming the faith of the American people in the soundness of their institutions and especially in the integrity of their courts."[38]

Despite the Court's eloquent language in *Powell*, the justices interpreted the right-to-counsel doctrine rather narrowly seven years later in a decision unanimously rejecting the contention that attorneys lacked adequate time to prepare a defense in a capital murder trial in rural Alabama, even though the lawyers were appointed only three days before the trial and were distracted by other business during part of that time.[39] Justice Black explained that there was less need for trial preparation in rural areas than in cities because "information concerning witnesses and events is more widespread." Denying that appointments of the attorneys were "mere formalities," Black found the attorneys had enjoyed time to exhaust "every angle" of the case and that they were "zealous and earnest" in their representation of the defendant.

The Court extended the incorporation process in *DeJonge v. Oregon* in January 1937, engrafting onto state law the First Amendment's guarantee of peaceful

36. "Address of Chief Justice Hughes," *American Bar Association Journal*, November 1932, 729.

37. "Chief Justice Hughes Addresses Judicial Conference of Fourth Circuit," *American Bar Association Journal*, July 1932, 446.

38. "The Scottsboro Case," *New York Times*, May 8, 1932, 22 (editorial).

39. *Avery v. Alabama*, 308 U.S. 444 (1940).

assembly, which the Court described as "a right cognate to those of free speech and free press."[40] In an opinion without dissent, the Court invoked the freedom of assembly and free speech clauses in overturning the conviction of a Communist, Dirk DeJonge, who had been sentenced to seven years in prison for violating Oregon's syndicalism statute. Speaking at a peaceable Communist Party meeting attended mostly by non-Communists, DeJonge had criticized the Portland police for harassing striking maritime workers, criticized county jail conditions, and called for greater efforts to recruit party membership. In his opinion for the Court, Hughes explained that the state could not prosecute a person merely for participating in a public meeting sponsored by Communists. DeJonge was "entitled to discuss the public issues of the day and thus in a lawful manner, without incitement to violence or crime, to seek redress of alleged grievances."[41] Although liberals naturally welcomed this decision, I. F. Stone remarked that "[i]t is indicative of how far we have drifted when we are so pleasantly surprised when the court begins to recognize the obvious," and Stone expressed alarm over the Court's suggestion that DeJonge could have been convicted for joining or promoting the Communist Party. "Some price must have been paid for the acquiescence" of the Four Horsemen, he feared.[42]

The Court circumscribed and delineated the incorporation process in its 1938 decision in *Palko v. Connecticut,*[43] refusing to incorporate the Sixth Amendment's prohibition against double jeopardy. The Court in *Palko* upheld the first-degree murder conviction and death sentence of a man who had been convicted in a state court of second-degree murder and sentenced to life in prison for the same crime in an earlier trial.

Justice Cardozo's opinion explained that the Fourteenth Amendment incorporated into state law only the basic core of the Bill of Rights. Cardozo defined these interchangeably at various points throughout the opinion as those that are "of the very essence of a scheme of ordered liberty," "implicit in the concept of ordered liberty," and "so rooted in the traditions and conscience of our people as to be ranked fundamental." He likewise tested incorporation by asking whether a state statute would produce "a hardship so acute and shocking that our polity will not endure it" and whether it violated those "fundamental principles of liberty and justice which lie at the base of all our civil and political institutions."[44]

In defining fundamental rights, Cardozo listed the First Amendment's freedoms of speech, press, religion, and peaceable assembly, along with the Sixth Amendment's right to trial by jury, at least in capital cases. As examples of rights that are not fundamental, Cardozo cited the Fifth Amendment's provision for

40. 299 U.S. 353, 364 (1937).

41. Ibid., 365.

42. Isador Feinstein, "The Supreme Court and Civil Liberties," *Nation,* February 6, 1937, 152. Feinstein later used the pen name I. F. Stone, by which he is better known.

43. 302 U.S. 319 (1938). Only Butler dissented, without opinion.

44. Ibid., 325, 328.

indictment by a grand jury and its privilege against self-incrimination, the Sixth Amendment's guarantee of a jury trial in criminal cases, and the Seventh Amendment's requirement of a jury trial in cases at common law exceeding twenty dollars. Cardozo also suggested that the Fourth Amendment's search and seizure provisions were not fundamental, nor were the other provisions of the Sixth Amendment, including the double jeopardy clause that was the subject of *Palko*.[45]

In defending this dichotomy against the admitted perception that it could appear "wavering and broken" to anyone who failed to undertake proper "[r]eflection and analysis," Cardozo claimed that his "ordered liberty" theory provided "a rationalizing principle which gives to discrete instances proper order and coherence." Though acknowledging that the right to trial by jury and the immunity from prosecution without a grand jury indictment "have value and importance," Cardozo claimed that "[f]ew would be so narrow or provincial as to maintain that a fair and enlightened system of justice would be impossible without them." Similarly, Cardozo contended that the immunity from self-incrimination "might be lost, and justice still be done." In contrast, free speech was "the matrix, the indispensable condition, of nearly every other form of freedom," and Cardozo contended that the other liberties that the Court had incorporated into state law were on a "different plane of social and moral values."[46]

In many respects, *Palko* is a model of judicial statesmanship because it is terse— only eight pages in length—elegantly simple in its style, resolute in a theme that is based upon bedrock moral and political principles, and is not muddled with dissent. Butler, the sole dissenter, wrote no opinion. The decision suffers, however, from a jurisprudential and historical relativism that ensured its transience. Although few would disagree that some of the liberties prescribed by the Bill of Rights are more fundamental than others, the Supreme Court during the 1960s found that many of the rights that Cardozo dismissed as less than fundamental were indeed so important that the Fourteenth Amendment's due process clause required their absorption into state law. In one sense, however, Cardozo's test has retained its vitality insofar as the Court has never incorporated all of the provisions of the Bill of Rights into state law and has incorporated only those rights that it regards as fundamental, even if its definition of what is fundamental has become much broader than *Palko*'s.

Five months after *Palko*, the Court offered an even more comprehensive vision of its expanding role in protecting civil liberties. In his celebrated footnote 4 to his opinion for the Court in *United States v. Carolene Products*, Justice Stone presaged the transformation of the Court's role from defender of economic liberties to protector of personal liberties.[47] After reiterating the Court's deference to economic legislation by holding that the Court would presume that Congress had a

---

45. Ibid., 325, 326.
46. Ibid., 325–26.
47. 304 U.S. 144 (1938).

"rational basis" for its statutory definition of adulterated milk, Stone wrote a foot-note indicating that the Court might exercise a more rigorous review of non-economic legislation that affected personal or political liberties.

In particular, Stone explained, "[t]here may be a narrower scope for operation of the presumption of constitutionality when legislation appears on its face to be within a specific prohibition of the Constitution," including those provisions of the Bill of Rights that the Court had incorporated into state law. Stone likewise explained, "It is unnecessary to consider now whether legislation which restricts those political processes which can ordinarily be expected to bring about repeal of undesirable legislation, is to be subjected to more exacting judicial scrutiny under the general prohibitions of the Fourteenth Amendment than are most other types of legislation." As examples, Stone cited restrictions on voting rights and dissemination of information, and interferences with political organizations and peaceable assemblies. Finally, Stone explained that the Court did not need to presently enquire "whether similar considerations enter into the review of statutes directed at particular religious . . . or national . . . or racial minorities" or whether there was need for "more searching scrutiny" of "prejudice against discrete and insular minorities" because such prejudice might constitute "a special condition, which tends seriously to curtail the operation of those political processes ordi-narily to be relied upon to protect minorities."[48]

Stone originally had proposed only the second and third prongs of the foot-note, but he accepted Hughes's suggestion to add the idea that legislation affect-ing specific constitutional rights might require higher scrutiny. Some proponents of judicial restraint have regretted the inclusion of Hughes's paragraph, arguing that heightened judicial scrutiny of legislation is justifiable only when there are impediments to redress of grievances through the political process.

Even though Stone's formulation is phrased only in tentative and hypothetical terms and obtained the endorsement of only four justices,[49] this "manifesto in a footnote"[50] has provided a jurisprudential blueprint for the Court's activism on behalf of personal liberties ever since 1938. Footnote 4 is important because it provides a succinct summary of countermajoritarian theory and was announced just at the time when the Court shifted its primary attention from economic issues to individual liberties, even though the Taft Court pioneered the civil liberties revolution.

Carolene Products's dichotomy between the Court's scrutiny of personal liberties legislation and economic regulatory legislation departed from pre-1937 doctrine as well as pre-1937 practice. In asserting that experimentation could not justify

48. Ibid., 152–53 n. 4.

49. In a concurring opinion, Black stated without explanation that he did not join the part of the opinion containing the footnote. 304 U.S. at 155 (Black, J., concurring). Butler con-curred on other grounds, McReynolds voted to affirm the lower court's judgment striking down the law, and Cardozo and Reed did not participate.

50. Leo Pfeffer, *This Honorable Court: A History of the United States Supreme Court* (Boston: Beacon Press, 1965), 340.

constitutional violations, Justice Sutherland, in his 1932 opinion striking down Oklahoma's regulation of the ice industry in *New State Ice,* had explicitly linked economic liberty with personal liberty. Pointing out that *Near* had not permitted censorship "to interfere with the fundamental doctrine of the freedom of the press," Sutherland declared that "[t]he opportunity to apply one's labor and skill in an ordinary occupation with proper regard for all reasonable regulations is no less entitled to protection."[51]

The impact of footnote 4 has been particularly manifest in decisions involving religious liberty, an area in which the Court had been slow to recognize civil liberties claims. Despite its indication in *Palko* that freedom of religion involved the "essence of ordered liberty" and its suggestion in *Carolene Products* that it would carefully scrutinize legislation that affected personal liberties or discriminated against "discrete and insular minorities," the Court by the end of the 1930s had not yet specifically nationalized religious freedom in any of its decisions. In contrast to the relative ease with which the Court incorporated freedom of speech, press, and assembly, the path to incorporation of freedom of religion was more circuitous. Just as the Taft Court had refused to consider the obvious religious dimensions of *Meyer* and *Pierce,* the Hughes Court was loath to recognize religious claims in a number of cases that invited incorporation of religious freedom.

In the first religious liberty cases to come before the Hughes Court, the justices by a vote of five to four rejected claims of religious freedom in sustaining the denial of naturalization to persons who were willing to bear arms for the United States only if they felt that it was morally justified.[52] These cases extended the doctrine of a 1929 decision[53] in which the Court had upheld denial of naturalization to an applicant who had stated that she would refuse to bear arms for the United States under any circumstances.

In the first case, *United States v. Macintosh,* the Hughes Court strictly construed the Naturalization Act of 1906, which required an applicant for citizenship to declare under oath that he or she would "support and defend the Constitution and laws of the United States against all enemies, foreign and domestic." Emphasizing that naturalization is a privilege rather than a right, Sutherland's opinion concluded that the Court had to interpret the statute in a manner that favored the government and that Macintosh had failed to meet his burden of showing that the statute permitted any exception. Treating the question primarily as an issue of statutory interpretation, Sutherland gave short shrift to claims of religious liberty. Although he declared that "[w]e are a Christian people, . . . according to one another the equal right of religious freedom, and acknowledging with reverence the duty of obedience to the will of God," he pointed out that, "also, we are a Nation with the duty to survive; a Nation whose Constitution contemplates war as well as peace; whose government must go forward upon the assumption . . .

51. 285 U.S. at 280.
52. *United States v. Macintosh,* 283 U.S. 605 (1931); *United States v. Bland,* 283 U.S. 636 (1931).
53. *United States v. Schwimmer,* 279 U.S. 644 (1929).

that unqualified allegiance to the Nation and submission and obedience to the laws of the land . . . are not inconsistent with the will of God."[54]

These decisions were at odds with the Court's general tendency to demonstrate solicitude for the civil liberties of those who were not political radicals—such as the German American Lutherans in *Meyer* and the Roman Catholics in *Pierce*—for neither petitioner lacked patriotism or presented any apparent threat to the political order. Douglas Clyde Macintosh, a Baptist minister, professor of theology at Yale, and chaplain to the Yale Graduate School, had served at the front during the war with the American YMCA and had made wartime speeches in support of the Allies. The petitioner in the companion case had nursed American soldiers in France during the war.[55]

Macintosh inspired what was perhaps Hughes's most impassioned dissent, in which he no doubt recalled the steadfast moral principles of another Baptist minister, his own father. Joined by Holmes, Brandeis, and Stone, Hughes argued for a statutory interpretation that would protect religious liberty. He pointed out that Congress had made exemptions for conscientious objectors in draft acts and observed that there were "other and most important methods of defense, even in time of war, apart from the bearing of arms," that would satisfy the statutory requirement of support for the Constitution against its enemies. Emphasizing that liberty of conscience was central to religious liberty, the chief justice found no evidence that Congress had intended to depart from its longstanding policy of "avoiding clashes with the dictates of conscience." In discussing the importance of freedom of conscience, Hughes declared that "[t]he essence of religion is belief in a relation to God involving duties superior to those arising from any human relation" and that Macintosh therefore "stated what is axiomatic in religious doctrine." Hughes observed, "The battle for religious liberty has been fought and won with respect to religious beliefs and practices, which are not in conflict with good order, upon the very ground of the supremacy of conscience within its proper field."[56] Hughes's interpretation of the statute became law fifteen years later, when the Court overruled its decisions in *Macintosh*.[57] In avowed defiance of *Macintosh*, an Ohio county judge in 1933 granted citizenship to a pacifist, a decision that met with widespread approval by newspaper editorials contending that such defiance was just, particularly because the Court's five-to-four decision was inconclusive.[58]

The Court similarly refrained from considering the religious aspects of *Hamilton v. Board of Regents*[59] in 1934, which upheld the University of California's expulsion of two students who refused to enroll in a compulsory course in military

54. Ibid., 615–20, 625.

55. For a detailed history of these cases, see Ronald B. Flowers, *To Defend the Constitution: Religion, Conscientious Objection, Naturalization, and the Supreme Court* (Lanham, Md.: Scarecrow Press, 2003).

56. *United States v. Macintosh*, 283 U.S. 634–35, 633–34 (Hughes, C.J., dissenting).

57. *Girouard v. United States*, 328 U.S. 61 (1946).

58. "Reversing the Supreme Court on Pacifists," *Literary Digest*, March 4, 1933, 21.

59. 293 U.S. 245 (1934).

tactics and science. The two students, active Methodists who were the sons of Methodist clergy, claimed that enrollment in these Reserve Officers Training Corps (ROTC) courses would violate their conscientious objection to war. The regional conference of their denomination had renounced war as an instrument of national policy, and the national and regional conferences of this church recently had petitioned federal and state authorities to exempt the church's members from participation in military training. Although Butler's opinion for the Court acknowledged that the youths had a constitutional right to entertain pacifist beliefs, the Court contended that they had no right to attend a state university. Accordingly, they had no right to object to the requirements of such attendance, particularly because the government, as the Court made clear in *Macintosh,* has a right to demand that citizens support the nation against its enemies.

The religious character of the claims was recognized by Cardozo in a concurrence joined by Brandeis and Stone, though this concurring opinion was scarcely less dismissive of the conscientious objection claim than was Butler's opinion. Expressing the assumption that the First Amendment's religion clauses were binding upon the states, Cardozo explained that the state did not establish a religion by insisting on military training and that such mere instruction did not violate liberty of conscience. Cardozo predicted that recognition of the right to object to military instruction could lead to "lengths that have never yet been dreamed of," including conscientious objection to pay taxes for war or any other public purpose.[60]

The Court finally incorporated the First Amendment's guarantee of the free exercise of religion in its unanimous decision in 1940 in *Cantwell v. Connecticut.*[61] *Cantwell* was anticlimactic because *Hamilton's* dicta supported incorporation, and *Palko* already had declared that freedom of religion was "implicit in the concept of ordered liberty." *Cantwell,* however, was the first decision in which the Court actually applied the free exercise clause, and it did so in a manner that demonstrated its willingness to give a relatively expansive application to that constitutional provision. Moreover, dicta in *Cantwell* stated for the first time in any Supreme Court opinion that the establishment clause was binding upon the states.

In *Cantwell,* the Court unanimously overturned the convictions of Jehovah's Witnesses whose proselytizing activities had resulted in convictions for breaching the peace and violating a statute that prohibited distribution of religious literature without a certificate of approval from a state official. One Witness, Jesse Cantwell, was arrested after he went into the streets of an overwhelmingly Roman Catholic New Haven neighborhood and played for two men a phonograph record that fiercely attacked Catholicism. Although the men had given Cantwell permission to play the record, its contents so incensed them that they were tempted to strike him. Cantwell immediately departed when they asked him to stop playing the record and to leave them alone.[62]

60. Ibid., 265–68 (Cardozo, J., concurring).
61. 310 U.S. 296 (1940).
62. Ibid., 300–303.

In his opinion for the Court, Roberts—without citing *Hamilton, Palko,* or any other authority—declared that both the establishment and free exercise clauses of the First Amendment were binding upon the states through the Fourteenth Amendment. In an early recognition of the close connection between the two religion clauses, Roberts suggested that the establishment clause ensures "freedom to believe," whereas the free exercise clause confers "freedom to act." Roberts explained that freedom of conscience is absolute but that "[c]onduct remains subject to regulation for the protection of society." Accordingly, a state has the power to enact nondiscriminatory legislation to "regulate the times, the places, and the manner of soliciting upon its streets . . . and may in other respects safeguard the peace, good order and comfort of the community." Roberts concluded, however, that the state could not preserve such order through a license because the licensing officer's discretion to withhold permission if he determined that the purpose of solicitation was not sufficiently "religious" constituted a "censorship of religion." The Court overturned the breach of peace conviction on the ground that Cantwell's activities posed no "clear and present menace to public peace and order."[63]

Cantwell accepted the concept, first sketched by the dissents of Holmes and Brandeis in the free speech cases of the 1920s and more fully developed in decisions after *Cantwell,* that robust discussion of controversial issues is essential for the maintenance of a free society. The Court pointed out that "sharp differences" naturally arise in the realms of religious faith and political belief and that in both religion and politics "the tenets of one man may seem the rankest error to his neighbor" and citizens who wish to win converts to their opinions sometimes resort to exaggeration, personal vilification, or false statement. As the Court explained, despite "the probability of excesses and abuses," the nation's history demonstrated that "these liberties are, in the long view, essential to enlightened opinion and right conduct on the part of the citizens of a democracy."[64]

The Hughes Court was less solicitous of religious liberty in its infamous "flag salute" decision, *Minersville School District v. Gobitis,* in which the justices rejected claims that a Pennsylvania statute requiring public school children to salute the American flag violated the religious liberty of Jehovah's Witnesses.[65] In his opinion for the Court, Frankfurter explained that religious liberty "has never excluded legislation of a general scope not directed against doctrinal loyalties of particular sects." He vigorously argued that the state had a powerful interest in inculcating patriotic values in youth, because national unity, of which the flag is the most important symbol, "is the basis of national security." Frankfurter characteristically emphasized that the Court should defer to legislative officials in determining how to instill patriotism in the young. Warning that the Court should not make pronouncements about "pedagogical and psychological dogma in a field where courts

63. Ibid., 303, 304, 305, 311.
64. Ibid., 310.
65. 310 U.S. 586 (1940).

possess no marked and certainly no controlling competence," he declared that "the courtroom is not the arena for debating issues of educational policy" and that the Court should not serve as "the school board for the country."[66]

Stone, the sole dissenter, sharply disagreed with Frankfurter's deference to the Pennsylvania legislature. In response to Frankfurter's reminder that "the remedial channels of the democratic process remain open and unobstructed," Stone warned against "the surrender of the constitutional protection of the liberties of small minorities to the popular will." Citing footnote 4 of *Carolene Products,* Stone now made explicit "the importance of a searching judicial inquiry into the legislative judgment in situations where prejudice against discrete and insular minorities may tend to curtail the operation of those political processes ordinarily to be relied upon to protect minorities." He pointed out that the Court in *Meyer, Pierce,* and *Tokushige* had "not hesitated similarly to scrutinize legislation restricting the civil liberty of racial and religious minorities although no political process was affected."[67] Stone contended that the state lacked any interest that would justify its effort to coerce children into expressing a sentiment "which violates their deepest religious convictions." In an early example of the search for "less restrictive alternatives" to oppressive legislation that has characterized modern civil liberties law, Stone pointed out that "there are other ways to teach loyalty and patriotism which are the sources of national unity."[68]

Stone's dissent became the law of the land only three years later, when the Court in *West Virginia State Board of Education v. Barnette* upheld a new Jehovah's Witnesses challenge to a West Virginia compulsory flag salute statute that was virtually identical to the law that the Court upheld in *Gobitis.*[69] The transformation of an eight-to-one decision to uphold the law into a six-to-three decision to strike down its counterpart was the result of changes in the thinking of Black, Douglas, and Murphy, the appointment of Robert H. Jackson after Chief Justice Hughes's resignation, and the substitution of Wiley B. Rutledge for McReynolds. Hughes presumably would not have changed his vote, for he congratulated Frankfurter on his dissent in *Barnette.* Hughes especially appreciated Frankfurter's emphasis on the voluntariness of public education.[70]

The significance of the doctrines that the Court had developed in the early incorporation cases and justified in *Palko* and the *Carolene Products* footnote were made manifest in numerous later decisions in which the Court explored the contours of freedom of speech and the press. In the 1936 *Grosjean v. American Press Co.* decision, five years after *Near,* the Court once again protected freedom of the press, this time unanimously, when it invalidated a Louisiana statute requiring newspapers with a circulation of more than twenty thousand to pay a license tax

---

66. Ibid., 594, 595, 597–98
67. Ibid., 605–6, 606 (Stone, J., dissenting).
68. Ibid., 601, 603.
69. 319 U.S. 628 (1943).
70. Merlo J. Pusey, *Charles Evans Hughes* (New York: MacMillan, 1951), 2:729.

of 2 percent of their gross receipts.[71] The statute had been enacted at the behest of Senator Huey Long and Governor O. K. Allen, who explained that because newspapers told a lie every time they earned a dollar, newspapers should pay two cents for every lie.[72] Finding that the law was enacted "with the plain purpose of penalizing the publishers and curtailing the circulation of a selected group of newspapers," the Court relied upon *Near* in concluding that the statute violated the First Amendment's guaranty of freedom of the press. Surveying the background of this guaranty, Sutherland's opinion emphasized that the Louisiana law closely resembled the taxation of newspapers decreed by the execrated British Stamp Act of 1765, which provided a major motivation for both the American Revolution and the adoption of the First Amendment's free press clause.[73]

Although Long's assassination five months before the Court's decision had freed Louisiana from much of the grip of his quasi dictatorship, the Court nevertheless perceived that the law threatened democratic values. In discussing the critical role of a free press in a free society, the Court observed that the nation's newspapers and magazines shed "more light on the public and business affairs of the nation than any other instrumentality of publicity; and, since informed public opinion is the most potent of all restraint upon misgovernment, the abridgement of the publicity afforded by a free press can not be regarded otherwise than with grave concern." The Court explained that the Louisiana law was "bad because . . . it is seen to be a deliberate and calculated device in the guise of a tax to limit the circulation of information to which the public is entitled in virtue of its constitutional guaranties. A free press stands as one of the great interpreters between the government and the people. To allow it to be fettered is to fetter ourselves."[74] The newspaper trade journal *Editor and Publisher* exulted that the Court "saved the press a few years ago by voiding the Minnesota gag-law. It now saves it from a tax that would cripple the industry."[75]

Two years after *Grosjean,* in 1937, the Court revisited free speech in *Herndon v. Lowry,* striking down the conviction of Angelo Herndon, an African American member of the Communist Party who had been prosecuted under Georgia's syndicalism statute.[76] The five-to-four decision found that Herndon's efforts to recruit party members, his solicitation of funds for the party, and his possession of party literature fell far short of incitement to insurrection. The Court held that the conviction deprived Herndon of his rights of free speech and assembly and that the statute failed to provide a reasonably definite standard of guilt. The justices explained that "[t]he power of a state to abridge freedom of speech and of assembly is the exception rather than the rule and the penalizing even of utterances of

71. 297 U.S. 233 (1936).

72. "Free to Print without Taxation," *Literary Digest,* February 22, 1936, 17 (quoting *Chicago Tribune*).

73. 297 U.S. at 244, 246, 251.

74. Ibid., 250.

75. "Free to Print without Taxation," 17.

76. 301 U.S. 242 (1937).

a defined character must find its justification in a reasonable apprehension of danger to organized government. The Court concluded that the statute, as applied by the Georgia courts, "amounts merely to a dragnet which may enmesh anyone who agitates for a change in government if a jury can be persuaded that he ought to have foreseen his words would have some effect in the future conduct of others."[77]

In a dissent joined by McReynolds, Sutherland, and Butler, Van Devanter insisted that the statute prescribed "a reasonably definite and ascertainable standard" for determining guilt and that Herndon attempted to induce others to forcibly overthrow the state government insofar as the Communist literature in his possession was rife with calls for violent revolution. Van Devanter suggested that the southern blacks to whom Herndon directed his recruitment efforts were particularly susceptible to Communist appeals because Communist literature "pictured their condition as an unhappy one resulting from asserted wrongs on the part of white landlords and employers."[78]

Despite their growing willingness to expand the contours of the Bill of Rights, the moderate and liberal members of the Hughes Court balked at using these liberties as a pretext for opposition to economic regulation. The Court therefore rejected the Associated Press's argument that its First Amendment right to freedom of the press exempted it from the National Labor Relations Act. The Court found that an order requiring the reinstatement of an editorial employee would not interfere with the Associated Press's ability to transmit news in a manner of its own choosing. Justice Roberts's opinion explained that a newspaper publisher "has no special immunity from the application of general laws. He has no special privilege to invade the rights and liberties of others."[79]

In dissent, the Four Horsemen demonstrated a passion for personal liberty that they normally reserved for economic liberty. Sutherland's opinion warned that Americans must "withstand all *beginnings* of encroachment" on First Amendment freedoms. "No one," Sutherland declared, "can read the long history which records the stern and often bloody struggles by which these cardinal rights were secured, without realizing how necessary it is to preserve them against any infringement, however slight." Sutherland contended that a news organization should have the right to dismiss a union activist to ensure that it could provide "fair and accurate information with respect to the contests between labor and capital."[80]

In addition to its free speech decisions, the Court had occasion to develop its nascent doctrines of freedom of communication in various decisions involving the distribution of handbills. In *Lovell v. Griffin* in 1938, the Court found prima facie invalidity in a municipal ordinance of a small Georgia town that required distributors of handbills and other publications to obtain a license from the city manager

77. Ibid., 258, 263–64.

78. Ibid., 264, 275 (Van Devanter, J., dissenting).

79. *Associated Press v. National Labor Relations Board*, 301 U.S. 103, 132–33 (1937).

80. Ibid., 141, 135, 138 (Sutherland, J., dissenting).

or risk prosecution for committing a nuisance.[81] In his opinion for the Court, Hughes observed that the ordinance contained no restriction with regard to time or place and thus was "not limited to ways which might be regarded as inconsistent with the maintenance of public order, or as involving disorderly conduct, the molestation of the inhabitants, or the misuse or littering of the streets." Hughes declared that the ordinance struck "at the very foundation of the freedom of the press by subjecting it to license and censorship," explaining that the "struggle for the freedom of the press was primarily directed against the power of the licensor." Finding that "liberty of the press is not confined to newspapers and periodicals," Hughes stated that "[i]t necessarily embraces pamphlets and leaflets. These indeed have been historic weapons in the defense of liberty, as the pamphlets of Thomas Paine and others in our own history attest. The press . . . comprehends every sort of publication which affords a vehicle of information and opinion."[82]

Although *Lovell* stated that a city could restrict public communication to prevent disorder such as littering, the Court narrowly construed the scope of this exception a year later in *Schneider v. State,* which reversed convictions for public distribution of handbills and leaflets in violation of ordinances in several cities throughout the nation.[83] Only McReynolds dissented. Rejecting arguments that these laws were valid exercises of the police power because they were intended to prevent littering, the Court explained that "the purpose to keep the streets clean and of good appearance is insufficient to justify an ordinance which prohibits a person rightfully on a public street from handing literature to one willing to receive it." Although the Court acknowledged that "a municipality may enact regulations in the interest of the public safety, health, welfare or convenience, these may not abridge the individual liberties secured by the Constitution to those who wish to speak, write, print or circulate information or opinion."[84]

Echoing its decisions in *Near* and *Lovell,* the Court declared that the exercise of freedom of speech and the press "lies at the foundation of free government by free men."[85] The Court's anxiety about the suppression of political communication was well placed because it probably was no accident that the antilittering campaigns of the burghers were directed against handbills supporting left-wing causes: a Los Angeles rally for republicans in the Spanish Civil War; a Milwaukee boycott against a meat market engaged in a labor dispute; and a Worcester, Massachusetts, meeting to protest the administration of unemployment insurance.

The Court in *Schneider* also reversed the conviction of a Jehovah's Witness for distributing booklets in violation of an Irvington, New Jersey, ordinance similar to one the Court nullified in *Lovell,* which required permission from the chief of police for canvassing, soliciting, or distributing circulars. Refusing to justify the

81. 303 U.S. 444 (1938).
82. Ibid., 669.
83. 308 U.S. 147 (1939).
84. Ibid., 162, 160.
85. Ibid., 151.

statute even as a means of preventing fraudulent appeals in the name of charity and religion, the justices explained that "[t]o require a censorship through license which makes impossible the free and unhampered distribution of pamphlets strikes at the very heart of the constitutional guarantees."[86]

Fulfilling part of the prophecy of the *Carolene Products* footnote, the Court in *Schneider* indicated that it was undertaking an exacting scrutiny of the Los Angeles, Milwaukee, and Worcester ordinances because they impinged on fundamental rights that affected the operation of political processes. The majority explained that "[m]ere legislative preferences or beliefs respecting matters of public convenience may well support regulation directed at other personal activities, but be insufficient to justify such as diminishes the exercise of rights so vital to the maintenance of democratic institutions." Embracing a role in the review of personal liberties legislation that it had so recently rejected in the context of economic regulation, the Court stated that "the delicate and difficult task falls upon the courts to weigh the circumstances and to appraise the substantiality of the reasons advanced in support of the regulation of the free enjoyment of the rights."[87]

In *Schneider,* the justices also limned the modern First Amendment doctrine of "less restrictive alternatives" by considering the extent to which the cities could have exercised their police power in a manner that was less intrusive than an outright ban on public distribution of handbills. The Court observed that there were "obvious methods of preventing littering" other than such a ban, including "the punishment of those who actually throw papers on the streets." Similarly, the Court explained that prosecutions for fraud and trespass would be appropriate remedies for some of the wrongful activities against which the Irvington ordinance was directed. It explained that while such prosecutions might be "less efficient and convenient" than prior restraint by police officials, "considerations of this sort do not empower a municipality to abridge freedom of speech and press."[88]

Several of the Court's civil liberties decisions had relevance for the Court's post-1937 solicitude for the rights of organized labor insofar as the justices used the First Amendment to strike down laws that impeded the exercise of free speech and assembly by labor organizers. The justices extended the doctrine of free speech to embrace picketing in its 1940 decisions in *Thornhill v. Alabama* and *Carlson v. California,* which held that antipicketing statutes were facially invalid.[89] In his opinion for the Court in *Thornhill,* Murphy found that an Alabama law left "room for no exceptions based upon either the number of persons engaged in

86. Ibid., 162, 160, 151, 164. In *Gobitis,* Frankfurter distinguished *Schneider* on the grounds that national security "presents a totally different order of problem from that of the propriety of subordinating the possible ugliness of littered streets to the free expression of opinion through the distribution of handbills" and that the Court "was concerned with restrictions cutting off appropriate means through which, in a free society, the processes of popular rule may effectively function." 310 U.S. 599 n. 6.

87. 308 U.S. 151.

88. Ibid., 162, 164.

89. 310 U.S. 88 (1940); 310 U.S. 106 (1940).

the proscribed activity, the peaceful character of their demeanor, the nature of their dispute with an employer, or the restrained character and the accurateness of the terminology used in notifying the public of the facts of the dispute." Rather, the statute prohibited virtually every practicable means by which critics of a business could "enlighten the public on the nature and causes of a labor dispute." Murphy remarked that "[f]reedom of discussion, if it would fulfill its historic function in this nation, must embrace all issues about which information is needed or appropriate to enable the members of society to cope with the exigencies of their period."[90] In *Carlson,* Murphy expressed similar objections to the California statute.[91]

Murphy observed in *Thornhill* that "[t]hose who won our independence had confidence in the power of free and fearless reasoning and communication of ideas to discover and spread political and economic truth. Noxious doctrines in those fields may be refuted and their evil averted by the courageous exercise of the right of free discussion." Murphy explained that "[a]bridgement of freedom of speech and of the press . . . impairs those opportunities for public education that are essential to effective exercise of the power of correcting error through the processes of popular government." Such an abridgement, Murphy stated, could be justified only if the "clear danger of substantive evils arises under circumstances affording no opportunity to test the merits of ideas by competition in the market of public opinion." Murphy concluded that "the danger of injury to an industrial concern is neither so serious nor so imminent as to justify the sweeping proscription of freedom of discussion" in the statute.[92] Only McReynolds dissented.

Because both *Thornhill* and *Carlson* involved labor disputes, the decisions were significant victories for organized labor, which so frequently used picketing as a means of calling attention to its grievances. Referring to *Stromberg,* Murphy declared in *Carlson* that "[t]he carrying of signs and banners, no less than the raising of a flag, is a natural and appropriate means of conveying information on matters of public concern." Accordingly, Murphy concluded that "publicizing the facts of a labor dispute in a peaceful way through appropriate means, whether by pamphlet, by word of mouth or by banner, must now be regarded as within that liberty of communication which is secured to every person by the Fourteenth Amendment against abridgement by a State."[93]

In some instances, however, the Hughes Court in its later years rejected civil liberties claims. In the same case in which the Court held that the Norris–La Guardia Anti-injunction Act permitted federal courts to enjoin picketing that could cause violence, the justices also sustained a state's right to enjoin union picketing that generated violence.[94] Frankfurter explained that, although

90. Ibid., 99, 104, 102.
91. 310 U.S. at 109–13.
92. Ibid., 95, 104–5.
93. 310 U.S. at 112–13, 113.
94. *Milk Drivers Union v. Meadowmoor Dairies,* 312 U.S. 287 (1941).

"[p]eaceful picketing is the workingman's means of communication," "[i]t was in order to avert force and explosions due to restrictions upon rational modes of communication that the guarantee of free speech was given a generous scope. But utterance in a context of violence can lose its significance as an appeal to reason and become part of an instrument of force."[95] In dissent, Black, Douglas, and Reed averred that the Fourteenth Amendment prohibited the state from issuing the injunction without a stronger showing of the likelihood of violence, particularly because the labor dispute involved an issue of public concern.

The Court's willingness to uphold regulations that promoted public safety and convenience without unduly impinging upon free speech likewise was demonstrated in 1941 in the Court's unanimous decision in *Cox v. New Hampshire*, upholding an ordinance that required public paraders and marchers to obtain a license from the city.[96] In his opinion, Hughes explained that the license gave city officials discretion only to regulate the "time, place, and manner" of the processions to prevent undue traffic congestion and that the license fees were adjusted to pay for policing and administrative expenses. Hughes found no evidence that city officials had administered the statute in other than a "fair and non-discriminatory manner." He stated that "[c]ivil liberties, as guaranteed by the Constitution, imply the existence of an organized society maintaining public order without which liberty itself would be lost in the excesses of unrestrained abuses."[97]

Although the Court's decisions nationalizing the Bill of Rights generally were based on the theory that the Fourteenth Amendment's due process clause nationalized various provisions of the Bill of Rights, the Court in 1939 held that the Fourteenth Amendment's privileges and immunities clause made the First Amendment's free speech and freedom of assembly clauses binding on the states when the state sought to repress speech about a federal statute. In that decision, *Hague v. C.I.O.*,[98] the justices held that a Jersey City ordinance requiring approval from the chief of police for public meetings and forbidding the distribution of printed matter violated the rights of the Congress of Industrial Organizations, which was convicted of distributing literature and conducting a public meeting without a permit in connection with its efforts to publicize the rights of labor under the National Labor Relations Act. The Court observed that "[c]itizenship of the United States would be little better than a name if it did not carry with it the right to discuss national legislation and the benefits, advantages, and opportunities to accrue from citizens therefrom."[99]

In a concurring opinion joined by Hughes, Stone contended that the Fourteenth Amendment's due process clause was sufficient to void the ordinances as violations of free speech and freedom of assembly. Stone pointed out that the

95. Ibid., 293.
96. 312 U.S. 569 (1941).
97. Ibid., 576, 577, 574.
98. 307 U.S. 496.
99. Ibid., 513.

Slaughter-House Cases had limited the scope of the privileges and immunities clause to those arising out of the relationship of United States citizens to the federal government.[100]

In other decisions protecting personal liberties, particularly those involving criminal procedure, the Court continued to rely upon general theories of due process. Its use of due process rather than the specific guarantees of the Fifth, Sixth, and Eight Amendments in criminal cases probably reflected the Court's reluctance to intrude in an area that was primarily local in character and over which states traditionally enjoyed a high degree of sovereignty. The Hughes Court therefore addressed the most glaring abuses of criminal procedure on an ad hoc basis pursuant to general notions of due process. Although the use of due process rather than the Bill of Rights theoretically gave the Court more discretion to interfere with the actions of state officials—this may have been one of the reasons why the Court had begun to nationalize the provisions of the First Amendment— confinement of judicial review to due process in only the most egregious cases would leave the states more control over their criminal procedure.

In one significant decision, *Brown v. Mississippi,* the Court relied on a general theory of due process in unanimously reversing judgments against three African Americans whose murder convictions were based upon confessions that a deputy sheriff had coerced through torture.[101] The deputy did not deny that he subjected all three defendants to searing whippings, and one of the defendants, whom the deputy had twice hung from a tree limb, appeared at trial with rope marks plainly visible on his neck. The brutality was so grisly that one of the dissenting justices of the Supreme Court of Mississippi exclaimed that "the transcript reads more like pages torn from some medieval account, than a record made within the confines of a modern civilization which aspires to an enlightened constitutional government."[102]

In his opinion for the Court, Hughes acknowledged that a state generally was free to prescribe its own criminal procedure and that most of the procedural protections of the Bill of Rights did not bind the states. He explained, however, that a state was nevertheless bound by due process and could not use tactics that offend core principles of justice. As Hughes observed, "[b]ecause a State may dispense with a jury trial, it does not follow that it may substitute trial by ordeal. The rack and torture chamber may not be substituted for the witness stand. The State may not permit an accused to be hurried to conviction under mob domination—where the whole proceeding is but a mask—without supplying corrective process." Because he believed that "[i]t would be difficult to conceive of methods

100. Ibid., 519–21, 524–27 (Stone, J., concurring), citing 16 Wall. 36 (1876).

101. *Brown v. Mississippi,* 297 U.S. 278 (1936). For an account of the case, see Richard C. Cortner, *A "Scottsboro Case" in Mississippi: The Supreme Court and Brown v. Mississippi* (Jackson: University of Mississippi Press, 1986).

102. 161 So. 465, 470 (Miss. 1935) (Griffith, J., dissenting), quoted in Hughes's opinion at 297 U.S. 282.

more revolting to the sense of justice" than those used to extract the confessions in *Brown*, the state clearly had violated due process. Hughes also rejected Mississippi's argument that counsel for the defendants had waived objections to the admissibility of the confessions because they had failed to move for their exclusion after the court admitted the evidence over their objections. Again, Hughes explained that the denial of due process was so fundamental that "the proceeding thus vitiated could be challenged in any appropriate manner."[103]

Brown was the first decision in which the Court struck down a state criminal conviction on the basis of coerced confession. Although Hughes and his fellow jurists struck down several other convictions on the same basis, the Court did not nationalize the self-incrimination clause of the Fifth Amendment until 1964.[104]

Four years after *Brown*, the Court unanimously reached a similar result on similar facts in *Chambers v. Florida*,[105] in which it invoked the Fourteenth Amendment's due process clause as grounds for reversing the convictions of four African Americans whose convictions for murder of a white man were obtained in part through coerced testimony. Although there was sharp conflict in the record about the extent to which the defendants were subjected to physical violence, in his opinion for the Court Justice Black explained that there was no dispute about "the dragnet methods of arrest on suspicion without warrant, and protracted questioning and cross-questioning of these ignorant young colored tenant farmers by state officers and other white citizens, in a fourth floor jail room, where as prisoners they were without friends, advisers, or counselors, and under circumstances calculated to break the strongest nerves and the stoutest resistance." Brushing aside the argument that brutal law enforcement procedures sometimes are necessary to uphold the law, Black observed that the "Constitution proscribes such lawless means irrespective of the end." Black declared that "[c]ourts stand against any winds that blow as havens of refuge for those who might otherwise suffer because they are helpless, weak, outnumbered, or because they are non-conforming victims of prejudice and public excitement."[106]

Even though *Brown* in many ways presented a stronger factual and legal case for reversal because there was no clear evidence of physical abuse in *Chambers* and the confession was not the sole basis for the convictions, the rhetoric of *Chambers* was much bolder in deploring the abuse of the defendants and emphasizing the Court's role as the champion of society's dispossessed. Although this may in part reflect the difference in style between the authors of the opinions, the cerebral Hughes and the passionate Black, it also may reflect the impact of the judicial revolution. Although the Court no longer needed to prove its liberalism on social issues to appease critics of economic due process, it no longer needed to take so much account of the sensibilities of southerners who had been useful in stemming

---

103. Ibid., 285–86, 286, 287.
104. *Malloy v. Hogan*, 378 U.S. 1, 3 (1964).
105. 309 U.S. 227 (1940).
106. Ibid., 238–39, 240–41, 241.

Court-curbing tides provoked by the Court's antiregulatory decisions during the early decades of the century.[107] In a larger sense, the magisterial tone of *Chambers* is an example of the transformation of the Court's role from principally a guardian of property rights to primarily a bulwark of personal liberties. In recognizing the racial and socioeconomic context more explicitly than did *Brown, Chambers* was one of the earliest examples of the Court's exercise of the countermajoritarian function envisioned by Stone in his *Carolene Products* footnote.

In four later decisions, the Hughes Court relied upon *Chambers* in reversing the capital convictions of other southern black defendants on the ground that their confessions were coerced. Although the defendants in all but one of the cases alleged that they were beaten, state officials in each case denied physical abuse. The Court therefore relied only upon evidence of psychological coercion or questioned the credibility of small-town southern law enforcement officials.

Three per curiam decisions reversed the convictions of an Alabama defendant who confessed to murder after several late-night interrogations in secluded woods,[108] another Alabama defendant who confessed to murder after a six-hour interrogation following his week-long confinement in the dark basement of an Alabama jail in which the walls were lined with whipping straps,[109] and a Texas defendant who confessed to raping a white woman after one interrogation during which he was naked and another in which he was not permitted to sit down for several hours.[110]

In a fourth case, *White v. Texas,* the state admitted that Texas Rangers had taken the defendant, an illiterate black farmhand, into the woods for questioning on several nights before he confessed to raping a white woman, though the state denied the defendant's allegations that he was beaten during these interrogations.[111] The Court apparently was not impressed with the state's argument that the nocturnal excursions were required because the Beaumont jail, which had at least eight floors, was too crowded for private interrogations. The Court found that the prisoner, who confessed at 2 A.M. after four hours of interrogation, had no lawyer and "was out of touch with friends and relatives."[112]

The Court's reversal of the defendant's conviction did not spare him from execution, however, because the husband of the alleged rape victim shot and killed the defendant in open court during the jury selection for his retrial after

107. See Ross, *A Muted Fury,* 185, 239–40.

108. *Vernon v. Alabama,* 313 U.S. 547 (1941). See Bennett Boskey and John H. Pickering, "Federal Restrictions on State Criminal Procedure," 13 *University of Chicago Law Review* 285 (1946).

109. *Canty v. Alabama,* 309 U.S. 629 (1940). See Boskey and Pickering, "Federal Restrictions," 285.

110. *Lomax v. Texas,* 313 U.S. 544 (1940). See Boskey and Pickering, "Federal Restrictions," 285.

111. 310 U.S. 530 (1940).

112. Ibid., 532.

learning that acquittal was probable without the confession. Although the husband was tried for murder, the jury followed the *prosecution's* recommendation of acquittal.[113] This bizarre sequel to *White* tragically illustrates the pervasiveness of the racial and class prejudice that poisoned justice in many courtrooms throughout the South while Hughes sat as chief justice. It helps to explain why he was particularly scrupulous about reviewing petitions for habeas corpus and why the Hughes Court was willing to hear numerous appeals from state criminal courts despite the Court's traditional reluctance to interject itself into state criminal cases.

In addition to its decisions using due process to strike down coerced confessions, the Court likewise relied on a general theory of due process in suggesting that a state's knowing use of perjured testimony to obtain a criminal conviction would violate the Fourteenth Amendment's due process clause.[114] Similarly, in a 1941 decision, the Court reversed a conviction on the ground that the state had failed to inform the defendant of the charges against him, had tricked him into pleading guilty, and had denied him counsel.[115] Justice Black's opinion, which found that the state's conduct in its totality constituted a denial of due process, did not make clear whether the denial of counsel alone in this noncapital case would have provided grounds for reversal.

In a 1934 decision, the Court held that a state did not deny due process to a defendant who was absent from an inspection of a crime scene by a judge, jury, prosecutor, and defense counsel.[116] Cardozo's opinion declared that "gossamer possibilities of prejudice" should not require the Court to "set the guilty free."[117] In one of the most anomalous coalitions in the history of the Hughes Court, Roberts wrote a dissent joined by Brandeis, Sutherland, and Butler. Arguing that the danger of prejudice was significant, Roberts declared that the Fourteenth Amendment requires not only that "a just result shall have been obtained," but also that the result "shall be reached in a fair way."[118]

In addition to its decisions expanding the rights of criminal defendants in state litigation, the court also extended the scope of constitutional guarantees in federal cases. In a 1941 decision, the Court required lower federal courts to hold a hearing on any habeas corpus petition if the allegations and answers raised a question of fact.[119] In another decision, the Court held that habeas hearings must be held before a court rather than merely before a court-appointed commissioner.[120]

---

113. Boskey and Pickering, "Federal Restrictions," 266, 286, 286 n. 67.

114. *Mooney v. Holohan*, 294 U.S. 103 (1935). The Court denied without prejudice a habeas corpus petition filed by a California prisoner who had served eighteen years of a sentence for first-degree murder, holding that the petitioner had not yet exhausted his state remedies.

115. *Smith v. O'Grady*, 312 U.S. 329 (1941).

116. *Snyder v. Massachusetts*, 291 U.S. 97 (1934).

117. Ibid., 122.

118. Ibid., 137 (Roberts, J., dissenting).

119. *Walker v. Johnson*, 312 U.S. 275 (1941).

120. *White v. Johnson*, 313 U.S. 538 (1941).

In these decisions the Hughes Court also reaffirmed that the defendants had a right to counsel. In several instances, the Court imposed upon federal courts procedural requirements that it did not require of state courts until the 1960s. In 1938 the Court in *Johnson v. Zerbst* held that the Sixth Amendment's "assistance of counsel" clause required federal courts to provide indigents with counsel in all cases in which the Sixth Amendment guaranteed counsel, unless a defendant waived assistance of counsel.[121] In reversing the convictions of two U.S. Marines who were sentenced to four years in prison for counterfeiting, the Court declared that the Sixth Amendment's "assistance of counsel" clause "embodies a realistic recognition of the obvious truth that the average defendant does not have the professional legal skill to protect himself when brought before a tribunal with power to take his life or liberty."[122] Not until 1963, in its celebrated *Gideon v. Wainwright* decision,[123] would the Court make the Sixth Amendment's guarantee of counsel generally applicable to the states.

The Hughes Court likewise broadly interpreted existing restrictions on the federal government's power in criminal actions. In 1931 and 1932 decisions imposing Fourth Amendment limitations on searches and seizures, the Court held that Prohibition agents could not conduct exploratory searches to gather evidence in support of a crime during the course of an arrest.[124] Both of Butler's opinions for the Court expressed indignation over the high-handed tactics of law-enforcement officers and emphasized the sanctity of private premises. In the 1932 decision, the Court for the first time explicitly linked the Fourth Amendment's prohibition against unlawful searches and seizures with its requirement of a warrant for searches. As Butler explained, "Security against unlawful searches is more likely to be attained by resort to search warrants than by reliance upon the caution and sagacity of petty officers while acting under the excitement that attends the capture of persons accused of a crime."[125] In another of its many Prohibition cases, the Court unanimously found that federal agents violated the constitutional guaranty against unreasonable searches when they broke into a garage merely because they smelled whiskey and noticed numerous cardboard boxes when they peeped through a small opening.[126]

In a 1941 decision, the Court also protected the rights of aliens, invalidating a Pennsylvania statute requiring registration of aliens on the ground that Congress had preempted the subject of immigration and naturalization by enacting the Federal Alien Registration Act of 1940.[127] In his opinion for the Court, Black explained that Congress intended "to protect the personal liberties of law-abiding

121. 304 U.S. 458 (1938).

122. Ibid., 462–63.

123. 372 U.S. 335 (1963).

124. *Go-Bart v. United States*, 282 U.S. 344 (1931); *United States v. Lefkowitz*, 285 U.S. 452 (1932).

125. *United States v. Lefkowitz*, 285 U.S. 464.

126. *Taylor v. United States*, 286 U.S. 1 (1932).

127. *Hines v. Davidowitz*, 312 U.S. 52 (1941).

aliens through one uniform national registration system, and to leave them free from the possibility of inquisitorial practices and police surveillance that might not only affect our international relations but might also generate the very disloyalty which the law has intended guarding against."[128] In a dissent joined by Hughes and McReynolds, Stone pointed out that the Fourteenth Amendment protected the rights of aliens, and he concluded that Congress did not intend to preempt the subject and that the state law did not interfere with the federal statute.[129]

Although its decisions on criminal procedure and freedom of expression in many ways laid important foundations for the Warren Court's activism on behalf of civil liberties, the Hughes Court provided no precedents for the controversial reapportionment revolution that was one of the Warren Court's most important and durable legacies. Advocates of electoral reform were disappointed by a decision delivered by Hughes shortly before the 1932 election in which the Court overruled a district court order enjoining Mississippi from conducting congressional elections for malapportioned districts. It held that a 1911 federal statute requiring congressional districts to be contiguous and roughly equal in population was inapplicable because Congress had not reenacted these provisions in its 1929 apportionment statute.[130] Critics of the Court predicted that the decision would enable the Republican-dominated New York legislature to gerrymander Democrats out of their seats and would help conservative Democrats in border states to wrest control from Republicans in mountain districts.[131] Not until *Baker v. Carr*,[132] thirty years later, would the Court express willingness to adjudicate issues of malapportionment.

The Court likewise endorsed a broad view of federal power in a 1939 decision, *United States v. Miller*, which upheld the constitutionality of a federal statute requiring registration of firearms transported in interstate commerce.[133] In a unanimous decision by Justice McReynolds, the Court held that the statute did not invade the reserved powers of the states. The Court also held that the statute did not violate the Second Amendment because the Court could not take judicial notice that the sawed-off shotgun that was the subject of the case bore any reasonable relationship to a preservation of the efficiency of a well-ordered militia and therefore could not say that it infringed the right of citizens to keep and bear arms.[134] Since *Miller* is the Supreme Court's most recent decision interpreting the Second Amendment, this case receives much attention in the ongoing controversy over gun control. Advocates of gun control argue that it supports their position that there is no

---

128. Ibid., 74.

129. Ibid., 74–81 (Stone, J., dissenting).

130. *Wood v. Broom*, 287 U.S. 1 (1932). In a separate opinion, Cardozo, Brandeis, Stone, and Roberts contended that the Court should not have reached the question of whether the 1911 statute was applicable because the parties had not presented the issue. They nevertheless favored dismissal of the challenge for want of equity. 287 U.S. 8–9.

131. "The Supreme Court and the Gerrymander," *Nation*, November 9, 1932, 443–44.

132. 369 U.S. 186 (1962).

133. 307 U.S. 174 (1939).

134. Ibid., 177–82.

individual right to bear arms, while opponents contend that it demonstrates that individuals have a right to bear arms that could be used in connection with military activities.[135]

The Hughes Court's civil liberties decisions were the product of many forces. Like the Taft Court's decisions, the First Amendment decisions of the Hughes Court tended to arise out of repressive legislation that reflected fear of radical political movements. Unlike the Taft Court's decisions, however, many of the Hughes Court's decisions overturned the convictions of political radicals. The Hughes Court seemed to recognize, though, that its "liberal" decisions on civil liberties could have a "conservative" impact. As one commentator observed in 1931, radical forces "would be much more dangerous to the established order if the so-called radicals felt that the cards were stacked against them in advance when they came before the nation's highest tribunal. . . . Far from being a threat to our institutions, the 'liberalism' of the Supreme Court may well prove to be a safety valve against a destructive radicalism."[136] Moreover, the Court may have perceived that protection of personal liberties, so essential to a free society, was itself conservative insofar as it embodied the bedrock principles upon which the nation was founded.

The Hughes Court's dedication to a free society was reflected in its caution in reviewing the constitutionality of legislation that allegedly infringed upon civil liberties. Although even before 1937 it accorded less deference to legislation in personal liberties cases than in cases involving economic regulation, the Court never strayed far from the *Palko* doctrine that it would protect only those rights that were essential to an "ordered liberty." It is significant that political conservatives rarely complained about the Hughes Court's civil liberties decisions, except for its decisions about racial issues. Similarly, the Hughes Court's considerable expansion of federal judicial review of state laws affecting personal liberties never provoked the controversy that the Warren Court's civil liberties decisions inspired, even though the Hughes Court provided so many precedents upon which the Warren Court built. Although the Hughes Court for the most part had occasion only to adjudicate cases involving flagrant abuses of state power, decisions such as *Palko* and its one apportionment decision indicate that the Court might not have wished to go further even if opportunities had presented themselves. As one scholar has aptly observed, the Hughes Court attempted to achieve a "proper balance . . . between a bulwark of protection for our fundamental liberties and a deference to democratic participation in the definition of those liberties."[137]

135. Michael C. Dorf, "What Does the Second Amendment Mean Today?" in Carl T. Bogus, ed., *The Second Amendment in Law and History: Historians and Constitutional Scholars on the Right to Bear Arms* (New York: New Press, 2000), 249–51.

136. Oliver McKee Jr., "A Liberal Supreme Court: The Position of Chief Justice Hughes," *Outlook and Independent*, October 7, 1931, 189.

137. Merle William Loper, "The Court of Chief Justice Hughes: Contributions to Civil Liberties," 12 *Wayne Law Review* 595 (1966).

The decisions of the Hughes Court also may have reflected the Court's revulsion against the growing suppression of freedom by Fascist and Communist governments in Europe. As Black remarked in *Chambers* in overturning a coerced confession, "Today, as in ages past, we are not without tragic proof that the exalted power of some governments to punish manufactured crime dictatorially is the handmaiden of tyranny."[138] Similarly, Hughes reminded the American Law Institute in 1941 that "[t]he lamps of justice are dimmed or have wholly gone out in many parts of the earth, but these lights are still shining brightly here," and he contended that judicial institutions had an important role in maintaining standards of justice that would help to turn the tide against Fascism.[139]

The Court's growing solicitude for personal liberties also reflected Hughes's influence. With the exception of *Gobitis* and a few of the handbill cases, Hughes stood on the side of civil liberties in every case that came before the Court. In trying to explain the chief justice's liberalism in both civil liberties and economic regulatory cases, one observer argued in 1931 that, while Hughes had championed progressive causes throughout his career, the chief justiceship enabled him to express his liberal tendencies even more forcefully. "As Chief Justice," he wrote, "Mr. Hughes finds himself emancipated from the bonds of party discipline. . . . He has moved into the realm of justice, where the air is purer than in the political firmament, and where he is free to follow the still, small voice of his legal conscience. Certainly this Hughes of 1931 is more human and more approachable than the Hughes who was the choice of his party in 1916. He has lost the ancient austerity and coldness of manner; in his new office he exhibits a buoyancy and geniality which did not rest upon him of old. Quite clearly, his new freedom agrees with him."[140]

138. 309 U.S. at 241.
139. "'Address of Chief Justice Hughes," *American Bar Association Journal*, June 1941, 335.
140. McKee, "A Liberal Supreme Court," 171.

7

ERODING OLD BARRIERS

Steps toward Racial Equality

Although the Hughes Court did not render any landmark decision altering the fundamental legal doctrines that consigned blacks to second-class citizenship in large parts of the nation, more than a few of its rulings significantly eroded legal barriers that perpetuated racial injustice. Much of the revolution in civil rights law during the 1940s and 1950s was rooted in the evolutionary decisions of the 1930s. By imposing stricter standards of due process on criminal trials, the Hughes Court helped to ameliorate the use of criminal law to perpetuate the socioeconomic suppression of blacks who were disproportionately the victims of terror tactics and slipshod procedures in criminal proceedings. The Hughes Court also helped to empower blacks by eliminating at least some of the ruses by which southern Democratic primaries deprived blacks of their right to vote. Moreover, the Court helped to lay the foundation for desegregation by requiring more rigid standards for the application of the "separate but equal" doctrine. Finally, the Court's nationalization of the First Amendment freedoms of speech, press, and assembly helped facilitate the burgeoning civil rights movement by protecting blacks and other minorities from laws that muzzled efforts to organize the movement, publicize its activities, and protest injustices.

The Court's modest steps toward erosion of legal barriers to racial justice were consistent with the general tenor of the 1930s, a time when blacks made moderate but important economic and political progress. As Michael J. Klarman has observed, "One cannot say whether the Supreme Court's race decisions were ahead of or behind the pace of extralegal change, but they certainly were not far out of step in either direction."[1] The Depression slowed but did not stop the mass migration of blacks to the cities of the North, where blacks received better jobs and enjoyed more favorable economic, social, and political conditions than they had known in the often desperately poor backwaters of the plantation South from which so many came. Meanwhile, the National Association for the Advancement of Colored People (NAACP) and other civil rights organizations escalated their

---

1. Michael J. Klarman, *From Jim Crow to Civil Rights: The Supreme Court and the Struggle for Equality* (New York: Oxford University Press, 2004), 169.

efforts to challenge racial inequality, and found whites increasingly receptive to their pleas for justice.

Even though Roosevelt personally maintained a discreet silence about racial issues to avoid offending the southern constituents of his coalition, his administration quietly made significant strides in improving the condition of blacks. In contrast to previous Democratic presidents, especially Woodrow Wilson, Roosevelt did not systematically exclude blacks from federal employment, and African Americans, along with whites, joined the federal payroll in unprecedented numbers in the proliferating New Deal agencies. A handful of blacks received prominent positions, including William H. Hastie, the first African American federal judge. Because blacks were disproportionately poor, those who remained jobless or underemployed were among the principal beneficiaries of federal relief programs. Moreover, several prominent administration officials, as well as Eleanor Roosevelt, were outspoken in their defense of the civil liberties of blacks. But blacks never shared equally with whites in the largesse of the New Deal. African American employees of federal relief programs typically received less pay than their white counterparts, the Tennessee Valley Authority employed only a smattering of blacks, the Civilian Conservation Corps discriminated against blacks in its selection process and segregated most of its work camps, and no southern black served on any Agricultural Adjustment Act county committee.[2] Although support for federal antilynching legislation grew during this period, southern Democrats continued to block various bills, which Roosevelt failed to champion.

Racial discrimination reached even into the Marble Palace itself, where the cafeteria manager sometimes refused to serve African Americans. On at least one occasion, Brandeis personally intervened to seat a black lawyer who had come to argue a case.[3] When the Court's marshal, Thomas E. Waggaman, complained to Hughes that blacks were using the cafeteria, Hughes instructed him to step outside the building to look at the portal and to read the words, "EQUAL JUSTICE UNDER LAW." Hughes warned Waggaman that he would be replaced if he failed to understand the meaning of those words.[4]

Hughes's attitudes toward race were forged in the Baptist parsonage of his father, who supported abolitionism before the Civil War. As president of a philanthropic society, Hughes once incurred criticism when he invited the prominent black educator Booker T. Washington to the society's annual dinner and personally escorted Washington and his wife to their seats. Hughes later recalled that he

2. Harvard Sitkoff, *A New Deal for Blacks: The Emergence of Civil Rights as a National Issue,* vol. 1, *The Depression Decade* (New York: Oxford University Press, 1978), 49–55; Olen Cole Jr., *The African American Experience in the Civilian Conservation Corps* (Gainesville: University of Florida Press, 1999).

3. A. Leon Higginbotham and William C. Smith, "The Hughes Court and the Beginning of the End of the 'Separate but Equal' Doctrine," *Minnesota Law Review* 76:1104 (1992), based in part upon Judge Lois Forer's recollection.

4. Ibid., based upon Judge Higginbotham's interview with Thurgood Marshall in July 1990.

"thought this criticism ridiculous and ignored it."[5] As we have seen, Hughes's tenure as an associate justice from 1910 from 1916 was notable for his championship of racial justice. In the Court's 1914 decision in *McCabe v. Atchison, Topeka, & Santa Fe Railway,* Hughes had joined the five-to-four majority in holding that a Jim Crow railroad that provided "separate but equal" facilities for the races could not fail to regularly provide first-class accommodations for African Americans, despite a paucity of demand.[6]

Hughes's enlightened views were generally shared by his brethren. Like Hughes, Brandeis, Cardozo, Stone, and Sutherland had long records of advocating racial justice. Neither Hughes nor any of his associates, however, had devoted any special attention to African American causes. Even Brandeis, who gave so generously of his time and ample financial resources to so many liberal movements, lent little more than passive support to black institutions and aspirations.[7] Although fidelity to judicial restraint and federalism did not prevent Brandeis from voting to strike down racially discriminatory legislation, he did not address racial inequality with the passion and creativity he had demonstrated in his seminal dissents on free speech.

While the White Court never had fewer than three members from the Deep South and the Taft Court had two, McReynolds remained as the sole southern member after Sanford's death in 1930 and the Senate's defeat of the Parker nomination. Never shedding the prejudices of the Tennessee plantation on which he was raised, McReynolds was the only blatantly racist member of the Hughes Court. There is no reason to suppose that McReynolds ever significantly altered the opinion of blacks that he expressed as a twenty-one-year-old Vanderbilt student, when he described them as "ignorant, superstitious, immoral, and with small capacity for radical improvement. They are improvident, lazy, . . . have a low order of intellect, learn with difficulty, and apparently make small use of what attainments they have acquired."[8]

Because African Americans naturally hoped, along with liberals, that Roosevelt's appointments would make the Court more sympathetic toward their aspirations, Roosevelt's selection of Hugo Black came as a bitter disappointment. Although African Americans did not dare to hope that the president would name a civil rights advocate, they had reason to suppose that he at least would not nominate a Klansman. Roosevelt's apparent lack of concern about rumors of Black's erstwhile Klan affiliation during the confirmation process and his silence when Black's Klan membership was verified after his confirmation provided a biting

5. David J. Danelski and Joseph S. Tulchin, eds., *The Autobiographical Notes of Charles Evans Hughes* (Cambridge, Mass.: Harvard University Press, 1973), 112–13.

6. 235 U.S. 151 (1914).

7. See Philippa Strum, *Brandeis: Beyond Progressivism* (Lawrence: University Press of Kansas, 1993), 141–42.

8. James E. Bond, *I Dissent: The Legacy of Chief [sic] Justice James C. McReynolds* (Fairfax, Va: George Mason University Press, 1992), 126.

reminder of the administration's insensitivity toward blacks and the relative unimportance of the black vote, notwithstanding the role that blacks had played in defeating the Parker nomination in 1930. Though Black eventually became a rigorous advocate of civil rights, it naturally took a while for African American misgivings over his appointment to subside.

Roosevelt appears to have taken African Americans no more into consideration in making his second appointment, Stanley Reed of Kentucky. Never a race-baiter, Reed still had imbibed the prejudices of his home state, never becoming an ardent judicial advocate of civil rights and indeed voting with the majority in *Brown v. Board Education* only with the greatest reluctance. Perhaps Roosevelt supposed that Reed's experience in the Roosevelt administration as solicitor general would help blunt his prejudices. In contrast, two other Roosevelt nominees, Felix Frankfurter and Frank Murphy, were prominent advocates of justice for black Americans. Both had served as members of the NAACP's legal advisory committee.[9] Roosevelt's other nominee, William O. Douglas, was a blank slate on racial relations at the time of his appointment. Reared in Washington state, which had few blacks, Douglas does not appear to have given much thought to race before joining the Court even though he eventually became one of the Court's most forceful advocates of civil rights. Four of Roosevelt's five nominees during the Hughes Court era therefore made major contributions to the Court's racial jurisprudence, though nearly all of their decisions on this subject were rendered during the post-Hughes era.

Although the Hughes Court rendered important decisions striking against racial discrimination in voting, jury service, education, and public transportation, the criminal justice decisions of the Hughes Court perhaps had the most significant racial impact, even though these decisions did not explicitly involve racial issues. Because the criminal laws often were used as a means of intimidating southern blacks from more aggressively seeking political and economic opportunity, the many decisions of the Hughes Court overturning the criminal convictions of blacks who were denied the most elementary elements of a fair trial had profound implications for the burgeoning civil rights movement. At a time when law enforcement officials not only in the South closed their eyes to lynchings and the Roosevelt administration refused to actively support antilynching legislation, the Supreme Court was the only organ of government that helped to check terrorism against blacks in the criminal justice system. The Court's criminal procedure decisions subjected the Court to less controversy than its other decisions on race because even many of the staunchest advocates of racial segregation admitted that southern states often subjected black criminal defendants to gross injustices.[10]

During his travels in America during 1938–1940 to study race relations, the Swedish sociologist Gunnar Myrdal was "amazed to see how carelessly the Negro

9. Klarman, *Jim Crow to Civil Rights*, 193.

10. Gunnar Myrdal, *An American Dilemma: The Negro Problem and Modern Democracy.* 20th anniversary ed. (New York: Harper & Row, 1962), 550, 556.

defendants—and sometimes also defendants belonging to the lower strata of whites—are sentenced upon scanty evidence even when they emphatically deny the charge. There is an astonishing atmosphere of informality and lack of dignity in the courtroom, and speed seems to be the main goal."[11]

The most dramatic of the Hughes Court's criminal justice decisions was *Powell v. Alabama,* discussed at length in the previous chapter. Although the case was immediately important for its requirement of meaningful assistance of counsel in capital cases at a time when the death penalty was commonly applied, especially to black defendants, the decision also was important because the Court implicitly recognized the racial prejudice inherent in the Scottsboro trials. As one commentator has observed, the rhetoric of Justice Sutherland's opinion "captures the sociopolitical drama behind the legal questions to which the Court's judgment is addressed: It notes the convergence of race, gender, age, and class, and it uses the statement of facts to presage the outcome."[12] Similarly, Leon Higginbotham and William Smith explained that the Hughes Court's criminal procedure decisions helped subvert the "separate but equal" doctrine by demonstrating "that courts treated black criminal defendants far more harshly than their white counterparts, and that this harsher treatment was not a figment of blacks' imaginations. These cases demonstrated that in many areas of the country the treatment of blacks was both separate and *un*equal."[13] They aptly pointed out that the disparate treatment of blacks that the justices observed in criminal procedure cases must have suggested to them that "a political system that permitted such gross discrimination even within its halls of justice would probably have similar inequalities in its segregated schools, universities, and public facilities, and in other aspects of its public and private culture."[14]

Likewise, the Court tacitly acknowledged the racial context of its decision in *Brown v. Mississippi,* reversing the convictions of three black men who were tortured into confessing to murder. Although Hughes's opinion did not directly mention race, it approvingly quoted at length from the dissent of a Supreme Court of Mississippi justice who pointed out that the defendants were uneducated African Americans, that their torturers were white, and that the deputy sheriff had testified at trial that one of the defendant's whippings was "[n]ot too much for a negro."[15]

In striking down another coerced confession four years later in *Chambers v. Florida,*[16] the Court was much more explicit about the racial and socioeconomic implications of the case. In addition to pointing out that the defendants were "ignorant young colored tenant farmers" and that their tormenters were white,

11. Ibid., 552.
12. Kendall Thomas, "*Rouge et Noir* Reread: A Popular Constitutional History of the Angelo Herndon Case," 65 *Southern California Law Review* 2691 (1992).
13. Higginbotham and Smith, "Hughes Court," 1112.
14. Ibid., 1112–13.
15. 297 U.S. 281, 282, 284 (1936).
16. 309 U.S. 227 (1940).

the opinion emphasized that the due process clauses were inspired by a long and tragic history of tyranny over "populations of different races and beliefs" and oppression against "the poor, the ignorant, the numerically weak, the friendless, and the powerless." Black concluded his opinion by declaring that no "higher duty" rested on the Court than to make due process a reality "for the benefit of every human being subject to our Constitution—of whatever race, creed or persuasion."[17]

The Court's rejection of coerced confessions may have had little immediate impact on interrogation procedures because the justices could not prevent remote tyrants from torturing prisoners, most of whom lacked the evidence, knowledge, counsel, courage, or funds needed to successfully invoke the Court's rulings at trial or on appeal. At least, however, the Court's decisions provided cautionary warnings to southern sheriffs and judges. Such decisions also generated hope, energy, and public support for the burgeoning civil rights movement. As Klarman has pointed out, the grisly facts of these cases inspired widespread revulsion against racism, while these and other decisions of the Court helped to stave off demoralization of civil rights activists by providing them with salient victories during a decade that otherwise was more a time of sowing than one of harvest.[18]

In addition to protecting blacks from coerced confessions, the Hughes Court made significant strides in preventing jury prejudice against blacks. In one of its early decisions, the Court held that an attorney for an African American who was tried in the District of Columbia for the murder of a white policeman was entitled to query prospective jurors about racial prejudice.[19] Hughes's opinion, from which only McReynolds dissented, failed to cite any constitutional provision, but the Court presumably contemplated the Fifth Amendment's due process clause and the Sixth Amendment's right to a fair trial. Pointing out that even the supreme courts of Mississippi, North Carolina, and Florida had reversed convictions of black defendants whose attorneys were denied requests to question jurors about racial bias, the Court observed that "[t]he practice of permitting questions as to racial prejudice is not confined to any section of the country, and this fact attests the widespread sentiment that fairness demands that such inquires be allowed." The Court concluded that "[n]o surer way could be devised to bring the processes of justice into disrepute" than to deny inquiries about racial prejudice.[20] McReynolds contended that threat of racial prejudice was unduly speculative and that queries about racial prejudice would impose excessive burdens on a criminal justice system that already was staggering in the face of a rising crime rate.[21]

17. Ibid., 233, 237, 238, 241.
18. Klarman, *Jim Crow to Civil Rights,* 167, 168, discussing opinions during 1930s.
19. *Aldridge v. United States,* 283 U.S. 308 (1931).
20. Ibid., 313, 315.
21. Ibid., 315–18.

The Hughes Court also rendered important decisions reaffirming that states could not systematically exclude blacks from juries. Many advocates of racial justice believed that placement of blacks on juries was even more important than providing defendants with counsel.[22] Three years after *Powell*, the Court in *Norris v. Alabama* and *Patterson v. Alabama* overturned the convictions of two Scottsboro defendants on the ground that Alabama had unconstitutionally excluded blacks from the juries that reindicted and retried them.[23] These decisions established no new doctrine, but they breathed new life into the Court's long line of earlier decisions holding that exclusion of African Americans from juries on the grounds of race was unconstitutional.[24] In decisions that turned on evidence rather than on law, the Court simply could not accept Alabama's protests that the counties in which the defendants were indicted and tried did not systematically exclude blacks from grand and petit juries. In *Norris*, the Court found a prima facie case of denial of equal protection on the grounds that no black had served on any jury within the memory of any witness, that local blacks had served on federal juries, and that numerous blacks who were well qualified for jury duty resided within the counties. The Court observed that the "general attitude" of the jury commissioner of one of the counties was demonstrated by his testimony that he knew of no black in the county "who is generally reputed to be honest and intelligent and who is esteemed in the community for his integrity, good character and sound judgment, who is not a habitual drunkard, who isn't afflicted with a permanent disease or physical weakness . . . and who can read English, and who has never been convicted of a crime involving moral turpitude." The Court found it "impossible to accept such a sweeping characterization of the lack of qualifications of negroes in Morgan County." Stripping away the legal technicalities and formalism behind which racist officials so often took refuge, Hughes announced that the Court had a duty to inquire not merely whether state officials had expressly denied a federal right, "but also whether it was denied in substance and effect."[25] No justice dissented, though McReynolds did not participate in the cases.

The Court reaffirmed *Norris* in several later cases. In a 1935 per curiam opinion, the Court tacitly rejected Oklahoma's argument that it could exclude blacks from juries as part of its general policy of racial segregation.[26] Perhaps, as one commentary has observed, "the Court could not see any practical way to establish separate but equal juries."[27] In a 1938 case from Kentucky, the Court found a

22. Klarman, *Jim Crow to Civil Rights*, 154.

23. *Norris v. Alabama*, 294 U.S. 587 (1935); *Patterson v. Alabama*, 294 U.S. 600 (1935).

24. *Strauder v. Graham*, 100 U.S. 303 (1880); *Virginia v. Rives*, 100 U.S. 313 (1880); *Ex parte Virginia*, 100 U.S. 339 (1880); *Neal v. Delaware*, 103 U.S. 370 (1881); *Carter v. Texas*, 177 U.S. 442 (1900); *Rogers v. Alabama*, 192 U.S. 226 (1904).

25. Ibid., 598–99, 599, 590.

26. *Hollins v. Oklahoma*, 295 U.S. 394 (1935). For reference to the state's argument, see Merle William Loper, "The Court of Chief Justice Hughes: Contributions to Civil Liberties," 12 *Wayne Law Review* 562 (1966).

27. Loper, "Court of Chief Justice Hughes," 562.

presumption of denial of equal protection insofar as no black had served on the local jury since at least 1906 and all members of the jury wheel were white even though seven hundred blacks were qualified for jury service.[28] Similarly, the Court in a 1939 case from Louisiana ordered the dismissal of a murder indictment of a black who was prosecuted in a county in which no black had served as a juror between 1896 and 1936, despite the fact that blacks constituted as much as half of the population.[29]

In a later decision, *Smith v. Texas*, the Court made clear that good faith or lack of actual knowledge of qualified black jurors was no justification for excluding blacks from juries.[30] In *Smith*, only five blacks were among the 384 grand jurors who served between 1931 and 1938 in a county that was more than 20 percent African American. Speaking for a unanimous Court, Justice Black found that "[c]hance and accident alone could hardly have brought about the listing . . . of so few negroes from among the thousands shown by the undisputed evidence to possess the legal qualifications for jury service." Expressing impatience with one jury commissioner who claimed that he did not know any qualified blacks and another who said he knew no blacks at all, Justice Black explained that "discrimination can arise from commissioners who know no negroes as well as from commissioners who know but eliminate them." Any discrimination, "whether accomplished ingeniously or ingenuously," would constitute a ground for reversing a conviction. In bolder language than the Hughes Court ordinarily used to speak about racial discrimination, Black declared that exclusion of qualified groups from jury service was not only unconstitutional but was "at war with our basic concepts of a democratic society and a representative government."[31]

The Hughes Court's decisions clearly helped to discourage racial discrimination in jury selection, even though a 1940 survey found that "the vast majority of the rural courts in the Deep South have made no pretense of putting Negroes on jury lists, much less calling or using them in trials." Blacks served, probably increasingly, as jurors in federal courts and in state courts in the larger cities, and the threat of appeals to federal courts encouraged even some rural courts to use black jurors, at least in capital cases.[32] After decades in which the Court had acquiesced to defiance of its decisions requiring blacks to serve as jurors, the Hughes Court's renewed vigilance helped to increase public awareness of racially discriminatory juries and emboldened advocates of change. The Court's decisions also reminded discriminatory officials that they were lawbreakers and that their actions were vulnerable to review by the Court, even if this was a risk that many preferred to bear.

28. *Hale v. Kentucky*, 303 U.S. 613 (1938).

29. *Pierre v. Louisiana*, 306 U.S. 354 (1939).

30. 311 U.S. 128 (1940).

31. Ibid., 131, 132, 130.

32. Myrdal, *An American Dilemma*, 549–50, citing Arthur Raper, "Race and Class Pressures" (1940), 79, 80, an unpublished manuscript prepared for Myrdal's study.

As was explained earlier, the Hughes Court significantly assisted African Americans in labor disputes in its 1938 decision in *New Negro Alliance v. Grocery Co.*,[33] which held that allegations of racial discrimination in employment could constitute a "labor dispute" within the definition of section 13 of the Norris–La Guardia Act. Because the Act generally prohibited the issuance of injunctions in labor disputes, the Court held that a lower federal court had improperly enjoined a civil rights group from picketing a District of Columbia store that employed no blacks. Pointing out that "[t]he Act does not concern itself with the background or the motives of the dispute," the Court observed that "[r]ace discrimination by an employer may reasonably be deemed more unfair and less excusable than discrimination against workers on the ground of union affiliation."[34]

In a dissent joined by McReynolds, Butler found it "unbelievable" that Congress intended to "encourage mobbish interference" with the liberty of business enterprises to prefer "helpers of one color or class." Butler predicted that such interference with liberty could eventually harm "the very people whom present petitioners claim to represent," as "prefigured by the grievous plight of minorities in lands where the law has become a mere political instrument."[35]

The Hughes Court's record on voting rights was more mixed. Voting was perhaps the most important right because it was the means by which blacks could achieve political and social equality. It is therefore not surprising that southern states assiduously abridged this right, even though the Fifteenth Amendment is more explicit in spelling out this right than is the Constitution's enunciation of any right of racial equality other than freedom from slavery. In 1940, fewer than 5 percent of adult blacks in the eleven states of the old Confederacy were registered to vote.[36]

The Court had begun to dismantle racial barriers to voting in its 1927 decision in *Nixon v. Herndon,* holding that Texas could not exclude African Americans from voting in a primary because such prohibition constituted state action denying equal protection of the laws in violation of the Fourteenth Amendment.[37] In response to *Herndon,* the Texas legislature enacted new legislation to permit the executive committees of political parties to prescribe the qualifications of their members and determine who would be eligible to participate in primary elections. Pursuant to the statute, the executive committee of the Democratic Party in Texas promptly adopted a resolution permitting only whites to vote in the party's primary. In its decision in *Nixon v. Condon* in 1932, the Court ruled that the committee's racial discrimination violated the equal protection clause because it

33. 303 U.S. 552 (1938).

34. Ibid., 561.

35. Ibid., 563, 564.

36. David M. Kennedy, *Freedom from Fear: The American People in Depression and War, 1929–1945* (New York: Oxford University Press, 1999), 19.

37. 273 U.S. 536 (1927).

constituted state action within the meaning of the Fourteenth Amendment.[38] Cardozo explained that the legislation lodged the power to prescribe voting qualifications in a committee, "not by virtue of any authority delegated by the party, but by virtue of an authority originating or supposed to originate in the mandate of the law" and that the party's convention, which was the party's principal governing body, had never expressed any intention to exclude blacks from the party's primary. "Delegates of the State's power have discharged their official functions in such a way as to discriminate invidiously between citizens white and black," Cardozo wrote. "The Fourteenth Amendment, adopted as it was with special solicitude for the equal protection of members of the Negro race, lays a duty upon the court to level by its judgment these barriers of race."[39] McReynolds spoke for all four of the Horsemen in arguing that the statute was content neutral, merely delegating power to the executive committee in a manner that the committee could exercise independently of the legislature.[40]

In its 1935 decision in *Grovey v. Townsend,* however, the Court unanimously held that the Texas Democratic Party could exclude blacks from its primary if it acted in the absence of state legislation, even though the state was substantially involved in the regulation of primary elections.[41] Although it acknowledged that state law "elaborately provided for the expression of party preferences" on ballots and "attempted in minute detail" to prevent fraud in primary elections, the Court explained there was no "state action" because the political parties privately financed the primaries and counted primary votes. Although the Court did not deny "that in Texas nomination by the Democratic party is equivalent to election," it held that the argument that this proved unlawful discrimination confused "the privilege of membership in a party with the right to vote for one who is to hold a public office."[42] Critics of the decision argued that the Democratic Party performed a critical political function that was organically connected with the state-sponsored election.[43]

In deploring *Grovey,* liberals emphasized that suffrage was by far the most effective way for blacks to eliminate racial injustice. "It is hard to magnify the tragedy

38. 286 U.S. 73 (1932).

39. Ibid., 84, 84–85, 89.

40. Ibid., 89–106 (McReynolds, J., dissenting).

41. 295 U.S. 45 (1935).

42. Ibid., 50, 54, 55.

43. "Black Justice," *Nation,* May 1, 1935, 497; "Should Negroes Vote?" *New Republic,* May 8, 1935, 357. As the *Nation* stated, the Court's opinion lay "in a rarefied atmosphere of dialectic far removed from political actuality. It seems irrelevant to the court that a party performs a political function, that the Democracy of Texas includes the great mass of electors, that the primary has usurped the place of the election, and that the exclusion from the primary robs the Negro of his suffrage." The *New Republic* remarked that "the obtrusion of the legislature spoiled the ceremonial of denial" of suffrage to African Americans in *Nixon v. Condon* and *Herndon* but that in *Grovey* "the two houses remained discreetly in the background—and the trick worked."

of the decision," the *Nation* declared. "Its denial to a minority—particularly when that minority is a racial group—is tantamount to exclusion from civic life." Although the Court could protect African American rights in other contexts, as it had done in its second *Scottsboro* decision on the same day it decided *Grovey*, the Court's acquiescence to voting restrictions reduced the African American to "a ward of the judiciary." As the *Nation* observed, "An alien body at the nation's capital is called upon to do for the Negro what he ought to be able to do for himself. The tedious, decorous, and uncertain processes of the law are substituted for direct action at the ballot box."[44] Similarly, the *New Republic* likened the Court to "Old Mother Hubbard," casting blacks in the role of the "Poor Doggie" to whom the Court had thrown a little bone in the recent *Scottsboro* decision while withholding a far greater one in *Grovey*. "The right to a little fairer trial affects only the exceptional person; the denial of a political right is of concern to a whole people."[45]

In one of its final decisions, *United States v. Classic*, the Hughes Court interpreted state action more expansively, holding that state officials who altered and falsely counted ballots in a congressional election were subject to prosecution by federal authorities because state law had made the primary an integral part of the process of choosing congressional representatives.[46] Although this decision involved not discrimination against blacks but rather a corrupt New Orleans congressional primary, it effectively rejected *Grovey*'s artificial distinction between state recognition of primaries and state legislation concerning them.

Throughout the period of the Hughes Court, states also disenfranchised African Americans through the poll tax and literacy tests, both of which disproportionally affected blacks. The Court unanimously upheld the validity of Georgia's poll tax in a 1937 case brought by a white who alleged that it violated equal protection by partially exempting women, as well as persons younger than twenty-one and older than sixty.[47] Although Butler's opinion concluded that it was "fanciful to suggest" that "the law is a mere disguise under which to deny or abridge the right of men to vote on account of their sex,"[48] he failed to consider that it was not fanciful that the poll tax was intended in large measure to discriminate against blacks. Although the tax was only one dollar per year, this was sufficient to inhibit voting by southern blacks, most of whom supported families on annual incomes of less than one thousand dollars.

The Hughes Court refused, however, to permit states to apply literacy tests in a blatantly discriminatory manner. In 1939 in *Lane v. Wilson*, the Court invalidated an Oklahoma voter registration law that discriminated against African Americans.[49] The state had enacted the statute in the wake of the Court's 1915 decision

44. "Black Justice," *Nation*, May 1, 1935, 497.
45. "Should Negroes Vote?" *New Republic*, May 8, 1935, 357.
46. 313 U.S. 299 (1941).
47. *Breedlove v. Suttles*, 302 U.S. 277 (1937).
48. Ibid., 284.
49. 307 U.S. 268 (1939).

in *Guinn v. United States*, which struck down an Oklahoma "grandfather" clause that waived a literacy test for anyone entitled to vote on January 1, 1866, or then residing in a foreign country, and their lineal descendants.[50] The new statute disenfranchised any person who did not vote in 1914 or who did not register within a short period of time during 1916. In an opinion from which only McReynolds and Butler dissented, Frankfurter stated that the Fifteenth Amendment "nullifies sophisticated as well as simple-minded modes of discrimination. It hits onerous procedural requirements which effectively handicap exercise of the franchise by the colored race although the abstract right to vote may remain unrestricted as to race."[51]

Although most of the cases that dismantled racial segregation lay in the future, the Hughes Court began to shake the foundations of school segregation in 1938, when its decision in *Missouri ex rel. Gaines v. Canada* held that Missouri had unconstitutionally deprived Lloyd Gaines, an African American,[52] of the opportunity to obtain a legal education in his home state of Missouri. The Court held that Missouri's offer to pay his tuition at the law school of any public university in any adjacent state did not fulfill the requirements of the Fourteenth Amendment's equal protection clause insofar as the state denied blacks the privilege of attending law school in their home state solely on account of their race. Although Hughes's opinion acknowledged that Missouri could establish a separate law school for blacks, Hughes found no evidence that the state had any imminent plan for starting one, and he explained that its stated intention of doing so was not enough to comply with the demands of the Fourteenth Amendment. Nor could the state fail to provide a separate law school for blacks merely because there was insufficient demand for such a school. Here Hughes relied upon the Court's 1914 decision in *McCabe*, which had held that a railroad that insisted upon separating the races could not use lack of demand as an excuse for refusing to provide separate luxury cars for blacks.[53] Hughes likewise brushed aside Missouri's argument that the law schools of the adjacent states of Kansas, Nebraska, Iowa, and Illinois were comparable in quality to Missouri's law school. He explained that "[t]he question here is not of a duty of the State to supply legal training, or of the quality of the training which it does supply, but of its duty when it provides such training to furnish it to the residents of the State upon the basis of an equality of right." Missouri's offer to send black students to adjacent states "may mitigate the inconvenience of the discrimination but cannot serve to validate it."[54] In holding that payment of out-of-state tuition could never pass constitutional muster, the Court's opinion went beyond the scope of a 1936 decision by Maryland's

50. 238 U.S. 347 (1915).

51. 307 U.S. at 275.

52. 305 U.S. 337 (1938).

53. *McCabe v. Atchison, Topeka & Santa Fe Railway*, 235 U.S. 151 (1914).

54. 305 U.S. at 349, 350.

highest court, which had required Maryland to admit blacks to its state law school because out-of-state scholarships for blacks were underfunded.[55]

In a dissent joined by Butler, McReynolds urged deference to the state, which had made a "fair effort" to resolve "grave difficulties." Presaging arguments made two decades later by southern opponents of *Brown v. Board of Education*[56] who contended that northerners failed to understand relations between the races in the South, he declared that Missouri "should not be unduly hampered through theorization inadequately restrained by experience." The Court's decision, McReynolds believed, presented Missouri with the cruel choice of either closing its law school or integrating it "and thereby, as indicated by experience, damnify both races." McReynolds insinuated that Gaines's real purpose was to challenge racial segregation rather to obtain admission to a law school, and he hinted that the Missouri court on remand could defy the Court's decision by refusing to issue a writ of mandamus to require Gaines's admission to the law school.[57] McReynolds similarly demonstrated his contempt for Gaines's case even before he wrote his dissent, when he turned his back to Howard Law School dean Charles Hamilton Houston, Gaines's attorney, and stared at the wall during Houston's oral argument.[58]

The Hughes Court likewise eroded the "separate but equal" doctrine in a 1941 decision, *Mitchell v. United States,* unanimously holding that a railroad violated the antidiscrimination provisions of the Interstate Commerce Act by forcing Arthur W. Mitchell, a black Illinois congressman, to move from a first-class Pullman car into a second-class segregated coach as the train approached the Arkansas border.[59] As in *McCabe,* the Court determined that railroads that segregated passengers by race must provide separate but equal luxury accommodations for blacks who were willing to buy first-class tickets, despite a paucity of demand. Insisting on strict equality, Hughes rejected the argument that black passengers should make reservations far enough in advance to ensure the availability of first-class accommodations. Finding that the discrimination was "palpably unjust," Hughes rejected the need "for administrative or expert judgment with respect to practical difficulties."[60]

Although *Mitchell* was based upon statutory construction rather than the Fourteenth Amendment, its reaffirmation of the reasoning of *McCabe* demonstrated that the Court would continue to carefully scrutinize all forms of segregation to ensure that accommodations for blacks were truly physically and logistically equal to those provided to whites. The decision also illustrated the Court's determination to subject racial discrimination to strict scrutiny insofar as the Court departed

55. *Pearson v. Murray,* 169 Md. 478, 182A, 590 (Md. 1936).

56. 249 U.S. 294 (1954).

57. 305 U.S. at 354, 353, 353–54, 354 (McReynolds, J., dissenting).

58. Higginbotham and Smith, "Hughes Court," 1110, reporting recollection of Judge Robert Carter, who witnessed the argument.

59. *Mitchell v. Interstate Commerce Commission,* 313 U.S. 80 (1941).

60. Ibid., 96, 97.

from its newfound deference to administrative agencies in reversing a district court's affirmation of the Interstate Commerce Commission's dismissal of Mitchell's complaint. Even though the decision discouraged segregation since the lack of demand for luxury accommodations among African Americans made it uneconomical for railroads to provide separate first-class coaches for blacks, liberals complained that the decision perpetuated the detested separate but equal doctrine.[61]

In response to *Gaines*, the state of Missouri opened a poorly funded law school for blacks in a ramshackle building in a poor St. Louis neighborhood. The NAACP could not challenge the constitutionality of this school without commencing a new lawsuit because Gaines had mysteriously and forever disappeared.[62] Lacking the funds to start fresh litigation, the NAACP had to wait nearly another decade before successfully challenging the constitutionality of the inferior law school that Oklahoma provided for African Americans.[63] Ironically, *Gaines* did not discourage other states from establishing "scholarship" programs to send African Americans to sister states for professional education. The number of states that tried to evade the "separate but equal" doctrine in this manner increased from five before *Gaines* to eleven in 1943 and seventeen in 1948.[64]

Even though *Gaines* did not deny the validity of the "separate but equal" doctrine, it established a more rigorous standard for its application. The decision therefore began to lay the doctrinal foundation for the Warren Court's ultimate rejection of school segregation in *Brown*. Paradoxically, the Court was dismantling the separate but equal doctrine in the very cases in which the Court perfected it. By raising the standards of equality, the Court made it more difficult for states to maintain segregated facilities. Moreover, these cases nudged the law closer to the Court's ultimate determination in *Brown* that separation never can constitute equality because racial segregation tended to instill in blacks a sense of inferiority.

Although racial issues were not a significant part of the Hughes Court's docket, Stone presumably was mindful of racial discrimination in his *Carolene Products* footnote. All three elements of the footnote promoted racial equality. Stricter scrutiny of legislation affecting "discrete and insular minorities" obviously could accord greater judicial opportunity to nullify laws that overtly or covertly discriminated on the basis of race. The footnote's reference to legislation that impeded the political process provided broader scope for judicial examination of barriers to voting. And the heightened scrutiny of legislation impeding liberties protected by the Bill of Rights could help shield racial minorities from abuses of the criminal process and facilitate their efforts at political activism by protecting their rights of speech and assembly.

61. *Nation,* May 10, 1941, 542–43.

62. Kevin M. Kruse, "Personal Rights, Public Wrongs: The *Gaines* Case and the Beginning of the End of Segregation," *Journal of Supreme Court History* 125–26 (1997).

63. Klarman, *Jim Crow to Civil Rights,* 204–5.

64. Ibid., 161.

Despite its promotion of racial justice, the Hughes Court's scattered decisions did not erase the Court's many earlier decisions that had tolerated, and sometimes even advanced, social and political repression of African Americans. It is therefore not surprising that African Americans failed to join other major minority groups in defending the Court as a haven for liberty during the Court-packing episode and that some prominent blacks supported Roosevelt's proposal. This does not mean, however, that the Hughes Court's decisions on race did not facilitate the nascent civil rights movement. As Klarman has observed, "It is possible that civil rights litigation [during the interwar years] was more important for its intangible effects: convincing blacks that the racial status quo was malleable, educating them about their rights, providing focal points for organized protest, and instructing oblivious northern whites about the egregiousness of Jim Crow conditions."[65] By the end of the Hughes Court era, both black and white Americans recognized that the Court had made significant advances in securing and restoring the constitutional rights of African Americans. Few could have foreseen, however, that these decisions would establish a foundation for much bolder decisions in the not so distant future.

65. Ibid., 163.

8

A JOVIAN PRESENCE

Hughes as an Administrator

The Supreme Court's success in preserving its power and prestige during the political and economic upheavals of the 1930s is attributable in great measure to the wise leadership of Chief Justice Hughes. Hughes's formidable political and administrative abilities ameliorated hostility toward the Court even when its decisions were controversial. In addition to crafting opinions in a manner that helped to deflect criticism, Hughes helped to maintain public confidence in the Court during a time of legal transition through his masterful management of the Court's docket, its courtroom, and its internal conferences. Hughes's powers of diplomacy also helped blunt conflicts and promote harmony among his brethren even when they were deeply divided over points of legal doctrine. As the chief officer of the federal court system, Hughes also helped ensure that the lower federal courts operated in a fair and efficient manner, and he effectively presided over major modernization of their procedures. Although Hughes's imperious manner and his sometimes self-serving motives frequently annoyed even his political allies, and his critics have not unfairly suggested that he might have done more to avert the crisis of 1937, it is difficult to imagine that anyone else would so successfully have navigated the federal judiciary through such treacherous shoals.

Much of Hughes's success was attributable to his commanding personality. His calm demeanor and mien of rectitude and certitude seemed to many Americans to exemplify ideal judicial temperament. As Paul Freund recalled, "His Jovian figure seemed to occupy the central seat by natural right."[1] Felix Frankfurter found that Hughes "radiated authority, not through any other quality than the intrinsic moral authority which was his."[2] When Hughes retired, Robert H. Jackson declared that "[e]ven more than by his judgments this man imparted strength to the Court during our time by his character."[3]

Hughes was particularly successful in managing the Saturday conferences at which the Court discussed and decided the outcome of cases that attorneys had

1. Paul Freund, "Charles Evans Hughes as Chief Justice," 81 *Harvard Law Review* 38 (1967).

2. Felix Frankfurter, "Chief Justices I Have Known," 39 *Virginia Law Review* 901 (1953).

3. Robert H. Jackson, "The Judicial Career of Chief Justice Charles Evans Hughes," *American Bar Association Journal*, July 1941, 408.

argued before the Court. Meeting nearly every week during the Court's term from October to June, the Court during Hughes's chief justiceship annually conducted approximately thirty conferences, which each lasted approximately five hours.[4] Frankfurter recalled that Hughes,

> guided discussion by opening up the lines for it to travel, focusing on essentials, evoking candid exchange on subtle and complex issues, and avoiding redundant talk. He never checked free debate, but the atmosphere he created, the moral authority he exerted, inhibited irrelevance, repetition, and fruitless discussion. He was a master of timing; he knew when discussion should be deferred and when brought to an issue. He also showed uncommon resourcefulness in drawing elements of agreement out of differences and thereby narrowing, if not always escaping, conflicts.[5]

Hughes conserved conference time by limiting the time that the justices spent discussing certiorari petitions. Although each of the justices reviewed all of the petitions for certiorari,[6] Hughes before each conference circulated a list recommending denial without discussion in an average of 60 percent of these petitions. In eleven years, Hughes's brethren presented only a half dozen of these blacklisted petitions at conference.[7] Mindful that Chief Justice White's failure to limit discussion on certiorari petitions had often deprived the Court's conferences of sufficient time for discussion of important argued cases, Hughes attempted to dispose as rapidly as possible of remaining certiorari petitions, jurisdictional statements on appeal, and miscellaneous issues so the Court could devote approximately three of its five conference hours to argued cases. This permitted only about three and a half minutes for each certiorari petition.[8] Observing the "rule of four," the Court would grant certiorari on the concurrence of four justices "and, not infrequently, when three, or even two Justices strongly urge[d] the grant."[9]

Shortly before his death, Hughes confided to Frankfurter that any virtues he had as chief justice were derived from his determination to avoid the failings of White. Although Hughes praised the kindly White for fostering excellent personal relations with his brethren, Hughes recalled that White often was indecisive and unprepared and that he failed to begin discussions of cases by presenting his own views in a manner that would provide guidance and structure for the Court's conferences.[10] Hughes also may have felt that White permitted conferences to become

4. Edwin McElwain, "The Business of the Supreme Court as Conducted by Chief Justice Hughes," 63 *Harvard Law Review* 14 n. 15 (1949).

5. Felix Frankfurter, " 'The Administrative Side' of Chief Justice Hughes," 63 *Harvard Law Review* 3, 4 (1949).

6. "Address of Chief Justice Hughes," *American Bar Association Journal,* June 1934, 341; "Address of Chief Justice Hughes," *American Bar Association Journal,* June 1940, 472.

7. Merlo J. Pusey, *Charles Evans Hughes* (New York: MacMillan, 1951), 2:672.

8. McElwain, "Business of the Supreme Court," 14; Pusey, *Charles Evans Hughes,* 2:672–73.

9. "Address of Chief Justice Hughes," *American Bar Association Journal,* June 1937, 431.

10. Joseph P. Lash, *From the Diaries of Felix Frankfurter* (New York: W. W. Norton, 1975), 313–14.

too discursive. As Hughes stated in his 1928 Columbia lectures, "harmony does not always wait on argumentation."[11] Hughes explained after his retirement that he made "an independent study of each case" and presented "to the conference accurately and comprehensively, but succinctly, the questions presented" and then stated his own views, "seeking thus to afford a basis for the discussion of essential points."[12] Frankfurter later recalled that a conference led by Hughes "was not a debating society but a place where nine men do solos."[13]

According to some accounts, however, Hughes maintained too tight a rein over conferences. One critic complained that conference discussion was "a statement of conclusions more than it was an exchange of mutually stimulating ideas. Some of the apparent unanimity in the Hughes Court derived . . . from the superficiality of the discussion which glossed over rather than illuminated difficulties. "[14] Brandeis famously remarked that the conferences "lasted six hours, and the Chief Justice did all the talking."[15]

As a former law professor, Stone particularly regretted the lack of opportunity for the justices to debate one another and consider complicated issues in a more leisurely manner. Stone derogated Hughes for conducting conferences "much like a drill sergeant,"[16] and he complained privately in 1932 that "discussion of our cases should be much fuller and freer, and that in many instances an adjournment over for a week after preliminary discussion might produce more satisfactory results."[17] At one conference, Stone expected that Hughes would postpone announcement of the Court's decision on a full faith and credit issue for at least a week after Stone presented a memorandum criticizing Brandeis's majority opinion. Instead, Hughes brusquely exclaimed, "Very powerful memorandum. Case goes down on Monday."[18] Stone also believed that Hughes could have spared the Court embarrassment during the controversy over the New Deal decisions if he had allowed more time for consideration of cases. For example, he complained that the Court's consideration of the constitutionality of the Agricultural Adjustment Act in *Butler* "was characterized by inadequate discussion and great haste in

11. Charles Evans Hughes, *The Supreme Court of the United States: Its Foundation, Methods, and Achievements: An Interpretation* (New York: Columbia University Press, 1928), 72.

12. Danelski and Tulchin, *Autobiographical Notes,* 301.

13. Alpheus Thomas Mason, *Harlan Fiske Stone: Pillar of the Law* (New York: Viking Press, 1956), 789, quoting author's interview with Frankfurter, April 14, 1952.

14. John P. Frank, *Marble Palace: The Supreme Court in American Life* (New York: Alfred A. Knopf, 1958), 112, quoting "Confidential communication to the author from someone in a position to observe the pre-1937 Court."

15. Freund, "Hughes as Chief Justice," 40. As Barry Cushman has pointed out, however, "Brandeis may here have been referring only to conferences at which petitions for review were considered." Barry Cushman, *Rethinking the New Deal Court: The Structure of a Constitutional Revolution* (New York: Oxford University Press, 1998), 267 n. 98.

16. David M. O'Brien, *Storm Center: The Supreme Court in American Politics* (New York: W. W. Norton, 1986), 187, citing Memorandum of Howard Westwood, Stone Papers, Library of Congress.

17. Mason, *Harlan Fiske Stone,* 790, citing Stone to John Bassett Moore, May 17, 1932.

18. Ibid., 789.

the production and circulation of the opinions."[19] To permit more discussion of cases, Stone sometimes may have met at his home on Friday afternoons with other justices, including Frankfurter, Douglas, Roberts, and Murphy.[20] Douglas recalled that this "rump conference seemed to bring Stone satisfaction because he could express himself."[21]

Hughes's tendency to administer conferences as a commanding chief executive rather than as a colleague who was merely primus inter pares was characteristic of a man who was accustomed to wielding great power and whose executive experience was superior to that of any of his brethren. Having served as governor of the nation's most populous state, as secretary of state under two passive presidents, and as senior partner in major law firms, Hughes was used to having his own way. Moreover, it is natural that a man who almost had been elected president and had served on the Court as an associate justice long before most of his brethren took their seats would not greatly defer to his colleagues. This was not inevitable, however, for Taft by most accounts was a more collegial chief justice.[22]

Despite criticisms of his method of managing the conferences, Hughes apparently did not perceive that he was unduly imperious. In a conversation with Frankfurter after Hughes's retirement, Hughes laughed when Frankfurter told him that he had a reputation for having kept conferences brief by throttling discussion. Hughes explained that he could not have inhibited discussion by his strong-minded brethren even if he had wished to do so.[23]

Hughes was as commanding in the courtroom as he was in the conference room. Jackson, who had ample opportunity as attorney general to observe Hughes, stated that "[t]he majestic presence of Chief Justice Hughes as a presiding officer shed a native and simple dignity upon all of the Court's proceedings. A keen and experienced advocate at the bar, he knew the problems and the arts of the working lawyer. No one ran away with his Court. He was helpful and patient with the inexperienced, but he despised the tricky statement and the bombast that is sometimes used to cloak poor preparation—and he knew how to deflate it. Even when passions were running high and his own associates were in sharp division, he never lost his poise. He was an ideal presiding judge."[24] Similarly, Frankfurter declared that "to see him preside was like witnessing Toscanini lead an orchestra."[25] Hughes's effectiveness in understanding courtroom dynamics owed

19. Cushman, *Rethinking the New Deal Court,* 102, citing Memorandum Re: 401, *United States v. Butler, et al., Receivers of Hoosac Mills Corporation,* box 62, Harlan Fiske Stone Papers, Manuscript Division, Library of Congress (hereafter cited as Stone Papers).

20. Mason, *Harlan Fiske Stone,* 790.

21. William O. Douglas, *The Autobiography of William O. Douglas: The Court Years, 1939–1975* (New York: Random House, 1980), 222. For discussion of whether such conferences occurred, see page 28, note 118.

22. Mason, *Harlan Fiske Stone,* 317.

23. Lash, *Diaries of Felix Frankfurter,* 315.

24. Robert H. Jackson, "The Judicial Career of Chief Justice Hughes," *American Bar Association Journal,* July 1941, 410–11.

25. Frankfurter, "Chief Justices I Have Known," 901.

much to his background as a trial lawyer, for Hughes argued twenty-five cases before the New York Court of Appeals between 1894 and 1904.[26]

Freund recalled that Hughes "kept the courtroom taut, but not tense. His equanimity and his cool power of analysis were reserves against explosive pressures."[27] Even though Hughes had little patience with poorly prepared attorneys, he tried to concentrate their minds and help focus their arguments rather than deliberately intimidate them. Edwin McElwain, one of Hughes's law clerks, recalled that he "was always conscious of the limitations of counsel, usually sizing them up a split second after the first word was uttered. Once conscious of such limitations, he would make every effort to keep counsel on the track and direct his attention to the important points at issue."[28] Because Hughes often knew the case better than the lawyers, "it was not uncommon to hear him state the case, argue both sides of it, and then indicate his opinion in a subtle fashion, all through a series of genial questions from the bench."[29] Similarly, Freund found that Hughes's questions to counsel "showed a remarkable capacity to bring an argument into focus, to go for the jugular."[30]

Hughes believed in the importance of questions from the justices. As he explained in his Columbia lectures, "Well prepared and experienced counsel . . . do not object to inquiries from the bench, if the time allowed for argument is not unduly curtailed, as they would much prefer to have the opportunity of knowing the difficulties in the minds of the Court and attempting to meet them rather than to have them concealed and presented in conference when counsel are not present. They prefer an open attack to a masked battery."[31]

Consummate preparation was a major source of Hughes's mastery of conferences and the courtroom, as well as his ability to influence decision making and facilitate relative harmony among the justices. Hughes brought the same mastery to obscure patent or tax cases that he demonstrated in adjudicating major constitutional issues. He once commented upon "the vast importance of the work of the Court which, unspectacular and hence largely unnoticed by the press and the public, goes on from day to day demanding unremitting industry and technical competence. The public are naturally interested in the great divisive cases in constitutional law, but these are few and constitute but a small part of the burden which the Court constantly bears."[32]

Hughes's thoroughness in studying cases awed numerous observers and encouraged similar preparation by other justices. As McElwain recalled, "[S]eated at the head of the conference table with records, briefs, and law books (all with innumerable bookmarks) piled high about him, he somehow exuded complete

26. McElwain, "Business of the Supreme Court," 8.
27. Freund, "Hughes as Chief Justice," 38.
28. McElwain, "Business of the Supreme Court," 16.
29. Ibid.
30. Freund, "Hughes as Chief Justice," 13.
31. Hughes, *The Supreme Court of the United States,* 62.
32. "Address by Chief Justice Hughes," *American Bar Association Journal,* June 1938, 431.

preparation and conveyed the impression that anyone who disagreed with him had better know *all* the facts and know them well."[33] Similarly, Frankfurter found that "[y]ou just didn't like to talk unless you were dead sure of your ground, because that gimlet mind of his was there ahead of you."[34] During conferences, "his preparation was so thorough as to discourage challenge without equal preparation by the challenger, and his very thoroughness resulted in his views being given great weight."[35] As a journalist reported in 1934, "[H]is resounding exposition of the law is said to be an awe-inspiring event. Whatever influence he enjoys derives from his having the last and longest word, and not from his titular eminence."[36]

Hughes's high level of preparation reflected his formidable powers of concentration, his prodigious memory, and his ability to identify the most important points in the mounds of petitions, briefs, and records that crossed his desk. Observing that the "Supreme Court is a student's life," Frankfurter recalled that Hughes could "disembowel a brief and a record" because "all his life he had been a student."[37] Understanding that even Supreme Court decisions often turn more on the facts than on the law, Hughes made a point of mastering the facts of every case. Douglas described Hughes as "like a terrier after a rat—intent on cornering every fact" and "almost ravenous as he ransacked records for the essential facts." Indeed, Douglas observed that the chief justice spent more time on the records of cases than on the briefs.[38] Hughes's preparation also reflected the sheer number of hours he devoted to his work. Freund remarked that Hughes "had learned that an official in Washington must choose between the attractions of its social life and the demands of the job, and he made a resolute choice. He and his wife accepted no evening engagements except for Saturday nights."[39]

Hughes was particularly careful to make certain that the Supreme Court kept abreast of its work. He once remarked to the American Law Institute that "progress in the courts may lie not so much in getting ahead but in not falling behind."[40] In maintaining a timely docket, Hughes benefited greatly from the work of his predecessor, Taft, who had persuaded Congress to enact the Judiciary Act of 1925, which gave the Court much more discretion over the cases it heard. By largely eliminating the mandatory appeals that had clogged the docket with insubstantial cases, the legislation freed the Court to devote more time to a smaller number of important issues. Thanks to the 1925 Judiciary Act and the 1928 revised rules of the Supreme Court, the Court was able to maintain control

33. McElwain, "Business of the Supreme Court," 14.

34. Frankfurter, "Chief Justices I Have Known," 902–3.

35. McElwain, "Business of the Supreme Court," 17.

36. Ray Tucker, "Court of the Last Guess," *Collier's*, July 7, 1934, 50.

37. Frankfurter, "The Administrative Side of Chief Justice Hughes," 4; Frankfurter, "Chief Justices I Have Known," 901.

38. Douglas, 215, 216.

39. Freund, "Hughes as Chief Justice," 39.

40. "Address of Chief Justice Hughes," *American Bar Association Journal*, June 1932, 368.

over its docket. The Court considered 984 cases in the 1929 term and 1,039 during the 1930 term, in contrast to the approximately 1,500 cases that it typically heard before 1928.[41] Addressing the American Law Institute in 1933, Hughes boasted that the justices were so much the "masters of our calendar . . . that at times we seem to be treading on the heels of the lawyers."[42] He "attached great importance to the Court's *per curiam* decisions, for he believed that clear expression of the reasons for the Court's summary dismissals or affirmances would result in a reduction in the number of insubstantial cases brought before the Court." To expedite their production, Hughes used standardized forms and citations for particular categories of cases.[43] According to G. Edward White, Hughes also "urged swift disposition of highly controversial cases, such as *Powell v. Alabama* . . . in order to cut down the amount of public attention focused on the Court."[44] To help the Court to maintain control of its docket and prevent hasty and unnecessary involvement of the Court in political controversy, Hughes, Brandeis, and Van Devanter appeared before the Senae Judiciary Committee in 1935 to testify against Senator Black's proposal to permit immediate appeals to the Supreme Court from lower federal court rulings that restrained compliance with federal statutes.[45]

Although the Judiciary Act of 1925 facilitated the Court's punctuality during the 1930s, the chief justice's administrative skills also deserve much credit. As Stone recalled at the time of Hughes's retirement, Hughes believed that "justice delayed is justice denied. During his term of office nothing which could be done today has been put off for tomorrow. . . . To his painstaking care and unflagging energy in ever pressing forward the disposition of the daily work of the Court and so preparing and presenting it for the consideration of the conference that no point should be overlooked or slighted, is due the thoroughness and dispatch with which the Court has done its work and the present fortunate state of its docket."[46] As was discussed in chapter 4, Hughes's success in keeping the Court's docket current played a critical part in the defeat of Roosevelt's Court-packing proposal in 1937.

As the chief officer of the federal court system, Hughes also worked to encourage lower federal courts to remain current in their work. In his annual address to the American Law Institute in 1933, Hughes complained about delays in federal courts, particularly in the completion of criminal appeals, which he attributed to unduly liberal stipulations and shortage of judges. Delay particularly troubled Hughes because large numbers of convicted felons remained free on bail during the appeals process.[47] Hughes's wish to expedite the movement of cases in federal

41. "Supreme Court Masters Its Crowded Calendar," *New York Times,* November 22, 1931, 16.

42. "Address of Chief Justice Hughes," *American Bar Association Journal,* June 1933, 325.

43. McElwain, "Business of the Supreme Court," 15.

44. G. Edward White, *The American Judicial Tradition: Profiles of Leading American Judges* (New York: Oxford University Press, 1976), 213–14.

45. Merlo J. Pusey, *Charles Evans Hughes* (New York: Macmillan, 1955), 2:755.

46. Harlan F. Stone, "The Chief Justice," *American Bar Association Journal,* July 1941, 407.

47. *New York Times,* May 6, 1932, 6.

trial courts helps explain his steadfast support for the adoption of uniform rules of civil and criminal procedure. He also encouraged increases in the number of federal judges. For example, Hughes wrote to Roosevelt in 1935 to strongly endorse the attorney general's recommendation of a fifth judge for the Ninth Circuit. "When a trial has been had and judgment rendered," he pointed out, "it is highly important that there should be no ground for the reproach that the ends of justice are defeated by delays in hearing appeals."[48]

In addition to increased control over its docket, the Hughes Court also benefited from another Taft legacy, the Court's own building. Recognizing that a coequal branch of government deserved its own headquarters and that the cramped chambers that the Court occupied in the Capitol impaired the institution's prestige and hindered the efficient discharge of its functions, Taft had successfully lobbied for the construction of a Supreme Court building. Authorized by Congress in 1929, the building was slowing rising when Hughes became chief justice. It opened in 1935. For the first time, the justices had their own office suites, along with a grand courtroom, modern administrative facilities, and a spacious library.

Speaking at the laying of the cornerstone in October 1932, Hughes pointed out that the new building would provide much-needed accommodations for the work of the justices, marshal and clerk, "for the vast accumulation of records," and for the temporary needs of lawyers and tourists. He emphasized, however that "the special significance of this edifice does not lie in its convenience" but rather in its "distinction as national symbol." Hughes declared that the templelike building embodied "the national ideal of justice in the highest sphere of activity, in maintaining the balance between the nation and the States and in enforcing the primary demands of individual liberty as safeguarded by the overriding guarantees of a written Constitution." He remarked that for such a symbol the people naturally "demanded the best that art and skill can furnish. They demanded that it should be worthy of themselves." Speaking at the nadir of the Great Depression at a time of grave economic and political uncertainty, Hughes asserted that "the Republic endures and this is the symbol of its faith."[49] In private correspondence, Hughes observed, "The service at the altars of justice has not been changed, although these altars are now established in a magnificent temple, with every convenience not only for the priests but for those who bring their sacrifices and petitions."[50]

48. Charles Evans Hughes to Franklin D. Roosevelt, February 22, 1935, reel 5, Papers of Charles Evans Hughes, Manuscript Division, Library of Congress (hereafter cited as Hughes Papers).

49. "Hoover Lays Supreme Court Cornerstone; Hughes and Davis Speak for Bench and Bar," *New York Times,* October 14, 1932, 1.

50. Charles Evans Hughes to Herbert Bayard Swope, October 12, 1935, reel 5, Hughes Papers.

Despite its beauty and spaciousness, the Marble Palace was not immediately popular with many of the justices. Several, including Hughes, continued to perform most of their work at home.[51] Brandeis, who feared that the grand surroundings would discourage judicial humility, refused even to set foot in his office suite.[52] Stone confided to Frankfurter shortly after the move that he was "not too happy in the new building. It is badly planned and inconvenient in most of its practical aspects, but apart from that I fear I shall never be reconciled to surroundings so pompous and pretentious."[53] Stone believed that it was "inappropriate . . . for a court with our traditions."[54] One justice, probably Cardozo, reportedly declared before the building opened that "the Chief should go in on an elephant and the rest of us on stilts."[55] Many members of the public shared these misgivings. During the Court-packing controversy in 1937, a journalist who conducted widespread grassroots interviews concerning Roosevelt's proposal reported that "a surprisingly large number were indignant at the Court because it had just been installed in a new $11,000,000 building."[56]

At the cornerstone ceremony, Hughes himself expressed "keen regret" at leaving the old chamber, with its "dignity . . . simplicity . . . and priceless memories," as well as nostalgia for the little conference room, which "had been quite large enough for the expression of views, whether harmonious or divergent."[57] At home, Hughes worked in a pleasant room furnished with two overstuffed chairs, a davenport, a plain mahogany desk, a high-backed desk chair he had used as governor, and books that covered two walls. The most conspicuous object was a bust of Lincoln, which faced Hughes from a high mantelpiece across from his desk. The room also contained pictures of Chief Justice White and John Stuart Mill, the latter a symbolic reminder that classical liberalism was the core of Hughes's intellectual universe. His secretary, Wendell W. Mischler, occupied an adjoining office.[58] The persistence of Hughes and the associate justices in working at home helped to preclude personal interactions that might have enabled them to resolve conflicts involving major cases. For example, Barry Cushman has pointed out that Hughes might have convinced Roberts to vote to sustain the New

51. Pusey, *Charles Evans Hughes*, 2:689–690.

52. Paul Freund, "Mr. Justice Brandeis: A Centennial Memoir," 70 *Harvard Law Review* 788 (1957).

53. Harlan Fiske Stone to Felix Frankfurter, October 18, 1935, reel 3, Felix Frankfurter Papers, Manuscript Division, Library of Congress.

54. Stone to Sterling Carr, October 10, 1931, box 8, Stone Papers.

55. Henry F. Pringle, "Profiles: The Chief Justice, III," *New Yorker*, July 13, 1935, 18. Professor Freund suggests that Cardozo was the source of this remark. Freund, "Mr. Justice Brandeis," 788.

56. Richard L. Neuberger, "America Talks Court: John Q. Citizen Has Definite Opinions and Speaks Out on the Judiciary Issue," *Current History*, June 1937, 33.

57. "Hoover Lays Supreme Court Cornerstone; Hughes and Davis Speak for Bench and Bar," *New York Times*, October 14, 1932, 1.

58. Pusey, *Charles Evans Hughes*, 2:667.

York minimum wage law in *Tipaldo* if Hughes and Roberts had spent more time in the Court building.[59]

In addition to administrative efficiency, the Hughes Court also operated smoothly because of the chief justice's personal courtesy toward his colleagues and his general avoidance of favoritism and intrigue. In his *Autobiographical Notes,* Hughes stated that he "was careful not to identify myself with any group in the Court" and that "[v]ery rarely, and then only very casually, did I discuss cases with any Justice in advance of the conferences of all of the Justices."[60] When Hughes retired, Stone stated that "[i]n his relations with his colleagues he has been friendly to all, but partial to none. No differences of opinion have been allowed to disturb that fortunate relationship. He has provoked no resentments and cherished none."[61]

Of course, no chief justice can satisfy all of his colleagues all of the time. In addition to alleging that Hughes conducted conferences in an imperious manner, his critics complained about the manner in which he assigned opinions, a sensitive issue that has tested the diplomacy of all chief justices. The assignment of opinions, which a chief justice may make when he votes with the majority, is virtually the only direct power that a chief justice has over the associate justices, and the selection of who will write an opinion often affects the substance of the opinion and its perception by lawyers and the public. Hughes's assignment of opinions was an especially sensitive responsibility at a time when the Court often was closely divided on significant issues, there was considerable divergence of opinion even among justices who voted with the majority, and the Court's opinions often inspired a particularly high level of public controversy. Hughes described his assignment of opinions as his "most delicate task." He explained that he "endeavored to do this with due regard to the feelings of senior Justices and to give each Justice the same proportion of important cases while at the same time equalizing so far as possible the burden of work."[62]

Because no justices were incapacitated for prolonged periods of time, Hughes—unlike so many of his predecessors—usually was able to spread the writing workload fairly evenly among all nine of the justices. Van Devanter was the only justice who never carried his full share. Suffering from chronic writer's block, he sometimes failed to produce opinions Hughes had assigned to him. Hughes reassigned the opinions in a discrete manner, taking care to avoid hurting Van Devanter's feelings.[63] With an ability to identify and cultivate the talents of those with whom he worked, Hughes recognized that Van Devanter compensated in conference for what Sutherland called his "pen paralysis."[64] After Van Devanter's

---

59. Cushman, *Rethinking the New Deal Court,* 267 n. 105.
60. Danelski and Tulchin, *Autobiographical Notes,* 301.
61. Stone, "The Chief Justice," 408.
62. Danelski and Tolchin, *Autobiographical Notes,* 302.
63. Pusey, *Charles Evans Hughes,* 2:667–68.
64. Danelski and Tolchin, *Autobiographical Notes,* 171.

retirement, Hughes recalled that the justice's "wide experience, his precise knowledge, his accurate memory, and his capacity for clear elucidation of precedent and principle, contributed in a remarkable degree to the disposition of the Court's business" in its conferences. Hughes also praised Van Devanter's special expertise in public land law.[65]

In making writing assignments, Hughes remained mindful of his dedication to expediting the Court's business. In 1934 a journalist reported that "some resentment still smolders against Mr. Hughes's driving, dictatorial manner in requiring quick write-ups of decisions assigned to certain members."[66] A notable exception was Cardozo, who produced opinions so rapidly that Hughes feared for his fragile health. Hughes waited until Monday to assign opinions to Cardozo because he knew that his colleague would labor throughout the weekend if he assigned him an opinion after the Saturday conference.[67] Hughes recalled in his memoirs that he "often had in mind the special fitness of a Justice for writing in the particular case."[68] Hughes explained to his biographer, however, that "every judge should have a chance to demonstrate through the writing of opinions the wide range of his reasoning powers and not be kept before the public as an extremist or specialist working one particular groove.[69] Hughes assigned each associate justice to write on a broad range of topics.[70] Chafing at this system, some justices complained that it prevented them from developing expertise in particular subjects.

Like all chief justices, Hughes often made assignments based on strategic considerations. As G. Edward White has observed, Hughes "took pains to assign opinions in such a way as to blunt the identification of any Justice with a partisan position."[71] When the Court was divided, Hughes sometimes assigned the case to the most centrist justice.[72] For example, he assigned Roberts to write the Court's decision in *Butler,* invalidating the Agricultural Adjustment Act. To promote the sense that the Court was united, Hughes also assigned liberal decisions to conservative justices and vice versa. The widespread perception that Sutherland was more moderate than were his fellow Horsemen encouraged Hughes to assign to him some controversial opinions, including *New State Ice Co. v. Liebmann, Jones v. SEC,* and *Carter Coal.* As Drew Pearson and Robert S. Allen observed in 1937, Hughes often chose Sutherland as "the spearhead of the reactionary attack" because "[t]he dynamite-laden reaction which falls from his mild, scholarly lips

65. "Address by Chief Justice Hughes," *American Bar Association Journal,* June 1938, 431.

66. Tucker, "Court of the Last Guess," 50.

67. O'Brien, *Storm Center,* 249 (citing conversation with Paul Freund); William O. Douglas, "Mr. Justice Cardozo," 58 *Michigan Law Review* 549 (1960).

68. Danelski and Tulchin, *Autobiographical Notes,* 302.

69. Pusey, *Charles Evans Hughes,* 2:678 (based on October 17, 1946 interview with author).

70. McElwain, "Business of the Supreme Court," 18. McElwain explained that Hughes "did not believe that the Court should be made up of tax experts, admiralty experts, patent experts, bankruptcy experts, or any other particular sort of expert." Ibid.

71. White, *The American Judicial Tradition,* 213.

72. See McElwain, "Business of the Supreme Court," 18.

creates a more profound impression . . . than the hotheaded blasts of McReynolds or Butler. Sutherland can wrap the poison in a pill of sweet and sonorous pontification."[73]

Hughes, like other chief justices, often assigned the most important decisions to himself, particularly when they were likely to have significant political impact. Accordingly, Hughes wrote the opinions in *Blaisdell*, the Gold Clause decisions, *Panama Refining Co. v. Ryan, Schechter Poultry, Ashwander v. TVA, West Coast Hotel v. Parrish*, and *Jones & Laughlin Steel*. Hughes also wrote a disproportionate share of the major decisions in which the Court expanded the constitutional scope of personal liberties, including *Stromberg v. California, Near v. Minnesota, Norris v. Alabama, Brown v. Mississippi, DeJonge v. Oregon*, and *Missouri ex rel. Gaines v. Canada*. In moving back and forth between the Court's factions, Hughes's vote determined the Court's decision in many cases in which the Court upheld regulatory legislation, notably the Gold Clause cases and *West Coast Hotel*. In contrast with Roberts, however, Hughes never provided a critical fifth vote for a major decision invalidating regulatory legislation. Alpheus Thomas Mason alleged, without providing specific examples, that Hughes sometimes switched his vote to the "liberal" side if the liberals "had a majority without him."[74]

Hughes's critics have argued that the chief slyly cultivated an undeserved reputation as a liberal by writing mostly liberal opinions while assigning conservative opinions to others. As Mason charged, "Hughes attempted to "run with the hares and hunt with the hounds."[75] In a much-discussed article published near the end of the Court-packing struggle during the summer of 1937, Irving Brant found that Hughes had accomplished this sleight of hand by writing a disproportionate share of liberal opinions in cases in which there were at least two conservative dissents but writing virtually no opinions in the larger number of cases in which he was part of a conservative majority in decisions with at least two liberal dissents. Brant calculated that Hughes had written for the Court in the thirteen of the forty-three cases in which he was part of such a liberal majority but had written only one opinion in the fifty-one decisions in which he joined such a conservative majority. He also found that Hughes had written seven dissents in the fifteen cases in which he had voted against a conservative majority. Brant concluded that when "Hughes is a liberal, he proclaims it to the world. When he is reactionary, he votes silently and allows somebody else to be torn to pieces by the liberal dissenters."[76] Pointing out that Hughes had joined with the conservatives in fifty-one of the sixty-six decisions in which there were at least two liberal dissents, Brant alleged that Hughes had "never deviated an inch from his policy of making America safe for reactionary business." According to Brant, Hughes's veneer of liberalism helped to blunt

73. Drew Pearson and Robert S. Allen, *The Nine Old Men* (Garden City, N.Y.: Doubleday, Doran, 1937), 199, 200.

74. Alpheus Thomas Mason, "Charles Evans Hughes: An Appeal to the Bar of History," 6 *Vanderbilt Law Review* 15 (1952).

75. Ibid., 9.

76. Irving Brant, "How Liberal Is Justice Hughes?" *New Republic*, July 21, 1937, 296.

liberal attacks on the Court and won for Hughes approbation from the liberal intelligentsia, which he craved.[77] Privately, Brant complained to Frankfurter that Hughes's record was "much worse than that of Justice Roberts, because the basis of his inconsistency appears to be craft, while that of Roberts is just plain confusion."[78]

Critics also charged that Hughes sometimes assigned liberal opinions to himself so that he could write them in the most conservative manner. For example, Mason complained that Hughes "could be as harmful to a broad construction of the Constitution when writing for a liberal majority as in dissenting from it. There is hardly a case where the chief justice could speak for the Court without rousing the so-called liberal justices to protest." For Mason, the "most characteristic feature of Hughes's leading opinions" was "the escape hatch through which he might move in whatever direction expediency may seem to demand." In this way, his opinions would not seem so inconsistent, and he could legitimately claim that *Jones* did not conflict with *Schechter* and *Carter Coal*.[79] Hughes rankled Stone by withholding major assignments from him,[80] perhaps because Hughes feared that he would write unduly liberal opinions. Stone also alleged that Hughes deliberately tried to create disunity among the liberal justices. He once complained to Roosevelt that, if even a small divergence of opinion developed at conference between two of the liberal justices, Hughes would "get his big toe in and widen the cleavage."[81]

Hughes, however, did not always assign opinions to himself to restrain the Court's liberalism. Most notably, Hughes apparently asked Stone to write the *Darby* opinion sustaining the constitutionality of the Fair Labor Standards Act because he had reservations about the statute's constitutionality.[82] Hughes also assigned to Cardozo several of the Court's most significant decisions, particularly the Social Security Act decisions and *Palko v. Connecticut*, which Cardozo wrote with a breadth that Hughes seems to have made no effort to stifle.

Hughes likewise attracted criticism for crafting even conservative opinions in a manner that made at least rhetorical concessions to liberals. Hughes presumably included such dicta in an effort to placate losing parties. In *Crowell*, for example, Hughes presented a long discourse supporting the constitutionality of the Longshoremen and Harbor Workers' Compensation Act, only to circumscribe the fact-finding power of administrative officers. In the wake of Hughes's opinion in that

77. Ibid., 332.

78. Irving Brant to Felix Frankfurter, June 12, 1937, box 7, Irving Brant Papers, Manuscript Division, Library of Congress.

79. Mason, "Charles Evans Hughes," 9, 13.

80. Mason, *Harlan Fiske Stone*, 316–17.

81. Harold L. Ickes, *The Secret Diary of Harold L. Ickes*, vol. 2, *The Inside Struggle, 1936–1939* (New York: Simon & Schuster, 1954), 552.

82. Mason, *Harlan Fiske Stone*, 551.

case, Stone declared that "whenever I read one of his opinions I feel as if I'd been through a cyclone with everything but the kitchen stove flying in my face."[83]

To Hughes's detractors, the chief justice's alleged efforts to conceal the extent of his conservatism and to blunt the liberalism of the Court's opinions were emblematic of their larger complaint that Hughes lacked consistent devotion to liberal principles and that he led the Court down a jagged constitutional path, frustrating unique opportunities for progressive reforms at a critical juncture in American history and needlessly bringing the nation to the brink of a constitutional crisis that splintered and exhausted the reform movement. Hughes's quest for moderation may have diminished his influence among his brethren. As White has observed, Hughes "was not able to influence any member of the Court to accept his jurisprudential views, with the imperfect and partial exception of Roberts," because Hughes "offered no real alternative" to either of the Court's blocs, "but simply blended them in an *ad hoc* fashion."[84]

Hughes might have had more success in influencing Roberts if he had not disdained personal appeals to his brethren. As Merlo J. Pusey explained, Hughes did not "solicit support for his views outside the conference. He had only contempt for the kind of chief who would take a judge aside and say, "Can't you see the tight spot we're in; you've got to help us out.""[85] Hughes's refusal to lobby his brethren may have represented more of a defect of leadership than a virtue. Although he correctly perceived that the strong-mindedness of his colleagues generally would doom such attempts to failure,[86] Barry Cushman has pointed out that Hughes's failure to communicate with Roberts in *Tipaldo* might have deprived him of an opportunity to convince Roberts to vote to sustain the constitutionality of the New York minimum wage law.[87] This surely would have spared the Court and the nation much anguish.

Like most chief justices, Hughes dissented more infrequently than most of the associate justices. Hughes wrote only seventeen dissents and six concurrences as chief justice, compared with more than two hundred majority opinions.[88] Believing that their role is to build a consensus that will enhance the institutional power of the Court by enabling it to speak so far as possible with one voice, Hughes and other chief justices have tended to regard their own dissents and those of their colleagues as a failure of leadership. Like other chief justices, Hughes also may sometimes have joined the majority so that he, rather than the senior associate

83.   Pearson and Allen, *The Nine Old Men*, 111. See also Mason, *Harlan Fiske Stone*, 339.

84.   White, *The American Judicial Tradition*, 214.

85.   Pusey, *Charles Evans Hughes*, 2:676.

86.   Ibid., 2:675–76.

87.   Cushman, *Rethinking the New Deal Court*, 101–3. Cushman contends that Hughes probably could have persuaded Roberts to vote to sustain the New York minimum wage statute if Hughes had understood that Roberts's objection was based upon his belief that the Court could not uphold the New York statute without rejecting *Adkins* and if Hughes had been willing to overturn *Adkins* rather than distinguishing it. Ibid.

88.   Freund, "Hughes as Chief Justice," 38.

justice, could assign the writing of the Court's opinion. "Hating dissents . . . he strives earnestly, evangelically, to reconcile warring views," a journalist observed in 1934.[89] Nevertheless, although Hughes tried to avoid dissents, he recognized that they were inevitable and often had value. Wistfully expressing admiration for the absence of dissenting opinions in ALI Restatements, which he believed enhanced the authority of the Restatements, Hughes nevertheless told the American Law Institute in 1933 that the law is never static and that "[r]eason has a way of playing havoc with 'authority.'" Hughes predicted that "[t]he dissenting opinions, if they exist, will undoubtedly find expression" among judges and lawyers.[90]

Similarly, Hughes in his Columbia lectures defended the usefulness of dissents. Although he acknowledged that dissents detracted from the force of a judgment, he insisted that they were essential to judicial independence. Hughes explained that "what must ultimately sustain the court in public confidence is the character and independence of the judges. They are not there simply to decide cases, but to decide them as they think they should be decided, and while it is regrettable that they cannot always agree, it is better that their independence should be maintained and recognized than that unanimity should be secured through its sacrifice." Although Hughes emphasized that "[n]othing is more distressing on the bench than the exhibition of a captious, impatient, querulous spirit," he believed that a "dissent in a court of last resort is an appeal to the brooding spirit of the law, to the intelligence of a future day, when a later decision may possibly correct the error into which the dissenting judge believes the court to have been betrayed."[91]

Similarly, Hughes remarked in his 1936 address to the American Law Institute that

> How amazing it is that, in the midst of controversies on every conceivable subject, one should expect unanimity of opinion upon difficult legal questions! In the highest ranges of thought, in theology, philosophy and science, we find differences of views on the part of the most distinguished experts. . . . The history of scholarship is a record of disagreements. And when we deal with questions relating to principles of law and their applications, we do not suddenly rise into a stratosphere of icy certainty.[92]

Although Hughes ostensibly was admonishing American Law Institute members not to fear disagreements of opinion within the institute, his remarks probably also were intended as a tacit rejoinder to widespread criticism of the Court for its many close divisions in cases testing the constitutionality of New Deal legislation.

Stone explained at the time of Hughes's retirement that the chief justice had "earnestly sought unanimity of decision by the removal of doubts and misunderstandings so far as that could be accomplished by exposition and discussion at

89. Tucker, "The Court of Last Guess," 50.
90. "Address of Chief Justice Hughes," *American Bar Association Journal,* June 1933, 326.
91. Hughes, *The Supreme Court of the United States,* 67–68.
92. "Address of Chief Justice Hughes," *American Bar Association Journal,* June 1936, 375.

conference. But he has never desired unanimity at the cost of the sacrifice, either for himself or for others, of strongly held convictions. He has recognized the part played in the development of the law by the dissenting opinion."[93]

It is somewhat ironic that the Hughes Court voted more cohesively before 1937 than it did after the so-called revolution. The proportion of unanimous decisions was highest during Hughes's first term, at 89.2 percent. It hovered in the low to mid-eighties during the next five terms before dipping to 79.2 percent during the 1936–1937 term. Although the Court seemed more united after 1937 because the Court no longer appeared to zigzag in economic regulatory cases, the proportion of divided decisions increased rather markedly. The percentage of unanimous decisions fell to 70 percent in 1937 and 64 percent in 1938–1939, before rising to 69.3 percent in 1939–1940 and 71.5 percent during the final term.[94] The consolidation of a liberal majority may actually have sharpened divisions within the Court, with neither liberals nor conservatives willing to accede to the majority in close cases. The increase in dissents also may reflect the growing prominence of economic regulatory decisions on the Court's docket.

Perhaps a better index of the Court's cohesion, however, is the number of decisions determined by the vote of only one justice. These ranged from two to eight during the first six terms of the Hughes Court before rising to thirteen among the 149 cases decided during 1936–1937. One-vote margins fell to three in 1937–1938 and accounted for six during the following year, four during 1939–1940, and five during the Hughes Court's final term.

More perhaps than many chief justices, Hughes was ever mindful that he was chief justice of the United States and not merely the chief presiding officer of the Supreme Court. In addition to encouraging lower federal courts to keep abreast of their dockets, Hughes regularly urged federal judges to maintain the highest standards. Hughes explained, "We are apt to look too far away for the accomplishment of reforms. Improvement is generally a personal and a local matter," and he looked "to the local bench and bar to remedy local defects in the administration of justice."[95] He also publicly denounced judicial corruption[96] and called for the creation of a permanent bureau within the Department of Justice for the collection and compilation of crime statistics.[97] Hughes also urged lawyers to assist judges in the expeditious conduct of trials, complaining in 1932 that "[i]n the lower courts, and in spectacular cases especially, counsel are at times prolix and, while occasionally the public may be entertained, promptness and efficiency are not served by their divagations."[98]

93. Stone, "The Chief Justice," 408.

94. Michael E. Parrish, *The Hughes Court: Justices, Rulings, and Legacy* (Santa Barbara, Calif.: ABC-CLIO, 2002), 25.

95. "Chief Justice Hughes Addresses Judicial Conference of Fourth Circuit," *American Bar Association Journal*, July 1932, 447.

96. "Hughes Denounces Court Corruption," *New York Times*, May 6, 1932, 5.

97. "Hughes for Bureau of Crime Statistics," *New York Times*, May 8, 1931, 6.

98. "Chief Justice Hughes Addresses Judicial Conference of Fourth Circuit," 448.

In attempting to enhance the general caliber of the law, Hughes was ever supportive of the American Law Institute's work. Commending its *Restatement of the Law of Contracts* in 1933, Hughes declared that "men and women in an ordered society . . . are entitled, so far as is humanly possible, to know the rules that govern them and to have these rules applied consistently. Clarity and certainty are thus desirable ends, but they cannot be attained . . . without cooperative efforts, in and out of courts, which seek to develop a coherent jurisprudence." Hughes predicted that the *Restatement* also would "foster analysis rather than displace it" and would "promote examination of principles, rather than discourage it."[99]

Hughes also was keenly interested in the improvement of administrative law, and he believed that federal courts could set an example. Acknowledging that "[o]f necessity these administrative boards have been entrusted with quasi-judicial functions," he warned that courts must serve as models of the competence and objectivity that such boards needed to emulate. "If courts—separate, distinctive tribunals—free from the intrusions of partisan demands, and as remote as possible from the play of particular selfish interests, fail in their mission, it is idle to expect that legislative or administrative agencies will conserve the essential interests of justice."[100]

Hughes's most important contribution to improvement of the law during his tenure as chief justice was his work in developing modern procedural rules for civil and criminal cases. After Congress in February 1933 enacted legislation authorizing the Supreme Court to prescribe rules for appeals in federal criminal cases, Hughes reviewed a study of existing procedures and conferred with senior court of appeals judges to obtain their suggestions before the Court promulgated the rules in May 1934.[101] In discussing these rules, Hughes averred that "[e]xperience shows, that rules of procedure should be as simple as possible. Numerous and involved procedural requirements with the force of statutes, breed controversial questions. The necessary flexibility of procedure under judicial guidance is lost in a maze of technicalities."[102]

Hughes similarly believed that the rules used for actions at law in civil cases in federal courts, which generally followed the rules of the state in which the federal court sat,[103] were encrusted with too many archaic technicalities and that rule variations among federal courts caused delay and sometimes frustrated justice. Although the American Bar Association during the late nineteenth century had begun to advocate uniform federal rules and every state bar association by 1912

---

99. "Address of Chief Justice Hughes," *American Bar Association Journal,* June 1933, at 326.

100. "Chief Justice Hughes Addresses Judicial Conference of the Fourth Circuit," *American Bar Association Journal,* July 1932, 446.

101. Pusey, *Charles Evans Hughes,* 2:683. See "Address of Chief Justice Hughes at the American Law Institute Meeting," *American Bar Association Journal,* June 1934, 342.

102. "Address of Chief Justice Hughes at American Law Institute Meeting," *American Bar Association Journal,* June 1934, 342.

103. Larry L. Tepley and Ralph U. Whitten, *Civil Procedure* (Littleton, Colo.: Fred B. Rothman, 1991), 21.

had endorsed such rules, federal legislation was stymied by state practitioners who did not want to have to learn two separate sets of rules.[104] Proposals to permit the Supreme Court to promulgate such rules, subject to congressional approval, encountered opposition from some liberal critics of the federal judiciary who questioned the constitutionality of congressional delegation of rule-making powers to the courts, opposed additional centralization of power in the federal government, and feared that the new rules would be unduly rigid.[105]

With Hughes and Attorney General Homer S. Cummings advocating federal civil rules and with the newly adopted criminal appellate rules serving as what Hughes described as an icebreaker, Congress in June 1934 finally authorized the Supreme Court to prescribe federal procedural rules.[106] The federal statute also permitted the Court to elect to establish a uniform procedural system for both actions at law and suits in equity, the latter of which already were governed by federal procedure.[107] A longtime advocate of the merger of law and equity, Hughes did not hesitate to encourage the Court to opt for uniform rules governing both.

Because Hughes believed "[i]t was manifestly necessary that the Supreme Court should have the most expert assistance in devising the new rules," the Court appointed an advisory committee consisting of law professors and experienced practitioners. The committee produced a preliminary draft that was distributed to judges and lawyers for discussion and debate in local conferences. It then prepared a final draft, which the Court adopted after making some changes. Congress approved the rules in 1938.[108] Among many other reforms, the rules effected a merger of the procedures of law and equity, which Hughes had vigorously advocated.[109]

Addressing the American Law Institute in 1940, Hughes expressed satisfaction with the operation of the new Federal Rules of Civil Procedure. He noted that the Court and the advisory committee it appointed strongly believed "that there should be as little tinkering with the rules as possible, that questions of construction could appropriately be dealt with as they arose in practice, and that nothing in the way of extensive amendments or revision should be attempted until demanded by adequate experience." Hughes also explained that, "while fully recognizing the power of Congress, we should endeavor to establish the tradition that the institution of amendments should remain with the Court, acting with the expert assistance of judges and members of the Bar." Hughes deplored the

104. Danelski and Tulchin, *Autobiographical Notes*, 314; Parrish, *The Hughes Court*, 219.

105. Edward A. Purcell Jr., *Brandeis and the Progressive Constitution: Erie, the Judicial Power, and the Politics of the Federal Courts in Twentieth-Century America* (New Haven, Conn.: Yale University Press, 2000), 31, 135–36.

106. Ch. 651, 48 Stat. 1064.

107. Danelski and Tulchin, *Autobiographical Notes*, 314–15.

108. Ibid., 315.

109. See "Address of Chief Justice Hughes," *American Bar Association Journal*, July 1935, 341.

"procedural monstrosities" arising in states that permitted legislatures to initiate amendments.[110]

In the wake of the success of the civil rules, Congress in June 1940 authorized the Court to prescribe rules of practice in all federal criminal proceedings prior to verdict, or a judicial finding of guilty or not guilty when a jury had been waived.[111] Again, Hughes strongly supported such rules, and the Court appointed an advisory committee that was still developing proposals when he retired in 1941. The rules were adopted in 1944 and promulgated in 1946. In commenting upon the complete uniformity of procedure that would be accomplished after these rules were adopted, Hughes declared in one of his last public pronouncements as chief justice that "we are making a frontal attack all along the line on procedural survivals unsuited to our time and we are seeking to sweep away the unjustified technicalities and opportunities for dilatory tactics which have obstructed the administration of justice in the federal courts."[112]

Although the uniform federal rules of civil and criminal procedure were major strides, Hughes believed that more was needed to improve the quality of judicial administration. "To secure promptness and efficiency in administering federal justice," Hughes recalled in his memoirs, "it was desirable to have machinery for constant and adequate supervision of the work of the courts."[113] Some such machinery already existed under a 1922 statute, enacted at the behest of Taft, establishing an annual Judicial Conference of Senior Circuit Judges (now known as the Judicial Conference of the United States), presided over by the chief justice and attended by senior court of appeals judges, to review administrative reports submitted by district judges and to make decisions concerning transfer of judges to overburdened courts and recommendations for the creation of additional judgeships. Hughes recalled after his retirement that he "was deeply interested in the work of this conference which gave a general view of conditions in the various districts, the number and kind of litigated cases, and the extent of delays in their disposition. It seemed to me that here was the nucleus of a supervisory organization." Hughes also found that voluntary conferences among judges in several circuits also were useful, but he believed "that there should be a more thoroughgoing organization." Hughes feared that complaints of delay and maladministration might generate legislation that would compromise judicial independence by placing federal courts "under direct executive or legislative supervision."[114]

In response to these concerns, Hughes in 1932 appointed a committee to work with the attorney general in developing a plan to transfer judicial administration

110. "Address of Chief Justice Hughes," *American Bar Association Journal,* June 1940, 472.

111. Sumners Courts Act of June 29, 1940, 76 P.L. 675, 54 Stat. 688, codified at 18 U.S.C. sec. 3771 et seq.

112. "Chief Justice Hughes before the American Law Institute," *American Bar Association Journal,* June 1941, 333.

113. Danelski and Tulchin, *Autobiographical Notes,* 316.

114. Ibid.

from the Justice Department to the federal courts themselves.[115] Beginning in 1936, Cummings supported a bill, of which he may have been the author, to create an administrative office of the federal courts. The legislation would have vested considerable additional administrative powers in the chief justice, particularly with regard to the budget, which the Justice Department at that time prepared, and the deployment of judges. Without committing himself, Hughes presented the plan to his brethren, who generally opposed it on the grounds that it would burden the chief justice with petty and politically controversial details. When Cummings advocated the bill during the Judicial Conference of Senior Circuit Judges in September 1938, Hughes expressed approval of removing budgets and other administrative operations from the Justice Department, but he opposed the chief justice's assumption of these duties. Instead, he urged the creation of judicial counsels in each circuit to administer housekeeping details, in cooperation with the judicial conference, aided by a permanent agency to gather statistics and perform other mundane administrative work. In response to Hughes's suggestions, the conference appointed a committee to draft a bill along such lines.[116]

Congress enacted similar legislation in 1939, creating the Administrative Office of the United States Courts.[117] The Supreme Court appoints its director and assistant director, and it reports to the Judicial Conference, which serves as its general supervisor. The office handles the business affairs of the federal courts, including budgets, audits of accounts, personnel issues, and procurement of supplies and facilities. It also assists judicial work through the Division of Procedural Studies and Statistics. The 1939 statute also provides for annual convocation of all district and circuit judges in each circuit to consider the state of business in the circuit.[118] As Cummings observed, the legislation enhanced judicial independence since the judiciary's "administrative work should not be handled by one of the executive departments, or be under the control of the chief litigant in the federal courts."[119] Cummings aptly explained that the statute's purpose was to "[l]et the judges run the judiciary."[120]

115. Cathy A. McCarthy and Tara Treacy, *The History of the Administrative Office of the United States Courts: Sixty Years of Service to the Federal Judiciary* (Washington, D.C.: Administrative Office of the United States Courts, 2000), 12.

116. Pusey, *Charles Evans Hughes,* 2:686; Danelski and Tulchin, *Autobiographical Notes,* 316–17; McCarthy and Treacy, *History of the Administrative Office,* 12–14.

117. Act of August 7, 1939, ch. 501, section 302, 53 Stat. 1223–25, codified at 28 U.S.C. section 601–13 (2000).

118. McCarthy and Treacy, *History of the Administrative Office,* 14–19; *American Bar Association Journal,* June 1940, 472.

119. McCarthy and Treacy, *History of the Administrative Office,* 13, citing Carl Brent Swisher, ed., *Selected Papers of Homer Cummings, Attorney General of the United States: 1933–1939* (New York: DeCapo Press, 1972), 225 (*Annual Report of the Attorney General, 1938*).

120. Gordon Bermant and Russell R. Wheeler, "Federal Judges and the Judicial Branch: Their Independence and Accountability," 46 *Mercer Law Review* 845 (1995), citing *Hearings before the Committee on the Judiciary, United States Senate, on S. 3212, a Bill to Establish the Administrative Office of the United States Courts, and for Other Purposes,* 75th Congress, 3d Session 31 (testimony of Homer Cummings).

Hughes worked closely with the Judicial Conference of Senior Circuit Judges and the Administrative Office of the United States Courts to ensure improvements in judicial operations. He remarked that "[j]udges with their continuous experience know where the technical shoe pinches and where procedure can be improved."[121] Hughes was ever ready to assist lower federal judges who sought his help in connection with judicial administration. In 1936, for example, he endorsed the proposal of the senior judge of the Eighth Circuit to stagger the vacation time of district judges in the Eighth Circuit so that at least one judge would be in each state throughout the summer.[122] Frankfurter observed that, although Hughes "gave creative guidance to the Conference of Senior Circuit Judges and the Administrative Office of the United States Courts in making the federal judiciary more responsive to the tasks of a civilized legal system, he avoided the temptations of a strong executive." Frankfurter explained that Hughes realized "that elaboration of administrative machinery is deadening to the judicial process, that the individual excellence of the judges, not paper efficiency, matters most."[123]

Addressing federal appellate judges in 1932, Hughes explained that "our business is to diminish friction in the machinery of justice, to improve that administration by preventing unnecessary delays, by dispensing with useless formalities, by cutting through a web of meaningless technicalities, by insuring speedy, expert, impartial, application of our laws."[124] Explaining that he was not one to "join in an indiscriminate attack on judicial administration," Hughes believed that "by and large, the history and accomplishments of the judicial department do not suffer in comparison with the other departments of our government."[125]

Like other chief justices during times of judicial controversy, Hughes made important contributions to amelioration of hostility against the Court. In helping to protect the Court from calumny and the loss of prestige and power, Hughes's most effective work was within the Court rather than in public defenses. In an address to the judges of the Fourth Circuit in 1932, he remarked that "[t]he best way to deal with criticism of the courts is to attend to our work and do it as well as we know how." He added, "The spectacle of a weak and incompetent judge in action, or in inaction, does more to undermine public confidence than abuse of the institution by hostile critics."[126]

Hughes wisely did not take criticism personally and recognized that criticism could have constructive benefits. He declared in 1932 that "[c]riticism of courts

121. *American Bar Association Journal*, July 1932, 447.

122. Charles Evans Hughes to Kimbrough Stone, June 2, 1936, reel 5, Hughes Papers, responding to letter from Kimbrough Stone to Charles Evans Hughes, May 29, 1936, ibid. Hughes suggested that special arrangements might be made for North and South Dakota since each of these states had only one district court judge.

123. Frankfurter, "'The Administrative Side' of Chief Justice Hughes," 4.

124. "Chief Justice Hughes Addresses Judicial Conference of Fourth Circuit," 447.

125. Ibid.

126. Ibid.

should never be confused with criticism of the judicial function. It is the imperfection of the discharge of that function that is the target. It is the adaptation, the operation, of the machinery, not its purpose, that is called in question. Criticism may be ignorant or captious, it may be informed and intelligent, but it generally reveals respect rather than disesteem for the ideal of the administration of justice. It is upon respect for that ideal that we have built our institutions."[127]

In his address to the American Law Institute in May 1938, Hughes acknowledged public criticism of the courts but attributed this to archaic procedures, pettifogging lawyers, and the occasional rogue judge rather than to any lack of harmony between judicial decisions and the political temper of the times. Despite these flaws in the legal process, Hughes insisted that "the judicial tradition stands forth in testimony to the endeavor of the people to be just and to maintain their rights against the varied opportunities for partiality and oppression in administration."[128]

He also generally remained silent in the face of political attacks on the Supreme Court. The only significant exception to Hughes's abstention from direct defenses of the Court was his letter to the Senate Judiciary Committee discrediting Roosevelt's contention that Court-packing was needed because the Court was reeling under an intolerable burden of work.

Despite his reluctance to respond directly to criticism, Hughes offered subtle defenses of the Court in numerous public addresses. Six weeks after sending his letter to the Senate Judiciary Committee, for example, Hughes informed the American Law Institute that the Court was abreast of its work.[129] Five years earlier, he had told the Fourth Circuit that the Constitution imposed limitations upon liberty "requiring a measure of freedom of opportunity that even legislatures must respect. We would be faithless to our judicial obligation in failing to recognize these boundaries of power because of individual conceptions of the value of new social schemes resting on coercion by a class, or upon unrestrained legislative will, as we would be in tightening conceptions to reinforce particular economic views." Hughes pointedly observed that "even those who appear to be disposed to decry other limitations, are not slow in invoking the aid of the courts to enforce their constitutional rights if freedom of speech or of the press is endangered."[130]

Just as Taft had used the unveiling of a statue of Chief Justice Salmon P. Chase in Cincinnati in 1923 as the occasion to draw parallels between attacks on the Chase Court and vilification of his own Court,[131] Hughes made remarks at the unveiling of a bust of Chief Justice Roger B. Taney in Frederick, Maryland, in 1931

127. Ibid., 446.

128. "Address by Chief Justice Hughes," *American Bar Association Journal*, June 1938, 431.

129. "Chief Justice Hughes Pays a Tribute to Elihu Root—The Supreme Court's Work—Measures for Improving Procedure—'The Success of Democratic Institutions,'" *American Bar Association Journal*, June 1937, 431.

130. "Chief Justice Hughes Addresses Judicial Conference of Fourth Circuit," 446.

131. William G. Ross, *A Muted Fury: Populists, Progressives, and Labor Unions Confront the Courts, 1890–1937* (Princeton, N.J.: Princeton University Press, 1994), 240.

that had obvious significance for contemporary politics. Hughes hailed Taney for unflinching dedication to duty and to the "constitutional right of personal liberty" in the face of "rancorous criticism" and the "gravest assaults." Recalling that Taney's nomination encountered widespread opposition because of Taney's record as a lawyer, Hughes pointed out that many critics of that nomination came to admire Taney's record as chief justice.[132]

As chief justice, Hughes, who served as president of the New York Legal Aid Society from 1916 to 1921, also continued his efforts to help ensure that the poor received justice in the nation's courts. Shortly after his retirement, the *American Bar Journal* commented, "To all the staff attorneys in legal aid offices and to their hundreds of thousands of clients it has been a constant source of inspiration and assurance that the highest judicial officer in the nation was concerned that legal aid should be supported and improved to the end that no man, woman, or child, however humble or poor, should be denied the equal protection of our laws."[133] Hughes took *in forma pauperis* petitions very seriously, particularly those that alleged violations of civil rights or injustice toward racial minorities.[134]

Despite his association with so many public-spirited causes during his long career, Hughes found his duties as chief justice so consuming that he limited his nonjudicial associations. In declining an invitation by the journalist Irwin S. Cobb to become a member of the board of governors of a new public interest group, Hughes explained, "I really have no time for anything outside my official work and the concerns which grow out of it." Although Hughes "retained a few old relations—chiefly with educational institutions," he "felt compelled to decline new connections."[135] Similarly, in rejecting a request to devote time to New York's Legal Aid Society, he stated, "The work I have in hand demands my attention during the Term and when the Term is over I must have a period of needed relaxation."[136] Other justices of the Hughes Court similarly conserved their energies. In declining Attorney General Murphy's invitation to a National Parole Conference, Stone explained that he would be glad to attend if he "were not chained to the wheels of another chariot." Stone expressed reluctance to undertake any nonjudicial responsibilities because he found the Court's work "so continuous and exacting."[137] Similarly, Sutherland told a Wall Street attorney two years before his resignation that he limited his public social appearances to the annual White House dinner because the Court's calendar "taxes me to the utmost and I am obliged to conserve my energy in every possible way."[138]

132. "Taney Great Jurist, Hughes Declares," *New York Times,* September 27, 1931, 8.

133. "Chief Justice Hughes and Legal Aid," *American Bar Association Journal,* September 1941, 553.

134. McElwain, "Business of the Supreme Court," 24.

135. Charles Evans Hughes to Irwin S. Cobb, March 25, 1932, reel 5, Hughes Papers.

136. Charles Evans Hughes to Clarence J. Shearn, May 3, 1937, reel 5, Hughes Papers.

137. Harlan Fiske Stone to Frank Murphy, March 16, 1939, box 76, Stone Papers.

138. George W. Sutherland to Alden S. Blodget, January 27, 1936, box 5, George W. Sutherland Papers, Manuscript Division, Library of Congress.

Hughes assiduously avoided efforts to ensnare him in political intrigues. When Harold Ickes accidentally solicited his assistance in depriving Hoover of the Republican nomination in 1932, Hughes replied with a terse and chilly letter of two sentences: "I am surprised to receive such a letter from you. You should know that I have nothing whatever to do with politics."[139]

Sensitive to the constitutional requirements of separation of powers, Hughes as chief justice always was guided by his keen sense of the Court's proper place in the constitutional system. Hughes believed that "[t]he supreme exercise of the judicial power of the United States is in maintaining the constitutional balance between State and Nation and in enforcing the principles of liberty which the Constitution safeguards against arbitrary power."[140] Accordingly, Hughes suggested in May 1941 that judicial institutions would help to defeat Fascism. "We are engaged in harnessing our national power for the defense of our way of life. But that way is worthwhile only because it is the pathway of the just. It is our high privilege, although our task may seem prosaic, to strengthen the defenses of our democracy by commending to public confidence and esteem the working of the institutions of justice in both state and nation."[141]

Similarly, Hughes believed that "a judge must represent authority, but he is the symbol not so much of power as of justice,—of patience and fairness, of a weighing of evidence in scales with which prejudice has not tampered, of reasoned conclusions satisfying a sensitive conscience, of firmness in resisting both solicitation and clamor. It is in the quality of judicial work—whether performed by courts or by agencies invested with judicial functions—in its expertness, thoroughness and impartiality, that the whole scheme of the law, of government by law, comes to the decisive test. And only as that test is successfully met will the foundations of a sound democracy be made secure."[142]

139. Charles Evans Hughes to Harold L. Ickes, March 17, 1932, reel 5, Hughes Papers, responding to Harold L. Ickes to Charles Evans Hughes, March 15, 1932, ibid. Ickes later apologized, explaining that his assistants had mistakenly included Hughes's name on a list of recipients of a form letter. Ickes to Hughes, March 18, 1932, ibid.

140. "Chief Justice Hughes Address Judicial Conference of Fourth Circuit," 446.

141. "Address by Chief Justice Hughes," *American Bar Association Journal,* June 1941, 335.

142. "Address by Chief Justice Hughes," *American Bar Association Journal,* June 1940, 473.

CONCLUSION

The Enduring Enigma of the Hughes Court

With his legendary energy increasingly diminished by old age, the seventy-nine-year-old Hughes informed President Roosevelt on June 2, 1941, that he would retire from the chief justiceship on July 1. Although Hughes remained healthy, he had the wisdom and modesty to relinquish his power before his advancing years significantly interfered with his duties.[1] Roosevelt, whose expressions of regret over Hughes's departure appear to have been more than perfunctory, consulted Hughes on his choice of a successor and followed Hughes's recommendation of Harlan Fiske Stone.[2] The former chief justice lived quietly in retirement until his death at age eighty-six on August 27, 1948.

Hughes's retirement generated a torrent of tributes from diverse sources. Liberals who had execrated Hughes at the time of his nomination admitted that they had misjudged the man. The *Nation* remarked that "though he did not fully grasp the needs of a changing time . . . he refuted our fear that he would bring to the office the outlook of the typical corporation lawyer. . . . Hughes had the acumen to recognize the inevitable, and that is the larger part of statesmanship."[3] Similarly, the *New Republic* contended that Hughes was "a great judicial statesman" rather than a "great jurist in the technical sense" because "[i]t often looked as if he were considering issues, not as a devotee of some unchangeable absolute known as 'The Law,' but as a sort of moderator among vested interests and social forces."[4] Hughes was especially praised for his championship of civil liberties, particularly freedom of speech and the rights of African Americans.[5]

These tributes largely have withstood the test of time. Scholars today generally applaud Hughes for his judicial statesmanship during a time of political and constitutional crisis. Historians remain divided, however, about the extent to which external political forces influenced Hughes and Roberts, particularly in the

---

1. Merlo J. Pusey, *Charles Evans Hughes* (New York: MacMillan, 1951), 2:787.
2. Ibid., 2:787–88.
3. "Charles Evans Hughes," *Nation*, June 14, 1941, 685.
4. "Hughes, Judicial Statesman," *New Republic*, June 9, 1941, 776.
5. "Charles Evans Hughes," *Nation*, June 14, 1941, 685.

pivotal decisions of 1937 that forever ended the guardian review of economic legislation.

The amenability of Hughes and Roberts to economic regulatory legislation clearly had origins independent of the political pressures of the New Deal era, for the Hughes Court from its beginning was more deferential to such laws than the Taft Court had been. This change, clearly evident in numerous decisions during the first five years of Hughes's chief justiceship, is generally attributable to the chief justice's votes in various five-to-four decisions and his influence upon his brethren, particularly Roberts. The Hughes Court's record during its early years was consistent with Hughes's performance on the Court as an associate justice from 1910 to 1916, a period during which political progressives hailed the Court for its amenability toward regulatory legislation.[6] The Hughes Court's infamous hostility toward regulatory legislation manifest itself only through a period of a year and a half during 1935 and 1936, when the Court invoked restrictive theories of the commerce clause, due process, equal protection, the federal taxing power, and separation of powers to strike down several significant New Deal statutes and some state legislation.

Hughes, an old-fashioned progressive, and Roberts, a patrician with liberal instincts, were generally inclined to favor economic regulatory legislation and were not inherently hostile toward the New Deal's reformist spirit. Like many progressives, however, they were alarmed that the Roosevelt administration's programs disrupted the delicate balances of federalism and separation of powers. Having served as a governor and a cabinet member, Hughes was particularly sensitive to these issues, and many of his decisions rested upon his concern for proper balances between state and federal power and the distribution of power within the federal government. Both these considerations, for example, were integral in *Schechter Poultry*. Robert H. Jackson aptly praised Hughes when he retired for remaining ever mindful of the "interdependent destiny of governmental branches as well as of the appropriate separations of their powers. He knew that if needless obstructions were placed in the way of governmental efficiency and rendered our system unworkable, the most perfect logic of the most brilliant court would not save our society from disintegration."[7] Even members the Court's liberal bloc shared these concerns to one degree or another, for *Schechter Poultry* and *Radford* were decided by unanimous votes, whereas only Cardozo dissented in *Panama Refining*. It is likewise possible to attribute the Court's invalidation of some New Deal legislation, particularly the National Industrial Recovery Act, to hasty and inept statutory drafting and poor presentation of arguments to the Court, factors

6. The *Outlook* declared in July 1914 that the Court never had been more worthy of veneration. "A Great Court," *Outlook,* July 1914, 508. Similarly, another journal in 1914 remarked that "the Supreme Court . . . once regarded as the very stronghold of extreme constitutionalism, has steadily been setting an example of liberal construction." "The Majority Juggernaut," *Unpopular Review,* January 1914, 23.

7. Robert H. Jackson, "The Judicial Career of Chief Justice Hughes," *American Bar Association Journal,* July 1941, 410.

that in several decisions helped to convince even members of the Supreme Court's liberal bloc of the unconstitutionality of some New Deal nostrums.[8] The justices were hardly alone, for public opinion surveys indicate that substantial numbers of Americans remained skeptical about economic regulation even at the high water mark of the New Deal, despite the Democrtic triumph in the 1936 presidential and congressional elections.[9]

In addition to their concerns about federalism, separation of powers, and legislative craftsmanship, Hughes and Roberts may have shared an instinctively fundamental distrust of the New Deal itself. Hughes and Roberts, both Yankee Protestant Republicans who were devoted to the ideal of disinterested government, distrusted the Democratic Party because its power emanated from a coalition of corrupt urban political machines and feudal white southerners. For Hughes, Roberts, and their fellow progressives, activist government was a means of achieving social and economic ends rather a political end in itself. Two of their principal objectives were freedom of opportunity and economic competition, which moderate regulation could promote but which an intrusive federal bureaucracy could blight or even destroy. As one scholar has observed, "In Hughes's hierarchy of values, individual opportunity ranked higher than regulation, while the latter trumped corporate enterprise."[10] Hughes and Roberts, who shared the lofty progressive vision of a government that embodied the public interest and transcended the messier features of partisanship, likewise disdained the cacophony of the New Deal, which parceled favors to rambunctious interest groups in an unabashed political manner. Like other old-line progressives, their objections to the New Deal may have been as much cultural as political or jurisprudential.

Much of the legislation that the Court ultimately sustained was more consistent with the individualistic ideals of the progressives than were the more collectivist and corporatist measures of the early New Deal. The National Labor Relations Act, for example, imposed a high level of federal administrative regulation over labor-management relations and reduced union autonomy by permitting the National Labor Relations Board to certify—or decertify—a union as a representative of workers. By denying unions any stable or permanent role in representing workers, the statute promoted individualism, rejected collectivism, and drove a wedge between workers and unions that diminished working-class solidarity. On the basis of a theory of "responsible unionism" that progressive Republicans such as Hughes had championed, organized labor supported its enactment only

8. See Neal Devins, "Government Lawyers and the New Deal" (book review), 96 *Columbia Law Review* 240, 251–52, 257, 259–60, 266 (1966); Peter H. Irons, *The New Deal Lawyers* (Princeton, N.J.: Princeton University Press, 1982), 4–6, 10–13; Barry Cushman, *Rethinking the New Deal Court: The Structure of a Constitutional Revolution* (New York: Oxford University Press, 1998).

9. Barry Cushman, "Mr. Dooley and Mr. Gallup: Public Opinion and Constitutional Change in the 1930s," 55 *Buffalo Law Review* 7 (2002).

10. James A. Henretta, "Charles Evans Hughes and the Strange Death of Liberal America," 24 *Law and History Review* 115 (2006).

because unions supposed that they could manipulate it to their advantage.[11] Similarly, the Social Security Act, which pegged unemployment compensation and
pension benefits to contributions made by employees themselves, resembled a
mandatory insurance program rather than a welfare scheme or dole. It therefore
may make more sense to attribute the triumph of the regulatory state to a "congressional revolution" rather than to a "judicial revolution" insofar as Congress
during the so-called Second New Deal crafted legislation that the Court was able
to uphold within the framework of existing doctrines, at least when the Court
applied such doctrines more expansively and consistently.

The dissents of the Court's liberal members before 1937 were critically important in helping to shape the Court's decisions during and after the "revolution,"
for they provided doctrinal frameworks for the Court's later decisions. In addition
to developing useful constitutional theories, these decisions helped to blunt allegations of inconsistency. Although the Court always exposes itself to charges of
incoherence and instability when it reverses its position, the Court seems less
inconsistent if at least some justices had earlier supported the Court's new position. The efforts of Stone, Brandeis, and other liberal dissenters to construct an
intellectually unified opposition before 1937 helped to make the Court's later
decisions seem less revolutionary and more evolutionary. When Stone complained
to Yale law professor Karl Llewellyn in 1936 that he felt like Sisyphus because he
"slipped back more than he advanced," Llewellyn replied that Sisyphus failed only
because, unlike Stone, "he did not build his dissents together but rolled each one
separately."[12]

In contrast with the clear influence of such internal factors, the extent to which
the constant specter of Court curbing influenced the Hughes Court's decisions is
more problematical. Certainly many contemporaries perceived the hand of politics in many of the Court's decisions. Irving Brant, for example, believed that
public outcry over the Court's invalidation of the Agricultural Adjustment Act in
Butler in January 1936 helped to persuade the Court to refrain from disapproving
the TVA six weeks later in *Ashwander;*[13] the Court's validation of regulatory legislation in its decisions between the 1936 election and Roosevelt's announcement of

11. See Ruth O'Brien, *Workers' Paradox: The Republican Origins of New Deal Labor Policy, 1886–
1935* (Chapel Hill: University of North Carolina Press, 1998).

12. Harlan Fiske Stone to Karl N. Llewellyn, May 28, 1936, box 24, Harlan Fiske Stone
Papers, Manuscript Division, Library of Congress (hereafter cited as Stone Papers); Llewellyn
to Stone, July 10, 1936, box 24, Stone Papers.

13. Irving Brant to George W. Norris, August 25, 1936, box 7, Stone Papers. Brant confided
to Norris that "I was at the home of one of the liberal justices [probably Stone's] late in January,
after preliminary line-up on the TVA must have revealed itself in the court, and he talked about
the court's attitude toward New Deal legislation with an alarm concerning the future which
would have been illogical, or at least unlikely to manifest itself, if the court had then swung
even in part from the trend revealed by the AAA decision. I believe that public reaction . . . and
your presence in the Senate, persuaded the court to follow precedents and uphold the TVA on
the issues then before the court." Brant's assertion is highly questionable since *Ashwander* was
decided by a vote of eight to one, and a clear majority of persons surveyed by Gallup had

his Court-packing plan were widely perceived as responses to the election;[14] and the Court's decisions during the spring of 1937 were and continue to be regarded by many as responses to the pressure of the Court-packing proposal.[15]

Other observers, then and now, have been more doubtful. In the wake of the Court's November 1936 split vote upholding the New York unemployment insurance law, Wiley Rutledge, then dean of the University of Iowa's law school, told Brant that he failed to "see the occasion for all the press talk about this case as evidencing an effect of the election on the Court. Roberts and Hughes may have squinted sideways at the returns, but the Four Horsemen do not know that we had an election."[16] Because Hughes and Roberts, however, so often teetered between the Court's competing factions, even a mere glance at the election returns might have sufficed to tilt them over to the proregulatory side. Despite the absence of any "smoking gun," it is not implausible to believe that the specter of Court curbing influenced at least Roberts in some decisions, for his vote in *West Coast Hotel* is not easily squared with his vote in *Tipaldo*, and his vote to uphold the unemployment compensation features of the Social Security Act are not easily reconcilable with his opinion for the Court in *Butler*.[17]

In considering the reasons for the Court's apparent transformation during the 1930s, it also may be useful to consider the nation's transformation during the same period. Like the Court, most Americans became much more amenable toward economically activist federal and state governments. So sweeping were changes in attitudes toward regulation that Alfred M. Landon, the Republican presidential candidate in 1936 and Wendell Willkie, the GOP candidate in 1940, did not threaten to repeal major New Deal legislation. Despite grumbling about "me-tooism" among horsemen of the apocalypse within the GOP, Republicans tended to base their appeal on promises that they could administer the new reform measures more honestly and efficiently and with greater sensitivity toward separation of powers and states' rights.

Because Supreme Court justices are influenced by many of the same forces as other citizens, it is not surprising that the tragedy of the Great Depression may have affected the attitudes of the Hughes Court justices in the same manner as this catastrophe influenced the thinking of many other Americans. As William

---

indicated their hostility toward the AAA. Brant's observation is significant, however, because it may have been widely shared.

14. See chapter 4, notes 21 and 22.

15. See, for example, Roger Corley, "Was There a Constitutional Revolution in 1937?" in Stephen Shaw, William Pederson, and Frank Williams, eds., *Franklin Roosevelt and the Transformation of the Supreme Court* (Armonk, N.Y.: M. E. Sharpe, 2004), 36; William Lasser, "Justice Roberts and the Constitutional Revolution of 1937—Was There a 'Switch in Time'?" 78 *Texas Law Review* 1354–61 (2000).

16. Wiley B. Rutledge to Irving Brant, November 25, 1936, Irving Brant Papers, Manuscript Division, Library of Congress, box 13.

17. For the arguments of scholars, particularly Cushman and Friedman, who have argued that the decisions can be reconciled, see chapter 4, note 164.

Allen White remarked in 1937, "[T]he Supreme Court by and large . . . marches pretty steadily in line with the popular thought of the American people."[18] In the wake of the Court's landmark 1937 decisions, Justice Stone observed that "the Court has always shown a remarkable capacity to remedy its own mistakes."[19] Similarly, Robert G. McCloskey once observed that "what seems responsiveness to public opinion is something subtly different: *concurrence* with public opinion, arising from the fact that judges are themselves members of the public."[20] Furthermore, a modern study has concluded that "[j]ustices are no less susceptible than other individuals in society to influences by evolving societal norms and values."[21]

Although it is possible that the Court's greater receptivity to economic regulatory legislation reflected fears of at least Hughes and Roberts that the Court would lose some of its power or legitimacy, it is perhaps more likely that the ravages of the Great Depression helped to convince Hughes and Roberts, like millions of their fellow Americans, that there was a compelling need for more state and federal economic regulation and that it was possible to remove existing constitutional impediments to such laws largely within the framework of existing doctrines. As Daniel A. Farber has observed, "FDR and the Democratic tide may have helped push Justice Roberts along, but it would have been to no avail if he had not already been halfway converted and if some of his fellow Establishment Republicans had not themselves already seen the light."[22]

The general concurrence between the Court's decisions and the popular will reflected the keen political instincts that Hughes had honed during a lifetime of public service. He understood that the Court could not permanently remain at odds with the other two branches of government. In his Columbia lectures in 1927, the future chief justice stated that "far more important to the development of the country, than the decisions holding acts of Congress invalid, have been those in which the authority of Congress has been sustained and adequate national power to meet the necessities of a growing country has been found to exist within constitutional limitations."[23] Alpheus Thomas Mason aptly believed that "[a]side from his convictions as to civil rights, Hughes's mind was singularly devoid of ideological content or commitment"[24] and that his strength "was not in

---

18. William Allen White to Edward Rees, January 19, 1937, box C-270, William Allen White Papers, Manuscript Division, Library of Congress.

19. Harlan Fiske Stone to Gifford Pinchot, April 13, 1937, box 24, Stone Papers.

20. Robert G. McCloskey, ed., introduction in *Essays in Constitutional Law* (New York: Alfred A. Knopf, 1957), 16.

21. William Mishler and Reginald S. Sheehan, "The Supreme Court as a Countermajoritarian Institution? The Impact of Public Opinion on Supreme Court Decisions," 87 *American Political Science Review* 96 (1993).

22. Daniel A. Farber, "Who Killed Lochner?" 90 *Georgetown Law Review* 1006 (2002).

23. Charles Evans Hughes, *The Supreme Court of the United States: Its Foundation, Methods, and Achievements: An Interpretation* (New York: Columbia University Press, 1928), 95–96.

24. Alpheus Thomas Mason, "Charles Evans Hughes: An Appeal to the Bar of History," 6 *Vanderbilt Law Review* 17 (1952).

ideas but in a highly developed ear for the aspirations of the American people."[25] In adapting constitutional law to the changing needs of the nation, Hughes deflected a major threat to judicial independence and helped chart a new course for the Court.

To many observers of the Court, Hughes's performance as chief justice echoed his celebrated observation, made when he was New York's governor in 1907, that "[w]e are under a Constitution, but the Constitution is what the judges say it is."[26] The frequent quotation of this remark as the essence of legal realism embarrassed Hughes, who insisted in his memoirs that he did not intend to picture "constitutional interpretation by the courts as a matter of judicial caprice" or to talk "flippantly or in disrespect of the courts," and that the remark was ripped out of context.[27] As various commentators have observed, however, the context in which Hughes made this remark does not diminish its potency as an expression of legal realism, even if Hughes intended no disrespect to the judiciary. Hughes's own judicial decisions illustrated the aptness of his point.[28]

Even though the Court often had sustained the constitutionality of reform legislation before 1937, the Court's approval of such laws was never a foregone conclusion. The persistent threat of judicial nullification chilled efforts to enact state and federal reform legislation. After 1937, the Court's deference to regulatory laws removed this cloud from whatever remained of the reform movement. The Court's change in direction ultimately succeeded not so much because Hughes and Roberts became wholehearted converts to a theory of judicial restraint in economic cases, but rather because the numerous justices appointed by Roosevelt formed a permanent liberal majority. As Barry Cushman has demonstrated, both Hughes and Roberts frequently voted in dissent with what remained of the Court's conservative bloc in economic regulatory decisions for the remainder of their tenure on the Court.[29]

25. Ibid., 8.

26. Charles Evans Hughes, "Speech before the Elmira Chamber of Commerce, May 3, 1907," in *Addresses of Charles Evans Hughes, 1906–1916*, 2d ed. (New York: G. P. Putnam's Sons, 1916).

27. David J. Danelski and Joseph S. Tulchin, eds., *The Autobiographical Notes of Charles Evans Hughes* (Cambridge, Mass.: Harvard University Press, 1973), 143–44. Hughes pointed out that he declared in the very same sentence that "the judiciary is the safeguard of our liberty and of our property under the Constitution." Moreover, he emphasized that he had made the remark only in passing and that the actual point of the speech was to warn that the assignment of administrative questions to courts would swamp the courts with disputes that administrative agencies could more effectively handle and that such assignments would expose the courts to public criticism for meddling with issues that were more political than legal.

28. Mason, "Charles Evans Hughes," 17.

29. Barry Cushman, "Lost Fidelities," 41 *William and Mary Law Review* 95 (1999). In denying that the Court-packing episode produced a judicial revolution, Cushman and White contend that the most transformative commerce clause cases were *United States v. Darby*, 312 U.S. 100 (1941) and *Wickard v. Filburn*, 317 U.S. 111 (1942), both of which were decided several years after the Court-packing threat. Cushman, *Rethinking the New Deal Court*, 209–25; G. Edward White, *The Constitution and the New Deal* (Cambridge, Mass.: Harvard University Press, 2000),

Liberals were singularly fortunate that not even one of the five justices appointed by Roosevelt during the Hughes Court or the three others he later appointed, unlike so many justices throughout history, frustrated the expectations of the president by whom they were nominated and the senators by whom they were confirmed. In particular, they were fortunate that Black turned out to have been sincere about the populist economics he espoused as a senator, as well as insincere about the racism he projected to obtain and keep his Senate seat. Black's reliability helped to preserve the liberal momentum of the spring of 1937 until the appointment of other liberal justices secured a solid bloc of support for regulatory legislation and expansion of civil liberties.

The Hughes Court's abandonment of close scrutiny of economic legislation and its activism on behalf of noneconomic liberties commenced a new era that has continued to the present day. In this respect, the Hughes Court may be described as the first modern Court.[30] Although the Taft Court had pioneered personal liberty doctrines and had begun to incorporate the Bill of Rights into state law, the Hughes Court expanded this process both quantitatively and qualitatively in its decisions protecting freedoms of speech, press, assembly, and religion from intrusions by state governments. The Hughes Court also breathed new life into the equal protection clause in its decisions protecting racial minorities from discrimination. Here again, Hughes was a critical catalyst because his personal commitment to human freedom was so abiding.

Any consideration of Hughes also must consider that while he clearly was influenced by his commitment to civil rights and economic individualism, he always remained independent of rigid ideology and strove to do justice in individual cases. As one journalist observed during the summer of 1935, Hughes had "ruled against capital, against labor, against the farmer and for the farmer, against Congress and for Congress, against the president and for him. Each time he has been loudly praised or privately damned. Such, perhaps, is the proper role for the chief justice of the United States."[31]

202. Cushman believes that the turning point in due process occurred before 1937, in the Court's 1934 *Nebbia* decision, which rejected the doctrine that only businesses cloaked with a public interest were fitting subjects for public restraints pursuant to the police power. Cushman, *Rethinking the New Deal Court*, 72–83.

30. Michael E. Parrish, *The Hughes Court: Justices, Rulings, and Legacy* (Santa Barbara, Calif.: ABC-CLIO, 2002), 177.

31. Henry F. Pringle, "Profiles: The Chief Justice, III," *New Yorker,* July 13, 1935, 23.

Bibliography

MANUSCRIPTS

Henry J. Allen Papers, Manuscript Division, Library of Congress.
William E. Borah Papers, Manuscript Division, Library of Congress.
Irving Brant Papers, Manuscript Division, Library of Congress.
Felix Frankfurter Papers, Manuscript Division, Library of Congress.
Charles Evans Hughes Papers, Manuscript Division, Library of Congress.
La Follette Family Papers, Manuscript Division, Library of Congress.
George W. Norris Papers, Manuscript Division, Library of Congress.
George W. Norris Papers, State Archives, Nebraska State Historical Society, Lincoln, Nebraska.
Franklin Delano Roosevelt Papers, Roosevelt Presidential Library, Hyde Park, New York.
Harlan Fiske Stone Papers, Manuscript Division, Library of Congress.
George W. Sutherland Papers, Manuscript Division, Library of Congress.
Willis Van Devanter Papers, Manuscript Division, Library of Congress.
William Allen White Papers, Manuscript Division, Library of Congress.

BOOKS

Abraham, Henry J. *Justice, Presidents, and Senators: A History of the U.S. Supreme Court Appointments from Washington to Clinton.* Rev. ed. Lanham, Md.: Rowman & Littlefield, 1999.

Ackerman, Bruce. *We the People: Transformations.* Cambridge, Mass.: Harvard University Press, 1998.

Alsop, Joseph, and Turner Catledge. *The 168 Days.* Garden City, N.Y.: Doubleday, Doran, 1938.

Arkes, Hadley. *The Return of George Sutherland: Restoring a Jurisprudence of Natural Rights.* Princeton, N.J.: Princeton University Press, 1994.

Baker, Leonard. *Back to Back: The Duel between FDR and the Supreme Court.* New York: Macmillan, 1967.

Ball, Howard, and Phillip J. Cooper. *Of Power and Right: Hugo Black, William O. Douglas, and America's Constitutional Revolution.* New York: Oxford University Press, 1992.

Bond, James E. *I Dissent: The Legacy of Chief [sic] Justice James Clark McReynolds.* Fairfax, Va.: George Mason University Press, 1992.

Cole, Olen, Jr. *The African American Experience in the Civilian Conservation Corps.* Gainesville: University of Florida Press, 1999.

Cortner, Richard C. *The Jones & Laughlin Case.* New York: Alfred A. Knopf, 1970.

———. *The Supreme Court and the Second Bill of Rights: The Fourteenth Amendment and the Nationalization of Civil Liberties.* Madison: University of Wisconsin Press, 1981.

———. *The Wagner Act Cases.* Knoxville: University of Tennessee Press, 1964.

251

Culver, John C., and John Hyde. *American Dreamer: The Life and Times of Henry A. Wallace*. New York: W. W. Norton, 2000.

Currie, David P. *Federal Courts: Cases and Materials*. 3rd ed. St. Paul, Minn.: West, 1982.

Cushman, Barry. *Rethinking the New Deal Court: The Structure of a Constitutional Revolution*. New York: Oxford University Press, 1998.

Danelski, David J., and Joseph S. Tulchin, eds. *The Autobiographical Notes of Charles Evans Hughes*. Cambridge, Mass.: Harvard University Press, 1973.

Dawson, Nelson Lloyd. *Louis D. Brandeis, Felix Frankfurter, and the New Deal*. Hamden, Conn.: Archon Books, 1980.

Dinnerstein, Leonard. *The Leo Frank Case*. New York: Columbia University Press, 1968.

Douglas, William O. *The Autobiography of William O. Douglas: The Court Years, 1939–1975*. New York: Random House, 1980.

Dunne, Gerald S. *Hugo Black and the Judicial Revolution*. New York: Simon & Schuster, 1977.

Fassett, John D. *New Deal Justice: The Life of Stanley Reed of Kentucky*. New York: Vantage Press, 1994.

Feinman, Ronald L. *Twilight of Progressivism: The Western Republican Senators and the New Deal*. Baltimore: Johns Hopkins University Press, 1981.

Flowers, Ronald B. *To Defend the Constitution: Religion, Conscientious Objection, Naturalization, and the Supreme Court*. Lanham, Md.: Scarecrow Press, 2003.

Frank, John P. *Marble Palace: The Supreme Court in American Life*. New York: Alfred A. Knopf, 1958.

Frankfurter, Felix, and Nathan Greene. *The Labor Injunction*. New York: MacMillan, 1930.

Gallup, George H., William P. Hansen, and Fred L. Israel, eds. *The Gallup Poll: Public Opinion, 1935–1971*, Vol. 1, *1935–1948*. New York: Random House, 1972.

Gerhart, Eugene C. *America's Advocate: Robert H. Jackson*. Indianapolis: Bobbs-Merrill, 1958.

Glad, Betty. *Charles Evans Hughes and the Illusions of Innocence: A Study in American Diplomacy*. Urbana: University of Illinois Press, 1966.

Harris, Joseph P. *The Advice and Consent of the Senate: A Study in the Confirmation of Appointments by the United States Senate*. Berkeley: University of California Press, 1953.

Hendel, Samuel. *Charles Evans Hughes and the Supreme Court*. Reprint, New York: Russell and Russell, 1968.

Howard, J. Woodford, Jr. *Mr. Justice Murphy: A Political Biography*. Princeton, N.J.: Princeton University Press, 1968.

Howe, Mark DeWolfe, ed. *Holmes-Laski Letters: The Correspondence of Mr. Justice Holmes and Harold J. Laski, 1916–1935*, Vol. 2, *1926–1935*. Cambridge, Mass.: Harvard University Press, 1953.

Hughes, Charles Evans. *The Supreme Court of the United States: Its Foundation, Methods, and Achievements: An Interpretation*. New York: Columbia University Press, 1928.

Hyman, Harold M., and Leonard W. Levy. *Freedom and Reform: Essays in Honor of Henry Steele Commager*. New York: Harper and Row, 1967.

Ickes, Harold L. *The Secret Diary of Harold L. Ickes*. Vol. 1, *The First Thousand Days, 1933–1936*. New York: Simon & Schuster, 1953.

———. *The Secret Diary of Harold L. Ickes*. Vol. 2, *The Inside Struggle, 1936–1939*. New York: Simon & Schuster, 1954.

Irons, Peter H. *The New Deal Lawyers*. Princeton, N.J.: Princeton University Press, 1982.

Jackson, Robert H. *The Struggle for Judicial Supremacy: A Study of a Crisis in American Power Politics*. New York: Alfred A. Knopf, 1941.

Johnson, Donald Bruce, comp. *National Party Platforms*. Vol. 1, *1840–1956*. Urbana: University of Illinois Press, 1978.

Kaufman, Andrew L. *Cardozo*. Cambridge, Mass.: Harvard University Press, 1998.

Kennedy, David M. *Freedom from Fear: The American People in Depression and War, 1929–1945.* New York: Oxford University Press, 1999.

Klarman, Michael J. *From Jim Crow to Civil Rights: The Supreme Court and the Struggle for Equality.* New York: Oxford University Press, 2004.

Kyvig, David E. *Explicit and Authentic Acts: Amending the U.S. Constitution, 1776–1995.* Lawrence: University Press of Kansas, 1996.

Lash, Joseph P. *From the Diaries of Felix Frankfurter.* New York: W. W. Norton, 1975.

Lasser, William. *The Limits of Judicial Power: The Supreme Court in American Politics.* Chapel Hill: University of North Carolina Press, 1988.

Leonard, Charles A. *A Search for a Judicial Philosophy: Mr. Justice Roberts and the Constitutional Revolution of 1937.* Port Washington, N.Y.: Kennikat Press, 1971.

Leuchtenburg, William E. *Franklin Roosevelt and the New Deal, 1932–1940.* 1st ed. New York: Harper & Row, 1963.

———. *The Supreme Court Reborn: The Constitutional Revolution in the Age of Roosevelt.* New York: Oxford University Press, 1995.

Lisco, Donald J. *Hoover, Blacks, & Lily-Whites: A Study of Southern Strategies.* Chapel Hill: University of North Carolina Press, 1985.

Mason, Alpheus Thomas. *Harlan Fiske Stone: Pillar of the Law.* New York: Viking Press, 1956.

———. *William Howard Taft: Chief Justice.* New York: Simon & Schuster, 1964.

McCarthy, Cathy A., and Tara Treacy, eds. *The History of the Administrative Office of the United States Courts: Sixty Years of Service to the Federal Judiciary.* Washington, D.C.: Administrative Office of the United States Courts, 2000.

McCormick, Richard L. *From Realignment to Reform: Political Change in New York State, 1893–1910.* Ithaca, N.Y.: Cornell University Press, 1981.

McKenna, Marian C. *Franklin Roosevelt and the Court-Packing Crisis of 1937.* New York: Fordham University Press, 2002.

Mennel, Robert M., and Christine L. Compson, eds. *Holmes and Frankfurter: Their Correspondence, 1912–1934.* Hanover: University of New Hampshire Press, 1996.

Mullen, Arthur F. *Western Democrat.* New York: Funk, 1940.

Murphy, Bruce Allen. *Wild Bill: The Legend and Life of William O. Douglas.* New York: Random House, 2003.

Myrdal, Gunnar. *An American Dilemma: The Negro Problem and Modern Democracy.* New York: Harper & Row, 1962.

O'Brien, Ruth. *Workers' Paradox: The Republican Origins of New Deal Labor Policy, 1886–1935.* Chapel Hill: University of North Carolina Press, 1998.

Parrish, Michael E. *The Hughes Court: Justices, Rulings and Legacy.* Santa Barbara, Calif.: ABC-CLIO, 2002.

Pearson, Drew, and Robert S. Allen. *The Nine Old Men.* Garden City, N.Y.: Doubleday, Doran, 1937.

Pfeffer, Leo. *This Honorable Court: A History of the United States Supreme Court.* Boston: Beacon Press, 1965.

Polenberg, Richard. *The World of Benjamin Cardozo: Personal Values and the Judicial Process.* Cambridge, Mass.: Harvard University Press, 1997.

Pratt, Walter F. *The Supreme Court under Edward Douglass White, 1910–1921.* Columbia: University of South Carolina Press, 1999.

Pringle, Henry F. *The Life and Times of William Howard Taft.* 2 vols. New York: Farrar & Rinehart, 1939.

Purcell, Edward A., Jr. *Brandeis and the Progressive Constitution: Erie, the Judicial Power, and the Politics of the Federal Courts in the Twentieth-Century America.* New Haven, Conn.: Yale University Press, 2000.

Pusey, Merlo J. *Charles Evans Hughes*. 2 vols. New York: MacMillan, 1951.

Rosenman, Samuel I., ed. *The Public Papers and Addresses of Franklin D. Roosevelt*. 13 vols. New York: Random House, 1938–1950.

Ross, William G. *Forging New Freedoms: Nativism, Education and the Constitution, 1917–1927*. Lincoln: University of Nebraska Press, 1994.

———. *A Muted Fury: Populists, Progressives and Labor Unions Confront the Courts, 1890–1937*. Princeton, N.J.: Princeton University Press, 1994.

Schapsmeier, Edward L., and Frederick H. Schapsmeier. *Henry A. Wallace of Iowa: The Agrarian Years, 1910–1940*. Ames: Iowa State University Press, 1968.

Semonche, John. *Charting the Future: The Supreme Court Responds to a Changing Society, 1890–1920*. Westport, Conn.: Greenwood Press, 1978.

Shaw, Stephen, William Pederson, and Frank Williams, eds. *Franklin D. Roosevelt and the Transformation of the Supreme Court*. Armonk, N.Y.: M. E. Sharpe, 2004.

Sherwood, Robert. *Roosevelt and Hopkins*. New York: Harper and Brothers, 1949.

Sitkoff, Harvard. *A New Deal for Blacks: The Emergence of Civil Rights as a National Issue*. Vol. 1, *The Depression Decade*. New York: Oxford University Press, 1978.

Smith, Rixey, and Norman Beasley. *Carter Glass: A Biography*. New York: Longman, Green, 1939.

Sparks, George F., ed. *A Many-Colored Toga: The Diary of Henry Fountain Ashurst*. Tucson: University of Arizona Press, 1962.

Strum, Philippa. *Brandeis: Beyond Progressivism*. Lawrence: University Press of Kansas, 1993.

Swindler, William E. *Court and Constitution in the Twentieth Century: The New Legality, 1932–1968*. Indianapolis: Bobbs-Merrill, 1970.

Taft, Philip. *The A.F. of L. from the Death of Gompers to the Merger*. New York: Harper & Brothers, 1959.

Urofsky, Melvin, and Paul Finkelman. *A March of Liberty: A Constitutional History of the United States*, 2d ed. Vol. 2, *From 1877 to the Present*. New York: Oxford University Press, 2002.

Wallace, Henry A. *Whose Constitution? An Inquiry into the General Welfare*. New York: Reynal & Hitchcock, 1936.

Ward, Artemus. *Deciding to Leave: The Politics of Retirement from the United States Supreme Court*. Albany: State University of New York Press, 2003.

Wesser, Robert F. *Charles Evans Hughes: Politics and Reform in New York, 1905–1910*. Ithaca, N.Y.: Cornell University Press, 1967.

Wheeler, Burton K., with Paul F. Healy. *Yankee from the West*. Garden City, N.Y.: Doubleday, 1962.

White, G. Edward. *The American Judicial Tradition: Profiles of Leading American Judges*. New York: Oxford University Press, 1976.

Wiebe, Robert H. *The Search for Order, 1877–1920*. New York: Hill and Wang, 1967.

Wiecek, William M. *Liberty under Law: The Supreme Court in American Life*. Baltimore: Johns Hopkins University Press, 1988.

ARTICLES

Ariens, Michael. "A Thrice-Told Tale, or Felix the Cat." 107 *Harvard Law Review* 620–76 (1994).

Belknap, Michal R. "The New Deal and the Emergency Powers Doctrine." 62 *Texas Law Review* 67–110 (1983).

Benedict, Michael Les. "Laissez Faire and Liberty: A Re-evaluation of the Meaning and Origin of Laissez-Faire Constitutionalism." 3 *Law and History Review* 293–331 (1985).

Berman, Edward. "The Supreme Court Interprets the Railway Labor Act." 20 *American Economic Review* 619–39 (1930).

Boskey, Bennett, and John H. Pickering. "Federal Restrictions on State Criminal Procedure." 13 *University of Chicago Law Review* 266–99 (1946).

Buchanan, James M. "A Note on the 'Joe Cotton Story.'" *Yearbook 1981 Supreme Court Historical Society* 92–93.

Caldiera, Gregory A. "Public Opinion and the U.S. Supreme Court: FDR's Court-Packing Plan." 81 *American Political Science Review* 1139–53 (1987).

Cass, Ronald A. "Models of Administrative Action." 72 *Virginia Law Review* 363–98 (1986).

Chambers, John W. "The Big Switch: Justice Roberts and the Minimum-Wage Cases." 10 *Labor History* 44–73 (1969).

Currie, David P. "The Constitution in the Supreme Court: The New Deal, 1931–1940." 54 *University of Chicago Law Review* 504–55 (1987).

Cushman, Barry. "Lost Fidelities." 41 *William and Mary Law Review* 95–145 (1999).

———. "Mr. Dooley and Mr. Gallup: Public Opinion and Constitutional Change in the 1930s." 50 *Buffalo Law Review* 7–101 (2002).

———. "The Secret Lives of the Four Horsemen." 83 *Virginia Law Review* 559–645 (1997).

———. "Small Differences?" 55 *Arkansas Law Review* 1097–1148 (2003).

———. "Some Varieties and Vicissitudes of Lochnerism." 85 *Boston University Law Review* 881–1000 (2005).

Cushman, Robert E. "Constitutional Law in 1930–31: The Constitutional Decisions of the Supreme Court of the United States in the October Term, 1930." 26 *American Political Science Review* 256–84 (1932).

Dahl, Robert. "Decision-Making in a Democracy: The Supreme Court as a National Policy-Maker." 6 *Journal of Public Law* 279–95 (1957).

Devins, Neal. "Government Lawyers and the New Deal." 96 *Columbia Law Review* 237–68 (1996). Book review.

Dorf, Michael C. "What Does the Second Amendment Mean Today?" In *The Second Amendment in Law and History: Historians and Constitutional Scholars on the Right to Bear Arms.* Edited by Carl T. Bogus, 249–51. New York: New Press, 2000.

Farber, Daniel A. "Who Killed Lochner?" 90 *Georgetown Law Journal* 985–1005 (2002). Book review.

Forbath, William E. "The Ambiguities of Free Labor." 1985. *Wisconsin Law Review* 767–817.

Frankfurter, Felix. "'The Administrative Side' of Chief Justice Hughes." 63 *Harvard Law Review* 1–4 (1949).

———. "Chief Justices I Have Known." 39 *Virginia Law Review* 883–905 (1953).

———. "Mr. Justice Roberts." 104 *University of Pennsylvania Law Review* 311–49 (1955).

Freund, Paul A. "Charles Evans Hughes as Chief Justice." 81 *Harvard Law Review* 4–43 (1967).

———. "Mr. Justice Brandeis: A Centennial Memoir." 70 *Harvard Law Review* 769–92 (1957).

Friedman, Barry. "The History of the Countermajoritarian Difficulty, Part Three: The Lesson of Lochner." 76 *New York University Law Review* 1383–1455 (2001).

———. "The History of the Countermajoritarian Difficulty, Part Four: Law's Politics." 148 *University of Pennyslvania Law Review* 971–1064 (2000).

———. "The Turn to History." 72 *New York University Law Review* 928–65 (1997). Book review.

Friedman, Richard D. "A Reaffirmation: The Authenticity of the Roberts Memorandum, or Felix the Non-Forger." 142 *University of Pennsylvania Law Review* 1985–95 (1994).

———. "The Sometimes-Bumpy Stream of Commerce." 55 *Arkansas Law Review* 981–1008 (2003).

———. "Switching Time and Other Thought Experiments: The Hughes Court and Constitutional Transformation." 142 *University of Pennsylvania Law Review* 1891–1984 (1994).

Galloway, Russell W., Jr. "The Court That Challenged the New Deal (1930–1936)." 24 *Santa Clara Law Review* 66–109 (1984).

Galston, Miriam. "Activism and Restraint: The Evolution of Harlan Fiske Stone's Judicial Philosophy." 70 *Tulane Law Review* 137–86 (1995).

Gardbaum, Stephen. "New Deal Constitutionalism and the Unshackling of the States." 64 *University of Chicago Law Review* 483–566 (1997).

Gilman, Felix. "The Famous Footnote Four: A History of the Carolene Products Footnote." 46 *South Texas Law Review* 163–243 (2004).

Gordon, Colin. "Rethinking the New Deal." 98 *Columbia Law Review* 2029–54 (1998). Book review.

Graber, Mark A. "The Non-Majoritarian Difficulty: Legislative Deference to the Judiciary." 7 *Studies in American Political Development* 35–72 (1993).

Griffin, Stephen M. "Constitutional Theory Transformed." 108 *Yale Law Journal* 2115–63 (1999).

Hansen, Drew D. "The Sit-Down Strikes and the Switch in Time." 46 *Wayne Law Review* 49–133 (2000).

Heberle, Klaus H. "From Gitlow to Near: Judicial 'Amendment' by Absent-Minded Incrementalism." 34 *Journal of Politics* 458–83 (1972).

Henretta, James A. "Charles Evans Hughes and the Strange Death of Liberal America." 24 *Law and History Review* 115–213 (2006).

Higginbotham, A. Leon, and William C. Smith. "The Hughes Court and the Beginning of the End of the 'Separate But Equal' Doctrine." 76 *Minnesota Law Review* 1099–1131 (1992).

Hulsebosch, Daniel J. "The New Deal Court: Emergence of a New Reason." 90 *Columbia Law Review* 1973–2016 (1990).

Irons, Peter. "Politics and Principle: An Assessment of the Roosevelt Record on Civil Rights and Liberties." 59 *Washington Law Review* 693–722 (1984).

Kalman, Laura. "The Constitution, the Supreme Court, and the New Deal." 110 *American Historial Review* 1052–80 (2005).

———. "Law, Politics, and the New Deal(s)." 108 *Yale Law Journal* 2165–2213 (1999).

Kline, Stephen O. "Revisiting FDR's Court Packing Plan: Are the Current Attacks on Judicial Independence So Bad?" 30 *McGeorge Law Review* 863–954 (1999).

Kruse, Kevin M. "Personal Rights, Public Wrongs: The *Gaines* Case and the Beginning of the End of Segregation." 1997 *Journal of Supreme Court History* 113–30.

Kyvig, David E. "The Road Not Taken: FDR, the Supreme Court, and Constitutional Amendment." 104 *Political Science Quarterly* 463–81 (1989).

Lash, Kurt T. "The Constitutional Convention of 1937: The Original Meaning of the New Jurisprudential Deal." 70 *Fordham Law Review* 459–525 (2001).

Lasser, William. "Justice Roberts and the Constitutional Revolution of 1937—Was There a 'Switch in Time.'" 78 *Texas Law Review* 1347–76 (2000).

Leuchtenburg, William E. "Comment on Laura Kalman's Article." 110 *American Historical Review* 1081–93 (2005).

———. "When the People Spoke, What Did They Say? The Election of 1936 and the Ackerman Thesis." 108 Yale Law Journal 2007–2114 (1999).

Lively, Donald E. "The Supreme Court Appointment Process: In Search of Constitutional Roles and Responsibilities." 59 *Southern California Law Review* 551–79 (1986).

Loper, Merle William. "The Court of Chief Justice Hughes: Contributions to Civil Liberties." 12 *Wayne Law Review* 535–95 (1966).

Lusky, Louis. "Footnote Redux: A Carolene Products Reminiscence." 82 *Columbia Law Review* 1093–1100 (1982).

Mason, Alpheus Thomas. "Charles Evans Hughes: An Appeal to the Bar of History." 6 *Vanderbilt Law Review* 1–19 (1952).

———. "Politics and the Supreme Court: President Roosevelt's Proposal." 85 *University of Pennsylvania Law Review* 659–77 (1937).

McElwain, Edwin. "The Business of the Supreme Court as Conducted by Chief Justice Hughes." 63 *Harvard Law Review* 5–26 (1949).

Mendelsohn, Rona Hirsch. "Senate Confirmation of Supreme Court Appointments: The Nomination and Rejection of John J. Parker." 14 *Howard Law Journal* 105–48 (1968).

Mishler, William, and Sheehan, Reginald S. "Public Opinion, the Attitudinal Model and Supreme Court Decision Making: A Micro-Analytic Perspective." 58 *Journal of Politics* 169–200 (1996).

Nelson, Michael. "The President and the Court: Reinterpreting the Court-packing Episode of 1937." 103 *Political Science Quarterly* 267–93 (1988).

Olken, Samuel R. "The Business of Expression: Economic Liberty, Political Factions and the Forgotten First Amendment Legacy of Justice George Sutherland." 10 *William and Mary Bill of Rights Journal* 249–358 (2002).

———. "Historical Revisionism and Constitutional Change: Understanding the New Deal Court." 88 *Virginia Law Review* 265–326 (2002).

———. "Justice George Sutherland and Economic Liberty: Constitutional Conservatism and the Problem of Factions." 6 *William and Mary Bill of Rights Journal* 1–88 (1997).

———. "Charles Evans Hughes and the Blaisdell Decision: A Historical Study of Contract Clause Jurisprudence." 72 *Oregon Law Review* 513–602 (1993).

Parrish, Michael E. "The Hughes Court, the Great Depression, and the Historians." 40 *Historian* 286–308 (1978).

Pepper, David A. "Against Legalism: Rebutting an Anachronistic Account of 1937." 82 *Marquette Law Review* 63–154 (1998).

Perry, Matthew. "Justice Stone and Footnote 4." 6 *George Mason University Civil Rights Journal* 35–63 (1996).

Phillips, Michael J. "The Progressiveness of the Lochner Court." 75 *Denver University Law Review* 453–506 (1998).

Pope, Jim. "Worker Lawmaking, Sit-Down Strikes, and the Shaping of American Industrial Relations, 1935–1958." 24 *Law and History Review* 45–114 (2006).

Purcell, Edward A., Jr. "Rethinking Constitutional Change." 80 *Virginia Law Review* 277–90 (1994).

Rauh, Joseph L., Jr. "A Personal View of Justice Benjamin N. Cardozo: Recollections of Four Cardozo Law Clerks." 1 *Cardozo Law Review* 5–21 (1979).

———. "An Unabashed Liberal Looks at a Half-Century of the Supreme Court." 69 *North Carolina Law Review* 213–49 (1990).

Rosenberg, Gerald N. "Judicial Independence and the Reality of Political Power." 54 *Review of Politics* 369–98 (1992).

Ross, William G. "Participation by the Public in the Federal Judicial Selection Process." 43 *Vanderbilt Law Review* 1–84 (1990).

———. "The Resilience of *Marbury v. Madison:* Why Judicial Review Has Survived So Many Attacks." 38 *Wake Forest Law Review* 733–92 (2002).

———. "The Role of Judicial Issues in Presidential Campaigns." 42 *Santa Clara Law Review* 391–482 (2002).

———. "When Did the 'Switch in Time' Actually Occur? Re-discovering the Supreme Court's 'Forgotten' Decisions of 1936–1937." 37 *Arizona State Law Journal* 1153–1220 (2005).

Siegel, Stephen. "The Revision Thickens." 20 *Law and History Review* 631–37 (2002).

Somin, Ilya. "Voter Knowledge and Constitutional Change: Assessing the New Deal Experience." 45 *William and Mary Law Review* 595–674 (2003).

Sugarman, Joseph. "Note." 14 *Boston University Law Review* 419–20 (1934).

Thomas, Kendall. "*Rouge et Noir* Reread: A Popular Constitutional History of the Angelo Herndon Case." 65 *Southern California Law Review* 2599–2704 (1992).

Tushnet, Mark. "The New Deal Constitutional Revolution: Law, Politics, or What?" 66 *University of Chicago Law Review* 1061–80 (1999). Book review.

Urofsky, Melvin I. "Myth and Reality: The Supreme Court and Protective Legislation in the Progressive Era." *Yearbook 1983 Supreme Court Historical Society* 53–72.

Warren, Charles. "New Light on the History of the Federal Judiciary Act of 1789." 37 *Harvard Law Review* 49–132 (1923).

Watson, Richard L., Jr. "The Defeat of Judge Parker: A Study in Pressure Groups and Politics." 50 *Mississippi Valley Historical Review* 213–34 (1963).

White, G. Edward. "Cabining the Constitutional History of the New Deal in Time." 94 *Michigan Law Review* 1392–1421 (1996). Book review.

———. "Constitutional Change and the New Deal: The Internalist/Externalist Debate." 110 *American Historical Review* 1094–1115 (2005).

———. "The 'Constitutional Revolution' as a Crisis in Adaptivity." 48 *Hastings Law Journal* 867–912 (1997).

Wiener, Frederick Bernays. "Justice Hughes' Appointment: The Cotton Story Re-examined." *Yearbook 1981 Supreme Court Historical Society* 78–91.

Young, Gordon G. "Public Rights and the Federal Judicial Power: From *Murray's Lessee* through *Crowell* to *Schor*." 35 *Buffalo Law Review* 765–869 (1986).

Index of Cases

Subject Index